FURNITURE DESIGN

AN INTRODUCTION TO DEVELOPMENT, MATERIALS AND MANUFACTURING

For ROBM&C

LAURENCE KING

Published in 2013 by
Laurence King Publishing Ltd
361–373 City Road
London EC1V 1LR

T +44 20 7841 6900

enquiries@laurenceking.com
www.laurenceking.com

A catalogue record for this book is available from
the British Library.

ISBN: 978 1 78067 120 8

Designed by TwoSheds Design

Printed in the UK

Laurence King Publishing is committed to ethical and
sustainable production. We are proud participants in The
Book Chain Project®
bookchainproject.com

BOOK
CHAIN
PROJECT

Front cover: **Carbon Chair, Bertjan
Pot and Marcel Wanders for Moooi,
2004.**

Back cover: **ZA Stackable Bench
System, Shin and Tomoko Azumi
for Lapalma, distributed in the US
by Davis Furniture, 2003.**

FURNITURE DESIGN

Stuart Lawson

AN INTRODUCTION TO
DEVELOPMENT, MATERIALS
AND MANUFACTURING

Laurence King Publishing

CONTENTS:

Introduction

Intended to inspire and inform in equal measure, this book is primarily
written for students of design seeking to balance real-world process
with guidance about design methods and material and manufacturing
specifications for industrial production. No single approach to concept
origination or design development is prescribed. Rather, the book's
commentary and content aims to engender expansive and reductive thinking
around function, aesthetics, material selection, manufacturing and component
geometry. This book also provides an insight into furniture design for those
considering a tertiary education in product and industrial design.

Below: **Between its inception in 2003 and its launch in 2009, Studio 7.5 produced 30 different prototypes in the development of the Setu Chair for Herman Miller.**

Bottom: **Dieter Rams's 606 Universal Shelving System for Vitsoe + Zapf was launched in 1960 and uses extruded aluminium, folded steel and a laminated timber-board substrate.**

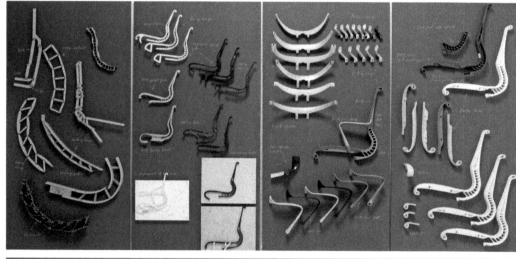

Furniture Design: An Introduction to Development, Materials and Manufacturing is primarily focused on industrial design for volume and mass production for the simple reason that nearly all furniture designers are employed within this realm. In addition to having keen and creative rationales, designers need a good understanding of materials and manufacturing parameters to communicate productively with engineers and ultimately to produce designs on brief and within budget for a client. *Furniture Design* is by no means an exhaustive guide to design and manufacturing, but as a companion for designers it provides an easy-to-access resource of furniture-design knowledge.

While choosing a material or a manufacturing process can be a rational and objective exercise, there is nearly always more than one solution to creating a form, structure and aesthetic, or to reducing costs or improving interaction. It can be revelatory for aspiring design students to discover that creativity exists in nearly all aspects of their design and development process, and that the designer's role is just one part of a long line of expertise that helps bring products to market.

The inspiration behind an idea and the focus of a brief will invariably be different, depending on the 'job' – if one exists – and the designer. The two example projects illustrated above and overleaf are both visually and technically innovative, but their designers had very different concerns during the course of each product's development. Both clients were high-end brands and so costs could be relatively high (but not rampant). The Joyn desk is manufactured in fairly high volumes and the Zip Zi table in low-volume batches. A designer would not necessarily approach the process using a graphic like the one that appears on the next page, but the need to conform to some kind of rationale is inherent in the subsequent development and, therefore, consciously or otherwise, the designer is guided by such parameters.

Few designers work to open, creative briefs; the vast majority of professional commissions are a balance between creative freedom and well-defined restrictions

Joyn Office Systems (single desk), Ronan and Erwan Bouroullec for Vitra, 2003.

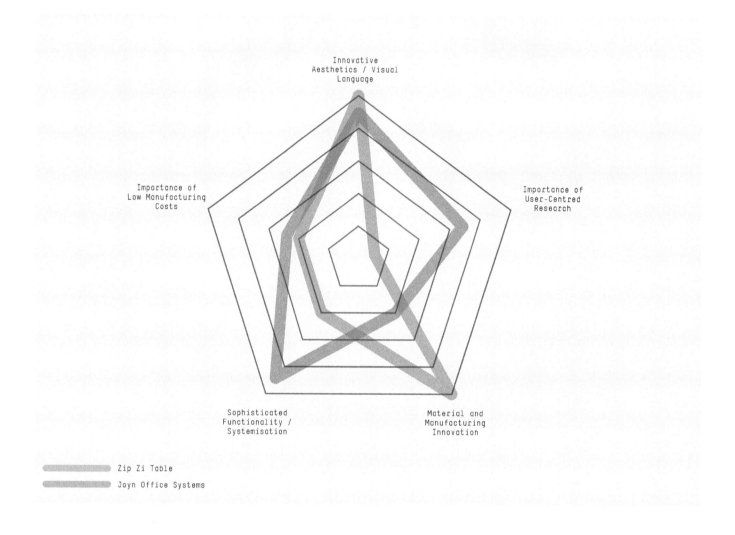

Innovative
Aesthetics / Visual
Language

Importance of
User-Centred
Research

Importance of
Low Manufacturing
Costs

Material and
Manufacturing
Innovation

Sophisticated
Functionality /
Systemisation

Zip Zi Table

Joyn Office Systems

of function, aesthetics, manufacturing capability and cost. Clients normally have sufficient ideas, market research or company feedback to understand that they need a certain sort of product, in a choice of certain materials and with a manufacturing and shipping cost below a certain price point. They may seek new manufacturing partners for innovative projects, but, on the whole, they will want to stick with their existing manufacturers to manage their risk. Companies with their own manufacturing capabilities are even less likely to step outside of what they know unless there is a clear commercial advantage. Central to any design process is the cost of manufacture in relation to the number of units to be produced and the target retail price. It is also imperative to consider the most suitable materials and approaches to manufacturing.

Choosing the correct manufacturing process for each component is paramount. The investment needed upfront for large-scale industrial manufacture

can be significant. Tooling for the likes of injection-moulded thermoplastics or for high-pressure die castings is extremely expensive and can be very risky considering that no sales will have been made of the product. Therefore, for small production runs, such technologies become untenable. Cheaper tooling costs for such methods as the rotational moulding of plastics or the sand-casting of aluminium may enable a project to get off the ground, as may the fabrication of components using adhesives or welding technologies. There are, however, restrictions and limitations when using lower-cost manufacturing technologies, both in visual refinement and in the tolerances available. The options for design and manufacture may at first seem vast, but once a client, a budget, an environment or a sustainability requirement is introduced, the decision-making process invariably becomes more straightforward.

Relative importance: factors that inform a brief and govern the design process.

Opposite: **Zip Zi Folded Paper, Michael Young for Established & Sons, 2007.**

Above: **Impossible Wood, Doshi Levien for Moroso, 2011. This armchair is injection moulded using a thermoplastic composite of 80 per cent wood fibre and 20 per cent polypropylene.**

Top right: **A Pile of Suitcases, Maarten De Ceulaer for Gallery Nilufar, 2008.**

Right: **Plastic Classic, 2009. Pili Wu's prototype combines a ubiquitous Taiwanese restaurant stool with a traditional Chinese loop-backed chair.**

Exploring the content

Chapter 1 provides a cultural and historical context for contemporary furniture design and outlines key functional, technical and aesthetic innovations since 1900. It goes on to study in more depth designers' rationales for seminal works, with a special focus on the furniture canon since the year 2000.

Design briefs and professional practice are covered in chapter 2, which also investigates anthropometrics, ergonomics and the governing principles of primary and secondary research. The chapter concludes with a series of case studies that underline the importance of concept development and testing.

Further case studies in chapter 3 explore material- and manufacturing-centred approaches to design and the issues surrounding sustainable and ethical design. The book's final section is a technical resource encompassing material properties and manufacturing processes, and is intended as a tool for readers to research their ideas' potential and to create basic specifications for manufacture.

Readers should digest this book in any way they like, but the following enquiries suggest the most productive and rewarding ways to navigate it. By cross-referencing the book's content, readers will begin to see how ideas, materials and processes can be allied to create visually and technically innovative solutions.

Precise enquiry

To research how to establish a project brief, explore 'Research for design' (2a) and 'Ergonomics, anthropometrics and spatial conventions' (2b).

To find the most appropriate manufacturing process for a project, based on known criteria such as shape geometry, manufacturing volume, possible materials, manufacturing tolerances (the possible accuracy of parts) and achievable detail definition, study the metal, plastic and wood manufacturing subsections in 3c.

To find the most appropriate material for a project, based on known criteria such as structural characteristics, environmental performance, aesthetic potential, achievable detail definition and durability, study the metal, plastic and wood materials subsections in 3c.

Broad enquiry

Explore chapters 1 and 2 and sections 3a and 3b and cross-reference the featured designs and commentary with the materials and manufacturing section of 3c.

Either by browsing 3c or with specific materials and manufacturing processes in mind, refer back to the previous chapters to find examples of a material, manufacturing process or surface finish.

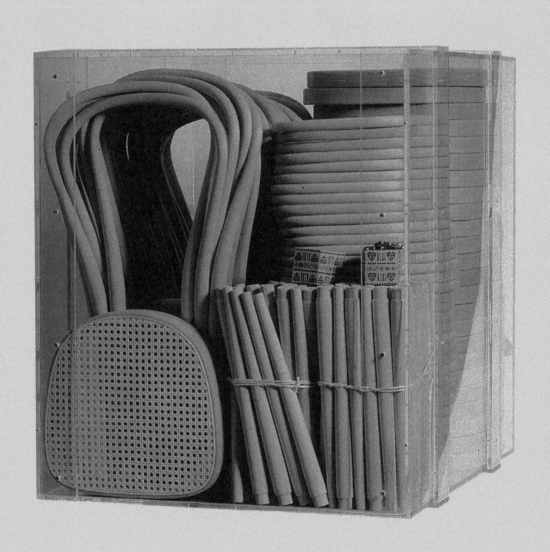

Chapter 1:

A survey of the development
of furniture design

1a: A cultural history
of furniture design

Within the realm of the designed object, the early twentieth century is characterized by the tension between mass industrialization and craft manufacture. By the end of the nineteenth century, architects, designers, craftspeople and artists had come together through societies, exhibitions and publications to imagine a new vision of the future in which new materials, new forms and new manufacturing processes would play a defining role. This chapter surveys the key milestones in this development, showing first how designers sought to bring together the old and the new, and then how newer materials and newer ways of manufacturing led to a break with past forms and a re-imagining of the way we live.

Following developments decade by decade, this section chooses significant works as exemplars of good design and innovation, linking with related contemporary activities and historical events. This selective approach means that these examples can be understood in terms of their manufacture as well as their aesthetic and historical context.

Significant first steps toward progressive design were taken in 1897 by the Vienna Secessionist architects Koloman Moser and Josef Hoffmann. The Secessionists were influenced by the latter stages of the Arts and Crafts Movement in the UK, and, in particular, by the work of Charles Rennie Mackintosh, whose highly original architecture, furniture and metalwork provided a bridge between the deconstructed vernacular of the 1890s and the imaginings of the Secessionists.

To establish an outlet for their work and to encourage a sharing of ideas between the city's most forward-thinking artists, craftspeople and architects, Moser and Hoffmann formed the Wiener Werkstätte (Vienna Workshops) in 1903. Following in the footsteps of William Morris and John Ruskin, proponents of the reform movement in the UK, the Werkstätte sought to pitch itself against a world that was increasingly populated by poorly designed industrialized products, through the craft manufacture of highly original art, textiles, metalwork, glass, ceramics, furniture and architecture. The Werkstätte was, therefore, a resolutely craft-focused enterprise and not an

example of integrated design for efficient mass manufacture, although Hoffmann and Moser did design furniture for Thonet. The Werkstätte's motto was: 'Better to work 10 days on one product than to manufacture 10 products in one day.'

Thonet was the first company to mass-manufacture furniture, and it has produced well-designed utilitarian products since the 1850s. Founded by Michael Thonet, a cabinet maker and entrepreneur from Germany, the firm's innovative approach to wooden furniture production (i.e. the division of labour to create affordable, refined products for the masses) and the fact that it worked with the very best designers meant that the Werkstätte voiced no objection. However, despite Thonet's considerable influence and achievements, the Werkstätte's output (particularly in the first five years) represents the beginning of truly progressive design due to its creation of a radical new aesthetic that became the style and substance of twentieth-century design.

In the USA, Charles Rennie Mackintosh had a great influence on the architect Frank Lloyd Wright, and he in turn undoubtedly inspired the Werkstätte. Of all Wright's work, his most uncompromising is the entirely metal furniture designed for the Larkin Building (1904) in Buffalo, New York. The Larkin Office Chair was one of the first indoor metal seats and, even though there are no accounts of its reception, it must have seemed Brutalist in its unforgiving use of materials and form. Despite Lloyd Wright's innovative interior design of glass doors, air

Opposite: **No. 14 Chair, Michael Thonet, 1859.**

Far opposite: **The Larkin Office Chair, Frank Lloyd Wright, 1904.**

1900s: Hoffmann to Lloyd Wright

1910   Eero Saarinen born/Early Fokker
         aeroplane uses tubular steel

1909   Mackintosh's Glasgow School of Art

1908   *Titanic* design approved

1907   Picasso's *Les Demoiselles d'Avignon*

1906   Richard Strauss's opera, *Elektra*

1905   Josef Hoffmann's Sitzmaschine Chair

1904   Frank Lloyd Wright's Larkin Building

1903   Wiener Werkstätte established

1902   Arne Jacobsen Born

1901   Koloman Moser's Bentwood Chair

1900   Paris Exposition Universelle

Sitzmaschine Chair,
Josef Hoffmann, 1905.

1910s: Klimt to Rietveld

1920   Eileen Gray's Pirogue Daybed/
                        Rietveld's Hartog Office Interior

1919   Bauhaus founded/Rietveld's Sideboard

1918   Gerrit Rietveld's Red Blue Chair/WWI ends

1917   De Stijl established/October Revolution in Russia

1916   Albert Einstein, Theory of General Relativity

1915   Alvin Lustig born

1914   WWI begins/Cologne Werkbund Exhibition

1913   Model T Ford launched

1912   *Titanic* sinks

1911   First aeroplane lands on a ship

1910   Eero Saarinen born/Early Fokker aeroplane uses tubular steel

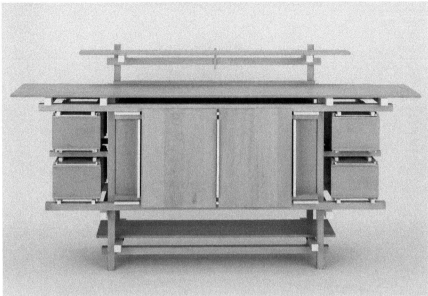

conditioning and built-in furniture, the Larkin Building was demolished in 1950.

During the first two years of the Werkstätte's existence, no work was more important than the Sitzmaschine Chair (Sitting Machine). Designed by Hoffmann in 1905, it went beyond the idiom of decorative innovation and, along with Wright's Larkin Office Chair, should be considered as one of the first 'modern' chairs as it made a significant break with the past and allied function with a restrained but expressive ornament. Both chairs herald the ascendance of functionalism and utility over adornment in radical design.

The advent of World War I and the October Revolution in Russia brought about seismic changes in Europe and the wider world, creating a collective desire for self-determination and a break with the past. Although a great many technological innovations took place during this period, furniture manufacturing development was delayed as a result of the war. Some advances were still being made in neutral countries, such as Denmark, and in the Netherlands, with Gerrit Rietveld's experimental work resulting in a new rationale. Rietveld's contribution to the reinvention of furniture was as significant as Picasso's engagement with abstraction or composer, Richard Strauss's increasing use of dissonance a decade earlier. Without the important influence of Rietveld and the art movement De Stijl (The Style), early Modernism would certainly have had a very different hue.

Although not as well known as his Red Blue Chair and its predecessor of 1917, Rietveld's Sideboard of 1919 is equal in its rejection and deconstruction of structure and decoration. However, furniture such as the sideboard still received a fair amount of criticism and even ridicule; it was referred to as a 'dust-catcher' with its excess of horizontal surfaces. Rietveld is recorded as finding this pedantic disapproval of his work amusing.

Despite the historical importance of Hoffmann's Sitzmaschine Chair and of Rietveld's structural experimentations, as a secession from the past, up until the 1920s, neither were designing specifically for mass production, although their work was of course rational in manufacturing terms. It is clear, therefore, that what exemplifies much of Modernism (in furniture design at least) was not the primary focus of their endeavours.

The years immediately after World War I saw the birth of progressive industrial design – a materials- and manufacturing-led approach that served function and efficiency of manufacture. Despite the Werkstätte becoming more of an Art Deco retail enterprise, Rietveld continued his work at the cutting edge, parallelled by the future demigods of Modernism. Collectively they created truly avant-garde but nonetheless logical products whose influence extended, in relative terms, as far as that of abstract art.

The interwar period saw rapid changes in manufacturing technology and the popularization

Left to right:
Prototype for the Red Blue Chair (unpainted), Gerrit Rietveld, 1917.

Sideboard, Gerrit Rietveld, 1919.

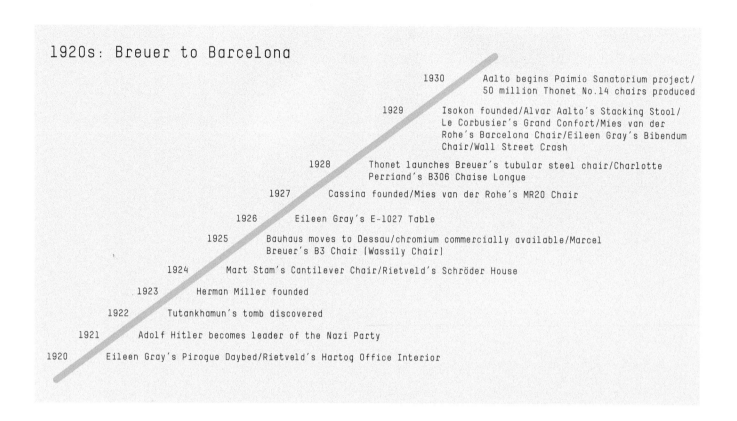

1920s: Breuer to Barcelona

1930   Aalto begins Paimio Sanatorium project/
50 million Thonet No.14 chairs produced

1929   Isokon founded/Alvar Aalto's Stacking Stool/
Le Corbusier's Grand Confort/Mies van der
Rohe's Barcelona Chair/Eileen Gray's Bibendum
Chair/Wall Street Crash

1928   Thonet launches Breuer's tubular steel chair/Charlotte
Perriand's B306 Chaise Longue

1927   Cassina founded/Mies van der Rohe's MR20 Chair

1926   Eileen Gray's E-1027 Table

1925   Bauhaus moves to Dessau/chromium commercially available/Marcel
Breuer's B3 Chair (Wassily Chair)

1924   Mart Stam's Cantilever Chair/Rietveld's Schröder House

1923   Herman Miller founded

1922   Tutankhamun's tomb discovered

1921   Adolf Hitler becomes leader of the Nazi Party

1920   Eileen Gray's Pirogue Daybed/Rietveld's Hartog Office Interior

of industrial materials for furniture. In 1919, the Bauhaus School was founded in Weimar, Germany, by Walter Gropius. The foundation of the Bauhaus education programme was an apprenticeship, which concentrated on free experimentation with colour, form and material. On completing an apprenticeship, students could choose one of the various courses in applied arts. The aim was for students to acquire an equal level of skill in art and hand-craft disciplines. For 13 years (before being shut down by the Nazi Party for its supposed Communist affiliations), the school taught the applied arts to some of the most important designers and architects of the twentieth century. They in turn, by example and through teaching, have influenced all that has happened since.

The most well-known and probably most important piece of furniture to be designed at the Bauhaus during this period was a tubular steel club chair, the B3, referred to latterly as the Wassily Chair (see p109). It is perhaps the greatest work from the German grand master of Modernist design, Marcel Breuer. While Thonet's mastery of mass production had preceded the Wassily Chair by almost 60 years, Breuer's chair was the first to attempt an alignment of 'new' material and manufacturing technologies with a radical and progressive approach to

functional design. Thonet's achievement was certainly no less important, but, at that time, a wooden chair could never have had the impact of chrome-plated steel.

Once the technical possibilities of tubular steel had been explored by Breuer, it was only a matter of time before the real potential of the material became apparent: the cantilever. Dutch architect Mart Stam is credited with producing the first chair of this kind, but once Breuer and his German-born contemporary Ludwig Mies van de Rohe heard what Stam had achieved, and realized its significance, they immediately developed their own versions. The dispute over who invented the cantilevered chair even ended up in the German courts in the late 1920s, with Stam being awarded the European patent by proving 'prior art' over Breuer.

Mies van der Rohe is widely considered to be the greatest of all Modernist architects and was also responsible for several groundbreaking furniture designs, the most significant of which were created in the 1920s. His variations on Stam's cantilever principle and his seminal works, such as the Barcelona Chair for the German Pavilion at the 1929 International Exposition in Barcelona, created a visually

Above: **Eileen Gray's adjustable-height E-1027 Table was designed as part of a collaborative architecture project with Jean Badovici in 1924.**

Right: **Mart Stam's tubular steel Cantilever Chair (contemporary version), licensed to L&C Arnold, 1927.**

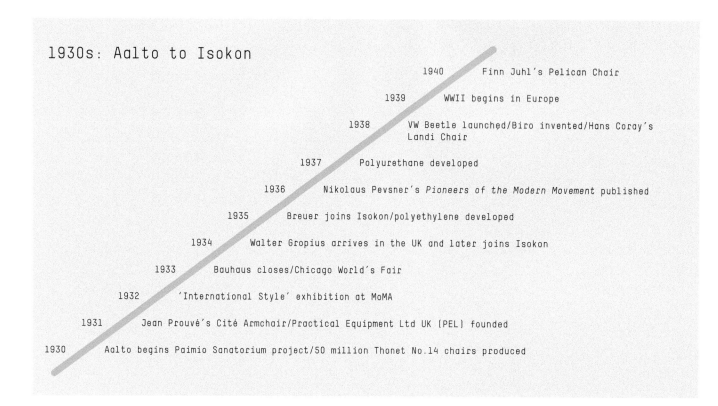

1930s: Aalto to Isokon

1940   Finn Juhl's Pelican Chair

1939   WWII begins in Europe

1938   VW Beetle launched/Biro invented/Hans Coray's Landi Chair

1937   Polyurethane developed

1936   Nikolaus Pevsner's *Pioneers of the Modern Movement* published

1935   Breuer joins Isokon/polyethylene developed

1934   Walter Gropius arrives in the UK and later joins Isokon

1933   Bauhaus closes/Chicago World's Fair

1932   'International Style' exhibition at MoMA

1931   Jean Prouvé's Cité Armchair/Practical Equipment Ltd UK (PEL) founded

1930   Aalto begins Paimio Sanatorium project/50 million Thonet No.14 chairs produced

extravagant, minimalist version of Modernism that has come to be seen as a defining view of the movement.

In partial contrast to Mies van der Rohe's visual opulence, French architects and designers Le Corbusier and Charlotte Perriand took traditional types of furniture and re-created them using a pared-down industrial aesthetic. The 'machine for living' (Le Corbusier, *Vers Une Architecture* [*Towards a New Architecture*], 1923) was a domestic interior where the shapes and styles of the past made way for the clean lines of new materials. Despite the prominence of Le Corbusier and Perriand's furniture in design history, their designs in tubular steel and glass were not particularly easy to manufacture and so had an inherently high cost. This was in contrast to the more 'democratic' designs produced by Breuer and Mies van der Rohe during the same period.

While Breuer, Stam, Mies van der Rohe and Le Corbusier dramatically changed design during the 1920s, Rietveld continued to make a significant contribution by experimenting with different materials and working on a major architectural commission in Utrecht: the Schröder House. Although rather overshadowed by the Bauhaus's

extraordinary output, Rietveld produced a broad range of furniture including two seminal chairs – one made entirely from aluminium pressings and the other with a seat and back formed from one piece of laminated plywood – pre-empting the work of Charles Eames more than 20 years later.

The 1930s saw a widespread acceptance of the modern aesthetic, as cinemas, transport and decorative objects all assumed the clean lines associated with what has become known as the style of the Modern Movement. The term Art Deco, derived from the 1925 Exposition Internationale des Arts Décoratifs et Industriels Modernes in Paris, gained currency through the early part of the 1930s. The glamorous world of Hollywood films and foreign travel influenced the Art Deco style with new designs in chrome, glass, laminates, lacquer and exotic materials such as animal skins, ivory and tortoiseshell. While not as meteoric as the 1920s, the pre-war period signified a maturing of Modernism and, importantly, the broad acceptance by designers of laminated furniture, despite being wood, as a worthy modern material.

In the UK, no company did more to support and promote technical innovation in furniture design

than the architecture and design practice Isokon, who as a replacement for the emigrating Walter Gropius, employed Marcel Breuer as director of design during his brief stay in London prior to the war. While Isokon was certainly producing innovative products in the 1930s, the Finnish architect Alvar Aalto had the greatest impact on subsequent manufacturing and design by achieving technically what no one before him had been able to – the lamination of large, complex, one-piece forms such as the Paimio Armchair. Throughout the 1920s, Aalto had conducted his own experiments with lamination and, after a fruitful collaboration with a manufacturer in Finland, he achieved a breakthrough while developing furniture for the now famous Paimio Sanatorium.

Craftspeople and furniture retailers in the UK and mainland Europe started to adopt the Deco style and, even though large-scale laminations were beyond the capabilities of most, the new visual language created by Aalto, Breuer and their British contemporaries Wells Coates and Arthur W. Simpson was interpreted using more traditional construction methods. The armchair designed by Arthur W. Simpson was one of the many iterations that became common in mainstream contemporary

Left to right:
A chair exhibited in the Red Rose Guild exhibition of 1935. Designed by Arthur W. Simpson, 1934.

Paimio Armchair, Alvar Aalto, 1930.

Below: **PEL tubular-steel stacking chairs with canvas seats and backrests (design RP6 & RP7), 1931–32.**

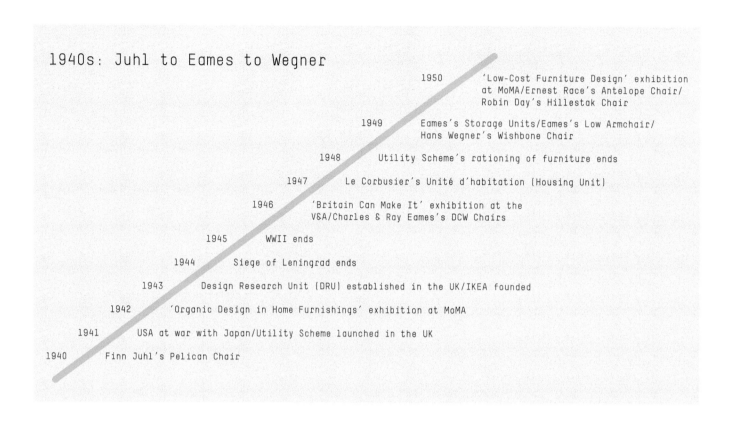

1940s: Juhl to Eames to Wegner

1950   'Low-Cost Furniture Design' exhibition at MoMA/Ernest Race's Antelope Chair/ Robin Day's Hillestak Chair

1949   Eames's Storage Units/Eames's Low Armchair/ Hans Wegner's Wishbone Chair

1948   Utility Scheme's rationing of furniture ends

1947   Le Corbusier's Unité d'habitation (Housing Unit)

1946   'Britain Can Make It' exhibition at the V&A/Charles & Ray Eames's DCW Chairs

1945   WWII ends

1944   Siege of Leningrad ends

1943   Design Research Unit (DRU) established in the UK/IKEA founded

1942   'Organic Design in Home Furnishings' exhibition at MoMA

1941   USA at war with Japan/Utility Scheme launched in the UK

1940   Finn Juhl's Pelican Chair

furniture before the war and which was still being reinterpreted into the 1950s.

Companies such as Practical Equipment Ltd (PEL, established in 1931) in the UK worked with designers like Wells Coates to produce 'Modernist' steel furniture of some sophistication for the mass market. Even though none of their products threatened the Bauhaus's innovative superiority, their presence in magazines like *The Studio* and in people's homes gave the wider public, whether enthusiasts for modernity or not, a clear vision of the future. As well as populating the living rooms of the relatively well off, at the onset of the Great Depression in the USA, PEL also produced a large volume of low-cost contract furniture that with the likes of its RP6 Nesting Chairs (1931–32) with tubular-steel frames and canvas seats and backs filled the civic halls and schools of a modernising nation.

In the USA, mainly in response to work shown at the Chicago World's Fair of 1933, designers such as Donald Deskey were heavily influenced by Modernist and Art Deco furniture. Firms like Howell Co. worked with designers such as Gilbert Rohde to produce predominantly tubular-steel furniture. Within a couple of years, the influence of

Breuer and his contemporaries had helped to create an entirely American style of Art Deco, which sowed the seeds for the USA's dominance in furniture-design innovation in the 1940s and 1950s.

Below: **'Britain Can Make It' exhibition, Victoria & Albert Museum, London, 1946. Utility table and three chairs, Clive Latimer.**

Although World War II hindered the ambitions of many manufacturers and designers, the material and manufacturing innovations that came out of the Allied and Axis countries made the next phase in furniture design as progressive and interesting as it had been after World War I. With plastics in their infancy, laminated wood and aluminium were the two main materials.

The use of new materials also influenced the aspirations and aesthetics of more traditional furniture manufacturing, and it is worth noting that not all important innovations were technical. For example, Finn Juhl's Pelican Chair from 1940 was probably one of the Danish designer's least technically advanced designs, but its sculptural visual language was entirely original and, from a modern perspective, well ahead of its time. Scandinavian design evolved in Denmark, Norway, Sweden and Finland. The central tenet of the movement was the production of low-cost, functional furniture that was also beautiful and used materials that could be mass-produced. Danish furniture design was certainly in ascendance from the 1930s onwards, with stars such as Bruno Mathsson, Finn Juhl and, probably the most famous of all, Hans Wegner.

Wegner's first great impact on European and American design culture was his Peacock Chair in

Low Armchair (contemporary version), Charles and Ray Eames, 1949.

Below: Pelican Chair (contemporary version), Finn Juhl, 1940.

Below left: Wishbone Chair (contemporary version), Hans Wegner, 1949.

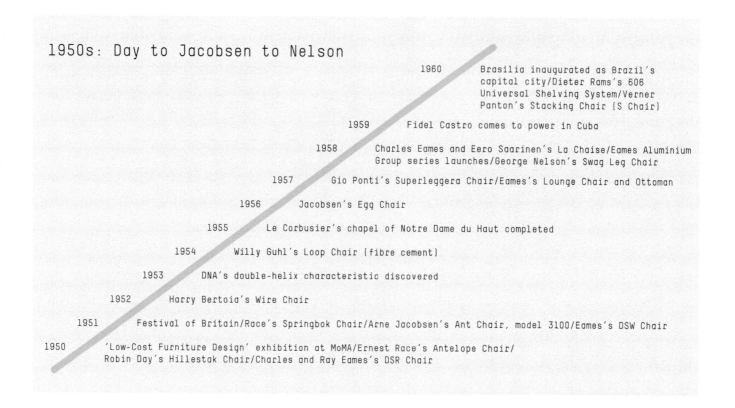

1950s: Day to Jacobsen to Nelson

1960	Brasília inaugurated as Brazil's capital city/Dieter Rams's 606 Universal Shelving System/Verner Panton's Stacking Chair (S Chair)
1959	Fidel Castro comes to power in Cuba
1958	Charles Eames and Eero Saarinen's La Chaise/Eames Aluminium Group series launches/George Nelson's Swag Leg Chair
1957	Gio Ponti's Superleggera Chair/Eames's Lounge Chair and Ottoman
1956	Jacobsen's Egg Chair
1955	Le Corbusier's chapel of Notre Dame du Haut completed
1954	Willy Guhl's Loop Chair (fibre cement)
1953	DNA's double-helix characteristic discovered
1952	Harry Bertoia's Wire Chair
1951	Festival of Britain/Race's Springbok Chair/Arne Jacobsen's Ant Chair, model 3100/Eames's DSW Chair
1950	'Low-Cost Furniture Design' exhibition at MoMA/Ernest Race's Antelope Chair/Robin Day's Hillestak Chair/Charles and Ray Eames's DSR Chair

1947, which although beautiful and highly original was still more rooted in a craft vernacular than the 'new world' being envisaged by the likes of the Eameses and Saarinen. However, in 1949, with the launch of his Wishbone Chair for Carl Hansen, Wegner created a mature style that strongly referenced the past but had entirely modern sensibilities (this was broadly true of Danish design during this period). Although well designed, the Wishbone Chair still required a significant amount of bench work and so, even though Wegner's design was significant, in terms of its cost in relation to mass manufacture, it was less successful. However, it was never intended to be a 'people's chair'. Its value, then and now, is about its evocation of refinement, quality and conservative modernity.

In the UK, material shortages and the necessity for efficient design and production led to the government's creation of the Utility Scheme in 1941 to oversee the manufacture of textiles and furniture. Much of the resulting furniture was restrained in style, but in terms of function, material use and manufacturing it often represented sound design principles. In contrast to much of the mass-market furniture of the pre-war period, the majority of the Utility Scheme's output was extremely well made and, in surprisingly contemporary terms, thoroughly sustainable.

The furniture scheme continued until 1948 and as part of the UK's immediate post-war reconstruction of society, economy and infrastructure, Utility furniture was exhibited at the 'Britain Can Make It' exhibition in 1946. While still conforming to strict guidelines about maximum material use, the exhibition previewed some remarkably 'modern' furniture for mass consumption. Compared to Charles and Ray Eames's output for the same year, the utility pieces are less noteworthy, but the Utility table and chairs designed by Clive Latimer for Heal & Son Ltd certainly stand up to contemporary scrutiny (particularly the cast-aluminium leg and plywood shell combination that became common currency for designers over the next two decades).

Without doubt, however, the stars of this period for admiring professionals and consumers alike were American designers Charles and Ray Eames. After studying under Eliel Saarinen, Charles developed a close working relationship with Saarinen's son, Eero, and in 1940 the pair prototyped a range of composite laminated furniture for which they won first prize in the MoMA design competition 'Organic Design in

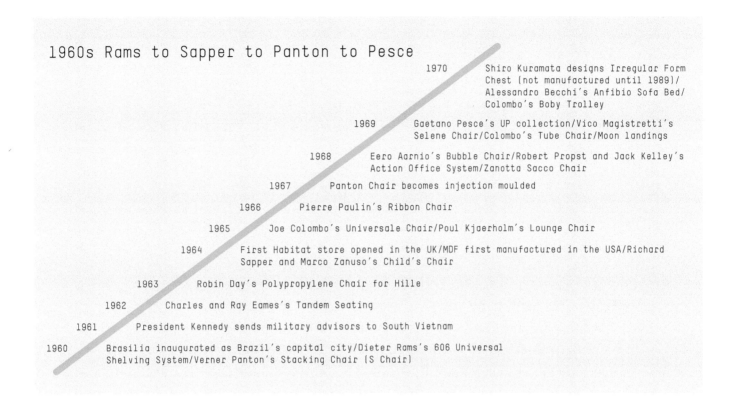

1960s Rams to Sapper to Panton to Pesce

1970	Shiro Kuramata designs Irregular Form Chest (not manufactured until 1989)/ Alessandro Becchi's Anfibio Sofa Bed/ Colombo's Boby Trolley
1969	Gaetano Pesce's UP collection/Vico Magistretti's Selene Chair/Colombo's Tube Chair/Moon landings
1968	Eero Aarnio's Bubble Chair/Robert Propst and Jack Kelley's Action Office System/Zanotta Sacco Chair
1967	Panton Chair becomes injection moulded
1966	Pierre Paulin's Ribbon Chair
1965	Joe Colombo's Universale Chair/Poul Kjaerholm's Lounge Chair
1964	First Habitat store opened in the UK/MDF first manufactured in the USA/Richard Sapper and Marco Zanuso's Child's Chair
1963	Robin Day's Polypropylene Chair for Hille
1962	Charles and Ray Eames's Tandem Seating
1961	President Kennedy sends military advisors to South Vietnam
1960	Brasilia inaugurated as Brazil's capital city/Dieter Rams's 606 Universal Shelving System/Verner Panton's Stacking Chair (S Chair)

Home Furnishings'. They also developed products for the US government's war effort, such as the now-iconic laminated leg splints for wounded servicemen. Their work represented the next great step forward, following on from the progress achieved by Alvar Aalto , Marcel Breuer and Mart Stam.

As peacetime afforded them more opportunities to pursue other projects, Charles began working more closely with Ray and, as the 1940s progressed, they produced some of their first legendary works, such as the Low Armchair, DCM and LCM furniture and Storage Units.

In the UK, Robin Day built on his and Clive Latimer's success in the 1948-49 MoMA furniture competition (which culminated in the 'Low-Cost Furniture Design exhibition of the following year) by becoming design director of Hille – a relationship that would last for decades and produce some of the most significant British design of the post-war period. Day's 1950 Hillestak Chair marked a shift in British design, which started an exploratory process that was to result in important innovations a decade later. Two main types of Hillestak Chairs were produced: a one-piece laminated ply shell with a tubular-steel leg frame and a second version of total

Child's Chair (Seggiolino 4999), Richard Sapper and Marco Zanuso, 1964.

laminate construction, which echoed the Eames's DCW Chair.

During this period in the USA, Charles and Ray Eames produced their greatest work. Their first revolutionary fibreglass-shelled chair (see p40) was launched by Herman Miller in 1949–50, and became the basis for a whole series of chairs created

Panton Chair (polyproplylene
version), Verner Panton, 1969.

throughout the early 1950s, culminating with La Chaise in 1958 (see p186, another Eero Saarinen collaboration). Despite being labour intensive, the chair shells were the precursor to the large-scale injection mouldings of the following decade and, at the time, represented the most efficient way of achieving such radical organic forms.

In parallel to this unequalled shift in visual language, Charles and Ray Eames were also developing the structural and material themes they had begun in the 1940s using plywood. Their Lounge Chair and Ottoman were originally intended as a one-off gift to film director and writer Billy Wilder. However, the design was eminently manufacturable, and ever since Herman Miller began its mass production in 1956 it has become a defining mainstay of office and domestic aspiration, mainly, it could be said, for men. Continuing with contract furniture and at that time, the male theme, in 1958 Herman Miller launched the most desired and copied office furniture to date: the Eames's Aluminium Group series (see p41).

Although not as well known as the Eames, George Nelson was one of the USA's foremost architects and designers during the 1940s and 1950s. His 1958 Swag Leg Chair used the Eames's patented fibreglass-moulding process to produce a chair shell in two parts, which were then glued together. The two mouldings and the chair's geometry provided good support and flexibility – an ergonomic feature that would be researched and exploited over the coming decades.

Driven by the emergence of consumerism and new buying patterns, the enormous progress in furniture manufacturing achieved during the 1950s was more than equalled in the 1960s, with an important technological breakthrough taking place in 1962. Robin Day and Hille managed to produce a one-piece, injection-moulded polypropylene chair shell of a size that had not been possible before (see p43). This development was significant for the UK as it was the first time since the 1930s and Isokon that such important technical innovation had taken place within its shores. Improvements to the process and the development of new plastic materials meant that laminated wood would no longer have the currency for designers that it had once had. Despite the large investment costs needed to create its tooling, the potential of plastic was so great that furniture design for mass manufacture would never be the same again.

In excess of 14million chairs of this kind have been sold since the Polypropylene Chair's launch in 1963, and Hille still sell more than 500,000 a year. It is testament to Robin and Lucienne Day's consummate design skills that the original version is still produced in such numbers and that it is one of the most comfortable chairs of its kind available.

The new aesthetics afforded by fibreglass, and later thermoplastics, heralded a new period in visual language that was not all 'organic' and was not all about chairs. The great German industrial designer Dieter Rams, who had a huge influence on product design from the mid-1950s onward, also made a significant contribution to the furniture canon with his innovative modular 606 Universal Shelving System for Vitsoe + Zapf (see p42), which was launched in 1960. Rams was certainly influenced by the likes of Mies van der Rohe and was possibly the first designer to be described as a minimalist. The simplicity and sensitivity to composition, proportion and materials in the Vitsoe system epitomized his work, and despite the wealth of referential versions designed since 1960, none improve its function and only some manage to parallel its elegance.

The development of injection moulding was being pursued across the manufacturing spectrum and even though the Hille chair represented a milestone, the goal for many designers and manufacturers from the mid-1950s on was to produce a one-piece (monobloc) injection-moulded plastic chair – what Saarinen called 'a structural total'. However, difficulties with material flow and tooling size meant that the first totally plastic chairs were assemblies of separate plastic parts (monocoques). Richard Sapper and Marco Zanuso's 1964 Child's Chair and Joe Colombo's Universale Chair (see p106) of the following year were both assemblies of this kind.

In such an atmosphere of technological and material furtherance, progress was dramatic, and so it was

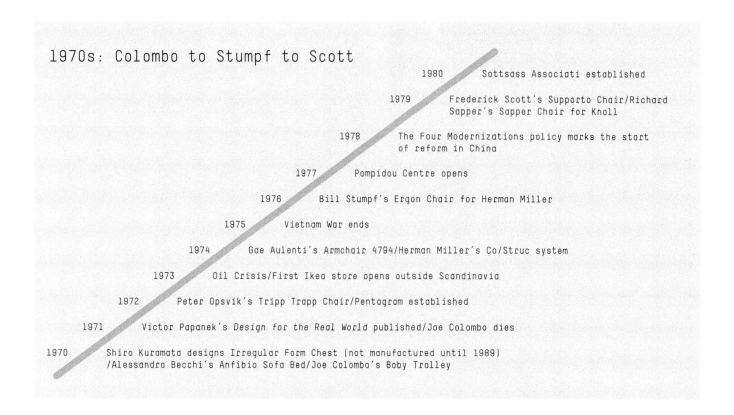

1970s: Colombo to Stumpf to Scott

1980   Sottsass Associati established

1979   Frederick Scott's Supporto Chair/Richard
        Sapper's Sapper Chair for Knoll

1978   The Four Modernizations policy marks the start
        of reform in China

1977   Pompidou Centre opens

1976   Bill Stumpf's Ergon Chair for Herman Miller

1975   Vietnam War ends

1974   Gae Aulenti's Armchair 4794/Herman Miller's Co/Struc system

1973   Oil Crisis/First Ikea store opens outside Scandinavia

1972   Peter Opsvik's Tripp Trapp Chair/Pentagram established

1971   Victor Papanek's Design for the Real World published/Joe Colombo dies

1970   Shiro Kuramata designs Irregular Form Chest (not manufactured until 1989)
        /Alessandro Becchi's Anfibio Sofa Bed/Joe Colombo's Boby Trolley

only two years later in 1967 when Verner Panton stunned his contemporaries with the first cantilevered, monobloc injection-moulded plastic version of the S Chair for Herman Miller at the 1967 Milan Furniture Fair, previously launched in fibreglass in 1960. Not to be outdone, the brilliant Vico Magistretti launched Selene, another of the first monobloc plastic chairs, with the prominent furniture-design company Cassina in 1969.

Also in 1969, Gaetano Pesce, a 30-year-old former fine artist from Italy, became the first designer to fully use the properties of polyurethane foam by producing the remarkable UP series of chairs, stools and footstools for C&B Italia (later B&B Italia). The open-cell structure of the foam enabled the UP range to be packaged and sold within a sealed vacuum-packed bag at a much reduced size. It visibly grew to full size once removed from its packaging and when the polyurethane foam had absorbed enough air.

During the early 1970s and following decades of experimentation with man-made materials, a number of designers became more aware of the need to source sustainable natural materials. This is historically evident in the resurgence of the designer-

maker and the popularity of Danish wooden furniture and semi-craft style. Alongside this revival came a new, although familiarly modernist, 'anti-aesthetic', in which structure was led by function. Designers such as Norwegian Peter Opsvik were not concerned with styling. In 1972, Opsvik launched his Tripp Trapp Chair – a universal chair (see p46) that was height-adjustable for children and adults, allowing everyone to sit at the same table. This theme of functionality was evident throughout the decade, as in the architectural icon the Pompidou Centre, designed by Italian architect Renzo Piano in partnership with British-born architects Richard and Su Rogers.

Undoubtedly, furniture design of the 1970s was not defined by the same material and manufacturing progress as in the 1960s, or indeed, the preceding six decades. Development was now more associated with electronics and IT. But this lack of progress seems to have become the catalyst for inspiring the loosely Postmodernism design revolution of the 1980s. The radical themes of the late 1960s were carried into the next decade by the likes of Joe Colombo and Alessandro Becchi. In spite of the more conservative work of certain designers like Poul Kjaerholm's who pushed the visual and conceptual ideas of Modernism into the 1970s,

Opposite: **Supporto Chair, Frederick Scott, 1979.**

1980s: Starck to Memphis

1990	Starck's Juicy Salif for Alessi
1989	London's Design Museum opens/Berlin Wall comes down
1988	Jorge Pensi's Toledo Chair
1987	Alberto Meda's Light Light Chair/Shiro Kuramata's How High the Moon Armchair/IKEA in the UK
1986	Norman Foster's Nomos series/Fernando Urquijo and Giorgio Macola's Mood Desk/Ron Arad's Well Tempered Chair
1985	Microsoft launches Windows operating system/IKEA in the USA
1984	Bill Stumpf and Don Chadwick's Equa Chair/Apple Macintosh launches a computer
1983	Formica launches ColorCore
1982	Philippe Starck's Costes Chair/Paolo Deganello's Torso Seating/Charles Pollock's Penelope Chair
1981	Memphis Group's debut exhibit at the Milan Furniture Fair
1980	Sottsass Associati established

Left to right:

1970s magazine advert for Moffat Kitchens (UK).

Armchair 4794, Gae Aulenti, 1974.

design historians, including the influential Penny Sparke, consider the design revolution of the 1960s as heralding the end of Modernism. While this is true in the main, Modernism did continue in work such as Frederick Scott's Supporto Chair, which was launched at the end of the decade. However, the diversity of minor design manifestos and products ensured that no single approach was king.

After its mainstream introduction in the 1960s, flat-pack (ready to assemble) furniture had become by the mid-1970s a commonplace way of buying furniture. For example, IKEA was building on its domestic popularity for this kind of furniture by expanding its operations outside Scandinavia. Board-surfacing processes such as foil wrapping and membrane pressing (see p209) would also impact on the flat-pack market by the end of the decade and would start to change the aesthetic range and pricing of low-cost panel-based furniture. However, for the majority of the decade, Formica and its offshoots were still the main components for board surfacing.

The Oil Crisis of 1973 had a big effect on the cost of plastics – the raw material rose suddenly by nearly 40 per cent. The intensive development of injection moulding in the 1960s was not continued into the 1970s, but with the invention of reaction injection moulding (RIM) in the mid-1960s and its subsequent

improvement in the 1970s through the development of a more versatile range of polyurethanes, there were great opportunities for more precise, complex and, in some cases, multi-density moulded polyurethane forms. By 1974, monocoque chairs with integral softness were possible, using the RIM process, as proven by the collaboration between home-furnishings company Kartell and Italian architect Gae Aulenti.

Modular work-based systems were nothing new but forward-thinking companies such as Herman Miller and Steelcase continued to conduct in-depth research into workplace requirements and worker behaviour, resulting in highly influential product ranges such as the Action Office System (see p44) and the Co/Struc healthcare range – both of which, as testament to the former company's insight and design ethos, are still widely specified and used today (see case study of one of Herman Miller's research programs, pp92–93).

Known as the designer decade, the 1980s saw a large-scale reappraisal of the history of design. International museums started to collect design, the first design museums were built and designers began self-consciously to reinterpret the past. Conversely, some designers, notably the Memphis Group based in Milan, sought to break with the past.

Left to right:
Costes Chair, Philippe Starck, 1982.

Torso Seating, Paolo Deganello, Cassina I Contemporanei Collection, 1982.

1990s: IKEA to Arad

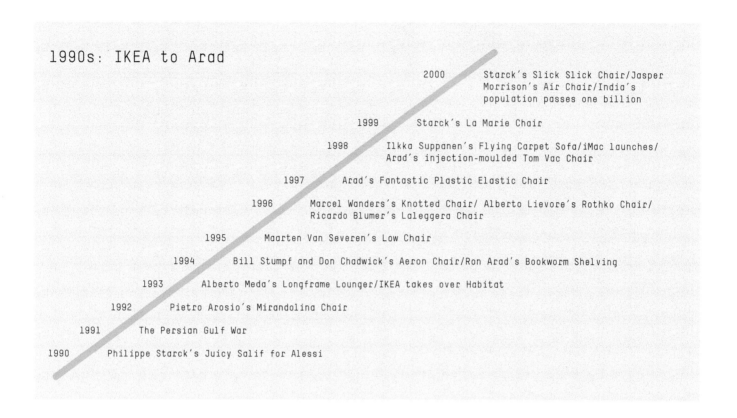

2000   Starck's Slick Slick Chair/Jasper Morrison's Air Chair/India's population passes one billion

1999   Starck's La Marie Chair

1998   Ilkka Suppanen's Flying Carpet Sofa/iMac launches/ Arad's injection-moulded Tom Vac Chair

1997   Arad's Fantastic Plastic Elastic Chair

1996   Marcel Wanders's Knotted Chair/ Alberto Lievore's Rothko Chair/ Ricardo Blumer's Laleggera Chair

1995   Maarten Van Severen's Low Chair

1994   Bill Stumpf and Don Chadwick's Aeron Chair/Ron Arad's Bookworm Shelving

1993   Alberto Meda's Longframe Lounger/IKEA takes over Habitat

1992   Pietro Arosio's Mirandolina Chair

1991   The Persian Gulf War

1990   Philippe Starck's Juicy Salif for Alessi

While the Memphis Group has an unassailable prominence in the history of furniture design and the 1980s, its direct influence is often overstated. It signified an ideological break from Modernism by its aesthetically singular designs and by the intellects of those involved, but its effect on Postmodernism was more akin to a starting gun than a lasting and transcending manifesto.

The 1980s heralded a diversification in design. So many different strands of cutting-edge design were part of an advancing front that the collective themes explored during the 1920s and 1930s were not parallelled in this decade of radical change. Perhaps the greatest influence was Philippe Starck, who had many successful products to his name before almost any other 'star' designer of the period. His products inspired designers, thrilled consumers and, along with those of Ettore Sottsass and Shiro Kuramata, helped to describe a new visual and conceptual language for furniture.

Although more visually original than technically radical, Starck's early furniture evolved throughout the 1980s and, by the end of the decade, was increasingly focused on technical and visual innovation. His first iconic and truly commercial

Below: **Longframe Lounger, Alberto Meda, 1993.**

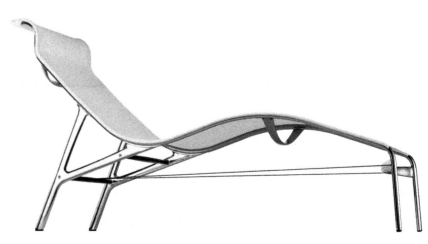

furniture design was the plywood and steel chair for Café Costes, which, despite its conservative use of materials, was an elegant portent of what was to come over the next ten years – most markedly in plastics.

A deconstructed and more obviously Postmodernist approach to design is evident in Paolo Deganello's 1982 sofa for Cassina, which, again, looks more original than it is technically radical, but also epitomizes the often idiosyncratic and witty language of Postmodern design throughout the mid-1980s. In parallel to this emerging sensibility, from the early- to mid-1980s, the one-off, almost 'anti-product' furniture designs of Ron Arad were a foil to the mass-consumed creations of Starck. However, despite an apparent gulf between the two designers, Arad increasingly brought his unique perspective to mass manufacture while Starck became more involved in pushing the boundaries of manufacturing materials and technologies.

The 1980s were not devoid of technical innovation, despite many notable steps forward being partially eclipsed by the brilliance of Starck and his up-and-coming contemporaries' visual creativity. Ergonomic office seating became one of the most progressive areas of furniture design. The Equa Chair (Herman

Miller, 1984) was an early partnership between Bill Stumpf and Don Chadwick, who a decade later would complete their ergonomic analysis for desk-working with the Aeron Chair. The Penelope Chair (1982) by Charles Pollock for Castelli was a significant manufacturing achievement, but despite the benefits of the air circulating through the mesh (an important, but differently resolved part of the Aeron Chair's innovation), the high manufacturing costs of the rigid mesh meant that it had few emulators. Norman Foster's Nomos office series for Tecno (1986; see p47) was as much a visual archetype as it was structurally innovative, and Alberto Meda's Light Light Chair from 1987 was as much an essay on structural possibilities as Gio Ponti's 1957 Superleggera Chair, although because of its labour-intensive manufacture Light Light was never intended to be mass manufactured.

If the 1980s were the decade of the designer, then the 1990s were when design entered the mainstream. Ron Arad, one of the enfants terribles of 1980s design, became a cornerstone of international design education as Professor of Design Products at London's Royal College of Art. This clear departure from the past was a reflection of broader trends leading UK product-design education away from

Flying Carpet Sofa, Ilkka Suppanen, 1998.

furniture and toward idiosyncratic design art.

The world's changing political map heralded a great many other changes, not least the start of the global environmental crisis. Consumers and the business community became aware of the profound need for an environmentally sustainable future, although, apart from the activities of a handful of forward-thinking companies, it was not until the end of the decade that such concerns were dealt with broadly and meaningfully by designers, manufacturers and retailers.

Early responses to the need for sustainability included craft furniture made directly from recycled objects and some batch and volume production using recycled sheet plastic. Work of this nature was prominent in publications, museums and galleries, but had little or no impact on mainstream or progressive furniture design and manufacturing. It was only when Herman Miller's Aeron Chair was launched in 1994 that the real issues of reuse and recycling were more completely understood by the wider design community. The Aeron was designed for longevity and disassembly, with 94 per cent of its structure using high-quality recycled materials. More than any other piece of furniture to that date, it represented a sincere and ecology-focused corporate ethos – a standpoint that in the 2010s is almost de rigueur for progressive brands.

The changing balance of world power, and in particular China's domination in manufacturing growth, meant that generic, low-cost products of all types were becoming increasingly cheap. While this made some well-designed consumables more accessible, the manufacture of 'new' furniture design (excluding copies of classics) became, by comparison, more expensive. The clamour and expectation for cheap furniture had, in part, begun a few years earlier with the opening of IKEA stores, first in the USA (1985) and then in the UK (1987), and although IKEA's market share (then and now) was relatively small, its influence over consumer taste and its competitors' product lines was disproportionately positive. What are generally accepted as design icons are rarely conceived or used as everyday furniture, yet certain products can

achieve a similarly iconic status simply due to their popularity and good function. Despite being a rather inelegant pastiche of Alvar Aalto's Chair 406, the ubiquitous IKEA Poäng Armchair has achieved just such a status by its vast sales since its launch in 1972. It is also probably one of the most interesting (in terms of structure and performance) pieces of contemporary furniture commonly found in domestic environments.

If there was an emerging theme from the 1990s, it was one that paralleled the interests of Starck and Arad: innovation inspired and led by a new or existing manufacturing process. Ricardo Blumer's polyurethane-injected plywood Laleggera Chair for Alias in 1996 and Pietro Arosio's 1992 extruded Mirandolina Chair for Zanotta certainly fit this approach, and the latter has obvious parallels with Ron Arad's Fantastic Plastic Elastic Chair (see p48) of 1997. The FPE Chair is probably one of Arad's greatest designs and represents a mastery of materials and processes echoed in his Tom Vac Chair (see p49). Not as lauded as Arad's output during this period, but nonetheless one of the most remarkable designs from the decade was Ilkka Suppanen's Flying Carpet Sofa, which was also launched at the Milan Furniture Fair in 1998.

IKEA catalogue spread (including Poäng Armchair), 1999.

2000s+: Grcic to The Bouroullecs to Diez

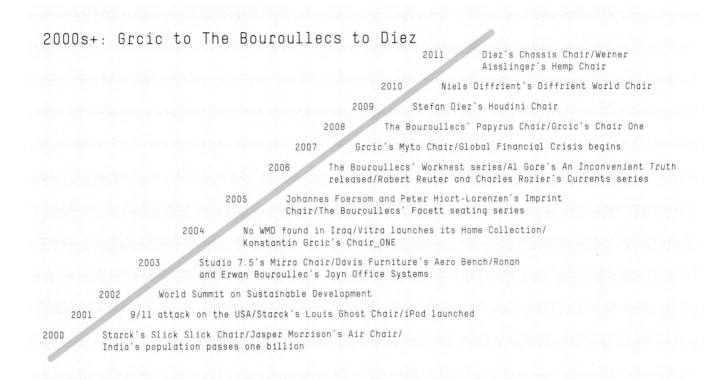

2011 — Diez's Chassis Chair/Werner Aisslinger's Hemp Chair

2010 — Niels Diffrient's Diffrient World Chair

2009 — Stefan Diez's Houdini Chair

2008 — The Bouroullecs' Papyrus Chair/Grcic's Chair One

2007 — Grcic's Myto Chair/Global Financial Crisis begins

2006 — The Bouroullecs' Worknest series/Al Gore's *An Inconvenient Truth* released/Robert Reuter and Charles Rozier's Currents series

2005 — Johannes Foersom and Peter Hiort-Lorenzen's Imprint Chair/The Bouroullecs' Facett seating series

2004 — No WMD found in Iraq/Vitra launches its Home Collection/Konstantin Grcic's Chair_ONE

2003 — Studio 7.5's Mirra Chair/Davis Furniture's Aero Bench/Ronan and Erwan Bouroullec's Joyn Office Systems

2002 — World Summit on Sustainable Development

2001 — 9/11 attack on the USA/Starck's Louis Ghost Chair/iPod launched

2000 — Starck's Slick Slick Chair/Jasper Morrison's Air Chair/India's population passes one billion

Supported by (resting upon) six sprung-steel rods, the sofa's seat is a layer of flexible steel sandwiched between two layers of 6mm (0.25in) felt. The resulting structure is dynamic, responsive, comfortable and quite unlike anything created before or since – a work of genius.

By the beginning of the new millennium, the decade of design had ingrained its sensibilities into mainstream culture (to be witnessed rather than necessarily consumed) to such a degree that new and established design festivals, in London, New York and Milan, also developed parallel subcultural events such as Designersblock in London's East End. At the same time, a movement of designer-makers emerged who worked at the intersection of design, craft and art. In turn, this led to the rise of furniture 'design art': one-off, idiosyncratic pieces created for a small market. Such work can be important for wider furniture design, but generally it has little to do with efficient, rational design for mass manufacture.

History shows that during the early 2000s, much of Europe and North America's education curricula and media output was more interested in the design-art end of the spectrum, and so industrial design for volume manufacture took a back seat in terms of exhibitions and publications. Design art was restricted to furniture and domestic products to a much greater extent than other product design. However, it is possible to draw a comparison between the rise of aestheticism in such products as the iPod and the fascination with entirely aesthetic and allegorical (rather than industrial) furniture design.

During the late 1990s and early 2000s significant development in thermoplastics – particularly polycarbonate and polypropylene – enabled the production of 'structural totals' (monoblocs) with significant new aesthetics. For example, Philippe Starck's groundbreaking La Marie Chair for Kartell in 1999 was the world's first clear plastic (polycarbonate) injection-moulded monobloc chair. Two years later, building on their technical expertise with the material, the same partnership produced the Louis Ghost Chair (see p179), which was perhaps the first mass-produced piece of furniture to establish the Postmodern principle of making historical forms contemporary.

In the 2000s, a new generation of international furniture design stars emerged, such as French designers Ronan and Erwan Bouroullec and London-based Konstantin Grcic. By 2002–03, both design

consultancies had experienced a step change in their commissions and clients and were undertaking work that was as technically innovative as it was clever or beautiful.

The Bouroullec brothers' intensely visual furniture has developed through a strong relationship with Vitra and Magis. Since developing the 2005 Facett seating series (see p110), they have increasingly pushed the boundaries of materials and techniques to create a paradigm shift in aesthetics. They have been highly influential ever since, particularly with their Worknest Chair (2006) for Vitra and their Papyrus Chair for Kartell (2008).

A more significant but less visual advance in plastic furniture during this period was Konstantin Grcic's Myto Chair. Grcic was fast becoming one of the most technically innovative furniture designers in the world and his Myto Chair of 2007, developed with BASF, used the new thermoplastic Ultradur, which enabled the creation of an enormously strong, cantilevered monobloc chair. Historically, Grcic is a worthy inheritor of Verner Panton's mantle after his injection-moulded Panton Chair.

During the 2000s, the major contract furniture players in Europe and the USA vied for pole position in ergonomic and sustainable innovation following the launch of Herman Miller's groundbreaking Mirra Chair designed by Studio 7.5 in 2003 (see p51). Steelcase, Knoll, Humanscale and Vitra all contributed significantly to the progress of workplace furniture and, in particular, task seating during this time. Humanscale's 2010 Diffrient World Chair (see p57) sets a new standard in energy-efficient manufacturing, reusability and recyclability, and illustrates the degree to which such 'moral positives' are now an unquestioned part of business accountability.

Design reflects the issues of the times and, at present, concerns about sustainability, ethical manufacture and responsible disposal are key. With greater design literacy than ever before and an ever-expanding furniture canon, consumers now expect high standards in both manufacture and performance. Maintaining these standards will be

the challenge for designers in the future. The tradition of manufacturing and material-led innovation that began with Thonet's revolutionary No. 14 Chair in 1859 (see p15), and which evolved with Breuer, Prouvé, Eames, Rams, Arad and Grcic, has continued. New design innovators persist in redefining furniture through aesthetic and technical enquiry, with examples such as Doshi Levien's bio-composite Impossible Wood (see p10) and Stefan Diez's deep-drawn Chassis Chair leading the way.

Papyrus Chair, Ronan and Erwan Bouroullec, 2008.

Opposite, top to bottom:
Myto Chair, Konstantin Grcic, 2007.

Chassis Chair, Stefan Diez, 2011.

1b: Innovations in materials and manufacturing processes

Many good designs display their designers' understanding of materials, manufacturing processes and ergonomics. Such works often represent paradigm shifts in awareness of material use and manufacturing. Marcel Breuer's use of tubular steel, Charles and Ray Eames's use of laminated veneers, Gaetano Pesce's expanding UP Chair or Don Chadwick and Bill Stumpf's Aeron Chair for Herman Miller – all changed the visual language and technical vocabulary of furniture.

As shown in the previous section, true innovation is nothing new; Jean Prouvé and George Nelson were as radical in their day as Ron Arad or the Bouroullec brothers are today. None are just stylists; all have innovated from a position of knowledge. To be able to design furniture well, it is necessary to study that which surrounds us and to, metaphorically, take it apart. Sound knowledge of design and manufacture enables designers to engage with or consciously throw away the rule book and embrace creativity.

Jean Prouvé's 1931 Cité Armchair displayed cutting-edge metal-forming and fabrication techniques coupled with a radical and dynamic visual language that would be enough in itself to justify its place in this chapter. Of equal visual but of greater cultural impact (through exhibition and media) were the Eames's fibreglass-shelled DSW and DSR chairs. Although the shell material has been superseded by thermoplastic, the chairs are still a significant part of furniture design's lineage for their technical and aesthetic innovation.

Dieter Rams's 1960 Vitsoe + Zapf 606 Universal Shelving System (see p42) was, and still is, an essay in elegant efficiency and adaptive, flexible design, which, barring a new age of ornament, will always be present in the minds of designers creating wall-storage systems.

Herman Miller's Action Office System (see p44) is over 40 years old but remains important today. There have been modifications to cope with developing technology use, but the core of the design thinking that went into Robert Propst and Jack Kelley's

system is still as relevant and sound today as it was in the late 1960s. Likewise, Peter Opsvick's 1972 Tripp Trapp Chair (see p46) rests at the top of the design pile through the addition of accessories that have addressed some of its limitations.

Aesthetic nuances and revelations will always supply a new style at the forefront of design; but it is affirming to know that it is still possible for new work such as Stefan Diez's Houdini Chair (see p56) to make an important contribution through its imaginative and introspective use of traditional construction techniques and materials.

The following case studies are examples of design excellence and also of diverse approaches to aesthetics, manufacturing, materials and efficiencies of all kinds.

Cité Armchair

Jean Prouvé (1931)

Jean Prouvé, one of France's foremost designers, used his metal-engineering skills to establish a significant manufacturing business in the late 1920s. His company produced architectural metalwork and progressive furniture such as the Cité Armchair. This highly original and dynamic design was developed using the most up-to-date metal-forming and welding processes of the time, which helped to create the Cité Armchair's radically new visual language.

The steel frame is stamped, pressed and welded into four sub-assemblies, which are powder-coated (originally enamelled). Integral metal connection fittings are fixed to the front of the tubular-steel seat frame, which supports a fabric sling cover. Cushioning is added to the sling and the whole assembly is enveloped in a fabric cover. Leather straps, tightened around the side frames, produce the armrests.

Contemporary version of the Cité Armchair manufactured by Vitra.

DSR Chair and DSW Chair

Charles and Ray Eames (1950, 1951)

Originally with a fibreglass shell, the DSR Chair
(the Eiffel-base version of these side chairs) was exhibited at
the 1950 'Low-Cost Furniture Design' exhibition at MoMA
and was the first industrially produced plastic chair. The
base frame of the DSR Chair was originally chromium-
plated, welded mild steel. In current versions the frames are
either chromed, galvanized or powder-coated (the latter two
for outdoor use).

The DSW version (wood base) was launched in 1951, with
turned beech legs that are braced using powder-coated steel
rod stays. This sub-assembly is connected to the shell using
steel brackets that are held within slots at the top of each wooden
leg. The components of the leg frame are screwed together.

Since the early 1990s Vitra has sold updated versions of both
chairs that use an injection-moulded polypropylene shell
with integral threaded inserts to which the different leg
frames are bolted.

**Contemporary versions of the DSR
& DSW chairs manufactured by Vitra.**

Aluminium Group

Charles and Ray Eames (1958)

Assembled from only six major components (or eight with armrests) the Aluminium Group offers many variations in seat material, base options and adjustment, ranging from the original rotating versions to gas-assisted height- and tilt-adjustable ones.

The system's main innovation is that rather than using a cushion over a substructure, the seat and backrest are suspended by being mechanically captured within each side frame and then tensioned apart by two cross braces. In addition to the leather seat cover over a polyester sling substructure, there is also Hopsak, a frequency-welded seat cover (100 per cent polyamide) and Netweave, a coated-polyester-thread sling.

All the main structural components (except for the seat) are made from die-cast aluminium, of which 95 per cent is recycled. These are either polished or chrome-plated.

The Aluminium Group is comprised of four chair types (Side, Lounge, Management and Executive), each with several material and component options.

606 Universal Shelving System

Dieter Rams (1960)

Designed in 1960 for Vitsoe + Zapf while Rams was head of design at Braun, the 606 Universal Shelving System is a highly flexible modular system, enabling set-ups ranging from a small alcove desk to library shelving. The system cantilevers from either a single extruded channel (E-Track) fixed directly to a wall, or from a structurally independent quatrefoil extrusion (X-Post) that runs from floor to wall or ceiling and can support units front and back as well as side to side.

The choice of extrusion system depends on the expected load, the quality of the available wall fixing (or whether there is a wall at all) or simply the aesthetic preference of the customer. Both systems can be used together. All the shelf, cabinet and desk units connect to the upright extrusions by

inserting aluminium pins through their fixing holes and through (perpendicular to) the extrusion.

The shelves are stamped and folded mild steel that is powder-coated. The cabinets are constructed from laminate-surfaced or beech-veneered MDF.

The wall-fixed version of the 606 Universal Shelving System.

Polypropylene Chair

Robin Day (1963)

Manufactured from polypropylene by Hille, this revolutionary chair could not be simpler in terms of technical design: one injection-moulded seat shell with four moulded fixing bosses to which a variety of leg frames are attached using screws. The geometry of the shell and, in particular, the lip around its edge, provides complete structural integrity, producing a chair that will last for many years of everyday use.

Although not indestructible, Day's super-tough chairs will only degrade as the result of serious abuse, typically causing deformation or surface damage to the leg frame.

Despite the large investment needed to manufacture an injection-moulding tool, once the tooling investment has been paid off, the profit margin significantly increases. Fibreglass equivalents of this single-piece shell were slow to manufacture and never became any cheaper to produce.

Hille's Polypropylene Chairs are familiar to many as the archetypal school seating.

Action Office System

Robert Propst and Jack Kelley (1968)

From the late 1950s, the balance of workplace activity in northern Europe and the USA began to shift away from manufacturing and, by the 1960s, office work was the dominant form of employment. Forward-thinking companies, such as Herman Miller, under the guidance of its design director George Nelson, began to research this trend in detail. In 1968, it launched the highly influential Action Office System – the first open-plan office furniture series.

With minor subsequent developments, this much copied series is still appropriate for today's office environments and technologies and continues to be a major part of Herman Miller's product line. Its longevity is a result of its flexibility, part of designer Robert Propst's original specification.

The Action Office System has three major component groupings: vertical panels, cabinets and work surfaces. An important advance has been the maximization of the panels' cable-management potential to keep up with the ever-changing demands of office technology.

Base cabinets are either floor based or, for lighter loads and display, they are cantilevered from the vertical panels. The wall cabinets are cantilevered in the same way. Work surfaces are available in the now-standard straight, 90° and 135° configuration and can be supported by the cabinets, panel system or leg options.

The Action Office System was the first furniture system for open-plan offices.

Tripp Trapp Chair

Peter Opsvick (1972)

The simplicity and flexibility of the Tripp Trapp Chair, manufactured by Stokke, creates a supremely functional seat that has never been equalled. The addition of the Baby Set and Play Tray have addressed some of its earlier limitations, and the design is now as current and as relevant as it ever was.

Assembled from nine major components, the chair gains its structural integrity by each of the two L-shaped sides being drawn on to two threaded bars, two backrests and a cross brace between the feet. The seat and the footrest are held tightly in place by this compression; but, with a slight loosening of the fixing bolts, these can be adjusted forward or backward or by height within the horizontal fluted slots, which have the same radius as the seat and back's edges.

The L-shaped sides are pre-glued, dowel-jointed, solid beech; the backrests are formed laminated beech and the seat and footrest are beech ply.

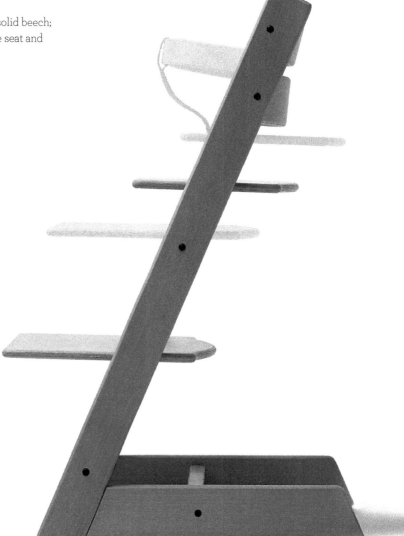

The original Tripp Trapp design, showing the Baby Set bar and strap.

Nomos Desk

Norman Foster (1986)

Developed from a concept by and for the architecture firm Foster + Partners' own offices in the early 1980s, the Nomos system encompasses an extensive series of modular desks and conference tables, all based around a system of glass tops with aluminium and steel leg frames.

The structural rationale behind Nomos parallels much of the architectural engineering that was being pioneered in buildings at the time, and all of the furniture is based on the same sophisticated structure and component system. The leg structure is an assembly of four major die-cast aluminium brackets and eight major fabricated sub-assemblies of tube, cast and machined elements.

Since its introduction, the finish options have increased significantly; as well as the original clear toughened glass and chromed-steel leg frame, its manufacturer Tecno offers a wide array of enamelled leg frames and colour-lacquered glass. The original collection's techno style epitomized mainstream designer furniture for much of the decade, yet, its aesthetic development has, in the eyes of this author at least, rendered it thoroughly convincing as 'new' contemporary design.

Updated finish options have ensured this 1980s classic retains its contemporaneity.

Fantastic Plastic Elastic (FPE) Chair

Ron Arad (1997)

Ron Arad's FPE Chair embodies a brilliant approach to design that seeks to express the characteristics of materials and manufacturing processes through arresting forms. Manufactured by Kartell, the chair uses no cross struts, simply employing the plastic seat to create a structure between the legs. The seat provides a good deal of rigidity, but there is still a reasonable amount of playful movement between the side frames; whether intentional or not, Arad drew attention to this dynamism when the chair was launched.

The FPE Chair was originally conceived as an entirely extruded product, but due to the constraints of the desired plastic's properties and finish and the design of the tool, it eventually became injection moulded.

The frame is extruded in a soft alloy and then milled part-way to separate the legs. It is then formed, age/precipitation-hardened and painted, after which the polypropylene seat is inserted.

The relative rigidity of the plastic seat replaces any need for cross members.

Tom Vac Chair

Ron Arad (1997, aluminium 'prototype' version; 1998, injection-moulded version)

The original Tom Vac Chair was financed by *Domus* magazine, which paid Ron Arad to produce a large-scale sculpture for the 1997 Milan Furniture Fair. Arad shrewdly used the funds to manufacture a CNC tool for superforming (see p169) 100 of the chair shells and manufacturing the leg frames from chromed-steel tube. These were stacked to a great height in a Milan square, and became the basis for the polypropylene versions produced by Vitra today.

As with the superformed version, today's shell gains a great deal of its strength from its large-scale wave texture. However, the mass-produced version is much more flexible and so relies on the leg frame for a central rigidity. The shell has integral threaded leg-frame fixings and a fine spark-eroded surface finish. It is available in five batch-dyed colours. The leg frames are either powder-coated or of chromed steel and have different types of glide feet, depending on whether they are for indoor or outdoor use.

A polished aluminium example from the 1997 'prototypes'.

Aero Bench

Alberto Lievore, Jeannette Altherr and Manel Molina (2003)

The Aero Bench's visual simplicity and ambitious use of
large-scale aluminium extrusions has made it one of the
best-known and most admired furniture innovations of the
2000s. Winner of the Delta De Oro and Red Dot Product
Design prizes, its notoriety is due in no small part to it often
being found in important transport hubs and high-profile
architecture projects.

Comprised of three longitudinally ribbed and anodized
extrusions (two identical and one unique), the Aero Bench is
intended to be used indoors since it features no drainage
system for rain. The three hollow elements telescope
together and are secured by the attachment of stainless-steel
end plates. The leg frame is bolted to threaded holes,
post-machined in the underside, while the legs are a
stainless-steel rod assembly which is inserted into cast-
aluminium feet.

The Aero series now includes optional cushions either in
self-skinned or upholstered polyurethane foam. There is also
a version without a backrest extrusion, which has a reduced-
height corner profile.

**Aero Bench, manufactured
by SELLEX.**

Mirra Chair

Studio 7.5 (2003)

Designed by German design group Studio 7.5, manufactured by Herman Miller and launched in 2003, the tasking Mirra Chair is a worthy successor to the industry-changing Aeron Chair, which had been launched a decade earlier. While the Aeron is an essay in adjustability, the Mirra achieves a parallel level of ergonomic excellence through active and passive adaptability at a lower cost. This is largely due to its highly sophisticated seat pan (the same PostureFit system made famous by the Aeron Chair), its highly adaptive Ultramid nylon TriFlex backrest form and structure and its overall material performance. A full range of manual adjustment options are possible, but not all come as standard. Seat height, depth, tilt (both its resistance and limit) and lumbar support, plus the armrest angle and height, can all be incrementally tuned to the user's needs.

Overall, the Mirra Chair is a fine example of efficient material use, and it still sets a high standard in terms of its design for repair, reuse and recycling.

The Mirra Chair's flexible backrest provides good postural support and allows air movement.

Imprint Chair

Johannes Foersom and Peter Hiort-Lorenzen (2005)

The Imprint Chair, manufactured by Lammhults, is a good example of material innovation. Even though it incurs a high unit cost in production, the investment required for manufacturing its tooling is less than a comparable injection-moulding tool. However, there is an additional cost for trimming the waste material from the shells if required, which comes as an option for purchasers.

The chair's shell is manufactured from cellulose (wood and bark fibre plus approximately 10 per cent of a polymer binder), which is produced in thin sheets and then compressed in a heated tool under great pressure, binding the laminations together and producing a very dense material with a fine surface finish. The resulting material – Cellupress – took the Imprint Chair's designers several years to perfect, and was only fully resolved with the help of Lammhults' technical expertise.

Offered trimmed or untrimmed, the chair shells are available with a loose felt cushion and are supported by a wooden leg frame.

The shell of the Imprint Chair's seat
is thermoformed from a flat sheet.

Currents Series

Robert Reuter and Charles Rozier (2006)

A complete office system, Knoll, Inc.'s Currents collection is comprised of desks, work tables, upstands, storage and screens. For any designer considering the needs of an office furniture series, Currents provides an excellent example of the ergonomic, functional and technical flexibility required in such a comprehensive system to enable its users to create free-standing workstations or working zones. Reuter and Rozier also designed Currents to be combined with other Knoll systems. Such an approach should always be considered by designers seeking to maximize the flexibility of their products while also keeping a rein on costs.

Desks and work tables are available in a wide range of shapes and modular options; they are either fixed or height adjustable for improved ergonomics. This (up to) 250mm (9.8in) range of adjustability can either be achieved by a lower-cost fixed pin or a more sophisticated and usable hand-cranked system.

The service wall system is a key component, working in conjunction with the desk and fence systems to facilitate the incorporation of large volumes of cables in an easily accessible panel system. Monitors and small storage elements can be hung from the fascias, which come in a range of materials.

The fence system is either a free-standing unit on a base, or a unit fixed to the back of the desks. A variety of height options and materials combines with two free-standing screen options to provide a broad range of permutations.

Storage options within the series are limited to mobile base cabinets. If users need overhead storage, they would use cabinets from Knoll's Reuters series, which is compatible with the service wall and fence system.

The Currents series can be integrated with other Knoll products.

Houdini Chair

Stefan Diez (2009)

Produced by e15, the Houdini Chair immediately achieved iconic status due to its innovative construction and unique look. Its high manufacturing unit cost means that it is probably the least 'democratic' chair in this section. However, as a volume-production craft piece, it will be more expensive to produce by definition, even though its investment costs are low.

The chair is constructed from solid timber and pre-laminated sheet plywood, glued and jointed together. The seat is made from solid timber, comprising a main block and a C-shaped ring that are glued together to provide a seat pan and enough of a gluing surface around its edge to form and glue a 4mm-thick (0.15in) plywood backrest. The legs are solid timber and are wedged and glued directly into mortices drilled into the base of the seat slab.

As well as the lacquered oak veneer and painted options, e15 also offers an upholstered armchair version.

Three Houdini Chairs alongside the armchair version

Diffrient World Chair

Niels Diffrient (2010)

In contrast to the complexity of most of the preceding decade's high-end task seating, Humanscale's Diffrient World Chair is a paragon of simplicity and function in design. Niels Diffrient's brief was to optimize performance and sustainability, while minimizing material use and the number of components and controls.

The chair – winner of the Red Dot 'Best of the Best' Award 2010 – has been developed since its launch, and only has two passive adjustments: seat height and depth. Its exemplary ergonomic performance is achieved through the reactive characteristics of its design, particularly the mesh seat and backrest support that adapts to any body shape, and its balanced recline, which gives support in any position without the need for adjustment.

Weighing in at 12.2kg (27lb), the Conference Chair/Task Chair version is almost half the weight of the Mirra (see p51). Combine this with its use of 100 per cent recycled aluminium and Niels Diffrient's offering was, at its launch, the most sustainable, high-performance task seat on the market.

The Diffrient World Chair is available with or without armrests.

Hemp Chair

Werner Aisslinger (2011)

Claimed as the world's first monobloc chair made from natural fibres, the Hemp Chair is made from 70 per cent hemp fibres in combination with 30 per cent Acrodur® (a water-based thermosetting glue that contains no phenols or formaldehyde). The impregnated hemp matting and glue is compressed under high pressure in a heated tool.

The composite material was first developed by BASF (makers of Acrodur®) and car company BMW for the manufacture of lightweight internal door panels. Although Hemp Chair is not an entirely bio-composite product, it achieves eco credibility through the high performance and non-toxic nature of its glue, which creates a durable, low-carbon alternative to petroleum-based polymer seating. These positives are slightly lessened by the fact that the composite is not currently recyclable, but the project still represents a milestone in eco-friendly composites since Acrodur® is also suitable for bonding a range of other materials, from wood to glass fibres.

The material and manufacturing technologies for Hemp Chair were developed for the automotive industry to provide an environmentally friendly alternative to thermoplastic internal door panels.

1c: New furniture – understanding innovation in contemporary furniture design

Much of the book's emphasis is on technical and functional innovation, but a great deal of the most popular contemporary furniture is predominantly visually original, or at least that is its most 'accessible' trait. As a consequence, the revolutionary use of a process, material, structure or function is largely ignored in mainstream discussion; aesthetics in furniture design will always be the most prominent and celebrated characteristic. For many consumers (even designers), the most useful semantic differential available to describe a piece of furniture would be somewhere between 'beautiful' and 'clever'. For those interested in what lies beneath, beauty is important, but without material, structural or functional expertise, many designers would consider this attribute to lack importance. Of course, the boundaries between technical and visual innovation are blurred; therefore, the furniture designs in this section have been grouped with some subjectivity in terms of the areas in which each piece excels.

Opposite: **A Pile of Suitcases, Maarten De Ceulaer, for Gallery Nilufar, 2008.**

Below: **Satellite Cabinets System, Edward Barber and Jay Osgerby, for Qoudes, 2006**

Since the designer decade of the 1980s, design has become more internationally ingrained into mainstream culture. As a result of the developed world's burgeoning interest in and broad acceptance of design, there is more design activity taking place now than at any other time in history. This is partly an impression created by the vast amount of design activity communicated through the Internet, but it is also a reality fuelled and inspired by this same resource. Allied to this, the first decade of the twenty-first century was significant in heralding an exponential increase in the number of leading-edge designers, design philosophies and design methodologies. Despite the resulting plethora of new designer furniture and the significant back catalogue of design classics, there was still an expanding market and (surprisingly) continuous innovation (although this progress was and still is more subtle than in preceding decades).

Some of the following groundbreaking work is visually, technically and functionally eloquent in equal measure, but the majority clearly excels in one category. The subsequent section identifies and discusses significant (although not necessarily commercially successful) and useful examples of visually and technically innovative furniture as a way of identifying strategies and approaches for new designers.

Visual language

Composition

Composition and proportional relationships are key factors in furniture design. The use of the 'Golden Section' and other 'divine' proportions is much less widespread than often supposed, with many designers instinctively approximating such proportional relationships in their work the majority of component arrangements and dimensions are decided through intuition and the interpretation of user needs. Barber Osgerby Associates' (BOA) modular, reconfigurable Satellite Cabinets System is described by its creators as: 'An exercise in graphic composition and organized volumes...about proportion, modularity and purity with character...a series of ideograms.' Although a great many furniture designs could be as loosely described as 'ideogramatic', i.e., representing an idea, most of BOA's statement succinctly express the system's compositional character.

Several modular combinations of Satellite are possible, although these are decided at purchase rather than being reconfigured by the customer. The cabinets themselves are not remarkable, yet the way that the leg frames obviously support the cabinets and their stark geometric contrast, elevates this system into a whole that is greater than the sum of its parts. The carcasses and doors are lacquered MDF and the leg frames are an assembly of two aluminium castings and tubing. The doors have cut-through, recessed handles with differently bevelled inside edges.

As much a lyrical piece of installation art as it is a piece of furniture, Maarten De Ceulaer's Pile of Suitcases is one of a series of suitcase-composed modular systems produced for Gallery Nilufar in Milan. Casamania is industrially producing a more economic, machine-made version using recycled leather called Valises. The freely arranged units, manufactured by the Brussels artisan Ralph Baggaley, are exquisitely and traditionally detailed. Their beauty could be said to supplant the need for more practicality – of course Valises could have shelves and be more structurally connectable, but the hanging rails are pure enough – any further interventions would erode the work's simplicity and visual power.

As with Satellite and Stack from Shay Alkalay, colour plays a significant role. Perhaps if the suitcases were an unremarkable brown, it would be easy to miss the significance of De Ceulaer's work, or perhaps it would simply be a pedestrian design. Such musings prove that there is value and meaning in being first, i.e., designing the previously unseen or unnoticed can appear profound.

Polder Sofa, Hella Jongerius, for Vitra, 2005.

While many designers' work is multidisciplinary, few have made such a broad impact as the Dutch designer Hella Jongerius. Along with her textiles for Maharam, her work for Vitra has been highly influential and has undoubtedly changed the way many designers approach aesthetics and material detailing. Named in figurative reference to the low-lying Dutch landscape, her Polder series of sofas uses traditional upholstery materials and techniques. The design was a radical aesthetic departure from tradition at its launch, but in the years since then, it has become possible to view its detailing, arrangements and colour palettes as heralding a new strand of aesthetics.

Polder is imbued with Jongerius's textile and ceramic design sensibilities and includes a button design with a large number of asymmetrically arranged threading holes. These create a range of thread patterns that also use different colour threads. Such attention to fine detail means that Polder is experienced very differently close up than at a distance. At the latter, Polder becomes an essay in composition and proportional relationships.

Milan-based multidisciplinary designer Patricia Urquiola has also had significant prominence since the 2000s, and in 2010 she was commissioned by Moroso to create an armchair and sofa system. The result was the Silver Lake project, which was inspired by the area of Los Angeles of the same name and famous for its Modernist architecture and, latterly, for its counterculture.

The range represents a new geometric investigation in the prolific Spaniard's work and is comprised of three sofas and two armchairs. The sofa and armchair are visual and material tours de force, although the chair without armrests is less visually successful, and seems to lack a clear systemization rationale. Nevertheless, the Silver Lake Sofa's convergence of materials, components and form is highly successful and original. The frame is constructed from hardwood, ply and steel and covered in variable density polyurethane foam. The optional arm cushions (not shown here) are filled with polyester fibre, while the armrests and leg frames are made from folded lacquered steel.

Silver Lake Sofa, Patricia Urquiola, for Moroso, 2010.

Elemental design

Simplicity and honesty to materials are recurring themes in furniture design. Ever since Gerrit Rietveld and Marcel Breuer's fundamental contributions set the tone for an entire century of design activity, understatement has been the order of the day. Such characteristics and comparisons to the early Modernists and Dieter Rams are often attributed to the work of British designer Jasper Morrison, and are no more clearly expressed than in his Cork Stools for Moooi.

These designs resonate with more significance as a result of Morrison's authorship than they ever could as a project by an unknown designer. Imagined or not, their importance and presence in this chapter underlines how elemental furniture design can be. Turned from agglomerate cork (bonded reject wine-bottle corks), these stools-cum-side tables are Morrison's most simple use of the material since he created a series of more geometric cork tables for Vitra in 2004. The grain size has as much impact on the overall effect as the form itself, so while this may not be a complex piece of design, a good understanding of the material is still needed, i.e., the scale of the detail in relation to the form.

Morrison's Cork Stools may be on the periphery of what the mainstream would consider as designed or even noteworthy, but there can be little disagreement about the beauty (though probably not the practicality) of Stack. If any piece of furniture stands for Established & Sons' early achievements it is this visual tour de force from Shay Alkalay, one half of London-based design group Raw Edges.

Where Stack succeeds most is in its organization of colour and reconfigurable nature. Each of the painted wooden drawers connects to the next with hidden runners to create either a straightforward stack or a multiple offset. Taller units were made for exhibition, but the units are sold as two standards: either four- or eight-drawer. Stack was never intended to function as well as it looks (with more colour-palette variations than illustrated here), but visually it is one of the new millennium's most influential forms. What is surprising about Stack,

however, is its scale – at 1780mm (70in) tall (the eight-drawer unit), it is at least twice the height that many would suppose based on photographs without an object for referencing scale.

In contrast to Stack's controlled splendour, the simplicity of Frank's Signal Cabinets belies their sophistication and originality. Inspired by railway-side metal boxes, the designers sought to elevate what is typically considered a utilitarian material and manufacturing process through aesthetic finesse. The cabinets are manufactured from press-braked steel and all have the option of either steel or wooden handles. Signal's angled base detail creates a distinct visual language that, coupled with the collection's lines, shadows and compositions, heightens its effect beyond simplicity to the exceptional. The effect of the base, however, is so important that within small spaces and without sufficient distance for viewers to fully appreciate this detail, the impact of the design is lost.

Below: **Cork Stools, Jasper Morrison, for Moooi, 2008.**

Opposite, clockwise from top left: **Stack, Shay Alkalay, for Established & Sons, 2008.**

Signal Cabinets, Frank, for Established & Sons, 2008.

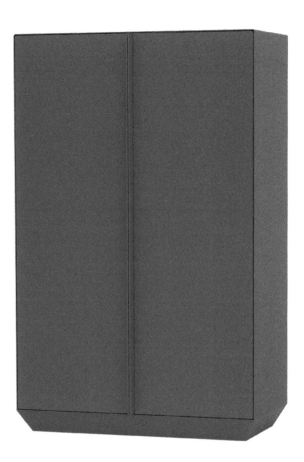

Piccola Papilio Chair, Naoto
Fukasawa, for B&B Italia, 2009.

Reframing the past

Naoto Fukasawa's influence on both product and furniture design has been important since the 1990s. His mastery of form is encapsulated in the Papilio Chair for B&B Italia, which although reminiscent of much that has gone before, in detail has something extra, particularly the Piccola Papilio, which is the more compact version of the Grande Papilio launched at the Milan Furniture Fair in 2009.

In the smaller version, the backrest has been reduced in height so that its scale is more appropriate for compact homes, and for many this change made it a more comforting design. Like its big brother, Piccola Papilio rotates 360° on its base. The internal frame is manufactured using tubular steel, padded with Bayfit flexible cold-shaped polyurethane foam. The fabric or leather cover, made from one piece of material, can be removed by using a zip that runs the height of the back. Piccola Papilio cannot be described as a radical innovation, but there remains great merit in such 'side steps' that reference and combine elements from the past.

Such subtle approaches to innovation as in the Piccola Papilio are rare and perhaps only get noticed when a designer has been truly radical in the past. New Antiques by Marcel Wanders is almost entirely down to his change in width of a 150-year-old design in relation to its other dimensions. Outside the context of contemporary design, it is possible to argue that Wanders's reinterpretations have not created anything new. However, what he has undoubtedly achieved is a convincing handling of decoration and form that would challenge many of his contemporaries.

The degree to which Wanders can claim the style of the details of New Antiques is unclear, but whether the result of in-depth research or direct referencing, the fact remains that the vernacular furniture of past centuries is very hard to emulate or develop convincingly.

New Antiques, Marcel Wanders, for Cappellini, 2005.

Alternative responses

So much of the furniture canon is made up of chairs and tables that designers often forget the opportunities for innovation presented by more unusual items, such as coat stands or escritoires. Certainly, student briefs for furniture such as the humble coat stand can be highly accessible and productive, not least because of the opportunity for highly aesthetic sculptural responses with far fewer functional requirements than for seating.

James Irvine's response to just such a neglected brief brought him back to some prominence as a furniture designer. Made from 3mm-thick (0.1in) steel, his iconic Dodici coat stand (meaning '12' in Italian and denoting the number of hooks) could, while uncovered, be perceived as both minimal and ornate. These are good qualities to have in a largely contract (non-domestic) market, where a modern middle ground probably has the broadest appeal. Dodici is manufactured by laser cutting, pressing and welding.

Although escritoires experienced a decline in popularity mirroring the rise of the home PC in the 1980s and 1990s, as a result of technological development and the laptop's pre-eminence, the relevance, prominence and desirability of such furniture has increased greatly once again. Michael Young's Writing Desk, designed for Established & Sons, is certainly more visually innovative than it is technically remarkable, but it still has depth beyond the aesthetic.

In many ways, the name Writing Desk is a misdirection – at first glance it appears rather straightforward, but once its concept and materials are revealed and its use experienced, it becomes something more elevated. The opulence of the die-cast aluminium legs combined with the unexpected softness of the felt back create a unique aesthetic that is enhanced when the light, hidden within the arching top, is switched on. Also, imagined or otherwise, the acoustics created by the felt, coupled with the softness of the light, make for a very welcoming environment. It is, however, likely that many users are mildly disappointed to discover that the felt top is not a moveable tambour to be scrolled down to cover the desk (as is suggested at first glance).

A great deal of high-end, volume-produced, designer furniture is complex to manufacture and excessively expensive, yet such characteristics do not necessarily mean that the designs themselves will be visually lavish. Such visual opulence is more likely to appear in the figurative and decorative aspects of

Art Deco, or of design art in the present day. However, it is still possible to conceive of such rich beauty as part of the mainstream. The Cupola Reading Table by Ed Barber and Jay Osgerby is just such an extraordinary and sumptuous design that turns on its head expectations about what furniture can be. The fragility of this piece does not matter – it is all about aesthetics, scale and a deep enjoyment of materials and manufacturing.

The table's lower base is made from black Belgian or white Carrara marble, while the main body and top are mould-blown glass. The opalescent glass main shaft encloses and filters the light, while the table top is made from mirror-polished, cast and spun white bronze. Certainly its materials make the Cupola what it is, but close parallels could be created with rotational and injection-moulded plastics.

The more mainstream products that adopt such radical visual language the better, perhaps with IKEA being best placed to sell and gain acceptance for such 'new' ideas.

Left: **Writing Desk, Michael Young, for Established & Sons, 2005.**

Above: **Cupola Reading Table, Ed Barber and Jay Osgerby, for Meta, 2008.**

Opposite: **Dodici, James Irvine, for Van Esch, 2006.**

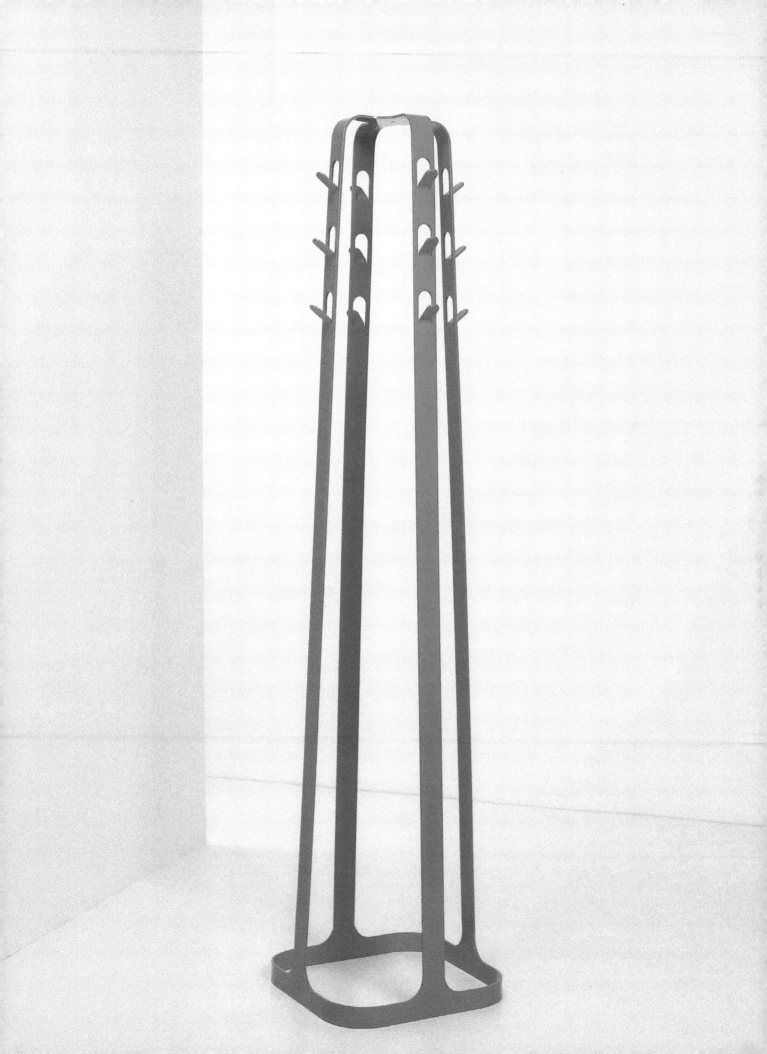

Technical and functional innovation

For all design projects other than the purely visual, it is important that the potential within ideas for improved functional performance, systemization, material and manufacturing innovation and cost reduction are all explored.

Interaction

Claudio Caramel's shelving system Hang was conceived with functional and manufacturing strategies running in parallel, each informing and furthering the other. The system is comprised of two aluminium extrusions: a wall-fixed long bracket extrusion, and the shelf itself that hooks on to the bracket. End plates cover the ends of the extrusions. The shelf would still have been strong enough had a folded steel or aluminium assembly been used, but such a manufacturing approach would not so easily provide opportunities for slotting in and supporting components.

The shelf can incorporate additional steel components that slide into and are captured within top and bottom slots on the extrusion. There are ten accessories available, including paper trays, hanging rails, hooks and book ends, the combination of which produces highly flexible storage that is as much about display and arrangement as utility.

A dynamic and functionally unique shelving system, Denis Santachiara's Booxx is made from folded steel. The use of laser-cut and press-braked (folded) steel achieves a structural excellence that would be difficult to improve on, given the steel's strength, ductility and weight. Booxx uses a scissor action to expand the shelves from a closed height of 350mm (13.8in) to a maximum open height of 2300mm (90.5in). Wall fixing is required at several points, including the top and bottom extremities once the shelves are at the required spacing.

Each folded steel shelf also forms a pronounced bookend at the left and a small lip at the other end, which denotes its intended shallow diagonal setting. Whether displayed as diagonal shelves with vertical central pivot points (as illustrated), or diagonally with the shelves horizontal, Booxx's limitations in terms of uniformed spacing are certainly balanced by the possible personalization of its installation. Even though the idea could be taken further, Santachiara's design is successful through being elemental and confident.

Exceptions to the rule

Useful quirkiness in mainstream furniture design is uncommon and eccentricities are more likely to appear in the form of obstreperous details that hinder rather than improve function. It is rare indeed to find an innovative bed, unless it transforms into something else. A notable exception to this 'rule' is the bed that forms part of Patricia Urquiola's Highlands seating and bed series. The upholstered headrests can be raised or folded down to provide an ergonomic backrest, also enabling the inevitable degrading of the lowered backrest to be hidden away when it is raised. The bed's frame is constructed from plywood that is upholstered with polyurethane foam, polyester fibre and a wide range of fabrics.

Opposite: **Hang, Claudio Caramel, for Desalto, 2008.**

Above: **Booxx Bookcase, Denis Santachiara, for Desalto, 2006.**

Highlands Bed, Patricia Urquiola, for Moroso, 2003.

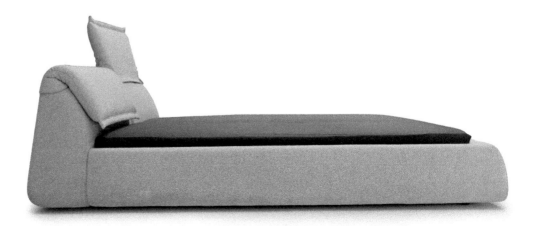

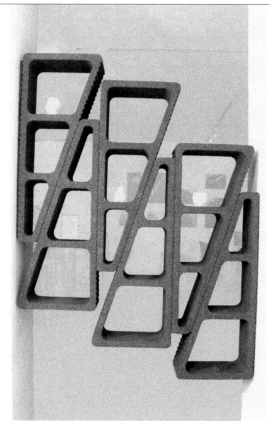

The headrest is also upholstered ply with a connecting steel mechanism to provide the change in position.

Occasionally, even on well-trodden paths of enquiry, a designer manages to throw a curve ball by creating something entirely singular. London-based designer and artist Peter Marigold managed to achieve just this in 2006 with his Make/Shift shelving system. Marigold rarely produces tooled products, but in this collaboration with Movisi, he sought to expand on a form he had explored in earlier work by using the properties of expanded polypropylene (EPP). The material's ability to be moulded with minimal draft angles (see p180) enables the units to be stacked or positioned vertically or horizontally.

Make/Shift's modularity allows it to expand to fit different widths (two modules can fit any width between 488 and 874mm / 19.2 and 34.4in) by interlocking its corrugated edges and slightly compressing the material, producing horizontal pressure that holds the units in place without any fixings and without causing damage to the walls. The system can also form free-standing structures by using clips to join each module, which works well enough as a solution, but the concept is undoubtedly more clearly expressed when the system is used without the clips.

Flexibility

There is a marked difference between the design requirements of shelving and seating in terms of performance and complexity of function. The Cobi Chair is an intricate response to a task seating brief, yet, in comparison to many other ergonomic chairs, Cobi is simple in that it has fewer components and user controls. Cobi's self-adjustment was conceived by PearsonLloyd in response to changes in working practice, leading to workers frequently sharing furniture and having no time or inclination to make manual adjustments.

Designed for Steelcase, Cobi uses an innovative rocking mechanism that adjusts itself to suit different users' centres of gravity rather than to react to their weight. The backrest is equally responsive but uses its structural and material properties to achieve this. The polymer backrest is vertically (and alternately) slotted and has an over-moulded elastomeric top band that controls the flexing and spread and flex of each rib between the slots. The flexibility and dynamism of the backrest means that there is no need for it to be padded.

Left: **Make/Shift, Peter Marigold, for Movisi, 2006.**

Below: **Cobi Chair, PearsonLloyd, for Steelcase, 2008.**

Opposite: **Sumo Chair, Xavier Lust, for Cerruti Baleri, 2008.**

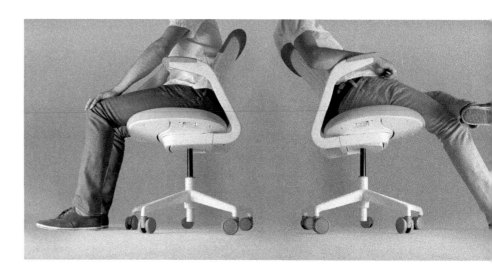

Injecting some humour

'Comfortable' does not necessarily mean 'ergonomic', yet the deep softness of Xavier Lust's Sumo Chair envelops the sitter and, as Lust intended, almost hugs them. Whether such softness is indeed ergonomic is open to question, but Sumo still allows the sitter a good deal of position adjustment, which in itself improves the enveloping, restrictive nature of the chair.

At somewhere between a cube and a sphere, Sumo is as welcoming as it is dynamic. The internal frame partly restricts the CFC-free polyurethane and helps create its bulging shape – not just moulded-in but also formed by its physical restriction. The seat and armrests are supported with internal straps, which give additional structure to the foam. The armrest straps are needed to support the weight of a sitter as Lust wanted the armrests to be 'stretchy'; without them, the foam would quickly degrade under such elongating stress.

Playfulness, as suggested by Sumo, is not common currency for most furniture designers, who prefer more serious and worthy traits in their designs. However, there are a handful of noteworthy designers such as Javier Mariscal and Ron Arad who thrive on pursuing such qualities. DoNuts, by Belgian designer Dirk Wynants, is arguably one of the most leftfield designs of the 2000s.

Its success is bolstered by the fact that it is supremely usable – providing you are under 40 and once you are sitting down. DoNuts can seat six, and is very easy to move (users can, for instance, keep up with the sun) and store away. Users can also sit facing outward and use the table as a backrest. The table is stable and the seat practical, but the inner tube must be inflated to almost exactly 0.15bar (2.18 lb/in²) – a gauge is helpfully provided. Given the correct mainstream retail opportunities such a broadly appealing system could surely become more widely appreciated?

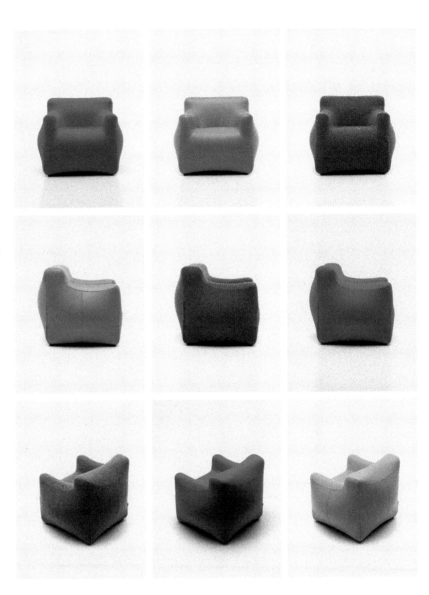

Top to bottom:
Joyn Office Systems, Ronan and Erwan Bouroullec, for Vitra, 2003.

MyBox, Iiro Viljanen, for Martela, 2008.

Workspaces

As technology advances and practices change in the workplace, designers need to research and understand changes in requirements for furniture, workspaces and document-management systems in order to design for what lies ahead. In the new millennium's first decade, the most significant early contribution is as visually innovative as it is responsive and functional. The Joyn Office Systems for Vitra include a synergy of single desks, screens, huts, active storage and technology storage. Ronan and Erwan Bouroullec intended Joyn to initiate 'new, productive forms of work based on communication and co-operation'.

The Modular Table System is centred on the table Platform, which is transformed into flexible, movable workspaces using a range of storage, support and display accessories. The Third Level component fits over the central cable channel to provide a low-level upstand. This in turn supports aluminium profiles and forms that 'hold screens, organisers, lamps and special adapters for flat screens'. Under the platform, Joyn features containers for PCs.

As a whole system and in parts, Joyn's originality lies in the fact that it formalizes more informal ways of working and encourages large-scale collaborative groupings.

In contrast to Ronan and Erwan Bouroullec's expansive office system, MyBox by Iiro Viljanen takes a more micro-view of working. Inspired by the designer's and his clients' needs, MyBox is intended for the office, but the principle of hiding away work also translates well to the homeworking environment. The concept behind Viljanen's desk is nothing new, and is a theme explored in many student design projects, but the way in which the designer has resolved the opening mechanism and the overall detail of the design is of note. Refined, die-cast aluminium brackets enable the lid to rotate and remain upright, and recessed plastic inserts allow storage of small untidy items while a lock provides security.

A lower overall height of 720mm (28.4in) and a reduced covering-box height would restrict what

Top to bottom:
IXIX, Sebastian Bergne, for Vitra, 1999.

LINK, PearsonLloyd, for MOVISI, 2007.

could be stored inside a little but, importantly, would enable the system to be used as a dining table as well as a desk. A wider top in relation to the leg frame would also improve its function in this regard, enabling a sitter at each end.

Function and flexibility

Flexible furniture items, such as temporary tables, are common, but the storage, volume and transport of such pieces is on the whole problematic. Such a straightforward problem would provide a perfect brief for student designers, but they should first consider Sebastian Bergne's eloquent solution. IXIX is a highly systemized task table with a transport and storage solution. Five tables are housed on a storage trolley that is lightweight, easy to manoeuvre and also has an inspired secondary function either as a projection screen or a whiteboard – a transformation that makes complete sense considering that the system is designed for spaces used for multiple purposes.

The die-cast aluminium legs pivot in a scissor action and clip into injection-moulded brackets on the underside of the table, using the flexibility of the polymer to lock them in place. To make deploying the tables as inclusive as possible, the top is made from ultra-lightweight MDF and the leg clip requires very little force.

The flexible use of a space often calls for partitioning. At the same time as designing its PARCS range (see p90) for Bene, UK design consultancy PearsonLloyd created an interesting project called LINK. Their focus was to create 'inspiring and productive' workspaces and informal meeting areas.

LINK is a simple modular element made from expanded polypropylene (EPP) that can be used to create meeting spaces, workspaces, room dividers or even sculptural interventions. While not strictly furniture, and only structural in that it is self-supporting, LINK is nonetheless an interesting spur to 'furniture design thinking', encouraging a more expanded view of furniture habitats than most

Top to bottom:
Lazy Seating Collection, Patricia Urquiola, for B&B Italia, 2004.

RU, Shane Schneck, for Hay, 2010.

designers are used to. Available in ten colours, 15 units are needed to create a 1m² (10.8ft²) wall and, even though a sturdy interference fit is achieved between the units, the structures need to avoid long straight runs for reasons of stability.

A material-based starting point for concept generation can be highly productive because it presents both opportunities and restrictions to the designer. Patricia Urquiola's Lazy Seating Collection for B&B Italia is not remarkable but is still an articulate response to a brief. Using a straightforward steel frame, the collection's seat pans and backrests are injection moulded with polyurethane cushioning, polyester fibre and either a leather or fabric covering (removable with a zip). Alternative versions for outdoors use a Textilene-type (woven, PVC-coated polyester) fabric sling. The series began with a chaise longue and was soon expanded to include high- and low-backed lounge chairs. Later additions to the collection include an armchair and two heights of stool, all of which follow the same material and construction principles.

Although complex to manufacture, a chair that truly follows the prescribed material and manufacturing process was designed at the invitation of Patricia Urquiola for the Promosedia International Design Exhibition. Stockholm-based designer Shane Schneck created a thoroughly original reappraisal of the laminated chair. Manufactured from seven glued components (three of which have 90° laminated bends at each end) that blend into each other, RU was inspired as much by Schneck's memories of school furniture as by his research. Intended for classrooms and cafés, RU is stackable and can be hung from a table to make cleaning the floor easier.

Just as materials and manufacturing can provide a great starting point for the furniture-design process, so can a clear scenario of application and use. One such project that focuses on flexibility and modularity for a variety of public, contract spaces is the ZA Stackable Bench System by Shin and Tomoko Azumi. This flexible system takes its name from 'Za', the Japanese word for 'sit', and is comprised of three modules that create a great deal of versatility and enable free-form arrangements.

ZA Stackable Bench System, Shin
and Tomoko Azumi, for Lapalma,
distributed in the US by Davis
Furniture, 2003.

Graduate System, Jean Nouvel, for Molteni & C, 2003.

Each module is easily connected with a sliding clamp. Cast-aluminium end frames are connected by tubular-steel rails that in turn are fixed to the laminated 3-D veneer shells. The system was conceived as either a temporary or permanent solution and, to aid the former application, the separated curved modules are stackable.

Technical stunts

Continuing on a material and manufacturing theme, another possible starting point for a project, particularly with a clear scenario of use, is a visual or technical stunt. Designers should beware of superficial whimsy in such realms and concentrate their efforts more on succinct visual one-liners. Opinions of such designs tend to more subjective than usual but, simply put, there are good and bad stunts: the good ones are honest and the bad ones make something look clever when in fact it is not – they fake it.

Although it contains some misdirection, Jean Nouvel's Graduate System is more honest than not. Its shelves are suspended from a cantilevered top shelf using very thin stainless-steel rods. Such a

system requires a very sound series of wall fixings, but if these are achieved then Graduate will support an evenly distributed 25kg (55lb) over a metre (39.4in) – strong enough for most loads.

The box-section top shelf conceals the wall-fixing bracket and, from its underside, suspends the steel rods that support the lower shelves. Graduate's very thin shelves are made possible by being aluminium extrusions with a decorative plywood edge. The shelves rest on concealed brackets that fix on to notches in the steel rods (these are at set distances rather than being adjustable). It is intended predominantly as a display rather than a library system.

Perhaps defining Graduate as a stunt-based design is unfair because its only fiction is the plywood shelf edge that is as likely to be there for aesthetic appeal as it is for misdirection. Also, in terms of the volume of materials used, Graduate's suspension system seems to be an efficient way of supporting the shelves compared to building a frame and transferring the weight to the ground.

A fine example of a purer design that expresses its materials, manufacture and principles more clearly is the winner of the 2005 Red Dot Design Award, Platten-Bau by Florian Petri. The self-assembly shelving system has a flexible storage and display system made from high-pressure laminate (HPL; see p199). The 4mm-thick (0.15in) boards are CNC-cut to a fine tolerance so that the system maintains its form and structural integrity. The vertical boards are joined by the end of an 'I'-shaped (on its side) component, the long shaft of which provides support under each horizontal shelf board. Top-pivoting doors and back panels can also be fitted.

Design fluency

Furniture with a complex function that is designed entirely in a single material will be a balance of concessions and benefits. The difficulty is to judge whether the elemental, single-material approach pays enough dividends in terms of concept for the final outcome to stand up to critical scrutiny. Platten-Bau succeeds in having a clear identity, but has limitations as a result.

More mainstream design solutions, whose audiences are less concerned with single-material challenges, expect function without concessions and a beautiful, less stark aesthetic to be more worthy of an award. However, for those in the world who appreciate fluent concepts, balanced between idea and utility, Platten-Bau and its parallels will always make sense. Sometimes, concepts that begin life as pure ideas end up being a little less neat; however, such 'imperfect' solutions are still worth pursuing.

Innovations in manufacturing processes

The practicality or comfort of a chair is high on most people's list of priorities if they are to sit on it every day, but as an object that is mostly to be regarded, such priorities can be reappraised. While the Carbon Chair by Bertjan Pot and Marcel Wanders provides very good comfort levels in terms of its ergonomic form, the gaps in the shell and the roughness of the fibre's inside edges do

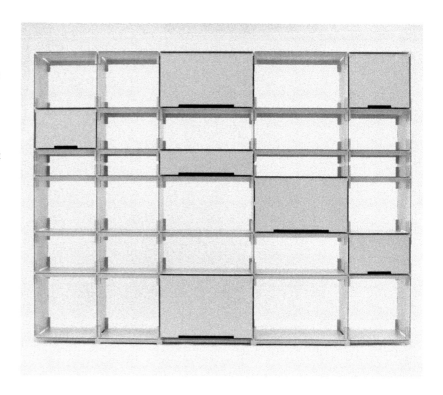

present problems for some clothing. However, such problems are small concessions made to achieve thoughtful, iconic furniture that is more about an idea and a look than utilitarian perfection.

The shell and leg frame of this Eames-referenced chair are made entirely of carbon fibre and resin, with only the threaded inserts and connecting bolts made out of steel. The principle of its construction is fairly straightforward, but the build itself requires great skill (the chair is manufactured in the Philippines by hand). The seat shell is made by wrapping a matrix of resin-dipped carbon fibres around a series of pins that runs around the edge of a positive convex mould. This creates a smooth tooled finish on the sitting side only. The leg frame is created in the same way but without a convex mould and is also coiled to produce greater structural integrity.

The chair's lightness (1.5kg / 3lb 5oz), material and aesthetics create a product with very broad interest and appeal, even though for reasons of cost it is not

Platten-Bau, Florian Petri, for Möbelbau Kaether & Weise, 2005.

Opposite: **Carbon Chair, Bertjan Pot and Marcel Wanders, for Moooi, 2004.**

Left: **Chair_ONE, Konstantin Grcic, for Magis, 2004.**

Steelwood Chair, Ronan and Erwan Bouroullec, for Magis, 2007.

found in many homes. In contrast, other chairs that have all the interest of Carbon may have much less appeal. Perhaps furniture that interests designers is the opposite of what less inquisitive observers base their decisions on: aesthetics.

Created at the time of Konstantin Grcic's ascendancy to design superstar, Chair_ONE represented a stylistic and material departure for its sponsor, Magis, and a significant challenge for Grcic. With the help of Stefan Diez, who was his assistant for several years, Grcic first used traditional modelling skills to develop the concept of a facetted geometric form. Then, in collaboration with Magis, tool makers and structural engineers, he finessed the design into a manufacturing-ready product. The shell is a high-pressure aluminium die casting that is galvanized and then powder-coated. The seat shell is available supported by three different bases: the original with extruded aluminium legs, the enigmatic concrete-based version and the beam-system version, Beam_ONE. The combination of such a singular aesthetic and an unforgiving material, makes for an archetypal designer's chair.

In visual contrast, the Steelwood Chair by the Bouroullec brothers is as much a designer's chair as Chair_ONE. Steelwood was a radical departure for the Bouroullecs at the time, not least because the

nature of its manufacturing processes and its materials echoed that of a product from the early twentieth century. Manufactured from stamped and deep-drawn steel with wooden legs, Steelwood illustrates the brothers' deep understanding and empathy with manufacturing processes. The chair becomes an essay in process (but not in easy manufacture), and as such can be an inspirational teaching aid for both industrial and conceptual understanding. The stamping and forming process of the frame was complex, requiring nine different stages before the armrests were finally bent perpendicular to the back. The legs were CNC-machined to achieve the precise fit needed to strengthen their union with the metal frame.

Chapter 2:

The design process

2a: Research for design

Design briefs and their underlying research occupy a position somewhere between creating an innovative new paradigm and reinterpreting a design standard, i.e., the development of a design or product type that already exists. As described in section 1c, whether an in-house or a consultant designer, the great majority of your design briefs are a balance between creative freedom and well-defined limitations of function, aesthetics, manufacturing capabilities and costs.

Those issuing a brief normally have sufficient understanding of the market and their own products to know that they need a particular type and style of product, made from specific materials and with a manufacturing and shipping cost below a certain price. Therefore, more often than not, the brief is the result of the commissioning company's research activities rather than the designer's. As a consequence, the designer's task is either to understand the context of a commission by examining the client's other products and their competitors' designs, or to investigate a subject or subjects in much more detail, through material, manufacturing, ergonomic, anthropometric or behavioural user-based design research.

Every furniture-design project requires some sort of research to establish or confirm ergonomic or anthropometric parameters (see section 2b), but this is mostly literature-based with subsequent application through test rigs and prototyping. Conversely, a large proportion of furniture-design projects do not require any kind of observational research. For those that do, the practice of collecting data about how things are or how they might be, is well established, following conventions and approaches that lead designers to gain insights that result in innovation and that, importantly, can be used to validate a design proposal to a client or a final product to consumers.

Gate is a reconfigurable dining table and work desk designed in response to a research study that analysed dining and home-working activity within compact environments. Prototype by Shu Aoki, De Montfort University, (Leicester, UK) 2010.

Researching the market

Although commercial research is not usually the preserve of designers, it pays for them to understand the business drivers and commercial principles behind such research and, ultimately, their and their client's motivation.

Product lines, such as PearsonLloyd's PARCS for Bene, are commissioned in response to clients either identifying a need themselves, or by commissioning a designer to tell them what they should be selling. Both approaches are driven by the same principle of establishing a market need. Commercially, a commissioning client would want to know whether a market exists and, if it does, how great is its potential? Next, they would want to establish how much the target consumer would be prepared to pay. Only when all of these questions have been answered can a designer be briefed.

Primary research

Before embarking on a primary-research study, designers should consider whether the information they need could be found by less demanding methods, i.e., perhaps some or all of the information exists already? It may be that although the information available is not specific enough for their needs, it may be sufficient to formulate a hypothesis that would direct the focus of subsequent research, as opposed to broad, exploratory research that tends to be the most labour intensive.

By assessing current provision, typical scenarios or the frequency of occurrences, for example, design researchers can gain an understanding that enables them to respond to an opportunity or need in a meaningful and sometimes innovative way. Nearly all research for design focuses on the collection and analysis of both quantities and qualities through observation or questioning. It is not useful however to consider quantitative- and qualitative-research approaches as separate – most research projects involve elements from both fields. Quantitative research creates numerical data using questionnaires or observational studies, whereas qualitative research records behaviour, opinions, emotions, etc.

In addition to the quantitative and qualitative data types, there are two distinct areas of research intent: descriptive research is concerned with understanding systems, behaviour and artefacts; normative research describes how systems, behaviour and artefacts could and should be. Normative research often relies on a descriptive approach for its foundation, i.e., collecting data about numbers of users, frequency of use, etc. Once a body of knowledge has been accrued, then hypotheses, experiments, interviews and further questionnaires should be created that will ultimately produce the understanding needed for a designer to offer a solution validated by research. Weaknesses in design research methodology – in the questions asked and in the interrogation of the data – are likely if a design researcher is inexperienced or unfamiliar with the subject, and asks either the wrong questions or not enough of the right ones. Therefore, it is vital that novice researchers follow the conventions established in ethnographic, sociological and psychological research (as outlined in this section).

Within both cultures of research there are three main methods of study:

_____ Re-examination of established research
_____ Exploratory research (broad descriptive study)
_____ Hypothesis-based study (broad descriptive or normative study).

The studies listed above can be pursued through:

_____ Observation of behaviour and processes to discover archetypes and variances
_____ Question-based studies – interviewing people who have an understanding of, or at least have experienced the focus of, a study
_____ Static object studies – studying and recording the characteristics of inanimate objects, often within a particular group, in order to establish their properties and parameters.

Observation is inherently visual. Observational studies record activities, behaviour and processes to discover models and variances. There are two types of observational study. Non-systematic observation studies simply record events and do not intervene in, influence or direct activities, behaviour or processes. Systematic observation studies are orchestrated experiments, as in simulations or role-playing exercises.

Before creating a questionnaire, it is vital for a researcher to have undertaken significant prior research to know which questions to ask. The questionnaire's purpose is to ascertain the frequency or prevalence of different category responses, which could be objective or subjective facts or opinions. As part of the preparatory process, researchers should always try out their questionnaires on a test group to observe any difficulty the respondents might have in answering the questions and to point out any failings in the data provided.

In question-based studies, the way questions are asked is critical. In interviews, for instance, it is possible to ask open-ended questions, but this is not an option for questionnaires. However, to accommodate situations where perhaps the researcher has not been as thorough as they might have been in their prior research, or for the truly unpredictable response, a useful final option in a questionnaire is 'Other'. Questions need to be concise, explicit and use a straightforward sentence structure and simple language.

As discussed, a researcher must have established enough of an understanding to be able to envisage all of the useful questions and, to a great extent, their possible answers. Therefore, questionnaires are ideal if:

_____ A large sample is required
_____ You require quantitative and, to a lesser extent, qualitative data
_____ You have a clear hypothesis
_____ The questions require mostly normative, factual responses
_____ The respondents might require anonymity for certain questions.

In all forms of question-based studies, researchers must be careful not to prejudice responses by asking leading questions or by offering the respondent a poor balance of answers. While expressing a question through a choice of check boxes on a scale between two opposites, i.e. 'Good' and 'Bad', can be straightforward, for more conceptual questioning, a more complex approach is required, such as the choice between 'Ugly' and 'Beautiful'. However, it is easy to confuse respondents with unfathomable language, so researchers beware!

Static object studies seek to establish the properties and parameters of inanimate objects or people, often within a particular group.

The extent of static object studies, i.e. how many objects or people (anthropometric data) will be assessed, usually determines the extent of detail to be registered. The smaller the number of objects studied would normally involve a higher level of enquiry and detail. However, an extensive study could also record a high level of detail.

Regardless of the extent of such studies, a simple trio of analytical tools will help categorise the assessed products' characteristics:

_____ Standard properties: characteristics that are the same in all of the systems or behaviours or artefacts
_____ Variable properties: characteristics that are different in all of the systems or behaviours or artefacts
_____ Singular properties: very unusual or remarkable characteristics that stand out

In addition to these more direct types of research, broader, contextual inputs can be as valuable, providing that they are supported by more valid data. PearsonLloyd's research for the PARCS project encompasses such a range of inputs (see following pages).

Furniture systems that enhance communication and cooperation

PARCS – New meeting environments developed for Bene by PearsonLloyd

PARCS was the result of two years of research and investigation into the needs and behaviour of what has become known as the 'knowledge worker', 'which in the broadest terms means [someone who] interacts to solve problems, serve customers, engage with partners, and nurture new ideas.' (McKinsey report, October 2009.)

Although the definition of knowledge workers is elastic, the opportunity that such working practices present to forward-thinking companies such as Bene is significant. The insights gained by design consultancy PearsonLloyd through its research created the opportunity for new concepts in furniture groupings and workplace layouts to be articulated through the PARCS system.

PearsonLloyd drew on its broad experience of managing complex environments (including transport hubs and aircraft interiors) to inform the concept development of PARCS. More diverse inspiration came from observing people's interactions and behaviour at places such as the Spanish Steps in Rome, while also studying broader anthropological perspectives, for example, the low-ceilinged meeting places of the Dogon people in Mali, Africa, where tribal elders have to sit and, as a result, avoid confrontational argument.

According to PearsonLloyd, the key aim of PARCS is to create productive and inspiring meeting and workspaces:

'A hybrid between architecture and furniture, PARCS offers a range of different types of places and spaces in which to conduct informal meetings and discussions; take a few minutes away from the desk to relax; give a casual presentation; or find a semi-private place for concentration or a personal call. PARCS makes sense of the open areas set apart from the open-plan desks and cellular meeting rooms. These places and chance encounters often produce moments of inspiration and positive actions.'

It would be possible to overstate the benefits of such a system but, since its launch, the multi-award-winning PARCS has received equally positive reviews from designers, architects and the press. Beyond the workplace, it has also been adopted in receptions, break-out areas and social spaces in the public and private sectors as well as hotels.

In PARCS, PearsonLloyd has achieved a system that is greater than the sum of its parts; simple elements that unify different parts of the system create an adaptable cohesion, increasing intimacy between users. Also, even though there is nothing new about a meeting hut, Toguna really does work because of its lighting, scale and acoustics.

The main elements of the system are:

Causeway: a series of varied-height, upholstered benches and fences that defines a type of semi-open space and encourages sitting, perching and leaning for a number of different uses.

Wing: armchairs, sofas and booths that afford comfort and privacy for small group discussions or concentration.

Toguna: a new definition of a semi-private meeting space.

The Idea Wall and Library augment Causeway elements, respectively providing audiovisual, information-technology presentation facilities and storage for periodicals and books. PARCS's flexibility is the key to its success – its components are deliberately easy to move and can create a wide range of meeting and working environments, aided by features such as subtle down-lighting that helps to define privacy and notions of boundaries.

Top to bottom:

The central premise of the PARCS concept was to create both productive and inspiring work and meeting spaces.

The optional bridging panel that connects the Wing sofas creates further intimacy between the sitters, providing them with either a view or simply a more cosseted enclosure.

Importantly for the client, PARCS interacts and complements much of Bene's other furniture ranges.

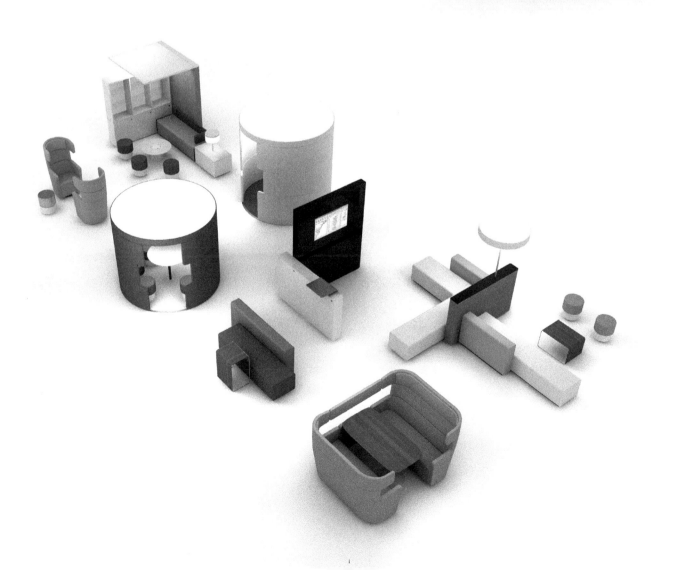

The evolving nature of working at home

Herman Miller research study

In 2008, Herman Miller commissioned several research studies that looked at behavioural and technology-led trends that could affect requirements and buying patterns for furniture. One of the most significant of these was concerned with how 'more and more people are getting to work without going to work'.

Such changes in work patterns and behaviour, coupled with constantly evolving technologies, mean that the way in which people are inclined to work and where in the home they do it is evolving. Designers concerned with responding to human need should regard such change as an opportunity for innovation.

Researchers studied a user group of 250 homeworkers, focusing specifically on how they worked – not on why they worked at home, which had already been established.

As more and more people are working for at least part of their week from home, what was once the preserve of the self-employed is now a common part of working life. As the potential for companies and workers to be carbon-taxed for travel, parking, etc., increases, the trend of homeworking is likely to grow. CoreNet Global suggests that during the decade following 2010 'just 40 per cent of all work will be done in corporate facilities. The remaining work will be done at home (40 per cent) and outside the office or home (20 per cent).'

These percentages may not yet ring true in terms of the time spent at work, but workers are increasingly more likely to take work home with them and, in particular, answer emails at home. Of course, 'home admin' accounts for a meaningful part of a household's 'homeworking' needs and because nearly all of this new and long-standing activity is viable using mobile technology, the traditional home office is becoming less common, or increasingly decentralized.

The Escritoire 'trestle' by Ett La Benn. Because of new technologies and the dominance of email and social media, the form and function of furniture standards such as bureaus and escritoires are worthy of reappraisal.

Herman Miller's study found that its subjects worked in an average of 2.4 different locations around the home. Of its 250 respondents, 87 per cent worked in dedicated home offices, 65 per cent worked in the living or family room and 48 per cent worked in a bedroom. Also, 43 per cent of women and 33 per cent of men worked from a kitchen counter.

Evidence shows that the dedicated home office desk is far from being in terminal decline, but it is true that the use of more informal, itinerant workspaces is in the ascendant – as is the trend for the digitisation of documentation. Such changes in the way we work and in our storage needs requires both paradigm-shifting and 'enhanced innovation' responses from designers. Perhaps the most pressing need is to adapt or re-specify the furniture used so that it provides good ergonomic posture for tasking while also being appropriate for its home-centred use. However, it has been established in several research studies that by working in different positions and postures throughout a day, damage to people's physiology is limited, even if the postures adopted are far from perfect. As a consequence, designers could be expected to have some freedom from anthropometric and ergonomic constraints, but since there is no way to prescribe such a rotation of

positions, designers still must respond to the homeworking phenomenon by designing for longer sessions of use. Aesthetics also play an important role in integrating such furniture into the home's most cherished and considered surroundings and, in parallel to the aims of truly inclusive design, this enhanced functionality should be unseen – certainly for the majority of users.

The Vitsoe + Zapf 606 Universal Shelving System's desk, originally designed for writing and typewriters, has enjoyed renewed and broad use with laptops and flat-screen monitors.

Below left: **The Bureau Office Desk (2008) is a variation on a series of computer workstations designed and manufactured by Martin Holzapfel.**

Below: **The Daybed Ergonomic Laptop Workstation is a 2007 concept designed for Humanscale by Manuel Saez.**

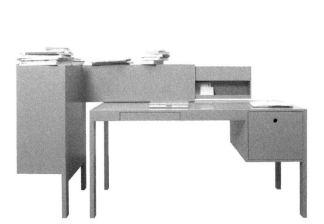

2b: Ergonomics, anthropometrics and spatial conventions

Ergonomics, or human factors, is the study and assessment of usability and how successfully or otherwise people interact with an environment or the objects within it. This tends to relate to work, but any task or action is relevant to ergonomic enquiry. Good ergonomic design seeks to improve the physical experience of interaction with objects and environments by reducing the effort required, or the fatigue or injury resulting from such interactions.

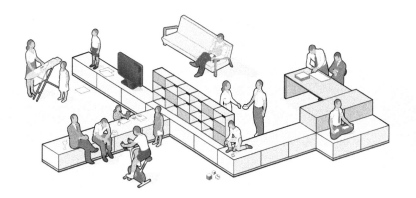

Regardless of any of its other characteristics, all furniture should be ergonomically correct and functionally fit for purpose.

Good ergonomics are determined through a range of assessments that, within environments, include efficient working triangles in kitchens and the set-up of office workspaces. For product-centred focuses, ergonomics can also relate to the comfort, adjustability and appropriateness of a tasking chair, taking into account such details as air circulation through its backrest or the user's interaction with its adjustment control knobs.

Anthropometry is the scientific study of the measurement and proportions of the human body, prescribing for the range of people's physical characteristics. It is fundamental to the study and improvement of ergonomics. Therefore, no design project should be undertaken without reference to personal research and scientifically validated ergonomic and anthropometric data.

Furniture design: ergonomic and anthropometric focuses

_____ Standing
_____ Sitting
_____ Reaching
_____ Moving
_____ Holding
_____ Lifting
_____ Gripping
_____ Adjustability
_____ Accessibility
_____ Arrangement/legibility

Furniture that is intended for use by adults should be designed for approximately 90 per cent of the adult population, i.e., between the 5th (female) and 95th (male) percentile of the population's physical characteristics. (For the anthropometric measure of height, the lower limit of the range is the height of a 1.52m / 5ft female and the upper limit is the height of

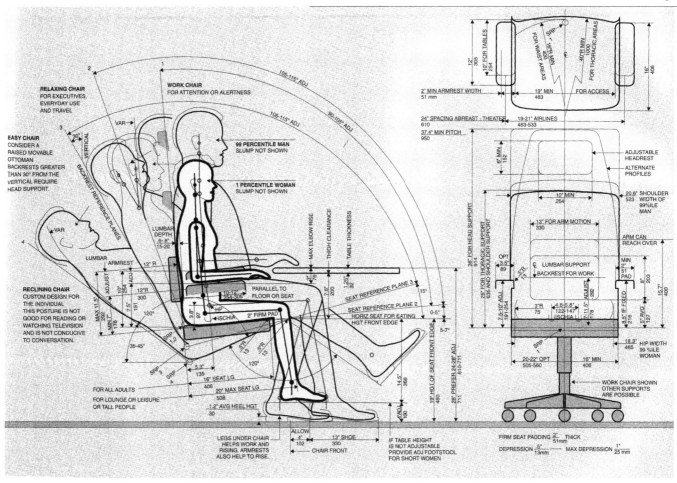

a 1.88m / 6ft 2in male). Furniture dimensions that are fixed (not adjustable), can be made ergonomic for the most common/50th percentile males and females. However, it is more usually appropriate to design for the upper end of the percentile range rather than the middle or most common, since oversized furniture can more easily be accommodated by users than that which is undersized. It is worth remembering that no one is an exact percentile in all measures, i.e., a certain height does not determine a corresponding leg length or arm reach – people are instead a combination of various arm lengths, elbow heights, lumbar depths, etc. Nor does the anthropometric data necessarily (unless stated or understood) take account of regionally prevalent physical characteristics such as obesity in the USA or tallness in Holland.

This chapter offers enough ergonomic and anthropometric information to begin most projects, but nearly all will require further reference to anthropometric tables and some kind of modelling to establish and confirm that a concept's particular combination of dimensions and features are correct.

In no project is such observance and care needed more than for chair design – an area of design that can be more challenging (and rewarding) than any other. One of the difficulties of designing all ergonomic furniture is that accurate test rigs or prototypes can be complex, time consuming and expensive. A 'sum of parts' approach using largely accurate rigs can achieve a great deal (see p104), but for projects such as Yves Béhar's Sayl Chair (see p128) or PearsonLloyd's Cobi Chair (see p72), complex rigs, rapid prototyping, RIM moulding and finite element analysis (FEA) are needed to test the properties of materials in relation to the design.

Furniture's dimensional parameters (anthropometrics) seem straightforward on paper, but it is very easy to combine separately correct dimensions to produce an incorrect whole. Also, a design's interaction with other furniture, with people's physical differences and with factors such as material properties and surface finishes all add up to a sizeable opportunity for designers to get it wrong.

Regardless of any of its other characteristics, a piece of furniture should be functionally fit for purpose. There are of course foibles, failures and annoyances in furniture performance that we are prepared to put up with – perhaps because the piece is beautiful, or useful in other aspects – but, overall, designers should have discovered and edited out these mistakes at the development stage, rather than

Since its first publication in 1959, *Measure of Man and Woman: Human Factors in Design* has been the most universally useful ergonomic and anthropometric resource for designers of space and products. A revised edition was published in 2002, from which these diagrams come, and, although some of the data is therefore not contemporary, any inaccuracies in relation to present-day percentile ranges are likely to be small. The book therefore remains the very best ergonomics reference for furniture designers.

discovering them in the final product when it is too late. Sometimes, changes happen that are out of the designer's control, for example, changes of material or a dimensional alteration in order to make a cost saving. Marcel Breuer's Wassily Chair (see p109) is not the most comfortable or ergonomic of chairs largely because the leather seat and backrest do not stretch and are slippery, making it difficult for the sitter to retain the right posture. The original prototypes used fabric in place of leather, which performed much better in this respect, but as the result of commissions that specified leather instead of fabric, the leather version gained popularity and publicity, putting a halt to the use of fabric.

Design students must familiarize themselves with the range of standard dimensions for furniture – not just the heights for seats, desks or dining tables but also such factors as user reach and accessibility. Considering the inclusive (universal) nature of design is also a critical part of the contemporary process; whether designing for a 35-year-old with rheumatoid arthritis or for the majority of people over the age of 70, considerations around organisation, layout and height should be central to research strategies and design thinking.

Ever since Bill Stumpf designed Ergon, the first ergonomic task chair, in 1976, significant inroads have been made into achieving similar levels of ergonomic performance but without the need for manual adjustment. To date, the most successful ergonomic and sustainable tasking chair is commonly thought of as being the 2010 Diffrient World Chair designed by the eminent ergonomist Niels Diffrient (see p57). Such progress in ergonomic seating development is as much driven by the need to produce new products as it is to improve ergonomics, but it is not a cynical exercise. Only incremental progress in ergonomics is, however, being made, although admittedly significant improvements in people's postures are being achieved with responsive self-adjusting chairs such as the Diffrient World and Cobi.

The developmental nature of ergonomics will continue, just as the exponential change in technology use will create new needs and opportunities for furniture designers. However,

Pierandrei Associati's Beta Workplace System for Tecno uses desks, storage and informal seating to create ergonomic and productive workspaces.

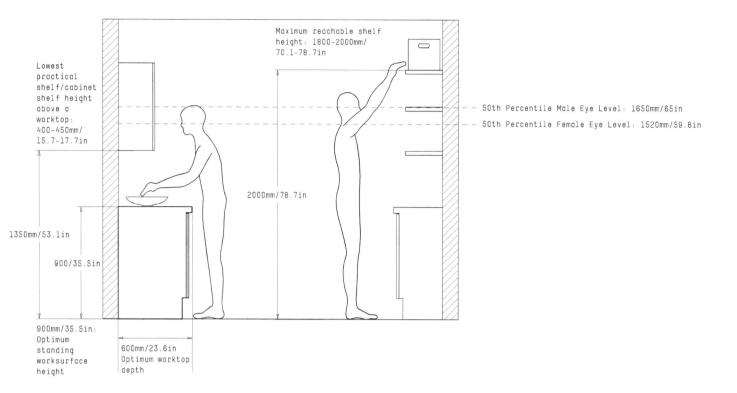

Maximum reachable shelf
height: 1800-2000mm/
70.1-78.7in

Lowest
practical
shelf/cabinet
shelf height
above a
worktop:
400-450mm/
15.7-17.7in

50th Percentile Male Eye Level: 1650mm/65in

50th Percentile Female Eye Level: 1520mm/59.8in

2000mm/78.7in

1350mm/53.1in

900/35.5in

900mm/35.5in:
Optimum
standing
worksurface
height

600mm/23.6in
Optimum worktop
depth

despite the mobility and flexibility of personal electronic devices, a significant proportion of work will still take place at a desk while sitting on a chair, and so any changes are more likely to meaningfully effect the organization of our working and living environments rather than the furniture itself.

Storage and workspace design

We most often interact with seating, desks and tables, but our need to organize, store and access possessions, work tools and other items means that storage and display furniture is as ubiquitous as seating. All rooms can be thought of as Le Corbusier's 'machines for living' and none more so than kitchens and workspaces. The arrangement of tasking areas, of storage for convenience and the organisation therein of their components is an important part of furniture design, which takes the discipline across the boundary and into interior design and architecture.

The main controls when designing accessible storage are reach, visibility, purchase and surrounding space. The above diagram illustrates the considerations that should be given to storage and workspaces, but designers should also be as careful to consider hand grips and access to drawer handles, particularly in relation to creating inclusive

(universal) design solutions that require less bending down, stretching, twisting and load bearing.

In addition to the ergonomic performance of the furniture in a kitchen or workspace, an area's layout and the resulting efficiency with which users can undertake tasks also plays a significant part in the machine's success or failure. The kitchen triangle is probably the most widely understood result of ergonomic analysis and was one of the earliest reported applications of the discipline. The triangle describes the path between the most often used parts of the kitchen: the hob, refrigerator and sink. According to *The Measure of Man and Woman* (by Henry Dreyfuss Associates), the sum of the triangle's three sides should not exceed 7015mm (276in) and should not be intersected by any through traffic.

Seating design

The posture we adopt when sitting matters a great deal, but its impact on people's physiology is also directly related to the amount of time spent in a particular position, or on a task or activity. As an example, in a study of seating provision in schools, a researcher would quickly discover that the ergonomics of the dining hall or library furniture matter a great deal less than that of the classroom. While a high standard of ergonomics is crucial in the classroom, so is the interactive relationship between furniture, such as chairs, desks and tables. More significantly,

Diagram of storage accessibility.

the range of ages of students using the furniture in a high school means that the needed scope for adjustability is greater than for adult percentile ranges.

The 5th to the 95th percentile range of anthropometric data for all seating is of limited use without specific examples related to different types of seating, such as dining chairs, public seating, office chairs and perch stools. The table on page 100 encompasses all major seating scenarios and should be used as a guide in conjunction with test rigs and further anthropometric data, because despite each example's more limited dimensional range, there is still room for error.

Importantly, if readers survey the market they will discover that the seat height dimensions outlined in this data for fixed-height chairs (all types except for the 'Office task chair') are rarely used. Instead, in accordance with British and international design standards, most seating of this type has a seat height of between 450 and 480mm (17.7 and 18.9in). Such seat heights are not ergonomic for a great many people, given the fact that the 50th percentile range between men and women is 390 to 430mm (15.4 to 16.9in). More succinctly, it is women that suffer the most in this case.

Fixed-height chairs are full of ergonomic concessions, and, as the British Standards and international comparators demonstrate, consensus seems to be that it is better for such chairs to be over-height rather than being a 410mm (16.1in) mean between 50th male and female percentiles. The best solution for non-adjustable chairs, therefore, should be to have two, three or four different overall sizes to reflect the great range of anthropometrics in the adult population. However, while this is theoretically practical, the reality is that most companies would not buy such a range and, if they did, users would find it difficult to differentiate between the products.

Despite all the arguments against dimensional ranges for universal chairs, design students need a straightforward guide to seating anthropometrics. Therefore, the data on page 100 should be used as both a reference for design segmentation and, with more careful judgements, universal seating. For the latter, and particularly for seat heights, a dimension at the higher end of the ranges listed will produce the most appropriate chair for the most people.

Occasional and dining chairs

While dining, conference and multipurpose occasional chairs do not tend to be used as intensively or as repeatedly as tasking chairs, such chairs in a domestic or contract setting can account for a significant amount of use by individuals. Dining chairs should feature a near horizontal seat and a relatively perpendicular backrest from between 5–10°. A more multifunctional chair, on the other hand, should have a backrest angle of 10–20° (from vertical), although if it is to be used for dining and tasking then the lower end of this range is most suitable. The profile or form of seat pans and backrests can significantly improve the experience of, and the fatigue resulting from, sitting. Upholstery, padding, surface finish and air movement all contribute to ergonomic performance and a sitter's comfort, but a well-designed rigid chair without any of the above can still be more comfortable than a badly designed, padded and upholstered chair, even with long-term use.

Occasional or multifunctional chairs are often better dining-room chairs than near-vertical-backed traditional dining chairs, given that eating is just one of the activities that take place at the table. However, too steep a seat angle and too great a backrest angle will produce a posture better suited to drinking in a bar than to eating or working.

A large radius or sloping front edge, often referred to as a waterfall front, provides the most ergonomic seating position on multifunctional chairs, not least because it reduces the pressure on the leg's femoral arteries and makes it easier to shift body weight forward to write. Also, given that most multifunctional chairs are too high for a large proportion of sitters, the waterfall front makes it easier and more comfortable for the toes to touch the floor.

Viewed from the front, raised seat-pan sides curving into the centre can produce a comfortable seating position, but if this form is too pronounced, the

The Alumno, a scaling school chair, automatically adjusts its seat depth relative to the chair's height, providing perfect ergonomics for students between the ages of 11 and 18. Designed by James Heywood, De Montfort University (Leicester, UK) and winner of the FIRA Ergonomic Excellence Award 2008.

Seating anthropometrics

SEATING TYPE	SEAT HEIGHT (mm/in) at front edge	SEAT DEPTH (mm/in)	SEAT WIDTH (mm/in) armrests require 480+mm /18.9i+n width space	SEAT ANGLE degrees from horizontal (+ denotes a forward tilt)	BACKREST HEIGHT (min) (mm/in) starting 150mm/5.9in above seat rear. Lumbar support area h230+mm/9.1+in x w370+mm/14.6+in	BACKREST ANGLE BACKREST ANGLE degrees from vertical value should increase relative to increase in '-' seat angle number	ARMREST HEIGHT (mm/in) from back of seat
Sofa/ armchair	370-400 / 14.6-15.7[a] max. 495/19.5	340-460 / 13.4-18.1[a] max. 430/16.9	450-600 / 17.7-23.6	-5 - -7	240 / 9.4	15-25	180-280 / 7.1-11
Dining chair	400-440 / 15.7-17.3 max. 495/19.5	340-400 / 13.4-15.7 max. 430/16.9	410-450 / 16.1-17.7	0 - -5	240 / 9.4	5-25	180-280 / 7.1-11
Occasional chair	390-430 / 15.4-16.9 max. 495/19.5	340-400 / 13.4-15.7 max. 430/16.9	410-450 / 16.1-17.7	-3 - -8	240 / 9.4	10-20	180-280 / 7.1-11
Office task chair	370-495 / 14.6-19.5[b]	340-400 / 13.4-15.7 max. 430/16.9	410-560 / 16.1-22	+3 - -10	180-290 /	0-15	180-280 / 7.1-11
Bench (backless)	400-450 / 15.7- 17.7 max. 495/19.5	300+ / 11.8+	450-600 / 17.7-23.6	0	n/a	0	n/a
Low stool (backless)	460-560 / 18.1-22 max. 600/23.6	200+ / 7.9+	450-550 / 17.7-21.7	0	n/a	0	n/a
High stool	590-740 / 23.2-29.1[c]	200-400 / 7.9-15.7	450-550 / 17.7-21.7	0	240 / 9.4	0-5	180-280 / 7.1-11

Key:

All white cells describe the full 5th-95 percentile range
Orange denotes the range between 50th male and female percentiles (maximum / male 95th percentile dimension given as 'max. xx').
a: Compressed upholstery/cushioning
b: Required seating range (height-adjustable chairs will require 125mm / 4.9in of adjustment)
c: Requires footrest

Diagram of chair anthropometrics.

(from left to right):
Sofa / Armchair
Occasional / Dining
Tasking / Office

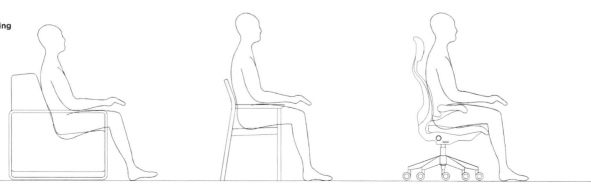

sitter's movement and capacity for self-adjustment will be restricted. Obviously, the narrower the chair, the more pronounced the effect. The overweight can also find themselves sitting on the high points on either side of such a chair, which causes discomfort and impeded blood flow. Equally, the backrest can benefit from a side-to-side curve and a rolled-back top edge. However, too tight a curve on the backrest restricts breathing and also restricts the sitter's ability to temporarily adjust his/her position to combat fatigue.

Office task chairs

In a wrongly sized or unergonomic chair, the best desk-working posture is one that changes constantly, since long-lasting physiological damage can be caused by repeated straining movements, particularly in relation to work surface height.

Primarily, an office tasking chair needs to support computer use, writing and relaxed working such as phone conversations. For this reason, tasking chairs need to be a combination of the manually adjustable and the self-adjusting in response to movement. The

retail cost of good ergonomic seating means that a great many workers sit on chairs that simply have seat-height and backrest-angle adjustment. Such provision is better than nothing, but to significantly reduce the impact of long-term computer use and other fixed-position tasks, finer adjustment (whether active or passive) is required. Primarily:

_____ Seat height: 360–520mm (14.2–20.5in)
_____ Seat angle: +3–-10°
_____ Backrest height: 920mm (36.2in) for head support and 630mm (24.8in) for thoracic support
_____ Backrest angle: 0–+15°
_____ Lumbar support (optional positive/negative adjustment): 180–290mm (7.1–11.4in)
_____ Armrest (optional) support height: 190–250mm (7.5–9.8in)
_____ Rotational movement: swivelling, stable base on five+ feet.

Far left: **As well as being highly sustainable, the Diffrient World Chair responds to the fact that people do not adjust their chairs as much as they should, requiring the chair to do it for them by being dynamically reactive.**

Left: **The Setu Chair by Studio 7.5 for Herman Miller has a sophisticated 'kinematic' spine that provides dynamic, flexible support to the sitter.**

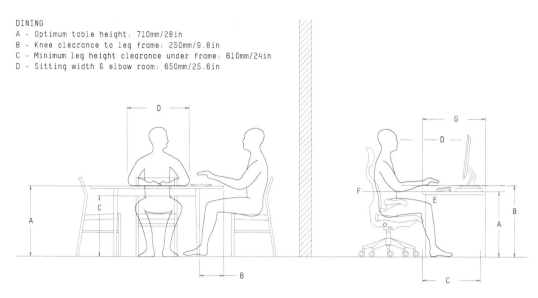

Desks and work tables

In spite of the year-on-year increase in laptop use and a general shift toward mobile technology and more informal working practices, the great majority of work still takes place at desks. However, with homeworking on the rise, scenarios such as the use of a laptop at a dining table with a dining chair often produces an ergonomically incorrect posture for a good number of users.

The optimum height (50th percentile combined men and women) for a dining table and for a fixed-height desk is 710mm (28in). However, British and other international design standards recommend that such desks should be in the region of 740mm (29.1in) high with an ideal thigh clearance (underneath) of 695mm (27.4in). Such dimensions suit men more than women since the 50th percentile desk height for women is 660mm (26in), as opposed to 720mm (28.3in) for men. The rationale for such compromise is rooted in the fact that it is easier to cope with a desk that is too high (by using a height-adjustable chair and a footrest) than it is with one that is too low. Such concessions are not ideal and so, whenever possible, designers should design and workers should sit at a height-adjustable desk.

In a survey (conducted by the author in 2011) of 20 dining tables selected at random from UK and US websites, an average height of 752mm (29.6in) was observed. In a survey of contract and domestic desks (without lower keyboard surfaces), each with a sample of 20 products, the contract office desks'

mean height was an 'appropriate' 721mm (28.4in), while the domestic desks' mean height was 737mm (29in). Both this and the 752mm (29.6in, dining-table average) dimensions produce further gender imbalances and posture-associated physiological problems, particularly for those who might work for long periods in such conditions.

Although not quite as important as desk height, the average provision for knee, thigh and toe clearance is very good for desks, but is less commonly right for dining tables. Minimum knee clearance (depth) for the combined percentile range is 393mm (15.5in), but in balance with the use of the 50th male percentile, knee clearance should be 440mm+ (17.3+in) to accommodate men. As mentioned, thigh clearance should be a minimum of 695mm (27.4in), with the distance needed between the highest seat surface and the lowest member of a table or desk at 200mm (7.9in) or more. Toe clearance of 605mm (23.8in) will be sufficient for 95 per cent of men and 99 per cent of women.

Ideal work-surface depths have changed since the advent of flat-screen technology, and so while it is possible to use a keyboard and monitor on a work surface that is 650mm (25.6in) deep, in order for there to be enough leg room for a 95th percentile man, a depth of 850mm (33.5in) is required. This reduced depth also makes it easier for users to reach any storage or panel system at the back of the desk without necessarily rising from their chair. In terms of the ideal width for a workspace, the more the better, but 600mm (23.6in) should be considered an absolute minimum space in which to type and use a mouse.

Left: **Diagram of desk and table ergonomics and anthropometrics.**

Opposite, top to bottom:
Airtouch by Steelcase is a height-adjustable workstation for both sitting and standing tasks.

Envelop Desk by Bill Stumpf and Jeff Weber for Herman Miller is a height-adjustable desk with an extendable top, designed to promote and improve different working postures. Left to right: reclined, relaxed and upright.

2c: Design-process skill set – concept development and testing

Developing a furniture concept from a sketch to a marketable concept presents huge challenges to both designers and industry. Dynamic concept sketches and sophisticated renders must be matched by well-researched manufacturing specifications and precise technical definition. Designers therefore require a great many skills, plus a great deal of detailed and peripheral knowledge to fulfil this often-complex role.

Between the inception and completion of any project, there exists an intense process of optimisation through which outcome-driven innovation can result. This rational developmental process also requires lateral thinking and compromise, presenting great tests to even the most experienced designers, since the result of improving a design's function, aesthetics, ergonomics or manufacturing rationale can also cause other previously well-thought-through attributes to be undermined. The resulting machinations can produce a drawn-out process with more side steps than forward movement, but it is through such salutary endeavours that good design prospers.

Early stage designers rely on their education, drawing on all of their conceptual and practical skills learned through intense study. As their experience grows, a more pronounced 'T-shaped' designer emerges, with a core, vertical shaft of applied skills balanced by a growing professional and commercial acumen. It is no surprise that many furniture designers' broadening skills lead them to become design or product managers – roles that encompass the commissioning of concept generation to manufacturing quality control. Experience becomes more relevant as a designer's career progresses, but without the core skills and experience of a formal design education, it would be very difficult for a designer to have broad

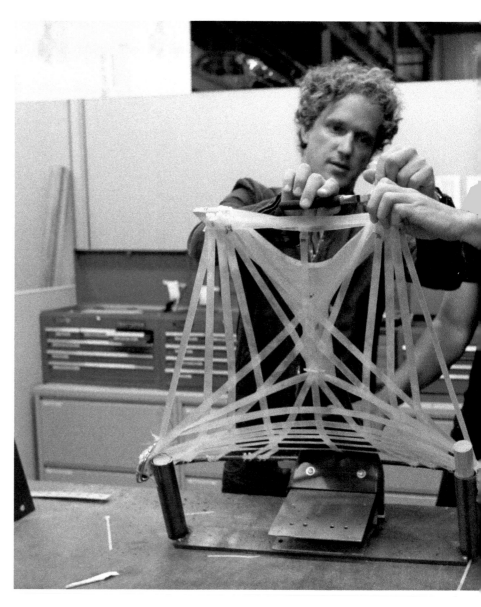

career possibilities beyond a specialism. However, within specialist areas of design and production, such as cabinetmaking, it is possible for talented individuals to circumvent the education system and develop their design and manufacturing knowledge through experience of work, although this would be limited in scope (but certainly not depth).

Yves Béhar used a series of increasingly complex test rigs in the development of the Sayl Chair.

'I prefer drawing to talking. Drawing is faster, and leaves less room for lies.' Le Corbusier (*Time* Magazine, 5 May 1961)

Drawing

In broad terms, drawing includes all forms of mark making, both digital and 'analogue', although referring to 'free' as opposed to 'measured' drawing techniques can make a clearer distinction. Drawing is a fundamental part of the design process and, in conjunction with scale models, test rigs, CAD models and prototypes, it plays an important role in the conception, development and resolution of successful design.

Drawing is the most accessible tool to designers – fast enough to keep up with thought processes and

Detailed illustrations, as well as quick sketches, play an important part in developing a design's visual language.

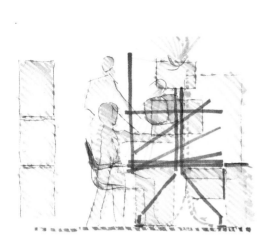

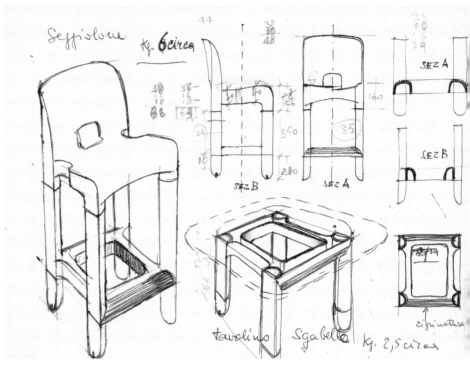

sensitive enough to describe the complexity or nuanced beauty of a detail. Therefore, a willingness to draw is essential, especially for budding designers who wish to interrogate and improve their ideas. However, without a good understanding of perspective and the skill to express three-dimensionality in form and detail, drawing can simply become an exercise in filling space.

Concept sketching

For concept origination and development, free sketch drawings should be the designer's first recourse – drawings that are a record of thoughts, potential and a means of rationalizing and furthering ideas. Initial sketches do not need to be to scale, have the correct perspective or be very polished, but as the idea development progresses, there exists an exponential need for accuracy in these drawings in order for a concept's potential to be assessed. Inaccurate drawings can make the impossible seem possible, the mundane seem interesting and the ugly seem beautiful. However, there is a caveat – drawing is by distinction, interpretive and inexact. Therefore, its inaccuracies can also be usefully ambiguous to a designer, aiding innovation by suggesting unthought-of constructions, materials and aesthetics.

Although the division between concept sketches and presentation drawings is blurred, first sketches illustrate an idea, a note to oneself – perhaps with annotations describing function, precise details and materials or manufacturing processes. As the idea is rationalized and turned into a concept, drawings increasingly illustrate what is known, gradually becoming more accurate descriptions or presentations of a whole idea. However, as they say, the devil is in the detail, and so what at this stage seems to unskilled observers to be a clear first concept, is

really just the first step on the long journey of product development, resolution and manufacture.

The use of traditional drawing skills and materials could be considered to be in decline, with computer-aided design (CAD) techniques being in the ascendancy; but it is certainly true that the accessibility of software can tempt designers toward measured 2-D and 3-D drawing techniques and away from pencils and paper too early. The control over developing ideas that free drawing provides is very rarely matched by a measured 2-D or 3-D CAD modelling interface, but the (optional) replacement of pencils and paper by digital pens, touch screens and software-based sketching tools are changing the way in which some designers work. Despite the ease with which a sketchbook can be kept close at hand while working on a computer, Illustrator, and latterly Sketchbook Pro and its descendants, encourage drawing and its enjoyment for the CAD-obsessed and desk-bound.

Above: **Detailed concept sketches for the Universale Chair by Joe Colombo, 1965.**

Left: **First sketches illustrate an idea or act as a note to oneself. This is the Nomos table concept sketch by Norman Foster.**

Presentation and definition

Presentation drawings describe rationalized concepts and, as such, should not be exploratory. Of course, drawn concepts that are presented early on to tutors or clients do not describe technically resolved designs, but they should illustrate a whole idea sufficiently enough to allow a single or composite choice to be made and a further development of the project to be subsequently commissioned. Later in this process, once the concept has been finalized in terms of function, aesthetics and manufacturing detail, a final presentation is created that includes more details in the form of both rendered (invariably, 3-D CAD drawings) and 2-D manufacturing drawings.

It is worth noting that striving for photorealism in initial concept presentations is not always advantageous. Principles of function and assembly should be expressed clearly, but there is also some advantage in the relative ambiguity inherent in illustrative sketches when it comes to aesthetics and materials. Certainly at the concept stage, clients and observers will sometimes interpret sketched, free drawings more favourably than seemingly resolved concepts as photorealistic CAD renders. It is, therefore, sometimes prudent to opt for a style of origination that is obviously a concept rather than a finished design.

Although 2-D drafting software is still widely used in the industry, engineering drawings using orthographic views of 3-D CAD models from solid modelling programs such as SolidWorks are a growing trend. The great advantage of this approach is that the product only has to be drawn once, rather than needing two versions of a product's data for direct or indirect manufacture. Also, providing that the 3-D CAD model is constructed correctly, it is easy to create cross-sectional views and exploded component drawings.

When it comes to creating manufacturing drawings, it is vital that conventions (drafting standards) are followed, so that a model maker or manufacturer can be sure of the information portrayed. Such drawings should be unambiguous and readable in any

country. Importantly, by so doing, such conventions will guard the designer against complaint or litigation should a part be manufactured incorrectly.

There is a great deal more information about ISO standards for engineering drawings than there is space in this chapter, and so readers who have not had the advantage of such technical training at a university or as part of their job should enquire with their country's standards institute for further information about standards and tolerances for drawing and manufacture.

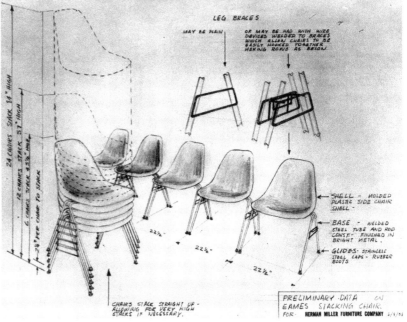

Top: **Final visualisations should invariably give context to a design's use and market and, while clarity is important, such presentations can benefit as much from a lyrical expression as from a pragmatic approach. Shown here is part of the Garden Seating presentation by Chris Berry at De Montfort University (Leicester, UK).**

Above: **A preliminary drawing by Charles Eames to explain to Herman Miller the stacking and linking principle for a variation of his Moulded Plastic Side Chair.**

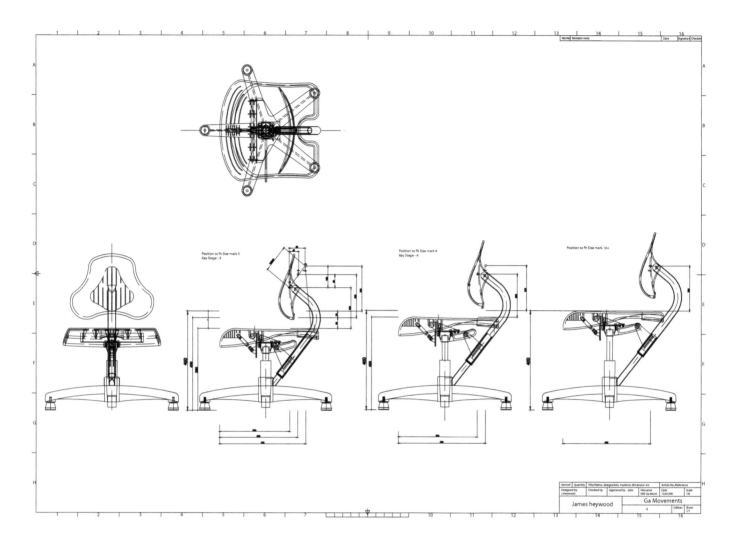

CAD-modelling software

CAD drafting and 3-D modelling software provides designers with enormously powerful definition and presentation tools, although they are not a total solution. CAD tools are best used in conjunction with drawing and physical modelling and prototyping. Nearly all 2-D and 3-D software can output files for CNC (computer numerical control) routing, laser cutting, etc. However, problems do arise from the use of polygon modellers because they are not accurate enough and produce faceted rather than pure curves, which slows the cutting of such details and, without a high resolution, these will become visible features.

Selecting a CAD package

CAD packages can be broken down into four distinct types that satisfy a range of design requirements. Often CAD packages provide some tools from a more advanced type of product, such as 2-D drafting packages, which have some simple 3-D modelling capabilities similar to those offered by solid modelling packages. The extent of these additional tools is usually restricted, ultimately forcing customers to upgrade their package when their ambitions and requirements evolve. AutoCad Inventor, SolidWorks and Rhino are the most commonly used programs.

2-D drafting packages (such as AutoCAD LT)

These drafting programs allow 2-D orthographic drawings to be created accurately. Drawings are produced at a 1:1 scale and scaled for printed output.

All designers must be able to produce clear, unambiguous technical drawings that follow international conventions if they are to communicate with manufacturers.

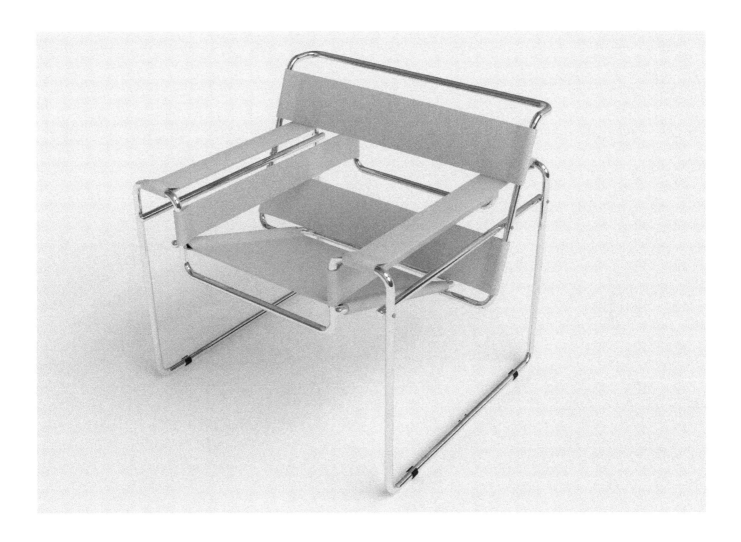

Solid modelling packages
(such as Autodesk Inventor and SolidWorks)

Designs are modelled in a virtual 3-D space using these programs and the software can make creating rational geometric-type forms easy. The model is created at 1:1, and the orthographic or section views can then be generated from the model along with renderings of the design with accurate representations of materials and surface finish.

Surface modelling packages
(such as Rhino 3D)

Such programs allow complex forms to be created that would otherwise be difficult or impossible using solid modelling techniques. Surface models tend to be used where the form cannot be defined with rational dimensions; for example, splines (curves) can have variable rates of change (similar to an elliptical curve) instead of a rational radius (like that of an arc).

Polygon modelling packages
(such as Maya, 3ds Max and SketchUp)

These packages describe forms and objects through surface approximation. This unfortunately means that models are not entirely accurate. It can be difficult or impossible to extract manufacturing-quality data from such models. They are used to communicate designs through visual renderings as they can create approximate models quite quickly.

Clients can interpret high quality, realistic renders as a visual contract and so designers should be careful when presenting such precise visual presentations.

Modelling, prototyping and testing

Test rigs, prototypes, visual models and the subsequent detailed analysis of material and structural performance and user interaction are all ways to 'proofread' a concept. Designers should expect to encounter problems and even significant flaws during this kind of rigorous enquiry, and so it would therefore be an act of folly to consider a concept as a finished design until it has been thoroughly tested. Granted, a product by a designer who is familiar with a furniture type and the materials proposed should not require significant testing, but any designer, whether a student or a seasoned professional who is pushing the limits of their ability and knowledge, will need to model and test their ideas.

Rapid prototyping (RP, both additive and subtractive processes) and accessible finite element analysis (FEA, via software) makes the prototyping and testing of plastic and metal components much more accessible. Such opportunities should, therefore, lead to a world populated by furniture that performs very well. Unfortunately, due to the high costs of RP in relation to build size and a lack of quality control in manufactured products, there is a great deal of furniture available that is not fit for purpose.

Sketching communicates a concept's potential, but such drawings lack the definition to be considered 'a design'. Likewise, CAD modelling can give the impression of a resolved concept with little more detail determined than in a sketch. In order for a concept to become a finished, manufacturing-ready design, its structure, ergonomics and aesthetics must be tested and assessed through a series of related rigs, models, interactions and software-based analysis; there is no all-encompassing prototype.

Unless designers have a good deal of time, funds and facilities at their disposal, full aesthetic models are not usually an efficient use of time and resources, so such visuals are best achieved as 3-D CAD models. However, test rigs and 1:1 approximation models are essential to the evolution of any piece of

furniture because aesthetics must always be supported by good function. Test rigs (proof-of-principle rigs) can be as simple as a quick cardboard model to assess a concept's scale or as complex as a prototyped seat-posture mechanism.

Testing the strength, stability, durability and safety of furniture is a necessary part of bringing a product to market. Most developed countries have their own standards for furniture performance that relate to particular types of objects such as chairs or bunk beds for domestic and contract environments. In the UK, for example, furniture with upholstery must be tested for flammability performance, whereas testing the strength of a chair is not a requirement. However, if retailers sell a dangerous product, they are liable for any problems caused by its failure and so all sizable retailers employ technologists or quality-assurance managers to monitor such issues. Often,

Simple scale models are often the best way to begin to engage with a project's technical challenges; shown here are Facett models by Ronan and Erwan Bouroullec.

problems simply relate to a dimension, such as a head trap or a strangulation risk on a child's bed, in which case, potential products can be assessed by measurement. Many agents or buyers will not supply furniture that does not meet these standards and so in order for manufacturers and their designers not to be exposed to litigious risk, independent third parties such as the Furniture Industry Research Association (FIRA) in the UK and the Business and Institutional Furniture Manufacturer's Association (BIFMA) in the USA provide facilities for testing furniture to provide legal and technical validation.

The development of functional and visual aspects of a concept can be achieved through a 'sum-of-parts' approach rather than using one model to develop all aspects together.

Top: Only once a final production model has been produced can it be truly tested so that any necessary improvements can be made prior to mass manufacture. Despite all of the virtual FEA testing of the Myto Chair, the first moulded prototypes with a range of Ultradur formulas were physically tested to assess their relative benefits.

Stefan Diez's Houdini Chair for e15

Since the launch of his Houdini Chair in 2009, Diez has progressed a range of seating for German brand e15 that expands on the constructional techniques used: Jean (a barstool), Eugene and Leo (lounge chairs), Bess (a sofa) and Bessy (a small lounge chair).

Diez developed this series by physical, hands-on modelling, firstly using cardboard and wood before moving on to entirely wood constructions for functional prototypes. Although the chairs' components are CNC-cut, their assembly is achieved by hand (in about two hours). However, because of this production limitation, there is no tooling needed for any of the components, which means that it is possible to manufacture the series without significant up-front investment apart from materials, stock, marketing, etc. This freedom enabled e15 to support the development of the collection.

1. Building 1:1 models of the chair (based on measured drawings) from card and wood.

2. Visual prototypes made from cardboard and wood.

3. Checking and laying out the parts for each chair in groups and in order of manufacture. The prototype chair's components are CNC-cut and machined by a partner company before being delivered as a kit of parts.

4. Gluing the lower backrest component to the base.

5. The legs are machined precisely to provide an interference fit with just enough of a tolerance for gluing.

6. A bracing support enables the first prototype to be tested.

7. A bracing jig supports the armchair while the glued legs dry.

8. A complex cramping and gluing procedure joins the lower backrest to the base and the seat to the base frame.

Houdini Chairs.

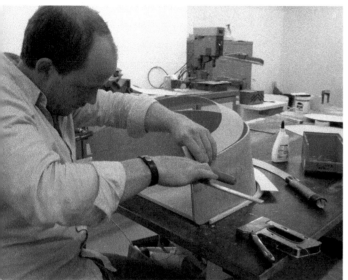

9: **Test fitting the backrest's lower and upper components.**

10: **Test fitting the upper backrest to the base.**

11: **Final gluing and cramping of the upper backrest.**

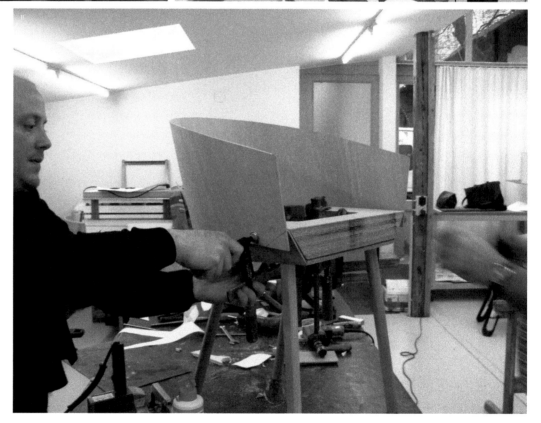

Konstantin Grcic's Myto Chair for Plank

Like his former assistant Stefan Diez, Konstantin Grcic centres all of his product development on drawing and modelling. For the groundbreaking Myto Chair, Grcic and his team used a mixture of traditional workshop-based prototyping alongside CAD modelling and finite element analysis (FEA) to evolve the concept. In spite of all of the virtual FEA testing of the chair (see picture 8, p117), the first prototypes were physically tested with a range of Ultradur formulas to assess their benefits. Testing included dropping heavy bags of raw materials from a height and also placing a 500kg (1102lb) block of steel on the chair – which it survived! The team also sat on the chair and noted each formula's particular peformance before selecting the final material.

The Myto Chair was developed in collaboration with BASF, using its innovative thermoplastic Ultradur.

1: In parallel with concept sketching, Grcic used Formetal, a perforated modelling material that is structurally superior to traditional modelling meshes, to develop the form of the chair. Grcic keeps additional materials to a minimum and uses insulating tape to mark outlines.

2: A quick test rig made from chair parts.

3-5: Red insulating tape is applied to manually take detailed dimensional measurements. This data becomes the basis for a 3-D CAD model.

6: Building a test rig (that relates to the CAD data and visual model) to evaluate and develop the chair's ergonomics. The team created a new visual model from wire and cardboard that described the developed form. The supporting rig was built to express its dimensions and form.

7: Grcic using insulating tape and marker pens to create the finalized mesh design. This aspect of the design was largely governed by the characteristics and flow mechanics of the plastic.

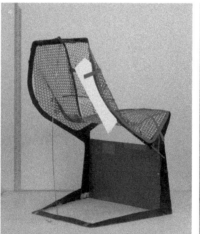

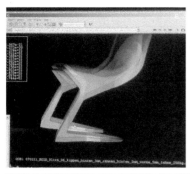

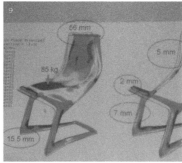

8-9: Using software to run dynamic and static stress analysis. The exchange of CAD data enabled all parties in the design and development process to remain in close contact. The BASF engineers also used flow simulations and testing to fine-tune the plastic (Ultradur) for Myto's particular needs.

10: Although a great deal of progress was made through modelling and test rigs, a CNC-cut model was necessary for comfort testing.

11: A rapid prototyped (selective laser sintering [SLS]) model also helped to identify issues with the moulding of Myto.

The first production run.

Ronan and Erwan Bouroullec's Vegetal for Vitra

Designed for Vitra, Ronan and Erwan Bouroullec's Vegetal took four years of complex development before it was ready for manufacture. The brothers' initial concepts were related to the idea of the 'grown chair' and were also informed by naturalistic styles of English cast-iron furniture from the nineteenth century. Rather than simply creating an ornamented chair, the brothers wanted to develop an innovative structure – and it was this objective that became the crux of the project.

While branching structures provided great freedom, the big challenge for the Bouroullecs was to maintain a naturalistic, convincing composition while also adhering to functionally sound leg positions.

After the development of a T-shaped profile for the seat shell 'branches' and after experimenting with a great many compositions and branch types, the Vegetal Chair was eventually prototyped by vacuum-casting high-density polyurethane within a CNC-cut mould. However, in spite of the progress that had been made and the great expense of this set-up, once the designers sat on the prototype, they realized that it was not comfortable due to the depth of the 'branches' overlap. They returned to the drawing board and eventually finalized the design using almost the same composition but with less pronounced overlaps.

Vegetal's front legs and seat shell are injection moulded from fibre-reinforced polyamide as one component, and the back legs are moulded separately before being screwed and glued to the fixing-point spurs.

Vegetal's apparently simple structure belies its complex development.

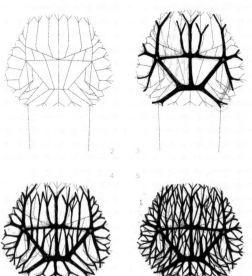

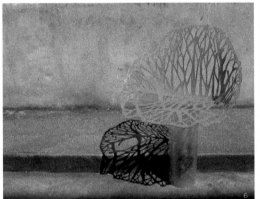

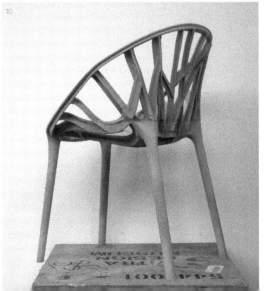

1. Initially, Vegetal was meant to be a chair that grew up from its legs, with its branches creating the seat and backrest. This early RP (stereolithography, SLA) model illustrates the degree to which the chair was developed.

2-5. The complexity of Vegetal's early forms created significant manufacturing and structural challenges.

6. An early visual model, created using glued paper.

7. Once the principles of the chair's structure had been defined, hundreds of variations were then explored.

8. Glued paper and Styrofoam 1:1 modelling helped to develop the concept's structural and aesthetic detail in parallel.

9. Testing different arrangements and widths of the branch structure using paper models.

10. For final prototyping, a mould was CNC-machined from high-density polyurethane in order for a resin model to be vacuum-cast. This prototype was produced to check the chair's comfort and to inspect overall details such as rib formation.

Material, ergonomic and safety testing

Designers' professional experience and testing of prototypes will give them and their client or employer some confidence in the material, ergonomic and safety performance of a design. However, without consulting design standards or without expert third-party validation, they could be risking both the time and the large sums of money involved in rectifying, withdrawing or replacing products as a result of failures and litigation.

Organisations such as the UK-based Furniture Industry Research Association (FIRA) and US-based Business and Institutional Furniture Manufacturer's Association (BIFMA) offer testing services and product certification, which most manufacturers and retailers are very keen to use in conjunction with their own technologists' endeavours. Regulations and guidance are often updated and because industry associations will help to create these improvements with organisations such as the British (BS), European (EN), American (ANSI and ASTM) and International Standards (ISO) committees, it is wise to at least monitor news output from them even if you are not a member.

Domestic furniture environs are considered to be very different from contract furniture environs, because the latter can range from low (such as schools) to high risk (such as prisons). The regulations for contract environs are therefore more complex than for the domestic, because they relate to a specific set of risks.

For further information about these areas, visit the following websites:

Ergonomics, human factors and safety:

_____ www.hfes.org
_____ www.ergonomics.org.uk
_____ www.bifma.com
_____ www.fira.co.uk
_____ www.iea.cc
_____ www.ergonomics.jp
_____ www.nist.gov
_____ www.osha.gov
_____ www.access-board.gov
_____ www.bsigroup.co.uk

Materials and manufacturing:

_____ www.iom3.org
_____ www.nist.gov

Tests and standards

A wide range of tests are applied to new products, including tests on/for adhesive, childcare products, flammability, formaldehyde, storage, table, wood-based materials, chairs and seating, ergonomics, foams, surface finishes and textiles. These tests are mainly concerned with establishing that a design is fit for purpose – that it will stand up to prolonged use without degrading or breaking and possibly becoming dangerous. Another aspect of testing checks whether the dimensional parameters of a country's design standards have been followed (although such problems should not exist beyond the concept-development stage).

The development and validation of explicitly ergonomic furniture (such as an adjustable desk or task chair) should involve (for commercial products at least) an ergonomics or human-factors expert; simply applying combinations of anthropometric

Performance testing is an important part of product validation.

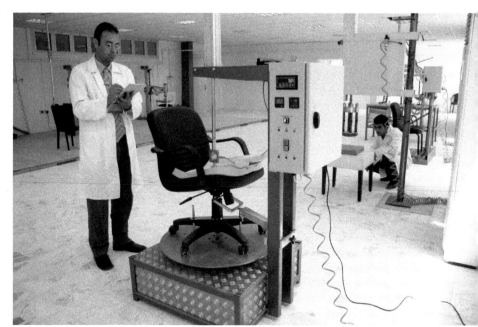

data to a design's development will not necessarily result in a product that is ergonomic or even fit for purpose. An ergonomist brings a great knowledge of established theories and current practice, and can help to create value in an ergonomic product by authenticating a premise or claim. All aspects of furniture design need some kind of usability or ergonomic testing that is often, although not always, associated with safety. All assessments of this kind should take place as part of the design-development process; some evaluations are immediately achievable with simple prototypes, whereas others require more complex testing and observation studies.

Simplistic judgements, such as whether a piece of furniture is comfortable or easily used, require much greater interrogation as part of a usability or ergonomics study. A super-soft sofa, for instance, may be comfortable initially, but could result in poor posture for the sitter. In turn, this effect could be physiologically damaging and exaggerated by prolonged and long-term use. Likewise, individual storage elements in an office environment might be easy to access, but as a system in normal use, their arrangement could be inefficient and create the risk of muscle strain or injury.

In addition to material and ergonomic testing, children's furniture and related domestic products have to be tested against the many international standards that relate to the risk of accidents caused by strength and stability issues, or the specific risks of suffocation, strangulation or crush injuries. Rather than general design guidance, these standards describe safe dimensional parameters for a wide range of furniture. For example, the minimum depth (mattress to top-rail height) of a cot is generally 500mm (26in mattress support to top-rail height in the US), which is enough to stop a small standing child from falling out. The bars have to be vertical to prevent a child from climbing and should have a gap of 45 to 65mm (a maximum of 2.38in in the US) between them to reduce the risk of a child becoming trapped and suffocating. For the same reasons, there should also be no gap of more than 40mm (1.6in) between the mattress and the bars. These parameters and many more besides are evidence-based regulations developed in response to accident analysis and theoretical testing. Therefore, no design project for children should be developed without consulting design standards, although students will probably only be able to access abridged versions since the full guideline documents are relatively expensive to buy.

Example test criteria

_____ Adhesive testing
This studies the quality of adhesive bonds. The failure of surfacing and edging bonds can result in cosmetic and structural faults.

_____ Chairs and seating testing
Encompasses a wide range of criteria. Each phase of these tests addresses issues such as strength, durability, stability and safety.

_____ Ergonomics testing
There are many international standards that relate to the ergonomics of product use associated with contract and educational realms.

_____ Flammability testing
Ratings for foam, padding and fabrics must conform to stringent regulations before products can be sold to the public.

_____ Formaldehyde testing
Most formaldehyde remains bonded within man-made timber boards, but small amounts of 'free formaldehyde' are emitted over time and under certain conditions. Strict limits govern the acceptable levels of free formaldehyde.

_____ Wood-based materials testing
Establishes man-made timber-board quality, analysing the board strength, screw holding, grit content and dimensional stability.

Chapter 3:

Materials, manufacturing and sustainability

3a: Material- and manufacturing-led design – case studies

When creating a concept or developing a design it can seem as if there is an overwhelming number of manufacturing options, but after considering volume, budget, sustainability, environment, longevity, materials and aesthetics, choosing the right approach is somewhat simplified and follows, at least in terms of narrowing it down, a straightforward rationale. This chapter explores material- and manufacturing-centred approaches to design and development through case studies, and through defining the sustainable and ethical issues surrounding furniture design. The final section of the chapter is a technical resource, encompassing material properties and manufacturing processes, and is intended as a tool for readers to investigate their idea's potential and to create basic specifications for manufacture. This section is by no means exhaustive, but it will give readers enough information to choose the right materials and processes and to understand the principles that govern their application. By cross-referencing this content with chapters 1 and 2, readers will also better understand how other designers think and innovate, while appreciating how ideas, materials and processes can be allied to create visually and technically innovative solutions.

Shanghai-based product designer Zhili Liu designed the Shrub Table for Belgian manufacturer Quinze & Milan. Shrub's leg frames are fabrications of aluminium rod that are assembled using machine screws and then powder-coated as an assembly.

Above: Oskar Zieta's unique FiDU technology (see p140) is currently a low-volume production method.

Above right: The main body of Benjamin Hubert's Pod Chair is formed using PET felt sheet.

Right: The Cobi Chair by PearsonLloyd uses a weight activated mechanism to automatically adjust itself to different users, who might not be relied upon to adjust the chair themselves.

Pressed Chair

Harry Thaler

H_770mm 30.3in	W_530mm 20.9in	D_530mm 20.9in
Aluminium		
Manufactured by Nils Holger Moormann		

Exhibited as a graduation project (from the Royal College of Art, London) in 2010, Harry Thaler's stacking aluminium chair represents a pure expression of a material and the mastering of a process. Pressed Chair is stamped from a 1m² (10.76ft²), 2.5mm- (0.1 in) thick aluminium sheet, with any waste material used to create three-legged stools. The chair is a true monobloc, whereas the stools are assembled by riveting three sections together.

The chair is stamped and pressed as a flat sheet before the back and legs are pressed or bent into different planes in a secondary forming process. The relatively soft alloy is transformed into a structural solution by being in constant three-dimensional transition – no surface is flat and this fact, coupled with the rigidifying splay of the legs, means that the chair can support the weight of almost five men. Rubber feet are fitted to each leg, which as well as preventing floor damage also serve to resist a spreading of the legs on slippery surfaces.

Structurally, the most significant detail is the pressed rib that runs from the backrest post into the seat pan. This is created during the secondary forming stage, at the same time as the concave forming of the seat pan. This element works in harmony with the backrest rib to brace the legs and to strengthen what would potentially be the weakest part of the chair – the backrest post.

From the outset, Thaler's intention was to design a chair that expressed a democratic and elementary approach to design, which for him was the logical outcome of a material- and process-led exploration. Trained as a goldsmith, and previously more of an experimental 3-D artist than industrial designer, Thaler states that his work is based on 'a foundation of traditional techniques and craftsmanship'. The chair and stool is now in volume production by Nils Holger Moormann.

Initial sketch for the Pressed Chair.

Weighing only 2.5kg (5.5lb), the chair is able to withstand 450kg (992lb) of vertical loading.

Below: Harry Thaler's chair is stamped and pressed from a flat sheet.

Sayl Chair

Yves Béhar

H_870-985mm 34.3-38.8in   W_622mm 24.5in   D_622mm 24.5in

Aluminium, steel, polyurethane, unspecified
elastomeric polymer

Manufactured by Herman Miller

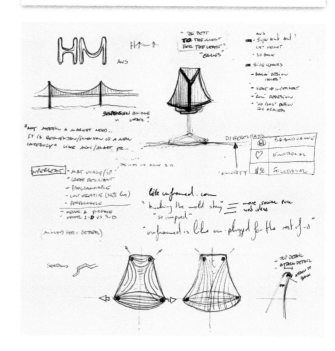

Yves Béhar's radical, 93 per cent-recyclable Sayl Chair was developed in partnership with Herman Miller as part of its ongoing quest for ever-more comfortable, sustainable and affordable seating. Béhar's designs use a minimum of materials to achieve high ergonomic performance; through the component design, the choice of materials and the manufacture, the chairs conform robustly to the cradle-to-cradle theory (see p152). The Sayl concept was inspired by the structural principles of suspension bridges – a notion that Béhar and the Herman Miller team developed into a tensioned backrest system with complex performance characteristics. The resulting Sayl project produced a work and a side chair, each using variations on Béhar's 3-D Intelligent™ backrest technology.

For the work chair, the backrest is comprised of a one-piece injection-moulded elastomeric matrix supported by a die-cast aluminium Y-strut. Five anchor points tension the frameless matrix. The firmest support is given where the tension is at its greatest – in the transition areas between the thoracic and lumbar zones. Above and below this area the backrest's resistance lessens to allow the sitter freer movement and adjustments to their position. A version of the work chair is available with an upholstered back but this accounts for nothing more than an aesthetic variation – underneath, the backrest technology remains the same.

The backrest of the side chair option is a variation on the work chair's elastomeric matrix but, instead of being tensioned between five anchor points, it is captured within a plastic injection-moulded frame around its entire perimeter. The form of the frame and the elastomeric web still gives 'dynamic' back support to the sitter, but the performance requirements of the side chair are less clear.

Above: **Over 1000 concept sketches were produced during the development of the Sayl Chair.**

Right: **The chair was inspired by suspension-bridge design.**

Opposite: **Five anchor points tension the frameless backrest matrix.**

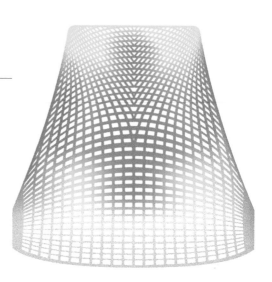

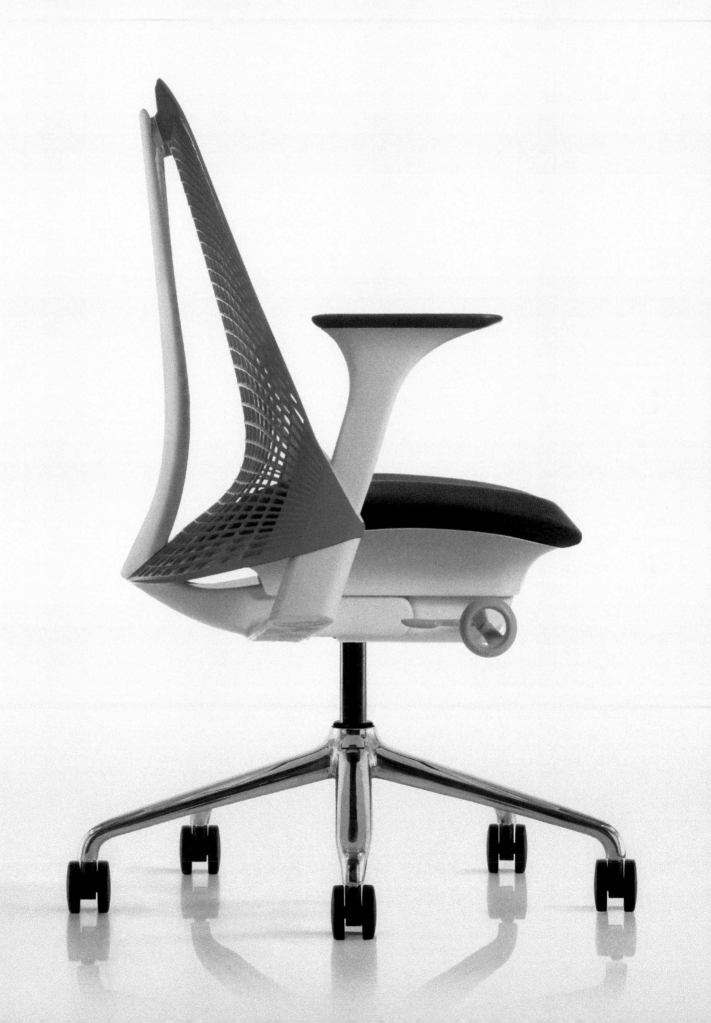

Hiroshima chairs

Naoto Fukasawa

H_684mm 26.9in	W_678mm 26.7in	D_640mm 25.2in
Beech and fabric/leather		
Manufactured by Maruni		

Since being founded in 1928, Japanese furniture manufacturer Maruni has commissioned designers to 'industrialize craftwork' by investing design for mass manufacture with craft sensibilities.

Naoto Fukasawa began collaborating with Maruni in 2008, with an ambitious aim of designing a 'decorative product standard, a chair that transcends the [Hans Wegner] Y Chair'. Using European beech wood, Fukasawa conceived the Hiroshima Armchair, which was created in empathy with the artistic, crafted element of Japanese wooden utility products. For Fukasawa, these uncoated objects made from Japanese cypress 'exalted a feeling of freshness, which seemed to disallow any kind of visual impurity'.

The Hiroshima series of tables and chairs evolved further with the introduction of the Hiroshima Dining Chair, which although very visually different from the armchair, has at its heart the same ethos. Both use the same potential of multi-axis CNC-routing technology for their manufacture. Due to the complex nature of the forms, it took Fukasawa and Maruni's technical team almost three months to programme the router's paths to develop the armchair design. Takeshi Yamanaka, of Maruni, maintains that the collaborative nature of such projects is vital and that, as with other designs they produce, 'it wasn't 100 per cent adherence to the desires of designers that made for truly good products, but the incorporation of knowledge and ideas based on the experiences of technical experts'.

The backrest is a sub-assembly: the lower part (referred to as the 'elbow') is CNC manufactured separately before its upper rim is dowelled and glued on to it. Then the whole assembly is unified with final CNC passes.

One challenge of creating such components as the backrest is that the wood must match in terms of colour and grain (end grain particularly) in the two or three connecting pieces. The wood for the whole chair frame, of course, needs to match while also providing the correct strength for its role in the structure. Therefore, the elbow is flat-sawn, the upper rim is quarter-sawn, and the seat frame and legs are all flat-sawn.

Below: **The Hiroshima Armchair and Table were developed after the introduction of the Hiroshima Dining Chair.**

Opposite: **The Hiroshima Dining Chair.**

Ovidio Table

Francisco Gomez Paz

H_720mm 28.3in   W_1600mm 63in   D_800mm 31.5in

Painted steel

Manufactured by Danese

Ovidio was the first of several folded-steel products designed by Argentine-born Francisco Gomez Paz for Italian design house Danese. The leg's tapering form and rear slots coupled with the seemingly ultra-thin top create a sophisticated visual language that elevates the table above the pedestrian essay in manufacturing that it could so easily have been.

Manufactured from 1.2mm-thick (0.05in) powder-coated mild steel, Ovidio is a testament to Gomez Paz's ability to refine a conceptual model into a table that is entirely resolved in terms of design for manufacture. The tabletop is a relatively simple structure and follows a straightforward rationale; but the leg and its seamless integration with the top is a highly complex piece of design that was determined through Gomez Paz's precise and iterative modelling, developed through a discourse with the manufacturer.

Keeping material to a minimum was an overarching concern, so, from the outset, Gomez Paz was keen to have the main expanse of the top unsupported from underneath. Consequently, throughout the design's early development there was a tension between the need for a thickness of steel sheet that had the structural integrity to span between the folded edges, while also being thin enough for it to be manipulated through the subsequent folding process to create the structural frame.

The nets (2-D flat patterns) for the top and leg components are laser cut before being CNC folded (press-braked) and welded into their structural forms. The tabletop includes additional welded, threaded nuts to receive the table leg bolts. The legs (made from 2mm / 0.08in thick steel) have extra welded fixing tabs through which to bolt them to the top.

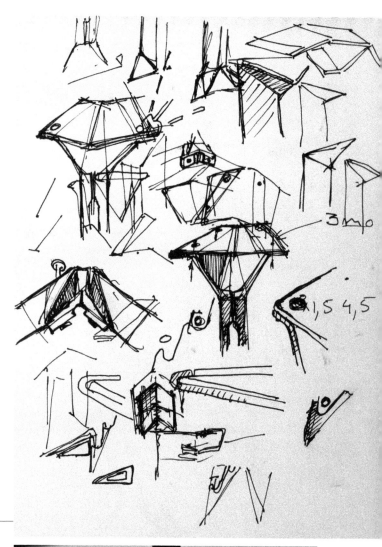

The design of the table leg and its sophisticated integration with the top required iterative development through accurate soft modelling.

Ovidio's complex geometry was developed through Gomez Paz's in-depth knowledge of the manufacturing process.

Nobody Chair

Komplot

H_780mm 30.7in	W_580mm 22.8in	D_580mm 22.8in
PET felt		
Manufactured by Hay		

The concept for the Nobody Chair was conceived in response to a brief from the Swedish prison administration requiring a chair that would be impossible to use in a fight, fashion into a weapon, hide anything in or be used to make loud noises. Komplot had already been experimenting with moulding and thermoforming PET felt while working on its second seating range for Danish company Gubi (see p138). It was an extrapolation of these ideas that led the design duo to experiment with a textile monobloc – no frame, no tubing, no assembly and no upholstery.

As the Nobody concept developed, so did its resonance with its designers. It began to evoke childhood memories of a summer cottage left for the winter, furniture covered with cloth for protection while the owners are away. Seen in this way, Komplot believes that: 'Nobody is...a representation of the object, not the object as such.'

The prison-chair brief lost its backing, but the challenge had so engaged Boris Berlin and Poul Christiansen that they pursued the idea independently, before Rolf Hay saw the concept while working with them on a different project. He fell in love with the singular nature of the chair and supported its final development into production. He even coined a slogan for its promotion: 'NOBODY is perfect'.

Hay has introduced a scaled-down version, Little Nobody, a chair for three to eight year olds, which Komplot describes as 'not just a light, friendly, noiseless children's chair, but a nice playmate as well'.

Nobody is manufactured using the thermo-pressing process, which transforms flat 'sheets' of semi-rigid felt into fused 3-D forms through the application of heat and pressure – no adhesives or fixings of any kind are involved. The felt is manufactured almost entirely from recycled drinks bottles and can in turn be recycled itself.

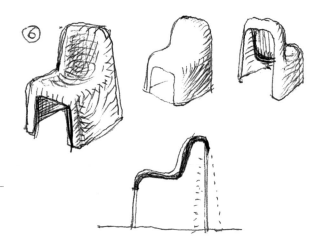

Sketches for the Nobody Chair.

Nobody is manufactured by thermo-pressing three sheets of PET felt matting between a two-part, aluminium tool.

Komplot explains: 'Nobody is not a chair as such; but a story about the missing chair.'

Myto Chair Part II (Part I, see pp115–17)

Konstantin Grcic

H_820mm 32.3in   W_550mm 21.7in   D_510mm 20.1in

Ultradur High Speed PBT
(Polybutylene terephthalate)

Manufactured by Plank and BASF

Myto was a collaboration between Italian furniture brand Plank, German plastics manufacturer BASF and Berlin-based designer Konstantin Grcic. Grcic understood that he had been offered the rare opportunity of working with highly specialized engineering plastics, affording the potential for structurally singular forms. In response, he began to reappraise the plastic monobloc, in particular, Verner Panton's cantilevered classic. It was a chance to create a true monobloc cantilever in a material that could be flexible and dynamic in ways that Panton's classic was never able to be.

BASF suggested using a plastic called Polybutylene terephthalate (PBT), otherwise known as Ultradur High Speed. PBT is very strong, flexible and has excellent flow characteristics when injection moulded, giving Grcic unparalleled freedom in the conception and development of this new chair. It enabled structural details that would not have been possible using polypropylene or ABS – not that this freedom would make the task easy or obvious.

Ultradur High Speed is innovative in several ways. Its performance at lower temperatures and its subsequent faster moulding process saves energy and makes it more sustainable. However, it was its strength and flowability that most appealed to Grcic. While the frame is immensely strong, it also flexes to a similar degree to tubular-steel cantilevered chairs and also actively responds to the weight and position of the sitter by the flexing of the seat pan and backrest, which are significantly thinner than the frame itself.

In spite of the inclusion of a reinforcing glass fibre (which counters a plastic's flowability), a secret ingredient – a nano-structured additive developed specifically for PBT – allows the plastic to achieve one of the best strength–flowability ratios of all thermoplastics.

Plastics manufacturer BASF proposed that its newly developed plastic – Ultradur High Speed – was used for the project.

Gubi Chair

Komplot

H_800mm 31.5in   W_540mm 21.3in   D_535mm 21.1in

3-D veneers, stainless steel

Manufactured by Gubi

The development of the 3-D veneer by German manufacturer Reholz enabled laminated plywood forms to be created without the 3-D limitations of traditional laminations. The Gubi Chair, designed by Danish partnership Komplot, was the first industrially produced product to use the material's capabilities, and represents a landmark in the structural and aesthetic development of laminated-wood furniture. The 3-D form of the shell creates a structural integrity that allows its 5mm (0.2in) thickness to be approximately half of, for example, an Arne Jacobsen Ant Chair. In turn, the thinner shell reduces the weight of the chair (it is only 1.88kg / 4.14lb). The need for fewer constructional veneers goes some way toward offsetting the high cost of the high-performance 3-D veneers, therefore enabling this radical chair to be more competitively priced.

As with all improvements, the thinner shell created its own challenges: the reduced thickness meant that there was too little material in which to fix a standard threaded insert (to which the leg frame is attached). Komplot, therefore, had to develop a unique fixing system that did not reveal any sort of sink marks on the top surface of the shell. The designers' solution was to create tooling for and mould a conical plywood component with threaded inserts (T-nuts) glued within it. These are glued into the milled 'nests' (recesses) on the bottom of the chair shell.

The Gubi Chair won a raft of design prizes on its launch in 2003 and, in 2004, won a Red Dot Award. The chair has since evolved into a large family that includes a range of similar and differently proportioned injection-moulded shells (manufactured from HiRek plastic – polypropylene with talc filler), either fully or face-only upholstered. The 3-D veneer has also been developed, most notably, with laminated ply legs. All are available with steel leg frames and swivel bases.

Opposite: **The form of the laminated chair shell created a structural integrity, allowing its thickness to be approximately half that of other contemporary ply chairs.**

Below: **A comparison between the 3-D veneer lamination on top and the one below, made using standard veneers.**

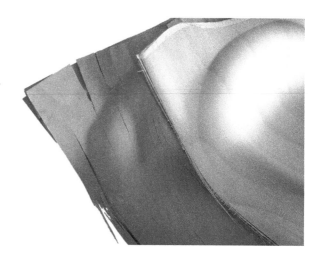

FiDU

Oskar Zieta

H_780mm 30.7in   W_400mm 15.7in   D_600mm 23.6in

Polished stainless steel, copper-plated steel

Manufactured by Oskar Zieta

Polish architect Oskar Zieta declares his FiDU (free internal pressure deformation technology) process to be a 'manifesto in technology'. His Plopp Stools and Chippensteel Chairs have been developed using this process and, although their manufacture uses laser-cutting and welding technologies, they are low-volume, batch-production items. Originally conceived as a low-cost hydroforming-style technology, FiDU uses low-pressure (up to 7 bar / 101.5psi) air from a standard compressor to inflate a welded assembly of two 0.8mm-thick (0.03in, approximately 22 gauge) laser-cut steel sheets into 3-D forms, which are then bent and welded.

In spite of its light weight (Plopp weighs 3.1kg / 6.8lb), Zieta's FiDU furniture is exceptionally strong. In the tradition of form following function, the features on FiDU furniture are there for a reason: the individual slats on Unterdruck, the studding on Chippensteel and the central hole in Plopp all control the expansion of the metal, its structure and form, and resolutely define the visual language of each piece.

Zieta's first prototypes were monobloc constructions that were bent into chair and stool forms, but the latest and final development of Chippensteel is a seamless welded assembly of inflated components that have allowed Zieta a greater freedom of form and facilitated a more streamlined manufacturing process. The Unterdruck Bench demonstrates FiDU's growing suitability for mass manufacturing through the 'component/assembly' approach. It also has a less overt visual language than its ancestors, potentially giving it a more mainstream appeal.

The FiDU collection is available in a variety of finishes, from lacquered mild steel and highly polished stainless steel to copper-plated steel and a range of powder-coated colour finishes.

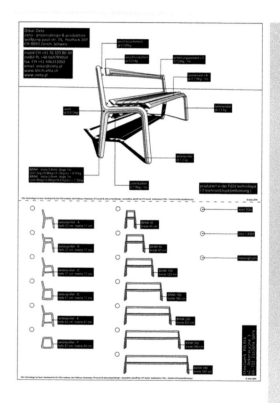

Above: **The Unterdruck Bench, launched in 2010, demonstrates FiDU's growing suitability for mass manufacturing through the use of self-assembly components.**

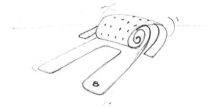

The Chippensteel Chair is part of
Oskar Zieta's development of FiDU
hydroforming-style technology.

Nomad Table

Jorre van Ast

H_750mm 28.5in	W_2400mm 94.5in	D_950mm 37.4in

Plywood, balsa wood, poplar, oak veneer, legs
solid ash

Manufactured by Arco

Lightweight honeycomb structures are nothing new,
but Jorre van Ast's Nomad Table for Dutch furniture
manufacturer Arco finesses the manufacture of the tabletop
assembly to such a degree that, in terms of cost, the
complexity of its component manufacture is balanced
out to produce a commercially viable product.

The seemingly thin tabletop tapers from 10 to 68mm
(0.4–2.7in) thick, and uses a vacuum-pressed 3-D veneer
(produced by Reholz) to sandwich a lightweight
substructure comprised of a cellulose-based honeycomb
matrix in conjunction with a balsa and poplar wood frame
and leg-locating blocks. This was the first time that 3-D
veneers had been used for such a large structural element
and a form such as this could not be achieved commercially
without them. The removable legs are solid ash, hexagonal
in section (partly to provide grip) and turned with a coarse
screw thread at one end.

In terms of its strength and structural integrity, the top could
probably be thinner and still able to support the weight of a
man. However, for the legs to have enough depth and
contact in their connection (so that the stress can be
distributed over enough of their length), the tabletop needs
to be at its current thickness. Also, the threads must have the
perfect tolerance – tight enough to distribute the load evenly,
but also loose enough to be easily assembled and to account
for expansion and contraction in the wood.

**A vacuum-pressed laminated
shell encapsulates a lightweight
cellulose-based honeycomb
substructure.**

Top right: **The solid wood legs are
removable for transportation.**

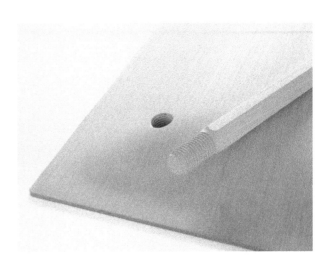

PS Ellan Chair

Chris Martin

H_810mm 31.9in   W_480mm 18.9in   D_660mm 26in

Wood plastic composite
(wood fibre and recycled PET/PVC)

Manufactured by IKEA

As a reliance on oil-based polymers becomes less tenable, designers and manufacturers are looking to increase the resource efficiency of their products by using recycled plastic and organic compounds for (particularly) injection moulding.

Stockholm-based British designer Chris Martin established a keen interest in materials and manufacturing when working with IKEA to develop the PS Ellan Rocker – a wood plastic composite (WPC) flat-pack rocking chair. WPCs are not in themselves radical, but at the time of this chair's development, they did not typically produce high-quality surface finishes.

A year-long collaboration with Swedish manufacturer Nolato Alpha led to the development of a suitably strong WPC using a combination of materials and moulding that had previously been used for road noise barriers. Manufactured by injection moulding the composite, the chair needed a lacquered final finish to raise the standard beyond the limits of the tooling. The WPC material is low cost compared to an equivalent 'virgin', and is lighter than pure plastic alternatives with the same structural properties.

Since 1961, IKEA had been selling a Thonet-style solid wood chair, but as a result of a push for more sustainable products and collaborations with Nolato Alpha, it is now manufactured from the same WPC material as the PS Ellan Chair.

The PS Ellan Chair is manufactured from a mixture of wood fibre (51 per cent) and recycled PET and PVC (49 per cent).

Opposite: One of Chris Martin's sketches for the PS Ellan Chair.

Woodware

Max Lamb

Various (chairs, tables and beds)

Various hardwood dowels, maple, walnut, ash, beech, cherry, tulip, oak, sapele and lime

Manufactured by Max Lamb

All items in British designer and artisan Max Lamb's Woodware series of dowel-jointed furniture conform to the same constructional rationale: drilled, perpendicular mortices of varying diameters that match other dowel diameters to create elemental furniture constructions. Although ostensibly a batch-production operation, sold through Gallery Fumi in London, Woodware's standardized manufacturing process lends itself to larger volumes, and Lamb has ambitions to expand output by involving other artisans in the project. This desire for Woodware to be 'affordable function' is reflected in other aspects of his work, which, he says, parallels potter Bernard Leach's commitment to utility and beauty and approach to craft production through the ideals of 'standard ware'.

The dimensional accuracy of the mortices are fundamentally important to the furniture's structural integrity, requiring that the dowels are manufactured to a high tolerance – within approximately 0.2mm (0.008in) relative to the Forstner drill bit used in manufacture. Such accuracies, however, demand that there is enough of a gap between the mortise wall and the tenon to allow the passage of the glue during assembly, while also allowing excess glue and trapped air to escape.

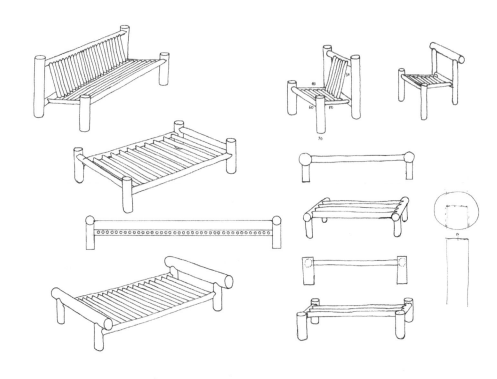

Right: **Woodware uses a range of dowel sizes, ranging from diameters of 16mm (0.6in) to 110mm (4.3in).**

Below: **The construction method requires great dimensional accuracy in the mortices and the components' alignment.**

3b: Ethics and sustainability

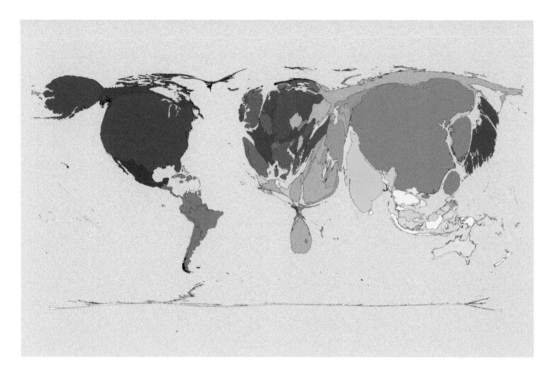

This cartogram illustrates the national per capita emissions of carbon dioxide as expressed through the countries' altered geographical proportions. It was created by Benjamin D. Hennig of the University of Sheffield, UK, in 2010 (www.viewsoftheworld.net).

Ideally, concerns about environmental sustainability should be central to all design practice, just as fair trade, ethical employment and sustainable manufacturing should be at the core of business. Global warming, resource depletion and environmental pollution are all fuelled by population growth and, importantly, by consumption, in which design plays a significant part. For designers, such far-reaching spheres of influence extend their impact on the world and create a professional responsibility beyond their individual selves – a role that may require commercial acumen and ethical cogency in equal measures. Although the terms 'ethics' and 'sustainability' are as overused as they are misappropriated, an understanding of their exact meaning is central to good design practice in both its philosophy and its methodology.

Whether based on conviction or obligation, the practice of ethical trade and employment, the use of renewable materials with low-embodied energy, the minimizing of components and designing for disassembly can all create a commercial advantage for businesses, as customers choose to 'buy into' more sustainable products to reduce their own carbon footprint or to promote fair trade. Within businesses that employ people and consume energy and goods, such strategic aims are becoming more common, although the commercial reality of global competition and increasingly tight margins mean that often businesses and designers focus more on profit than ethics and sustainability. This is not to say that products designed and sold by such businesses are unsustainable, but it is not unreasonable to assume that low-cost manufacture is more likely to involve either un-stewarded materials or carbon-heavy and convoluted global supply chains.

Sustainable design

There are several guiding principles that lead sustainable design methodologies and govern design practice. These include focusing on embodied energy, renewable resources, recyclability, design for disassembly, recycled materials, transportation reduction, weight reduction, longevity or durability, and the avoidance of hazardous and toxic substances.

The carbon footprint of a product, material or process is directly related to its embodied energy (although how that energy was produced has a bearing on it). So, the benefits of more energy-efficient manufacturing processes, whether of proprietary materials or finished products, is one of engineering's 'grand challenges'. For products that consume energy throughout their lifetime, the efficiency with which they do this, in relation to

their usefulness, has a greater impact and carbon footprint than products such as furniture, which are inert until they are reused, recycled or thrown away. For furniture design, the amount of invested energy in the materials used, and the embodied energy of final manufacturing are paramount.

Although renewable resources must ultimately replace the bulk of non-renewables, such as petroleum-based plastics, a balance is needed between the two supply streams so that the benefits of change are not undone by the impact of supplying renewables. For example, the production of carbon-neutral bio-diesel or significant forestation on a global scale would require a huge reduction in agricultural land available for food production, thus having the counterproductive effect of creating developed- and developing-world food shortages.

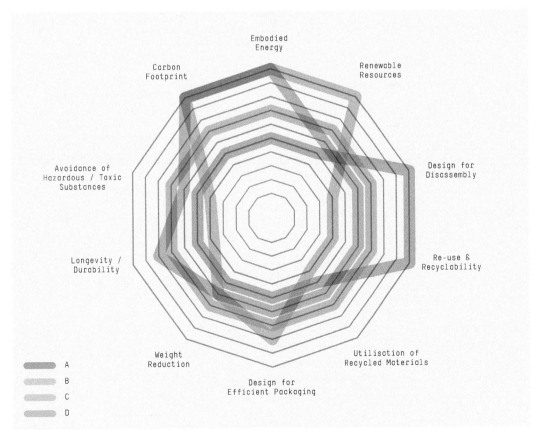

Emphases of sustainable furniture design. Although different design projects have a variety of emphases, adherence to as many of these principles as is relevant or possible is central to good design practice. Regardless of the difficulties of incorporating such principles into workplace hierarchies and established corporate cultures, many cost savings and commercial opportunities can result from their application.

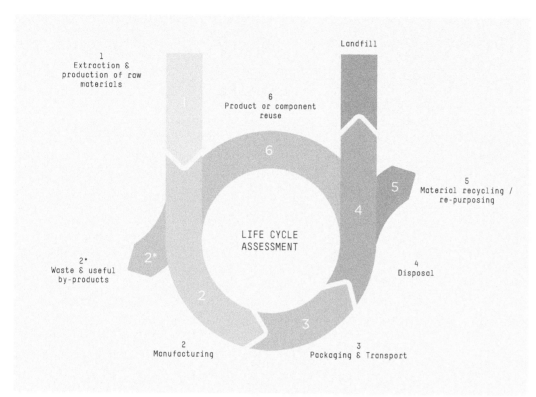

LIFE CYCLE
ASSESSMENT

Landfill

1
Extraction &
production of raw
materials

6
Product or component
reuse

5
Material recycling /
re-purposing

2*
Waste & useful
by-products

4
Disposal

2
Manufacturing

3
Packaging & Transport

A lifecycle assessment (LCA)
is a way of ascertaining the
environmental impact of proposed
or existing products. In more
detail, according to the
International Organisation for
Standardisation (ISO), an LCA is:
'A systematic set of procedures for
compiling and examining the
inputs and outputs of materials
and energy and the associated
environmental impacts directly
attributable to the functioning
of a product or service system
throughout its lifecycle.'

Below: **The ash-framed and
veneered Österlen Chair by Inga
Sempé for Gärsnäs.**

National and federal strategies for reducing external resource dependency and for countering future shortages are key to regional sustainability, but maintaining economic eminence requires guaranteed supplies that are difficult to ensure without resorting to the global market. A parallel driver for the nationalisation of material production is to reduce the carbon footprint of transportation. It is common practice to ship European and North American hardwoods to the Far East for manufacturing and then to transport the finished products back again for retail. Labour costs are the most important factor in this equation, but if a carbon tax were levied on the manufacturers and retailers of such products, then a very different material production and manufacturing economy could emerge and be supported in more regionally sustainable economic models. If, for example, the UK government encouraged the re-establishment of timber production capabilities by requiring that 50 per cent of all hardwoods used in the UK's furniture industry were grown within its borders, demand would very quickly outstrip supply. However, by the government taking legislative action and by pursuing long-term policy objectives that promoted and helped to optimize sustainable timber production, there could be engendered a more monetized tradition of

planting new trees. This more sustainable 'materials economy' could be further supported by the potential of wood-fired power stations and the carbon-capturing abilities of trees, which, added to a commercial and economic sum of parts, would mean that rationales for the augmented and widespread production and use of timber would increasingly make sense.

The use of recycled or organic materials does not always add up to a meaningful reduction in carbon dioxide emissions or less depleted natural resources. Mapping the invested energy and lifecycle of product concepts and sold products requires complex metrics for establishing the ultimate, measurable benefit of a product or system. It is, therefore, important that designers understand the true impacts of energy and material use early in the development phase so that their sincere endeavours are not undone by 'inconvenient truths'. The detail of material use and resource depletion within furniture production matters a great deal and can require

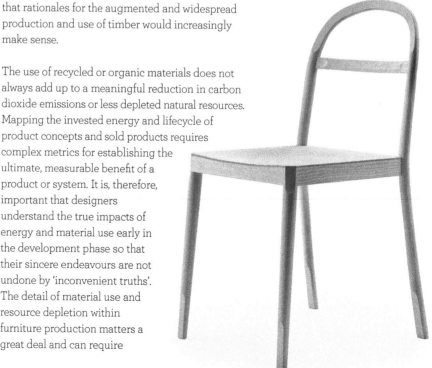

The responsible sourcing of timber
and man-made timber boards has
become easier through the activities
of organisations such as the Forest
Stewardship Council (FSC) and
Friends of the Earth (FoE).

Right: Bamboo is fast developing as
a furniture-making material and
although there are not yet any
low-cost laminated-board-based
solutions, manufacturing
technologies are improving.
The Hollow Dining Set by Brave
Space Design is made entirely
from bamboo.

in-depth interrogation via lifecycle assessment tools such as FIRA's Furniture Footprinter software. Advances such as the increasing use of renewable organic fibres combined with environmentally friendly resins or recycled and virgin plastics have some positive impacts on reducing resource depletion. Yet, unless the resulting products achieve the same material performance or longevity within broad, mass usage, a complete solution will not have been found, and their benefits will be much less profound than they might have appeared at first, particularly if the recycling chain is halted by unrecyclable composite materials.

Product and material recyclability is a significant area of manufacturing science that must run in parallel to all developments, although it is worth noting that problems of recycling are often caused as much by a lack of infrastructure as by a lack of suitable processing technologies. Ever since the dissemination of the cradle-to-cradle design and manufacturing strategy, many designers and businesses have embraced design for disassembly and the need for end-of-life products to be repaired, refurbished and recycled.

In the furniture industry, this was first essayed in 2003 by the launch of the easily disassembled Herman Miller Mirra Chair, made from 33 per cent recycled materials and 96 per cent recyclable overall. Its upholstery contains no PVC in its construction, and the foam is completely recyclable at the end of its life. In the ensuing years, such environmental credibility has, to varying degrees, become central to the business philosophies of prominent furniture suppliers, particularly the institutional or contract industry (most markedly in the US, where the top six control an estimated 83 per cent of the market).

Within broader markets, the use of recycled materials is largely driven by necessity and economics rather than ethics. The world's supply of raw materials cannot keep up with demand without plastics, metals, glass, wood and fabric entering the supply chain as secondary raw materials. However, the degree to which different materials can continue to be recycled without degrading varies.

Plastics are prone to UV degradation corruption in the re-melting process, so even the majority of the

Herman Miller's Mirra Chair by Studio 7.5 is made from 33 per cent recycled materials, is 96 per cent recyclable and disassembles easily. Its upholstery contains no PVC in its construction and the foam is completely recyclable at the end of its life. It adheres to McDonough Braungart Design Chemistry (MBDC) cradle-to-cradle design protocol.

1. PVC

2. PU, IPS, ABS, PC

3. FET

4. PE, PP

5. Biobased polymers

most reusable plastics (PETE, HDPE and PS) are down-cycled for use in lower-grade applications. Metals are the most recyclable materials, with approximately 40 per cent of 'new' steel and 32 per cent of aluminium being composed of recycled materials. Indeed, it is remarkable that in the region of '75 per cent of all aluminium ever produced since 1888 is still in productive use today', according to the International Aluminium Institute (IAI).

Secondary (recycled) raw materials also save a great deal of energy in their production. Recycled aluminium uses 95 per cent less energy and steel 25 to 40 per cent less compared to that mined and processed from virgin ore. Despite these impressive figures, according to a United Nations Environment Programme (UNEP) study published in 2011, less than one-third of some 60 metals had a recycling rate above 50 per cent, with 34 elements achieving below 1 per cent. A similar study of plastics recycling would reveal that, of total production, only approximately 5 per cent becomes secondary raw materials, in spite of the fact that the opportunities for energy saving through plastics recycling can achieve up to 40 per cent efficiency compared to virgin materials. However, the degree to which plastics are recycled locally within industry is unclear but, over the past decade, in response to increasing material costs and problems of supply, the plastics industry has increased its resource efficiency by minimizing its production waste and by recycling into its own production processes.

Craftspeople, engineers and designers have always focused on reducing materials and optimizing manufacturing processes, but the challenge today is for the same professionals to embrace more recycled and renewable materials while considering disassembly, invested energy and product longevity. In addition to consumers' personal responsibilities toward the environment and the global workforce, all companies that manufacture and sell products have an obligation to offset the impact of their

consumption by practising more sustainable and ethical business. However, because consumers of domestic and low-cost products are perhaps less able, obligated or willing to make ethical choices, carbon taxes and legislation that encourage better production and consumption behaviour are essential for the creation of significant change within parts of the industry that believe they cannot pass on the costs to their customers.

'The above is an attempt to rank the most common plastics in order of environmental and human health problems related to production, additives, product emissions and disposal and fires. The aim is to provide a basis for choosing and developing alternatives for PVC uses: the further you go down the pyramid, the less harmful the plastic is for the environment.'
www.greenpeace.org

Below: **The 20-06 Chair designed by Foster + Partners for Emeco uses 15 per cent less material than their Navy Chair, and is manufactured using 80 per cent recycled aluminium.**

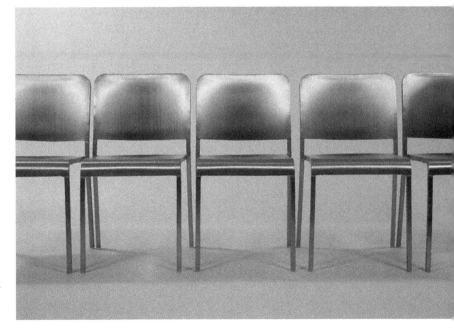

3c: Materials, manufacturing and assembly

Readers can simply browse the following sections, but by investigating specific structural, aesthetic, environmental or performance-related issues, it will be possible to work out the most appropriate materials and manufacturing process for a project, based on such criteria as:

———— Shape geometry
———— Manufacturing volume
———— Possible materials
———— Manufacturing tolerances (the possible accuracy of parts)
———— Achievable detail definition
———— Structural characteristics
———— Environmental performance
———— Aesthetic potential
———— Durability

Below: **Air Chair by Jasper Morrison for Magis. To achieve the necessary structural integrity and mouldability in such a structurally sparse and ambitious design, it was necessary to use gas-injection moulding combined with fibre-reinforced polypropylene.**

Below left: **The Trio Bench by Forms + Surfaces combines powder-coated cast-aluminium end frames with clear anodized aluminium slats.**

Opposite: **The Vitsoe + Zapf 606 Universal Shelving System by Dieter Rams uses anodized aluminium extrusions and stamped (blanked), press-braked and powder-coated steel.**

Metal

Metals

Metals are divided into two main categories: ferrous and non-ferrous (with/without a meaningful iron content). Within these groups there are very few pure metals that are useful on their own, but when alloyed together they achieve enhanced properties such as rigidity, ductility, malleability and corrosion resistance.

Although wrought iron is as close to a functioning pure metal as is possible, it is part of a family of iron-based metals that contain various amounts of carbon and other metals, which change their properties. These alloyed ferrous metals consist almost entirely of iron, which when mixed with varying percentages of carbon, become wrought iron (0.1–0.2 per cent carbon), cast iron (2–4 per cent carbon) and carbon steel (0.2–2 per cent carbon). Stainless steel includes up to 1 per cent carbon but is distinct by being alloyed with metals such as nickel, manganese and chromium to achieve high strength and corrosion resistance.

Many non-ferrous metals are used to alloy both ferrous and non-ferrous metals, but few are useful structural engineering metals, apart from aluminium alloys, brass alloys, titanium and zinc.

All metals can be cast or wrought. Cast metals are poured or injected into a mould and left to cool, whereas wrought (meaning 'worked') metals are either hot- or cold-worked. Wrought materials include sheet and other off-the-shelf commodity bars and rods, but they also describe secondary processing such as extruding, deep drawing, investment casting, roll forming, sand casting, spinning, swaging, stamping and superforming.

Aluminium alloys

Aluminium is produced from bauxite, one of the most abundant ores on the planet; it is lightweight, ductile and corrosion-resistant, although it is a great deal less rigid than steel. Because it is so soft in its natural state, aluminium is alloyed with materials such as manganese, copper, silicon and zinc to create performance characteristics for a range of applications and to make it more suitable for wrought production or casting. Once alloyed, the resulting materials exhibit greatly improved properties of strength and hardness, although to varying degrees all become slightly more prone to corrosion. There

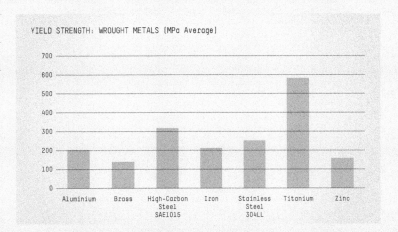

Yield strength is the point at which a material deforms permanently under a stress or load and is measured in megapascals (MPa).

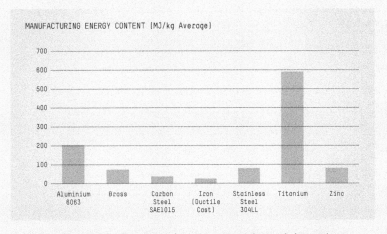

Manufacturing energy content measures the energy consumed or needed to produce a raw material, ready for use in manufacturing. It is measured in megajoules (MJ).

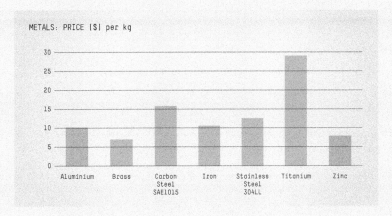

Average prices of metals in 2012.

are more than 300 aluminium alloys in production, but only 50 or so are commonly used. Of these, only eight alloys, see opposite, are normally used for the manufacture of furniture and furniture components.

Recycled aluminium accounts for a significant proportion of current production, in part because this has always been the case, but also because of the energy savings that its use creates. Recycled aluminium uses only 5 per cent of the production energy of aluminium smelted from ore. So manufacturers, who previously would have only used virgin materials, are now using alloys with more recycled content.

Applications: Aerospace, window manufacture, lighting, ladders, furniture components, domestic and office equipment.

Manufacturing: Aluminium can be wrought or cast. Because of its relative softness, aluminium is well suited to extrusion. It can be extruded, deep drawn, die cast, investment cast, laser cut, metal injection moulded, plasma cut, roll formed, sand cast, spun, stamped, superformed, water-jet cut or welded. All aluminium alloys can be welded and formed with ease or moderate difficulty.

The properties and performance of alloys can be altered by three processes of hardening and softening. However, only certain categories of alloy are appropriate for each process and the degree to which properties change has many variables. It is, therefore, essential to discuss the details of your requirements with a manufacturer.

Wrought alloys

The 3000 series alloys are hardened by cold working (rolling, bending, etc). The 6000 Series alloys react to heat treatment (annealing, etc) and age hardening (naturally hardening at room temperature).

Alloy 3003 is a soft, medium-strength material that is easily worked and welded and has very good corrosion resistance, particularly if polished. It is good for protective anodizing, but poor for aesthetic value.

Alloy 6060 is a medium-strength material and is the most widely used alloy, partly because of its potential

for high-quality surface finish. It is one of the most suitable alloys for anodizing and is used for window manufacture, lighting, ladders, furniture components, and domestic and office equipment.

Alloy 6061 is a medium- to high-strength material and resists corrosion well. Used in the aerospace industry, it is also popular for high-spec bicycle frames and components and relevant for high-performance furniture applications. Alloy 6061 welds easily and is good for protective anodizing, but poor for aesthetic value.

Alloy 6063 is a medium-strength material. Suitable for tubing or extrusions, it is particularly appropriate for furniture applications and all anodizing. Alloy 6063 also welds easily.

Cast alloys

Castings tend to be used as manufactured, without treatment to change their properties. However, in some instances heat treatment is appropriate to soften or harden alloy sand castings and gravity die castings, although pressure die castings can rarely be heat treated.

Alloy LM5 is a low- to medium-strength material appropriate for sand casting and gravity die casting. LM5 machines, polishes and anodizes very well. It is often used in marine applications because of its very good resistance to corrosion, and is also used for cooking equipment, architectural hardware and furniture.

Alloy LM6 is a medium-strength alloy appropriate for sand casting, pressure die casting and gravity die casting. It has good corrosion resistance, casts very well and is particularly suitable for large castings. Relative to other casting alloys, LM6 has a good degree of ductility and so small inaccuracies can be rectified easily. LM6 castings are particularly appropriate for welding. It is mainly used for marine applications, cooking equipment, domestic and office equipment, architectural components and furniture.

Alloy LM24 is a high-strength material appropriate for high-pressure die casting and, to a lesser extent, gravity die casting. LM24 is less resistant to corrosion than the above alloys, so needs painting or powder coating. It has very good castability and is mainly used for detailed, high-spec engineering applications.

Above: **The Aero Bench by SELLEX is assembled from two identical and one unique aluminium extrusion profiles.**

Right: **Chair_ONE by Konstantin Grcic is made from powder-coated die-cast aluminium.**

Far right: **Chiavari-style brass chairs are made up of brass-plated bars and tubes with sand-cast or die-cast backrest and legs.**

Although it outperforms LM6 mechanically, LM6 is generally preferred because of its superior corrosion resistance. LM24 is not suitable for welding.

Alloy LM25 is the most widely used high- to medium-strength material. It is appropriate for gravity die casting and investment casting. It has good corrosion resistance and has very good castability. Its excellent mechanical properties can be adjusted by heat treatment. LM25 is suitable for anodizing and welding.

Brass

Brass is an alloy of copper and zinc and is generally used because of its corrosion resistance, malleability, appearance and its low-friction coefficient (i.e., how easy it is to slide against itself or another material). It also has a low melting point and is non-magnetic. It is not commonly used for an entire item of furniture, but there is a long tradition of producing ornate, (partly) solid-brass chairs in the Italian town of Chiavari. More usually, however, (although rather out of fashion in recent years) brass plating is used on steel for structural furniture components such as occasional tables and bedsteads. Its low melting point makes it an excellent casting material and its relative softness translates to easy machining and forming.

Applications: Locks, furniture fittings, plumbing components, furniture, musical instruments.

Manufacturing: Brass can be wrought or cast. It can be extruded, deep drawn, die cast, investment cast,

laser cut, metal injection moulded, plasma cut, roll-formed, sand cast, spun, stamped, water-jet cut and brazed.

Iron

Iron is an almost pure metal and when mixed with various amounts of carbon its properties transform into cast iron (2–4 per cent carbon), ductile cast iron (3–3.4 per cent carbon), malleable cast iron (2.2–2.9 per cent carbon) and wrought iron (0.1–0.2 per cent carbon).

Cast iron is a rigid material, strong in compression and weak in tension. These characteristics produce a relatively brittle metal, but one that is ideal for some furniture applications such as garden furniture frames or as the heavy base of a pedestal table. Cast iron can be cast into complex shapes and can produce fine surface detail at least comparable to cast steel. It is also more corrosion resistant than steel. Cast iron cannot be welded easily, but machines well.

Ductile cast iron has properties more like steel than cast iron due to it being alloyed in its initial manufacture with materials such as nickel. It can be cast in very thick sections and is significantly more elastic and more impact resistant than cast iron. Malleable cast iron is an often-used alternative to ductile cast iron, but is less hard and elastic. In many ways malleable cast iron is comparable to low-carbon steel in its performance.

Although wrought iron formed the foundation of the Industrial Revolution, it has been almost entirely superseded by ductile and malleable cast iron and various steels.

Applications: Architectural components, furniture components, drain covers, cooking equipment.

Manufacturing: Iron can be wrought or cast. It can be plasma cut, sand cast, water-jet cut and welded.

WROUGHT AND CAST ALLOY TYPES SUITABLE FOR FURNITURE AND FITTINGS MANUFACTURE.

TYPE	YIELD STRENGTH (MPa) (average)	CORROSION RESISTANCE	US NAME
Wrought aluminium:			
Alloy 3003	36	Very high	Alloy 3003
Alloy 6060	90	High	Alloy 6060
Alloy 6061	112	High	Alloy 6061
Alloy 6063	213	High	Alloy 6063
Cast aluminium:			
Alloy LM5	99	Very high	514
Alloy LM6	142	High	A413
Alloy LM24	111	Moderate-high	380
Alloy LM25	91	High	A356

THE PROPERTIES OF BRASS ALLOYS

TYPE	YIELD STRENGTH (MPa) (average)	CORROSION RESISTANCE
Brass alloys		
Wrought (yellow)	122	High
Cast (sand)	98	High

THE PROPERTIES OF IRON

TYPE	YIELD STRENGTH (MPa) (average)	CORROSION RESISTANCE
Iron		
Cast iron	80	Poor
Ductile cast iron	400	Poor
Malleable cast iron	305	Poor

Carbon steels

Carbon steels are composed of iron and carbon. Mild steel accounts for the single greatest use of any steel sub-group, and carbon steels themselves – mild/low, medium, high and ultra-high – are the most widely used group. Mild or low-carbon steel is the lowest-cost and most malleable steel, but also has the lowest overall strength. Although not strong enough for high-stress machine parts, its properties mean that for the production of seam-welded steel tubing, for deep drawing and for welding, it performs very well. Mild or low-carbon steel is also used to make nails and, in the construction industry, for girders and reinforcing. Medium-carbon steel is a very good all-round engineering material. It is both tough and ductile. Although it can be hardened to a high degree through quenching in water, this process also makes it brittle. Medium-carbon steel is used to make screws and other fixings and fittings. High-carbon steel is unlikely to be used for furniture manufacturing, but instead is suitable for components that endure high and prolonged levels of stress, such as machine parts.

Applications: Carbon steels are used for a huge range of applications, ranging from concrete reinforcement to bicycle frames, and while not corrosion resistant, their low cost and tremendous range of mechanical properties makes these metals ubiquitous.

Manufacturing: Carbon steel can be wrought or cast. It can be extruded, deep drawn, investment cast, laser cut, metal injection moulded, plasma cut, roll formed, sand cast, spun, stamped, water-jet cut and welded. All carbon steels can be welded and formed with ease or moderate difficulty.

Wrought carbon steel: while it is important to know the carbon content of steel to predict its properties and suitability for different manufacturing processes, a more commonly discussed characteristic will be whether a steel has been hot rolled (HR) or cold rolled (CR). These two secondary processes create different properties of rigidity, ductility, etc, that are as significant as between different types of carbon steel. However, hot and cold rolling are just two of several secondary processes, such as normalizing and annealing, which complicate material selection (for non-engineers) even further. Therefore, the best approach to specifying carbon steel at the design

stage is to solicit advice of an experienced manufacturer as soon as the product's performance parameters are understood. Hot-rolled steel is softer and more ductile than cold-drawn or rolled, steel, which is more rigid.

Cast carbon steel, carbon alloys and stainless steels, can either be sand cast, investment cast or, on the periphery of furniture manufacturing, metal injection moulded (MIM). Cast steel is specified instead of cast iron because the latter is too brittle. However, the differences in performance between ductile cast iron and cast steel are smaller, so designers should make such a choice based on their project's particular requirements. If fine surface details and finishes, or high-strength products with complex geometries, are required (replacing the need for moulds with several parts), investment cast steel should be used.

Stainless steels

Stainless steels begin life as iron and carbon before being alloyed with metals such as nickel, manganese and chromium. The resulting material is corrosion resistant and more rigid and much harder than regular carbon steel. In spite of there being many different stainless-steel alloys, only a small number account for most usage. Some grades of stainless steel will rust (although not chronically) in the wrong environments, and so what is suitable for cookware or indoor furniture will not withstand a challenging maritime environment. Different grades also have varying degrees of strength and malleability. While it is important to understand the principle of these differences, it is vital to talk to an experienced manufacturer once your requirements are understood.

Although there are five types of stainless steel (ferritic, austenitic, martensitic, duplex and precipitation hardening), austenitic stainless steel accounts for most furniture manufacturing. The most widely used range is series 300 and the most commonly used within this is the 304 grade. Its popularity is based on the balance between its hardness and workability. It is also easy to weld. Although not suitable for marine environments, 304 can still cope well with temporary outdoor use. While 304 grade cannot be made more corrosion resistant (another grade should be chosen for this), there are

This late 19th-century table base is an assembly of three painted cast-iron components.

Xavier Pauchard's Tolix Chair 'A' is made from pressed/deep-drawn mild steel, which is resistance welded and galvanized.

PIPE was designed by Konstantin Grcic as part of a collaboration between Thonet and Muji. The desk and chair's frames are made from tubular, low-carbon steel.

The IKEA Lerberg Shelves are made from powder-coated steel. This lightweight (only 6.9kg / 15.3lb), low-cost shelving has only modest strength.

Ludwig Mies van de Rohe's Barcelona Chair has a welded and polished stainless-steel frame

useful variations in carbon content that affect its rigidity and yield strength; for example, 304 H grade (high carbon), 304 grade (medium carbon) and 304 L grade (low carbon). In theory, all grades of stainless steel should be available with three different carbon contents, but in reality this option is only applied to specific, widely used grades.

Applications: Kitchen equipment, outdoor furniture, cooking utensils.

Manufacturing: Stainless steel can be wrought or cast. Its relative hardness makes it difficult, or at least slow, to cut and machine. It can be extruded (with great difficulty), deep drawn, investment cast, laser cut, metal injection moulded, plasma cut, roll formed, sand cast, spun, stamped, water-jet cut and welded. All stainless steels can be welded easily and formed with varying degrees of difficulty.

Titanium

Titanium is an abundant raw material, but the high cost of its extraction and processing means that its alloys are approximately five times the price of aluminium alloys. However, its high strength and low weight make it ideal for high-performance aerospace applications and sports equipment, although it is less rigid than steel. Titanium has limited practical application in furniture design and manufacturing because its light weight and high cost would translate to an over-specification in most instances. Its use could, however, be perceived as appropriate for high-cost, high-status products but it would be difficult, ethically, to justify this.

Applications: Bike frames, spectacle frames, medical equipment.

Manufacturing: Titanium alloy can be wrought or cast (approximately 70 per cent is wrought and then machined or fabricated). Its hardness makes it difficult to cut and machine. It can be investment cast, laser cut, powder injection moulded, plasma cut and water-jet cut. Titanium alloys can be welded and formed with varying limitations and degrees of difficulty.

Zinc

The majority of zinc is used for galvanizing a process by which it is applied to carbon steel as a corrosion-resistant coating. However, when alloyed with metals such as aluminium, copper and magnesium, it is widely used in the production of furniture fittings, as a roofing material and, to a much lesser extent, as a surfacing material in the restaurant industry. Zinc alloys are ductile, have similar strengths to aluminium alloys and are approximately twice their weight. Zinc's low melting point makes it an ideal casting material, requiring cheap die-casting tooling and producing detailed components of moderate strength, suitable for cabinet hinges and handles.

A wide range of zinc alloys is available for wrought production and casting. These are generically known as Zamak™ alloys. Because of their low melting point and high strength, zinc alloys for casting can compete (in some applications) with plastics, not least because of their fast and, therefore, cheaper casting cycles (compared to other metals). These alloys are also able to achieve more complex geometries, thinner wall sections and higher quality surface finishes than aluminium alloys and brass.

Wrought sheets of zinc alloy are hot-rolled to produce a ductile, easily machinable material. Zinc alloys used for worktops are much purer than cast alloys (at c. 95 per cent zinc, rather than c. 70 per cent for casting).

Applications: Furniture fittings, roofing, worktops, galvanizing steel.

Manufacturing: Zinc can be wrought or cast. It can be investment cast, die cast, sand cast, extruded, roll formed, stamped, laser cut, plasma cut and water-jet cut. Zinc can be soldered, interference welded and specialist gas welded.

THE PROPERTIES OF STEEL

TYPE	YIELD STRENGTH (MPa) (average)	CORROSION RESISTANCE
Wrought steel:		
Low carbon SAE1015	315	Low
Medium carbon SAE1030	350	Low
Stainless 304L (low carbon)	255	High
Stainless 316L (low carbon)	250	High

THE PROPERTIES OF TITANIUM ALLOYS

TYPE	YIELD STRENGTH (MPA) (AVERAGE)	CORROSION RESISTANCE
Titanium alloys:		
Wrought	580	High
Cast	830	High

THE PROPERTIES OF ZINC ALLOYS

TYPE	YIELD STRENGTH (MPA) (AVERAGE)	CORROSION RESISTANCE
Zinc alloys		
Wrought	145	High
Cast	150	High

Metal finishes

Anodizing

Aluminium, titanium and magnesium can have their natural corrosion-resistant qualities enhanced through the process of anodisation. Aluminium forms a protective layer of surface oxidisation, which is extremely thin. Through the application of an electrical current to a piece that is submerged in a vat of sulphuric acid, the naturally occurring aluminium-oxide layer is thickened considerably to form a significantly more protective layer. This anodized layer is hard, reasonably abrasion resistant, can be clear or coloured and has a metallic sheen. It also allows for the improved adhesion of paint.

Electroplating*

This is a process whereby metal components are coated with a very thin layer of protective or decorative metal that forms a metallurgical bond, which can only be worn away and cannot be scratched off. Zinc or chrome plating is a very good way of protecting carbon steels, whereas chrome, nickel, rhodium and precious-metal plating are good for more decorative items such as door and cabinet furniture. These are usually plated on to wrought or cast base metals such as brass, which is cheap. Although some metals do not achieve a sufficient metallurgical bond to plate successfully, the addition of intermediate layers of copper or nickel enable this to happen.

*For electro-chemical galvanisation, see 'Galvanizing'

Enamelling (Vitreous)

Enamelling is an ancient surface-coating process that, although not often used for furniture, has potential because of its colourfastness and range, scratch resistance and its singular visual quality. Enamel coatings are essentially the same as ceramic glazes, but are applied to most metals. Powdered glass and colours are administered wet in a water suspension before being dried and then fired at very high temperatures. Surface finishes range from gloss to matt and are thicker than powder-coated or painted finishes. In comparison to these competing processes,

enamelling is more expensive in material and invested-energy costs, but its durability is unparallelled.

Sharp workpiece edges will be covered with the least amount of surface finish and so it is advantageous to reduce the sharpness of such areas prior to application.

Galvanizing

Galvanizing describes a small group of dipping and plating processes by which zinc is applied to the surface of carbon steels, cast irons and, to a lesser extent, aluminium. For furniture design and manufacture, hot-dip galvanisation and electroplating are the most commonly used; although they essentially do the same thing – protect ferrous metals from rusting – the two processes have different applications and visual characteristics.

Galvanized metals can be welded, but as this process damages the protective zinc layer, it is necessary to galvanize the joined components again, or simply to galvanize a bare-metal assembly or sub-assembly from scratch. Although the effect is not significant, it is worth noting that the brightness of new galvanized coatings dulls over time. Painted metals for exterior use are often galvanized first to add further protection against rust.

Hot-dip galvanisation can produce attractive crystal formations. The process involves dipping a workpiece into a molten vat of zinc, producing a protective layer.

Zinc electroplating (electro-galvanisation) produces a much smaller crystalline structure in a much thinner layer than hot dipping. This thinness has the advantage of allowing plated components such as nuts and bolts to still fit together, although only above certain thread or detail sizes.

Sharp workpiece edges will be covered with the least amount of surface finish and so it is advantageous to reduce the sharpness of such areas prior to application.

Painting

In industry, almost all metal paint is applied by spraying, because of its superior surface finish and its efficient use of materials. Quick-drying finishes are advantageous because they speed up output and reduce the risk of dust and particles settling on a still-drying surface.

However, there exists a great tension between the high performance of solvent-based paints and their damaging impact on the environment and human health. This downside is due to the evaporation of solvents containing volatile organic compounds (VOCs), which are gradually being phased out, although the difficulties in doing this are more pronounced in the manufacturing than in the building industry. Water-based paints contain no evaporating solvents but still include some VOCs.

When specifying paint finishes, performance and aesthetics will define the finishing products used. Ultimately, it is the ethical choice of the client as to whether a lessened performance is acceptable, but a designer may still exercise some influence by using their knowledge and the advice of expert manufacturing partners.

In the past, solvent-based paints were the most colourfast and produced the best surface qualities. However, the performance of water-based paints is now often comparable, although drying times are not as short. If water-based paints are used, carbon steels and cast irons usually need a solvent-based primer to prevent any oxidisation.

Sharp workpiece edges will be covered with the least amount of surface finish and so it is advantageous to reduce the sharpness of such areas prior to application.

Polishing

There are three metal polishing processes: mechanical polishing, chemical polishing and electropolishing. All three reduce surface roughness by abrading or dissolving its protrusions, although in so doing they also, to varying degrees, reduce detail definition. Mechanical polishing is both a mechanized

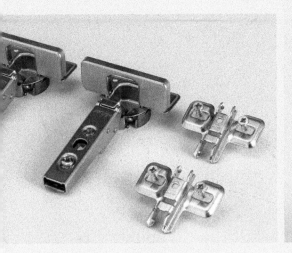

and manual process, requiring a great deal of time, skill and effort, making it the most refined and expensive of the three processes. While a workpiece's geometry determines how easy it is to polish, its original condition also defines its cost. As an example, a rough sand-cast aluminium component will require significant labour to polish it to a mirror finish and, in the process, will have a great deal of material removed. Unless the original shape is very easy to maintain, its detailed form will be lost and sometimes significant inconsistencies will exist between supposedly identical components.

The same concerns about loss of detail can apply to the much cheaper processes of chemical polishing and electropolishing, which are less accurate than mechanical polishing. However, because these two processes are automated, the results can be more consistent than mechanical polishing or that which employs low-skilled labour. Chemical polishing uses combinations of acids and heat to dissolve protruding parts and, of the three processes, produces the third-best surface refinement (a dull mirror finish). Electropolishing uses a combination of chemicals and electrical current to even out the surface in the same way as chemical polishing. Although slower, electropolishing produces a mirror finish, second only to mechanical polishing.

Powder coating

Powder coating is almost entirely used as a surface finish for metals and works as a result of the metal's conductivity. Rather than a liquid-sprayed paint that sticks directly to the surface of a workpiece, powder coating sprays an electrically (negatively) charged pigment and resin powder toward a positively charged or grounded workpiece. A uniform thickness of powder builds up through 'static electricity' on the workpiece, which is then transferred to an oven so that the powder melts and fuses with the metal surface. Powder-coating finishes can be applied as ultra-thin coatings or up to 1mm (0.4in) thick in one process. In spite of the energy used in baking the powdered workpieces, the process is low-cost compared to some painting or enamelling.

Close-facing surfaces can be problematic when powder-coating, as can sharp workpiece edges, which will be covered with the least amount of surface finish and so it is advantageous to reduce the sharpness of such areas prior to application.

Surface textures

Surface textures (patterns) can either be created by in-mould detailing or by secondary processing. The welding of materials with surface textures can be problematic if the weld visibly obscures the texture, or if the texture is removed when a weld is ground back. This is not such a problem for a brushed finish since the assembly can be reworked to either blend in the brushed weld or to brush the whole assembly from scratch. For non-linear, geometric textures, such reworking is not possible. Sheet materials may only be available with directional texturing lengthways or widthways, so when designing components using such materials, these factors need to be understood from the outset.

There are six main surface-texturing processes. Brushing uses rotary-applied abrasives to create circular or linear patterns with controllable grain coarseness. Acid etching employs a protective coating to resist the erosion of acid, which results in a recessed, coarse surface in exposed areas. Laser etching can produce textures of infinite complexity and cost if applied directly to a sheet material; it is more commonly used to etch a roller or die with which to texture metals. Electro-discharge machining (EDM) can either smooth or add texture (commonly known as a 'spark-eroded finish') to sheet or 3-D components. Rolling uses a hardened, textured roller to apply a repeat texture to the surface of sheet materials. Shot or bead blasting sprays a range of abrasive materials on to a workpiece to create a surface finish of determinable coarseness. These processes can be used in conjunction with masking to form patterns, but are more generally employed to remove old surface finishes or corrosion oxides and to prepare metals for painting, powder coating or enamelling.

Left to right:
Cabinet hinges are usually made from zinc- (electro-) plated steel.

Jasper Morrison's ATM system for Vitra combines powder-coated steel shelves with a composite aluminium and wood veneer structure.

Metal manufacturing processes

CASTING

There are three main metal casting processes in furniture manufacturing: die casting, investment casting and sand casting. Each one has specific and shared characteristics related to their outputs' size, complexity, detail, thickness and production volume that determine their use. There is also metal injection moulding, a powder-moulding technology that produces compacted powder forms, which are heated to fuse together (sinter) their composing particles. However, powder-moulding technologies are typically only used for small, high-specification engineering parts, so are not discussed in detail within this chapter.

Nearly all castings require some kind of machining to achieve a high enough tolerance to connect with other components accurately and without stressing the casting. For die castings or investment castings, machining is sometimes necessary, and the removal of material should equate to fractions of a millimetre, whereas for sand castings there could be inaccuracies of 1mm+ (0.04in) to remove.

It is also important to note that all cast parts shrink when cooling, and so patterns and CAD data supplied to manufacturers need to take this into account. The degree of shrinkage varies depending on the metal being cast, but an average of 1 per cent shrinkage from a nominal centre is a good rule of thumb. Ideally, discussions about shrinkage should take place with a manufacturer as soon as dimensions are known in order to reduce the need for redesign at later stages. For many parts, however, such small shrinkage rates can be accommodated within an assembly.

Die casting

Die casting is the equivalent of plastic injection moulding for metals. Used for casting small- to medium-sized detailed parts there are two processes: high-pressure die casting and gravity die casting.

SHAPES
Solid or thin-walled

METALS
Aluminium, zinc, magnesium

MANUFACTURING TOLERANCE
0.15–0.5mm (0.005–0.02in)

WALL THICKNESS (MIN–MAX)
1–8mm (0.04–0.3in)

MINIMUM DRAFT ANGLE
2–3°

MANUFACTURING VOLUME
5000–100,000+

Design guidance: Suitable for solid thin to medium wall thicknesses, die casting cannot produce hollow parts (unless a sand core is used in gravity die casting), but can create components that can be assembled into hollow forms. Of the two processes, high-pressure die casting is capable of achieving complex geometries, and the highest-quality detail, surface finish and dimensional accuracy, but it is also the most expensive process because of its high tooling costs. Gravity die casting is able to achieve a high-quality finish and surface detailing but is much less able to fill moulds with extended complex geometries.

Manufacture: High-pressure die casting is similar to plastic injection moulding in that molten metal is injected at very high pressure into a metal mould. Because of the pressures involved and the cost of tooling, high-pressure die casting is appropriate for high-volume manufacture only. Such castings tend to be small- to medium-sized, but the process is still used for larger complex and extended castings that require a high-quality surface finish.

Gravity die casting is capable of larger-scale castings than high-pressure die casting, but their geometry must be simple and limited enough for the metal to flow into. Tooling for gravity die casting is cheaper, but for the molten metal to achieve an appropriate flowability, it requires heating to a higher temperature and so uses more energy. Gravity die casting is, however, a cheaper overall process.

Investment casting

Investment casting is little changed from the process practised by ancient Mediterranean civilisations. Although an expensive production method, complex (solid or hollow) parts featuring undercuts and without draft angles can be made as one piece.

Left to right:

Chair_ONE by Konstantin Grcic is made from die-cast aluminium.

Tom Dixon's Lean Table Light is a powder-coated, one-piece iron casting.

The Trio Bench by Forms + Surfaces is made of clear anodized aluminium (extruded slats and cast frame).

Extruded aluminium profiles.

Naoto Fukasawa's all-aluminium Déjà-vu Stool for Magis combines extruded legs with a spun seat and a die-cast footrest.

SHAPES
Any shape (hollow or solid)

METALS
Aluminium, steel, titanium, zinc, brass and precious metals

MANUFACTURING TOLERANCE
Sectional: 0.1–0.4mm (0.004–0.02in)

WALL THICKNESS (MIN–MAX)
1–30mm (0.04–1.2in)

MINIMUM DRAFT ANGLE
None

MANUFACTURING VOLUME
1–1000+

Design guidance: Not often used for volume-production furniture components, investment casting (also known as 'lost wax casting'), nevertheless, is capable of producing complex solid and open hollow components that would not be possible to make to such a high quality using any other process (for a parallel process, see 'Sand casting' [full-mould casting], opposite). Part costs are still high, however, so the method is only suitable for high-cost product lines. High-quality surface finishes and fine surface details can be achieved easily with investment casting, although a fine-tooled finish will still require polishing.

Manufacture: Investment casting is able to produce very complex shapes in one process because each

part is cast within its own sacrificial ceramic mould. Each investment casting begins life as an injection-moulded wax pattern that is either attached to a wax 'tree' as a single casting, or one of several. These are repeatedly dipped into a ceramic slip to build up a thick shell before being left to dry. The air-dried shells are then heated to remove the wax and fired to harden the ceramic. Molten metal is poured into the voids left by the wax and allowed to cool. Finally, the shells are smashed from the casting before the parts are cut from the tree for finishing.

Sand casting

Sand casting encompasses two main manufacturing processes. Sand casting is the most widely employed to produce a broad range of complex solid and open hollow parts using two-part moulds. The second, full-mould (evaporative pattern) casting, is similar to investment casting and produces complex solid and open hollow parts using a sacrificial pattern. Both processes are labour intensive but with low tooling costs.

SHAPES
Hollow or solid

METALS
Aluminium, iron, magnesium, steel, zinc

MANUFACTURING TOLERANCE
1–3mm (0.04–0.1in)

WALL THICKNESS (MIN–MAX)
5–100mm (0.2–3.9in)

MINIMUM DRAFT ANGLE
2–3°

MANUFACTURING VOLUME
1–10,000+

Design guidance: Sand casting is suitable for the production of simple and complex parts that can incorporate varying thicknesses. Surface finishes are poor and castings often have significant flashing to be removed. Therefore, most parts require finishing and abrasive blasting before use.

The use of cores to create voids or undercuts adds to the set-up time and labour costs of sand casting and so these should be avoided if possible.

Because full-mould (evaporative pattern) casting uses

a sacrificial pattern, many of the usual part detailing rules do not apply because the pattern does not need to be withdrawn from the sand. Castings produced in this way do not need to include draft angles, can incorporate undercuts and have no split lines. Often this casting process is a more straightforward proposition than multi-cored sand casting, which can be very difficult to prepare.

Manufacture: Sand casting has the most ancient lineage of all casting processes and is based on the simplest of principles: creating a void within the compressed sand of two opposing moulds using a wood or metal pattern, and then filling this void with molten metal. This produces either solid castings by completely filling the void, or hollow castings by adding solid cores that are supported within or intersect the void. The metal flows between the wall of the void and around the core(s) to produce a hollow section or sections. Full-mould (evaporative pattern) casting uses a CNC-milled polystyrene pattern that is encapsulated by compacted sand. The poured molten metal vaporizes the polystyrene and fills the void.

EXTRUSION

Extrusions can be formed in a range of metals, of which aluminium alloys account for a large proportion. Extrusion enables the production of complex hollow and solid profiles. While a reasonable number of profiles are available off the shelf, by specifying their own, a designer can exploit the procedure's great potential to produce large and small components for innovative furniture.

Carbon and stainless-steel extrusions require very tough and expensive dies, so, while they are relevant to furniture manufacturing, the majority of their uses rely on fabrication using a range of standard extrusions. Aluminium, magnesium and zinc alloys are more likely to be used for visible furniture components, because it is easier and cheaper to achieve complex profiles with these alloys. Therefore, in the following section aluminium extrusion is described in detail. Most of the governing principles apply to all metal extrusion, but steel has more limited detail capabilities.

SHAPES
Hollow, solid and prismatic profiles

METALS
Aluminium (predominantly), steel, zinc

MANUFACTURING TOLERANCE
Sectional: 0.1–0.3mm (0.004–0.01in);
Longitudinal: 0.3mm (0.01in)

WALL THICKNESS (MIN–MAX)
0.4–3mm (0.02–0.1in)

MINIMUM DRAFT ANGLE
n/a

MANUFACTURING VOLUME
100–1000m+

Design guidance: A great many aluminium alloys with a wide range of properties are available, but for most furniture manufacturing, a small number of alloys are used (see pp157–59, 'Aluminium alloys').

Tooling costs for non-ferrous extrusions are comparatively low. However, minimum production runs are usually in the hundreds of metres and, where very accurate tolerances are required, more than one version of the die will typically need to be produced to make fine adjustments. Dies also suffer from wear and so have a finite life, the length of which depends on their shape, the type of alloy used and the desired surface quality of the product. In order to achieve a cost-efficient, optimized profile, a design needs to be as manufacturing-friendly as possible.

When designing an extrusion, it is important to keep within as small a circumscribing circle as possible, since this dimension is the characteristic most clearly related to the cost of the tool (i.e., the greater the dimension, the more expensive the tool becomes). Circumscribing circle diameters range between 3 to 400mm (0.1–15.7in). Solid profiles are normally cheaper to produce than hollow profiles (although cost savings should be discussed with a manufacturer since the more raw material used, the greater the cost per metre). Therefore, it is always better to design out cavities where possible, either by losing them altogether or by using solid profiles to create them.

A uniform wall thickness is desirable, but exceptions are not unusual. Depending on the design and the alloy used, minimum wall thicknesses vary. The speed with which the aluminium is extruded also affects possible wall thicknesses, as does the final

dimensional accuracy of the profile and its surface finish. Deep, narrow channels are very difficult to extrude if they are more than 1:3 in proportion, and so workarounds must be found if such features are essential. A solution might be two extruded sections joined together to produce the channel, or a one-piece 'open' extrusion that is then formed or rolled into the channel profile.

Radiused corners along all edges (internal and external) are a necessity to ensure a consistent level of detail. A minimum radius of between 0.5–1mm (0.02–0.04in) is sufficient.

Extrusions can be polished, brushed, anodized or painted (see p162 for finishing details), and can be joined in a variety of ways, including using screw ports, adhesives, threaded inserts, rivets and by welding. They can also be designed as male and female parts that telescope.

Produced by the die or tool, longitudinal ribbing can hide unavoidable imperfections such as heat zones and can protect the extrusion in application. Ribbing is also very useful in items such as shelving in which it resists objects sliding forward while also easing movement laterally.

CUTTING AND FORMING METAL

Lathe, milling, laser, plasma and water-jet cutting

For information about CAD software and file formats, see p108.

SHAPES
Metal lathe: hollow or solid, axisymmetric
Milling: hollow or solid
Water-jet, laser or plasma cutting: (primarily) flat, hollow or solid

MANUFACTURING TOLERANCE
Metal lathe: 0.05–0.5mm (0.002–0.02in)
Milling: 0.05–0.5mm (0.002–0.02in)
Water-jet cutting: 0.1–0.5mm (0.004–0.02in)
Laser cutting: 0.025–0.5mm (0.001–0.02in)
Plasma cutting: 0.1–0.5mm (0.004–0.02in)

MANUFACTURING VOLUME
1–10,000m+

MANUFACTURING SPEED
Slow to moderate (overall – see descriptions below)

UNIT COST
Moderate to high

TOOLING COST
None

SIMILAR PROCESSES
As above

All of the processes outlined below are available as 3-axis and 5-axis CNC technologies.

Overall, lathe machining, milling (CNC or manual) and cutting are slow processes. They have set manufacturing costs no matter what the volume and so their outputs do not become any cheaper. However, because they do not need the upfront tooling investment, CNC milling and cutting technologies are more accessible manufacturing processes.

CNC or manual lathe machining is used for short production runs and is ideal for components with re-entrant axisymmetric features and stepped axisymmetric profiles.

The CNC or manual milling of sheet metals should be avoided in favour of laser, plasma or water-jet cutting whereas, for the 3-D machining of plate or block metals, milling or possibly electrical discharge machining (EDM) are the best options.

CNC milling is used for producing relatively low volumes of parts and for machining moulding tools. The more material that needs to be removed via milling, the longer and more expensive the process, so designers should consider whether a fabricated part would be quicker and cheaper to manufacture. Cutting-tool length restrictions on milling depths can also affect the viability of a project. As a rule of thumb, a cutter's maximum milling depth is 8 to 12 times its diameter, while the minimum milling depth is 3mm (0.1in) in diameter, although smaller-diameter holes are possible using drill bits that are also part of a machine's interchangeable tool carousel set-up. However, when milling any sort of internal angle, the minimum radius possible with a cutter is equivalent to the cutter's own radius. Manual and CNC-milling technologies are used for fettling castings.

Laser cutting is the ideal process for cutting most thin sheet metals and creates the smoothest edge to the tightest tolerance. Laser widths can vary between 0.1 and 1mm (0.004–0.04in) diameters and can cut through carbon steels up to about 45mm (1.8in) thick, although at such extremes the cutting speed is low. Unless the laser's edge-finishing or detail-cutting qualities are essential, plasma cutting or water-jet cutting should be considered, particularly for materials over 12mm (0.5in) thick, on the grounds of cost and speed.

Plasma cutting does not result in the same high-quality edge finish as a laser, but for steel above 12mm (0.5in) thick, plasma cutting becomes increasingly economical (slower cuts produce a better edge finish). For unseen parts or for prototyping, plasma is ideal. However, as with all technologies, the plasma-cutting process is always improving and the latest developments produce moderately high-quality cuts that are beginning to compete with laser technologies.

Water-jet cutting is typically used for cutting thicker

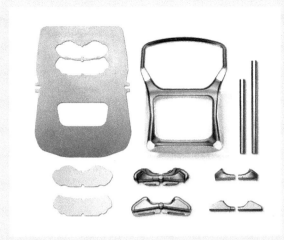

metals (steel up to 250mm / 9.8in) and can deliver a reasonably good-quality cut edge. An average jet diameter is 0.5mm (0.02in) and even though it gradually widens (1° maximum spread), the difference is negligible for thin sheet, although inaccuracies do increase with sheet thickness. It is advisable to consult with a manufacturer about this detail, since different cutting speeds, machinery and sheet thicknesses give different results.

Press forming

Press forming encompasses several sheet-working processes that are used to form or cut (or both) cold metals. These include stamping and deep drawing.

SHAPES
Shallow or deep, hollow, thin-walled

METALS
Steel and aluminium

MANUFACTURING TOLERANCE
0.2–0.5mm (0.008–0.02in)

MAXIMUM MATERIAL THICKNESS
5mm (0.2in)

MINIMUM DRAFT ANGLE
1–3°

MANUFACTURING VOLUME
100–1000+

Stamping

Design guidance: Stamping creates products and parts that either receive their entire form during the stamping process (such as a tray) or undergo stamping and a secondary forming and bending process. For designers, understanding the order of works in the stamping processes is less important than simply specifying achievable details and forms that can be removed from tools.

Manufacture: During stamping, sheet-metal blanks are pressed under great pressure between a male and female punch and a die. Simple, shallow forms can be shaped in one action, but parts with more complex geometries need to be formed in stages, potentially with further sections being punched out at a later time. Edge-forming

details such as hemming and swaging can also be carried out as one of the final processes.

Deep drawing

Design guidance: Deep drawing uses a different action to stamping, creating much deeper forms. Parts can be categorized as deep drawn when their depth dimension is more than half their diameter or widest dimension. Drawn products include laundry bins and stainless-steel sinks, and can have round profiles or radiused corners and straight or curved sides. Minimal draft angles are possible with this process. Limitations on the depth of draw depend on the part's width and depth or diameter and the thickness of the blank metal.

Manufacture: Different metals have different limits, but, as an example, a near parallel-sided steel cylinder can be drawn to a maximum depth equal to approximately five times its diameter. The deeper the draw, the more force is needed. A steel sink typically needs 200 tonnes of pressure whereas a deep laundry bin could require up to 500 tonnes. Even by applying such huge forces, deep-drawn parts are formed in several stages since even the most ductile of metals cannot be transformed to such degrees in one draw.

Punching and blanking

Punching and blanking describe one process, but with different outputs: punching creates holes and blanking produces cut-out shapes.

SHAPES
Flat, shallow

METALS
Steel and aluminium

MANUFACTURING TOLERANCE
0.2–0.5mm (0.01–0.02in)

MAXIMUM MATERIAL THICKNESS
5mm (0.2in)

MINIMUM DRAFT ANGLE
1–3°

MANUFACTURING VOLUME
100–1000+

Design guidance: There are few restrictions on punching or blanking details when creating a shape with a single tool, but when nibbling is used, clearance around the cut is needed so that material removal is possible. Also, as a general rule, channel or hole details have a minimum width of 1.5 times the material thickness.

Manufacture: Small punched and blanked shapes can be cut using a tool with that specific profile; however, the larger the shape, the more likely it is that the waste material will be removed by a process of nibbling using a smaller cutting tool. Although punching is a fast process, the increasing speed of laser-cutting machinery means that components punched from flat sheets are becoming less common, particularly when the pronounced burr edge of a punched part is undesirable. The mechanical punching of holes into 3-D forms as a secondary process (such as after deep drawing) is still much more common than laser cutting such objects. Blanked parts can be produced quickly and in high volumes. However, because they are invariably cut from a flat sheet, blanking is experiencing strong competition from laser cutting.

ROLL FORMING AND PRESS BRAKING

Roll forming and press braking are parallel processes that, in different ways, convert flat sheet into linear profiles and folded-sheet forms.

SHAPES
Thin-walled, hollow or open prismatic profiles

METALS
Steel and aluminium

MANUFACTURING TOLERANCE
0.2-0.5mm (0.01-0.02in)

MAXIMUM MATERIAL THICKNESS
5mm (0.2in)

MINIMUM DRAFT ANGLE
0°

MANUFACTURING VOLUME
100-10,000m+

Roll forming

Design guidance: Roll forming produces linear profiles with consistent wall thickness. Profiles range from seam-welded tubing to corrugated roofing sheets – all of which are typically manufactured in large volumes, because despite there often being limited tooling costs, the cost of setting up a production line is still significant. Therefore, while roll forming is not cheap, for many applications it is more commercially viable than extrusion (particularly of steel).

Manufacture: Specifying simple or commonly rolled profiles such as box-section tubing or lipping will probably not require new tooling. But, items that involve greater manipulation to achieve enclosed profiles or channel sections will need an extended and complex linear process that will entail high costs to develop and tool.

Press braking

Design guidance: Press braking is an important sheet-metal bending process (that results in folds rather than rolled bends), which is used for low- to medium-volume production. Its output would usually be welded or riveted together to create larger forms

and enclosures, which will always have been pre-dimensioned and detailed. As with other complex manufacturing processes, designers are not expected to understand the intricacies of press braking, but knowledge of its governing design principles will reduce the need for re-design. It is possible to form channels using press braking but their depth will be restricted by the reach of the tool and the surrounding geometry. The minimum internal radii of bends can vary between 0.5 to 1 times the material thickness (plus the material thickness for external radii). depending on the ductility of the metal used.

Manufacture: The length of a press-braked profile, plus the material type and its thickness, all impact on the machine strength needed. Some sequences of folds may not be possible using one part, and so it is often necessary to increase the number of components in order for them to be welded or riveted at a later stage. There are often no tooling costs for press braking because of the versatility in creating different profiles using a basic V die and limited range of punches.

SPINNING AND SWAGING

Spinning produces axisymmetric, open hollow forms by compressing and stretching a spinning flat metal disc on to a spinning mandrel. Swaging is a process by which the ends of metal tubing are either expanded or reduced in diameter. This diameter is either constant or in transition as a taper.

SHAPES
Shallow or deep, thin-walled, hollow or open axisymmetric profiles

METALS
Steel, aluminium

MANUFACTURING TOLERANCE
0.25-1mm (0.01-0.04in)

MAXIMUM MATERIAL THICKNESS
0.5-1.5mm (0.02-0.06in)

MINIMUM DRAFT ANGLE
0°

MANUFACTURING VOLUME
100-10,000+

Left to right:

The stainless-steel backrest of the Balance Bench by Forms + Surfaces is perforated using a stamping process as a flat sheet and then roll formed into the seat and back profile.

Roll forming a tube profile.

The Ball Joint Lamp and Indoor/ Outdoor Table by James Michael Shaw are made from spun and painted aluminium.

Spinning

Design guidance: Although spinning can be fully automated to increase its efficiency, it remains a slow process that is most suited to low- to medium-volume production. The minimum achievable spun radius is usually 3 times the thickness of the material, but it is possible to reduce this through secondary processing. The surface finish of spun components depends on the metal used, its thickness and, importantly, the speed at which it was formed.

Manufacture: Spun products with diameters ranging from approximately 50 to 1800mm (2–70.9in) are routinely manufactured, although larger diameters are possible. Mandrels can be either male or female depending on the desired geometry, and should feature a minimum draft angle of 1°. The use of male mandrels is most common, but female mandrels are used if a peripheral flange is required. Collapsible mandrels are sometimes employed to spin forms that capture the mandrel within a decreasing diameter, but these are costly and time consuming to operate. In order to speed up the process or to add features that are not possible with spinning, pre-formed components are used.

Rotary swaging

Design guidance: Tube swaging is most commonly used to create connecting male and female parts that usually locate and hold together with an interference fit. Swaging also produces long or short tapers for the likes of chair legs. By reducing the diameter of a tube, its wall thickness is increased, rigidifying and strengthening it.

Manufacture: Long, shallow swaged tapers that can be post-formed to become curved are time consuming and costly to produce. Yet these tapers are not achievable by any other method apart from casting, which for chair legs would be far too heavy. Swaging also creates solid, rounded ends on tapered tubing.

SUPERFORMING

Superforming describes a group of aluminium, magnesium and titanium vacuum thermoforming processes that produce open, thin-walled hollow forms.

SHAPES
Shallow or deep, thin-walled, hollow or open

METALS
Aluminium, magnesium, titanium

MANUFACTURING TOLERANCE
0.5–1.0mm (0.02–0.04in)

MAXIMUM MATERIAL THICKNESS
12mm (0.5in)

MINIMUM DRAFT ANGLE
2–3°

MANUFACTURING VOLUME
1–100m+

Design guidance: Tooling costs for superforming are moderate, but the slowness of the process results in high unit costs. However, the time or weight saved in manufacturing compared to fabrication can make the process viable, particularly in the automotive and aerospace industries. For furniture, superforming has been used only for the batch production of expensive seating (for the reasons outlined above), but there exists, nevertheless, great creative potential for this.

Manufacture: There are five different superforming sub-processes – back pressure, bubble, cavity, diaphragm and vacuum furnace – each with shared and specific characteristics suitable for different applications. For furniture manufacturing, bubble and cavity superforming are most relevant (Ron Arad's Tom Vac Chair shell is bubble formed). Superforming begins by heating aluminium, magnesium or titanium sheets, which are then forced down on to a male tool or up into a female tool using air pressure. Sheets of aluminium can be superformed up to 12mm (0.5in) thick.

TUBE, EXTRUSION AND SOLID-SECTION BENDING

Rotary draw bending and ring rolling form tubing, extrusions, wire and solid-section rods into tight radii and shallow bends. These bends can be anything from 1° to 180°, and are either a component with one bend or part of a sequence of bends. Technically speaking, every bend angle up to 179° is an elbow bend, and those of 180° are U-bends (although, at the upper end, U-bend is used as a general term).

Single bends can either be 2-D, with their ends on the same plane, or 3-D, with their ends on different planes. Wire forming can create complex 2-D and 3-D wire pieces with small radii bends with wire diameters typically up to 9mm (0.4in). Within this section, 'wire' is used to describe solid, circular-section metal up to 9mm (0.4in) in diameter; and 'rod' refers to solid-section steel of any profile, with a diameter of 3mm (0.1in) or above.

SHAPES
Hollow or solid, prismatic or axisymmetric

METALS
Steel and aluminium

MANUFACTURING TOLERANCE
0.5–1mm (0.02–0.04in)

MAXIMUM MATERIAL THICKNESS
Rod (typically) 12mm (0.5in); tube 32mm+ (1.3in+)

MANUFACTURING VOLUME
20–500m+

Design guidance: For the rotary draw bending of a sequence of 2-D and 3-D bends, it is important to know the minimum achievable distance between bends. This varies depending on the process and machinery used, and so it is essential to establish such parameters at the beginning of the design process. A simple, although potentially costly, solution to bends that are too close is for each bend to be achieved separately or in shorter sequences and then welded together, probably using a spigot (a solid or tubular male insert that slides into both tube ends) and either a weld or a grub screw.

The majority of rotary-draw-bending companies are only able to handle tube up to 32mm (1.3in) in diameter, with some having 75mm (3in) capabilities (only at certain wall thicknesses) and rod or wire up to 20mm (0.8in) in diameter. For most furniture applications, a rod diameter of 12mm (0.5in) is the thickest needed.

Rotary draw bending has two limitations: it can only bend tubes and rods with small diameters; and because it bends angles rather than curves, it requires dies of specific radii and tube diameters.

Ring rolling has the advantage of bending 2-D and 3-D shallow curves and sharp elbow bends without needing dies with specific radii. However, the process still needs rollers that feature the tube, rod or extrusion's profile. Ring rolling also bends and forms curves with very large diameters.

Manufacture: Rotary draw bending is the most commonly used method to curve hollow and solid profiles around a rotating die into tight and shallow 2-D bends. The ductility of metal, its sectional dimension and its wall thickness all influence the ease with which it can be bent. The rotary draw bending of hollow profiles uses an inserted mandrel to support the tube and to stop it from collapsing while being bent.

The same machinery used for tube bending, minus the mandrel, can be used for bending solid rod. The term 'mandrel bending', a form of rotary draw bending, is often wrongly used to describe the rotary draw bending of wire or solid rod (which cannot use a mandrel).

Wire-forming machines achieve 2-D and 3-D shapes by a very different process. Wire is propelled through a tight aperture and then directed in various ways by pins that are rotated on a CNC-controlled turret. For 3-D forms, the wire is also rotated in stages while being propelled.

Left to right:
George Nelson's Swag Leg Chair has tapering legs that are swaged from constant section tubing and then bent into the final leg form.

The original Tom Vac Chair's shell was manufactured from superformed aluminium.

The Tio series of tables and chairs by Chris Martin uses two thicknesses of carbon-steel rod that are welded together before powder coating.

Joining metal

WELDING AND BRAZING

Welding is the basis for most metal fabrication and is used to produce components, sub-assemblies or complete items. The suitability of each welding process to a particular job can be gauged by considering the intended materials, their thickness, the joint's geometry and the ease of access to the joining line. Also, the volume of production, the complexity of any holding jigs and the job's set-up time all have a bearing on the final choice of process, as does the amount of time the welding apparatus can be constantly used without overheating.

For many applications and businesses, welded fabrication represents the most cost-effective, efficient route for production, particularly for low-volume runs, because welding has limited, if any, upfront tooling costs. This is true in spite of the need for components to be additively or subtractively manufactured and being post-processed prior to being joined.

Components for welding are generally cheaper and easier to source as standard, off-the-shelf profiles and sections rather than special orders.

There are five types of welded joint – butt, corner, edge, lap and T-joint – each with variations that will be decided by a manufacturer depending on the directional stress that will be applied to the welded assembly.

There are five main categories of welding processes, some with several important sub-processes.

Arc welding

This category encompasses all processes that use an electric arc to provide heat.

As its name suggests, manual welding (MMA) is applied by hand. Only short, constant welds are possible without the operator pausing because of the length of the welding rods. The workpiece cools if the operator pauses, rendering the join weaker than if produced by automated, continuous methods. However, providing that it is skilfully applied to one-off and small-scale production MMA is appropriate for aspects of furniture manufacturing.

Instead of the limiting short welding rods of MMA, Metal inert gas welding (MIG) uses an automatically fed spool of welding rod that enables much faster, longer, stronger and more consistent welds than MMA or TIG.

Tungsten inert gas welding (TIG) is a more exact process than MIG and is suitable for thinner and more refined materials. It uses a non-sacrificial electrode (instead of a welding rod), which precisely melts the workpiece. Different gases and 'filler' materials (a separate welding rod) can be used to increase the size of the weld bead or the speed of the process.

WELDING PROCESSES AND BRAZING CHARACTERISTICS

WELDING PROCESS	PROCESS TYPE	SPEED	SET-UP TIME	WELDABLE METALS	MATERIAL THICKNESS
MMA	Manual	Moderate	Moderate	Steels, iron, nickel alloys, copper alloys	1.5-300mm / 0.06-11.8in
MIG	Manual/ automated	High	Moderate-high	Steels, aluminium, magnesium	1-12mm / 0.04-0.5in
TIG	Manual/ automated	Low	Low	Carbon steel, stainless steel, aluminium	0.1-6mm / 0.004-0.2in
PAW	Automated	Moderate	Low-moderate	Steels, copper, aluminium, magnesium, titanium, tungsten	0.1-6mm / 0.004-0.2in
LBW	Automated	High	High	Steels, copper, aluminium, magnesium, titanium	0.25-20mm / 0.01-0.8in
Friction	Automated	Low	High	All common metals	0.1-6mm / 0.004-0.2in
Resistance	Manual/ automated	Low	Moderate	All common metals	0.1-10mm / 0.004-0.4in
Oxy-acetylene	Manual	Moderate	Moderate	Steels, iron, nickel alloys, copper alloys	1.5-300mm / 0.06-11.8in
Brazing	Manual	Moderate	Low	All common metals with melting point above 650°C (1200°F)	1-100mm / 0.04-3.9in

Plasma welding (PAW) produces a more focused and precise weld than TIG, at varying powers. Depending on the strength of current used, a great range of material thicknesses can be joined – from very thin mesh to 6mm-thick (0.2in) steel plate.

Laser-beam welding (LBW)

LBW is a precise, powerful and fast way of joining metals up to approximately 20mm (0.8in) thick, and is usually applied to high-volume production. The laser is centred on a small area of 0.1 to 1mm (0.004–0.04in) in diameter, resulting in limited heating and distortion of the surrounding material in comparison to arc welding. However, such focused heat also requires that the mating components have precise joint gaps, and so LBW is only suitable for joining components capable of being manufactured to a high tolerance.

Friction welding

Normally associated with automotive manufacturing, friction welding has some potential for furniture-component assembly, not least because it is possible to weld differently derived or entirely different metals. There are two main friction-welding processes: rotary and linear.

In rotary friction welding (RFW), one or both components must be symmetrical in the plane in which it/they are rotated. The symmetrical part is rotated at high speed and then forced, in two stages, against the second component. The resulting friction and axial force heats and plasticizes both elements, producing a rim (flash) of molten metal on each. This weld flash can be ground off as a secondary process. RFW is particularly suitable for joining linear components, such as leg sections.

In the linear friction welding (LFW) process, one component is stationary, while the other is oscillated against it to plasticize and unify the metals. LFW is used for components that have an unsuitable geometry for rotary welding.

Resistance welding

This category includes spot welding, projection welding and seam welding, all of which pass a high-voltage current through two components to melt and join them together. The spot-welding and projection-welding processes are mainly used for thin sheet-metal fabrication, but have the potential to fuse components totalling up to 10mm (0.4in) in thickness and can be used to join different metals.

Spot welding is suitable for prototyping low-volume or mass production, although the process has speed limitations because only one weld point can be made at one time. However, because it is so well suited to welding objects with complex geometries and because little post-finishing is required to clean up the weld, it is still an efficient process.

Projection welding is very similar in principle to spot welding, but has the advantage of being able to produce several weld points at once by the use of an embossed form or additional metal insert on one of the components. Both of these features produce a route through which the electrical discharge can pass and so by using much larger electrodes, small clusters or shaped weld points can be welded.

Seam welding uses rotating electrodes that work in parallel to each other to continuously weld straight, mating surfaces, such as around radiators or fusing edges in the manufacture of steel tubing.

Left to right:

MIG and TIG welding can be both manual and automated processes.

Jean-Marie Massaud's resistance-welded Heaven collection for Emu.

An ultra-lightweight aluminium café chair. There are many variations on this design, all of which essay minimal material use and weigh between 1.6 and 2.5kg (3.53–5.51lb). The pressed seat and backrest slats are riveted to the extruded, bolted frame.

Oxy-acetylene welding

Not often used as a mass-manufacturing process due to its manual application, oxy-acetylene welding is nevertheless highly relevant for the fabrication of test rigs, prototypes, low-volume production and more craft-based furniture. The process mixes oxygen and acetylene to produce a flame of approximately 6300°F (3482.22°C), which is able cut through or weld a broad range of metals. The process is also able to join different metals. Generally, a welding rod is used to create the weld, although in skilled hands it is possible to join components by melting and fusing their surfaces.

Brazing

The brazing process produces medium-strength joints using filler materials (typically brass) with low melting points. The joint is formed within thin gaps between workpieces, which draw in the filler material once they have been heated to melting point. The process lends itself to joint geometries that have proportionally large mating surfaces and large joint tolerances, or for connecting thin materials. Also, importantly, the low melting temperature of filler materials means that the fabrication's components undergo little if any deformation changes when heated and cooled.

Welding and brazing applications: Tube, spigot or socket connections; low-volume or prototype components with mating surfaces rather than mating edges.

ADHESIVES

Metal adhesive technologies have improved enough for their use to become widespread in the automotive and aerospace industries. For furniture assembly, bonds between metals and other materials are likely to be more useful than metal on metal. Adhesives can be used if there are other materials to protect, or if there is limited access. Industrially, thermoset and thermoplastic adhesives are both used, but in most applications thermosets will give a superior bond and durability. There are many brand types, but only three chemically different types: acrylics, epoxies and urethanes.

METAL FIXINGS & FASTENERS

Riveting

Riveting mechanically compresses and permanently fastens materials together. It is typically used to fabricate thin sheet metal but blind rivets can also be used to fasten plastic and wood.

Applications: While there are several types of rivet and riveting processes, the majority are used in heavy engineering, infrastructure projects or the aerospace industry. For furniture manufacturing, the most broadly used processes are blind riveting and drive riveting, with some use of flush riveting for aesthetic reasons only. Materials between 2 and 25mm (0.08–1in) thick can be blind or drive riveted.

Blind rivets are inserted into pre-drilled holes and through the withdrawal of an integral mandrel the 'blind' end of the rivet expands, which in turn compresses the back of the workpieces and fastens them together. The mandrel snaps off in the process of withdrawal, leaving the open bore of the rivet visible externally. Visible blind rivet heads all look very similar at first glance, but they are available with a dome head, a wide flange head or a countersunk head. There are also several variations of body types for different fixing tasks, which enhance the rivets' performance for joining wood to metal or for joining brittle materials. All should, therefore, be investigated in detail.

Drive rivets consist of an expandable split collar and a pin. These connected components are inserted into pre-drilled holes, with the pin proud of the collar. The domed pinhead is then struck with a pneumatic hammer or hammer and punch to force the pin through the collar, expanding its split shaft and compressing the back of the workpiece.

Threaded fasteners

Sometimes, threaded fasteners are simply the best way to assemble metal furniture components and sub-assemblies, particularly when a product has been designed for disassembly. Their tendency to become loose can be countered by the use of locking nuts and thread-locking adhesives, although the latter will interfere with disassembly.

Hexagonal bolts feature an hexagonal head for use with spanners and socket wrenches. They are designed to be connected into a nut or a threaded hole.

Machine screws are, technically speaking, a threaded bolt with any kind of head and a total length of less than 19mm (0.7in). However, in common usage, machine screws tend to be fine-threaded bolts in a full range of lengths with a slot or socket head (either domed, pan or countersunk). They are designed to be connected with a nut or a threaded hole.

Grub (set) screws are headless screws designed to connect components such as a tube and a spigot by screwing through a threaded outer part and into either the threaded or un-tapped hole of the inner component. The head either has a hex-socket or a slot and sits flush with the outer surface.

Self-tapping screws are used with low-carbon steels and soft alloys such as aluminium and require a drilled hole rather than a tapped (threaded) hole.

Plastics

Plastics (polymers)

In terms of material performance, plastics have two categories: structural and elastomeric. Both types are made up of thermoplastics and thermoset plastics – distinctions that relate primarily to their manufacturing characteristics. There are further differentiations that relate to their use, namely engineering or commodity plastics.

Engineering plastics exhibit superior mechanical performance and function well in a range of temperatures. They are used in more specialized and demanding applications than commodity plastics, which are more likely to be used in lower-performance applications such as furniture and packaging. Nevertheless, for the purpose of this book and to simplify the material selection process for readers, the following section focuses only on plastics with a furniture pedigree or potential. Each plastic's performance can be altered when alloyed with other polymers. Such alloys are not discussed in detail and further research and discussion with manufacturers may be necessary to create a final specification for manufacture. The section entitled 'Biopolymers and bio-composites' (p183) encompasses both structural and elastomeric plastics, but because this group represents a particularly current and important realm, it has been given special prominence.

Structural and elastomeric plastics

It should be obvious to a designer whether they require a structural or elastomeric plastic. Structural plastics are mostly hard, rigid (although capable of flexing) and durable. Elastomeric plastics are, to varying degrees, stretchy, soft and able to be deformed and then returned back to their original shape.

In order to choose a plastic with the best range of performance characteristics for a specific application, it is always worth researching existing products with similar or parallel functions, rather than starting from scratch using only a chapter such as this for reference.

Opposite: **The Parapu children's chair (see p184).**

Thermoplastics and thermosets

Understanding the difference between thermoplastics and thermoset plastics is fundamental to design specification for manufacture.

Thermoplastics become soft when heated, either to a viscous state in which they can be moulded or extruded, or, at slightly lower temperatures, where they can be thermoformed. They are distinct from thermosets in their ability to be returned to their original raw material state when heated, enabling most to be recycled.

Thermoset plastics are resins that are cured either by heat or through a chemical reaction. In contrast to thermoplastics, thermosets cannot be returned to their original state through subsequent heating and so cannot be recycled. Thermosets cannot be post-processed by techniques such as thermoforming. Instead they are suitable for injection moulding, rotational moulding, resin-transfer moulding, pultrusion, compression moulding and casting.

UV resistance

Plastics are affected by ultraviolet light (UV) in different ways and to different degrees – the opacity of the material, its thickness and the addition or not of UV stabilizers all have a bearing on the level of degradation caused by exposure to daylight. Therefore, when specifying a plastic for prolonged or partial external use, it is important to obtain a material performance guarantee from the manufacturer. Readers should use the UV impact ratings in each section as a starting point for specification; only once a component's opacity and thickness have been established, combined with the benefits of an inhibitor, can a final performance be calculated.

Flame retardants

The flammability of plastics can be reduced by the addition of flame-retardant additives, which act in different ways, such as preventing a material catching fire, slowing or extinguishing burning, or protecting materials from heat.

Colour

Most plastics can take on a wide range of colours at the manufacturing stage. But, it is also possible to batch-dye components in such materials as polycarbonate to achieve a subtle range of colours at a much reduced cost compared to specifying the available colour range or special-order colours.

Fillers and foaming

As well as UV-inhibiting and flame-retardant fillers or additives, reinforcing plastics using particulate fillers or synthetic or organic fibres is common practice. Fillers do not give a high-quality surface finish and so in gas-assisted injection moulding (and some rotational moulding), it is normal to first create a skin using unfilled plastic before adding a thicker structural layer. Fibres increase the rigidity and tensile strength of plastics such as PP and polyamides, making the lean structures of products such as the Air Chair (p154) possible. The alignment of fibres does mean, however, that shrinkage rates are much greater perpendicular to the fibres than lengthways, although particulate fillers engender more even shrinkage rates in cooling.

Prior to moulding, most thermoplastics can be foamed using inert gas to reduce the amount of material used and the weight of the component, and to enable thicker sections to cool quickly (avoiding distortion and down time in the tool). Although the resulting mouldings have a lessened overall strength, this method is appropriate for many applications. The surfaces of foamed components are usually distinguishable from solid mouldings.

Structural plastics

Acrylonitrile butadiene styrene (ABS)

TYPE
Thermoplastic

CHARACTERISTICS
Easily moulded, durable, tough, recyclable

PRICE ($/KG)
Low

UV RESISTANCE
Low

ABS has a high-impact strength and moderately high tensile strength. Modifications to the material and its manufacture can improve these and other properties. For example, the inclusion of polyester fibres enhances its mechanical strength and being moulded at higher temperatures increases the quality of its surface finish. Its low resistance to ultraviolet light, however, means that it is not well suited to long-term external applications.

Applications: Chairs, chair shells, Lego, hard hats, casings for electrical appliances, storage trays, bowls and beakers.

Manufacture: ABS can be thermoformed, injection moulded (most commonly), rotational moulded, blow moulded, extruded, heat bent, sawn, machined, drilled, laser cut and water-jet cut. It can also be ultrasonically welded, thermo-welded and bonded with adhesive.

Acrylic or polymethyl methacrylate (PMMA)

TYPE
Thermoplastic

CHARACTERISTICS
Optically clear, UV resistant, recyclable

PRICE ($/KG)
Low

UV RESISTANCE
High

PMMA has light-transmission properties similar to polycarbonate, but has the advantage of being fairly scratch resistant, and is cheaper than polycarbonate (PC). It has low shock resistance and is consequently rather brittle; therefore, for monocoque chair designs PMMA would not be suitable (PC would be the best material). However, for storage components or as a replacement for glass, PMMA should be the first choice for designers.

Sheet rod or tube PMMA is either cast or extruded. Cast PMMA is stronger and has better optical qualities than extruded PMMA but is also more expensive.

Applications: Chairs, chair shells, aircraft windows, safety glasses, display cabinets, storage trays.

Left to right:
Verner Panton's second version of his Panton Chair was the first thermoplastic monobloc of its kind. Vitra's version uses polypropylene, but copies also use ABS.

The acrylic (PMMA) Magino Coffee Table by Karim Rashid.

PLASTIC TYPES

	THERMOPLASTICS	THERMOSETTING PLASTICS
Structural	ABS, acrylic solid surfacing, PMMA, polyamides, PC, HDPE, LDPE, HIPS, EPS, PS, EPP, PET/PETE, PP, tpUPVC	Polymer composites, PUR
Elastomeric	EVA, elPVC, TPU	tsPVC, butyl (synthetic) rubbers, natural rubber

The categorisation of plastic types featured within this section.

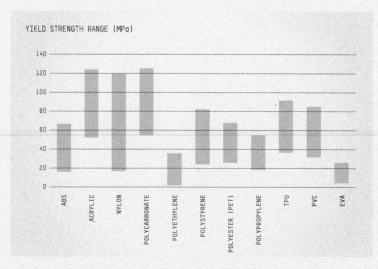

YIELD STRENGTH RANGE (MPa)

(Bar chart showing yield strength ranges in MPa, y-axis from 0 to 140 in increments of 20. Categories along x-axis: ABS, ACRYLIC, NYLON, POLYCARBONATE, POLYETHYLENE, POLYSTYRENE, POLYESTER (PET), POLYPROPYLENE, TPU, PVC, EVA)

Yield strength is measured as the point at which a material deforms permanently under a stress or load (measured in megapascals).

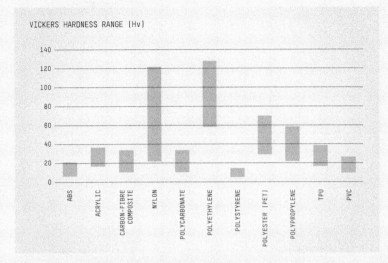

VICKERS HARDNESS RANGE (Hv)

Although the Vickers hardness scale is a measurement of several different attributes, it is most usefully applied to plastics as a measure of resistance to indentation and scratching.

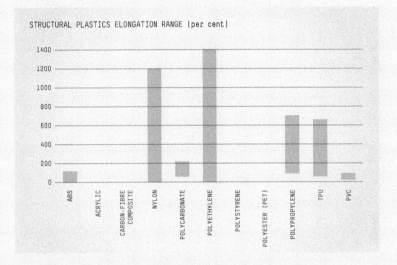

STRUCTURAL PLASTICS ELONGATION RANGE (per cent)

Elongation is a measure of the point at which materials break under tension. The length of this elongation prior to breaking is expressed as a percentage of the materials' original length.

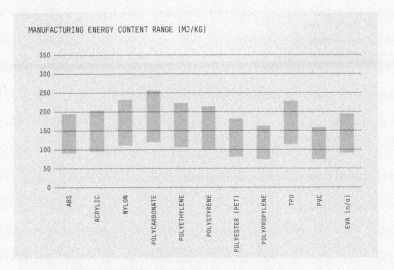

MANUFACTURING ENERGY CONTENT RANGE (MJ/KG)

Manufacturing energy content is a measure of the energy consumed or needed to produce a raw material ready for use in manufacturing.

Manufacture: PMMA can be thermoformed, injection moulded, blow moulded, extruded, heat bent, machined, sawn, drilled, laser cut and water-jet cut. PMMA can be ultrasonically welded, thermo-welded (although adhesives give better results) and bonded with adhesive.

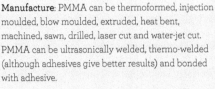

Acrylic solid surfacing (Corian®, HI-MACS™, etc.)

TYPE
Thermoplastic

CHARACTERISTICS
Non-porous, high UV resistance, resistant to most chemicals, non-recyclable

PRICE ($/KG)
High

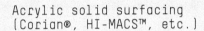

UV RESISTANCE
High

A range of solid surfacing products are available but the majority (including Corian® and HI-MACS™) are a mix of 20 to 25 per cent polymethyl methacrylate (PMMA) and between 70 and 75 per cent bauxite or aluminium trihydrate. Solid surfacing is specified as either sheet fabrications or fabrications of sheet products and thermoforms or injection-moulded or cast components. These are joined using adhesives that perfectly match the wide range of materials available. Solid surfacing has a low mechanical strength and is brittle. However, in applications such as worktops and exterior cladding it has a superior performance compared to other structural plastics.

Applications: Worktops, healthcare environments, signage and cladding for buildings.

Manufacture: Acrylic solid surfacing can be thermoformed, injection moulded, sawn, drilled, routed (the last three with specialized cutting tools), laser cut and water-jet cut. Components can be bonded with adhesive to produce seamless joins.

Polymer composites (polyester [and epoxy] and glass or carbon fibre)

TYPE
Thermoset plastic (component)

CHARACTERISTICS
Rigid, light, non-recyclable

PRICE ($/KG)
Very high

UV RESISTANCE
High (with UV-resistant gelcoat)

Broadly speaking, a composite is any material created by combining two or more materials. In this section, however, the focus is on man-made fibre-reinforced plastic.

Composites are a combination of resin and fibres that produce rigid (to varying degrees) or flexible hardwearing structures suitable for a wide range of environments. Glass, carbon or Kevlar fibres produce great strength in tension, being held in position by polyester or epoxy resin. The least strong, heaviest and cheapest combination is polyester resin and glass fibre (commonly known as fibreglass or GRP). Epoxy is a much stronger thermoset but is more expensive and usually only used in combination with carbon and Kevlar fibres (CF and KF), which in themselves are much stronger and lighter than glass fibre. Carbon and Kevlar fibres are also much more expensive and tend only to be used for high-performance sports and aerospace equipment.

Applications: GRP: Boat hulls, exterior seating, fishing rods, ladders; CF and KF: Chairs, high-performance sports equipment, fishing rods.

Manufacture: Since the hand lay-up of composites is time consuming and can produce variable results, faster processes that use resin injection and automated pressure have been developed. Resin infusion uses an aluminium tool, into which resin is injected at moderate pressure to infuse an enclosed fibre matrix. Vacuum-bag moulding uses atmospheric pressure to compress fibres and resin, removing air pockets. This is a low-cost option compared to resin transfer and autoclave moulding, which use high pressure and heat to improve the production rate and resulting integrity of the components. Filament winding is another process that produces such items as fishing rods, but which can also deliver less dense structures of a much larger diameter.

Nylons (polyamides)

TYPE
Thermoplastic

CHARACTERISTICS
Strong, durable, low coefficient of friction, recyclable

PRICE ($/KG)
Moderate to high

UV RESISTANCE
High

Nylon is the generic name given to a group of thermoplastics called polyamides. Their toughness, rigidity and low coefficient of friction mean that they are an ideal material for the contact surfaces of mechanical joints and for components that undergo a great deal of stress and abrasion in use. Nylon is available in many different forms, but for furniture specification there are three main types: Nylon6, Nylon66 and Nylon12. These can be further strengthened by the addition of glass fibres and can have their already low friction properties enhanced using graphite or oil additives.

Polyamide nylon is the usual material for SLS prototyping, which produces sintered plastic parts with high mechanical strength.

Applications: Bearings, rope, resilient product casings, structural chair components, handles, cable (zip) ties.

Manufacture: Nylon can be injection moulded, extruded, machined, sawn, drilled, laser cut and water-jet cut. It can be ultrasonically welded (but not to a high standard), thermo-welded and bonded with adhesive.

Left to right:
The Expression Table by Willem van Ast is composed of Corian sheet over a wooden substrate and frame.

Neo-Deco by Gareth Neal is made entirely of HI-MACS™ solid surfacing.

Alberto Meda's Light Light Chair is made from a carbon-fibre composite.

PearsonLloyd's Soul Chair for Allermuir features an injection-moulded polyamide seat frame, armrests and backrest.

Philippe Starck's visually groundbreaking Louis Ghost Chair is made from injection-moulded polycarbonate.

Polycarbonate (PC)

TYPE
Thermoplastic

CHARACTERISTICS
Clear, tough, high impact resistance

PRICE ($/KG)
Moderate

UV RESISTANCE
Moderate (high with surface coating)

PC has very high impact resistance (approximately twice that of ABS), a high tensile strength and light transmission properties that are almost as good as glass. Although anti-scratch coatings can be applied to improve polycarbonate's performance, its low scratch resistance means that for products that would encounter high abrasion or use, acrylic (PMMA) would perform better, although, of course, PMMA is weaker. PC has moderate UV stability but this can be improved significantly with the application of an inhibiting surface coating. PC can also be cold formed into bends (in a similar way to sheet metal) using a press brake, although typically only with sheets of up to 4mm (0.2in) in thickness.

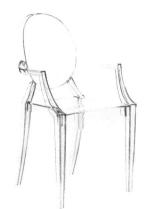

Applications: Chairs, chair shells, motorcycle helmets, protective screens, riot shields.

Manufacture: PC can be cold formed (using a brake press), thermoformed, injection moulded, rotational moulded, blow moulded, extruded, machined, sawn, drilled, laser cut and water-jet cut. It can be ultrasonically welded, thermo-welded and bonded with adhesive.

POLYETHYLENE

High-density polyethylene (HDPE)

TYPE
Thermoplastic
CHARACTERISTICS
Easily moulded, durable, low cost
PRICE ($/KG)
Low to moderate
UV RESISTANCE
Moderate

HDPE is mainly used for the manufacture of bottles and some helmets and kayaks. HDPE has good resistance to abrasion, a low coefficient of friction (third only to nylon and ultra-high-molecular-weight polyethylene [UHMWPE]) and very good impact resistance. It is particularly suited to blow moulding, while also being good for rotational moulding. Even though its resistance to UV is poor, the demanding strength requirements of products such as kayaks make it the ideal material for their production.

Applications: Food containers, construction helmets, kayaks, chopping boards.

Manufacture: HDPE can be thermoformed, injection moulded, rotational moulded, blow moulded, extruded, machined, sawn, drilled, laser cut and water-jet cut. HDPE can be ultrasonically welded and thermo-welded, but does not bond well with adhesive, although it is slightly better than HDPE. However, if bonding is the only option then there are some pre-treatments available that improve adhesion performance.

Low-density polyethylene (LDPE)

TYPE
Thermoplastic
CHARACTERISTICS
Easily moulded, durable, low cost
PRICE ($/KG)
Low to moderate
UV RESISTANCE
Low

LDPE's flexibility and toughness make it one of the most popular plastics for rotationally moulded furniture and blow-moulded children's toys (two processes for which it is very well suited). Compared to HDPE, LDPE is fairly scratch resistant but has a comparable UV performance, although this can be greatly improved using stabilizers.

Applications: Traffic cones, roadside bollards, blow-moulded children's furniture, rotational-moulded seating, polythene sheeting, plastic bags.

Manufacture: LDPE can be thermoformed, injection moulded, rotational moulded, blow moulded, extruded, machined, sawn, drilled, laser cut and water-jet cut. It can be ultrasonically welded and thermo-welded, but does not bond well with adhesive. However, if bonding is the only option then there are surface pre-treatments available that improve adhesion performance.

POLYSTYRENE

Expanded polystyrene (EPS)

TYPE
Thermoplastic
CHARACTERISTICS
Strong, low cost, lightweight
PRICE ($/KG)
Low
UV RESISTANCE
Low

Although EPS is primarily used as a packaging material, there has been some notable temporary or disposable furniture made from this material. Due to its very low density (up to 98 per cent air), it is structurally weak, but with the right geometries it can produce furniture with sufficient strength. For demanding applications such as seating, however, products would have to be a leg-less monobloc to survive any sort of use. Expanded polypropylene (EPP) has similar characteristics but has a wide density range and a better overall material performance (see p181).

Applications: Packaging, short-life furniture, floatation devices.

Manufacture: EPS is manufactured from compressed polystyrene pellets that, under high pressure, are injected with steam into an aluminium tool in which they expand to fill the void. EPS can be cut with a hot wire, a bandsaw or by water jet.

High-impact polystyrene (HIPS)

TYPE
Thermoplastic
CHARACTERISTICS
Clear, low cost, impact resistant
PRICE ($/KG)
Low
UV RESISTANCE
Low

Unlike polystyrene, and as you would expect from its name, HIPS has very good impact resistance. However, compared to ABS or PP, its tensile strength is low. Therefore, HIPS is not appropriate for major structural elements such as chair shells, but should be considered when specifying low load-bearing parts such as storage components. HIPS is used for fridge and freezer compartments and containers because it does not become brittle at low temperatures in the same way as most rigid plastics do. HIPS machines particularly well and is a cheap raw material compared to PP and HDPE, but does have some limitations of use due to its flammability (it burns rather than melts).

Applications: Toys, containers, fridge and freezer compartments.

Manufacturing: HIPS can be thermoformed, injection moulded, extruded, machined, sawn, drilled, laser cut and water-jet cut. It can be ultrasonically welded, thermo-welded and bonded with adhesive.

Polystyrene (PS)

TYPE
Thermoplastic

CHARACTERISTICS
Clear, low cost

PRICE ($/KG)
Low

UV RESISTANCE
Low

Polystyrene has limited use in furniture manufacturing because of its physical weaknesses. However, because it is a very cheap polymer, designers should consider its use as a way to reduce costs on a project. Its brittleness means that if UV inhibitors are added, then its strength is severely undermined. Therefore, PS should only really be specified where there is low stress, no impacts and no direct UV light.

Applications: Disposable cutlery, CD cases, plant pots, food packaging, clear low-cost or disposable items.

Manufacture: PS can be thermoformed, injection moulded (most commonly), rotational moulded, blow moulded, extruded, sawn and drilled (carefully), and laser cut and water-jet cut. PS can be ultrasonically welded, thermo-welded and bonded with adhesive.

Polyester/polyethylene terephthalate (PET/PETE)

TYPE
Thermoplastic

CHARACTERISTICS
Strong, low cost, transparent, high UV resistance

PRICE ($/KG)
Low

UV RESISTANCE
High

PET is used widely in the drinks-bottle and food-packaging industries, but also has a broader range of applications, including space blankets, chopping boards and, in fibre form, as sails. Its high mechanical strength means that very thin bottle walls can match the strength of glass, at a fraction of the weight and with less invested energy. The majority of PET production is of fibres for textiles and rope, with bottles and food packaging accounting for most of the remainder. PET's use in furniture was very limited until the launch in 2010 of Marcel Wanders's Sparkling Chair, which was manufactured in the same way as plastic bottles are, but with a greater wall thickness.

Applications: Textile fibres (woven and non-woven), bottles, carpets, flexible packaging, space blankets, chopping boards, boat sails.

Manufacture: PET can be blow moulded, injection moulded and extruded.

HDPE is widely used for rotationally moulding kayaks.

POLYPROPYLENE

Polypropylene (PP)

TYPE
Thermoplastic

CHARACTERISTICS
Durable, strong, low cost

PRICE $/KG
Low

UV RESISTANCE
Low

Polypropylene is cheaper than ABS and HDPE (its closest material competitors) and by the use of different polymers, catalysts and additive-based reinforcements, PP achieves high strength, rigidity and UV resistance. PP's toughness in combination with its flexibility means that it is one of the best plastics to use for manufacturing chair shells or entire monocoque chairs (using glass-reinforced PP). This flexibility also means that it is the best plastic with which to create live hinges.

Applications: Chair shells, monocoque chairs, electric kettles, storage tubs.

Manufacture: Polypropylene can be thermoformed (but good results are difficult to achieve in a workshop), injection moulded (most commonly), rotational moulded, blow moulded, extruded, sawn, machined, drilled, laser cut and water-jet cut. Polypropylene cannot be ultrasonically welded to a high standard and so thermo-welding or nitrogen welding are the best options. Specialized adhesives, good surface preparation and a proportionately large surface area are required to achieve a good bond; however, the welding options produce stronger joins.

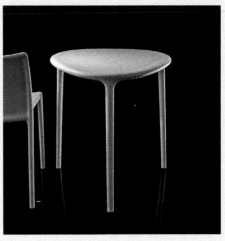

Expanded polypropylene (EPP)

TYPE
Thermoplastic

CHARACTERISTICS
Strong, low cost, lightweight

PRICE ($/KG)
Low

UV RESISTANCE
Low

Although manufactured by the same process as EPS (see p179), expanded polypropylene is a much more versatile material due to its range of densities. EPP's high impact resistance/absorption means that it is ideal for high-value packaging and suitable for protective clothing. In its more dense grades, EPP can be used for monocoque seating solutions and other furniture, but to achieve structural integrity these will need to be significantly thicker than for dense plastic manufacturing. Interestingly, because of material flexibility and shrinkage, it is possible to have 0° draft angles on some EPP products, which can be removed easily from the tool.

Applications: High-value packaging, protective clothing, seating, tables.

Manufacture: EPP is manufactured from compressed polypropylene pellets that, under high pressure, are injected with steam into an aluminium tool in which they expand to fill the void. The final product's density is dependent on the pellets used and variations in manufacturing set-up. EPP can be cut with a hot wire, a bandsaw or by water jet.

Thermoplastic polyurethane (TPU)

TYPE
Thermoplastic

CHARACTERISTICS
Durable, strong, flexible, recyclable

PRICE ($/KG)
High

UV RESISTANCE
High

TPU has a broad range of characteristics and, compared to PUR (see p182), it has increased mechanical strength and durability across its flexible and rigid range. It can also achieve a very high surface quality, emulate materials such as leather and rubber and, if required, be transparent. The use of TPU in furniture is largely limited to handles and feet, but there is good scope for its use in other components due to its load-bearing capabilities.

Applications: Car bumpers, insulation, drive belts.

Manufacture: Injection moulded, extruded. Denser or harder grades of TPU can be machined, sawn and drilled. Some grades can be thermo-welded, and all can be bonded with adhesive.

Top, left to right:
Tom Dixon's EPS chairs were given away as part of the London Design Festival in 2006.

The lightweight (1kg / 2.2lb) PET Sparkling Chair by Marcel Wanders. The chair achieves its strength by its components being filled with high-pressure air.

Jasper Morrison's Air chairs and table for Magis are manufactured in two stages using gas-injection-moulded polypropylene. The outer layer is pure PP but within it is a fibre-reinforced, partly hollow PP body.

Above, left to right:
The world's first one-piece, injection-moulded PP chair shell by Robin Day for Hille.

Ronen Kadushin's LYTA Chair is a two-part EPP structure with an upholstered cover.

Textilene® is a PVC-coated woven polyester fabric, ideal for exterior applications such as seating.

Elastomeric plastics

Polyvinyl chloride (PVC)

TYPE
Thermoplastic or thermoset plastic

CHARACTERISTICS
Low cost, durable

PRICE ($/KG)
Low

UV RESISTANCE
High

A great range of material performance is available from PVC, which encompasses hard, rigid structural plastics called UPVCs and softer elastomeric PVCs called elPVCs. PVC has received a great deal of bad press due to the toxicity of vinyl chloride and the inclusion of a range of phthalates (which soften unmodified UPVC). However, if produced and managed correctly using current European and US safety guidelines there should not be a problem; its less regulated manufacturing in the Far East is the main cause of concern. Phthalates are being phased out and phthalate-free PVC must now be used for all children's products and should be a first choice for all interior applications.

Applications: UPVCs: plumbing pipes, windows, guttering; elPVCs: fabric covering, swim floats, fake leather.

Manufacture: UPVC can be thermoformed, injection moulded, extruded, machined, sawn, drilled, laser cut and water-jet cut. It can be ultrasonically welded, thermo-welded and bonded with adhesive. elPVC can be cut, ultrasonically welded, thermo-welded and bonded with adhesive; elPVC is also the main material used for profile-wrapping and membrane-pressing processes (see p209).

Butyl (synthetic) rubbers

TYPE
Thermoset plastic

CHARACTERISTICS
Strong, durable

PRICE ($/KG)
Low

UV RESISTANCE
Moderate

While there are many types of elastomer that are commonly referred to as 'rubber', only butyl rubbers can truly be described as such. Butyl rubbers have very similar properties to natural rubber but perform better with prolonged exposure to UV and lubricants. Ozone cracking is another degradation problem affecting synthetic rubbers and is caused by their reaction to sunlight. Without being reinforced, butyl rubbers can lack the strength needed for certain high-stress applications.

Because of the material's potential flexibility, it is possible not to include draft angles in some aspects of component design and still be able to remove the component from the tool. However, such an approach is dependent on the product's shape, geometry and the particular rubber's flexibility. In such matters, always consult with a manufacturer first.

Applications: Tyres, hosepipes, inner tubes, seals.

Manufacturing: Synthetic rubbers are either injection moulded or extruded.

Polyurethane resin (PUR)

TYPE
Thermoset plastic

CHARACTERISTICS
Abrasion & tear resistant, lightweight

PRICE ($/KG)
Moderate

UV RESISTANCE
Moderate

Thermosetting polyurethanes are manufactured by casting, vacuum casting, or through the reaction injection moulding (RIM) process. Thermosetting PURs have properties ranging from elastomeric (elPU) Lycra and soft upholstery foam to semi-rigid reinforced drive belts and rigid, hard mouldings (tsPU). PUR is also a very useful prototyping and low-volume production process using vacuum casting and RIM. Foams (40 per cent of total production) can either be open or closed cell and range from hard to soft grades. Upholstery uses either 'converted' sheet or block foam or moulded (RIM) PU, which can be skinned (coated) by prior spraying of the moulding tool or even afterward on the exterior surface.

Applications: Furniture cushioning, either as sheet foam or moulded into a form, with or without a structural armature inside.

Manufacture: Cast, vacuum cast, or reaction injection moulded. Denser or harder grades of PUR can be machined, sawn, drilled and bonded with adhesive; elPU can be cut using a knife or with specialized blades for power saws.

Ethylene-vinyl acetate (EVA)

TYPE
Thermoplastic

CHARACTERISTICS
Durable, strong, lightweight, flexible

PRICE ($/KG)
Low

UV RESISTANCE
Moderate

Although not widely used for furniture manufacture, EVA's tactile softness and mouldability make it worth considering for a range of applications. EVA can be manufactured with a broad array of characteristics – from dense and translucent tubing to lightweight, low-density foam. The foams can be very soft and rubbery or semi-hard.

EVA is not in itself fire retardant, but with additives it achieves fire-safety ratings suitable for aerospace and automotive applications. However, as constructional or upholstery foam, it is not classified as safe in the UK, and designers should check their country's safety

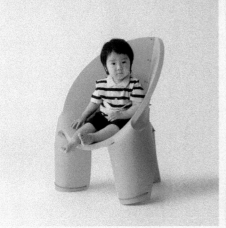

regulations. Denser varieties of EVA can still have soft tactile qualities that make it ideal for moulded handles or armrests.

Applications: Flip-flops, running shoes, toolbox linings, swim floats, fishing-rod butts and reel handles.

Manufacture: EVA can be thermoformed, injection moulded, extruded, water-jet cut and bonded with adhesives.

Natural rubber

TYPE
Thermoset plastic

CHARACTERISTICS
Durable, strong, flexible

PRICE ($/KG)
Low to moderate

UV RESISTANCE
Low

Derived from the sap (latex) of the rubber tree, natural rubber is manufactured through the addition of sulphur and by curing with heat. This process of vulcanisation can be altered to affect the rigidity or flexibility of the resulting parts. Natural rubber is widely used, but in certain environments does not perform as well as synthetic rubbers – it degrades in contact with oil, UV light and, to a lesser extent, through oxidisation. Ozone cracking is another

degradation problem that can be caused by volatile organic liquids (VOLs) reacting with sunlight. However, natural rubber is still a very good choice for a great many applications, not least because it is cheap, non-toxic and largely produced from renewable resources.

Applications: Tyres, seals, toys.

Manufacture: Natural rubber is either cast, injection moulded or extruded. Because of the material's potential flexibility, it is possible not to include draft angles in some aspects of component design and still be able to remove the component from the tool. However, such an approach is dependent on the product's shape, geometry and the particular rubber's flexibility. In such matters, always consult with a manufacturer first.

Biopolymers and bio-composites

Type: Thermoplastic and thermoset plastics

Biopolymers can be structural or elastomeric thermosets or thermoplastics made from organic, renewable materials, with the majority being derived from plant cellulose. The research and development of biopolymers and bio-composites by companies such as BASF represents the leading edge of materials science, and, although not entirely carbon

neutral, biopolymers and bio-composites are still the least impactful or most renewable materials available for mass-produced mouldings. Market forces help drive such material research and so furniture designers have a responsibility to stay abreast of these developments and to specify their use in their designs.

Biopolymers are often confused with bio-composites and vice versa. Bio-composites are typically composites of petroleum-based polymers and a considerable amount of reinforcing organic fibre (see Chris Martin's wood plastic composite [WPC] PS Ellan Chair [p144] or Impossible Wood [p10] by Doshi Levien). However, it is possible to use a biopolymer and an organic fibre to produce a biodegradable composite.

The Hemp Chair by Werner Aisslinger (see p58) is something else altogether. The chair is 70 per cent natural hemp fibre bonded with an environmentally friendly water-based glue called Acrodur® that contains no phenols or formaldehyde. Because Acrodur® is man-made, it does not necessarily mean that the Hemp Chair is less green or worthy than a purely biopolymeric chair. Also, because of Acrodur's high performance and longevity, products made in this way will become serious alternatives to petroleum-based non-renewables and play a significant part in a more sustainable future. Biopolymers and bio-composites may not be recyclable; check with manufacturers for details.

Manufacture: Check manufacturing options with each specific material's manufacturer. Bio-composites such as those used for the Hemp Chair can only be compression moulded. Most biopolymers and some bio-composites can be injection moulded, thermoformed, compression moulded and rotational moulded. CNC machining, and water-jet and laser cutting are also likely to be possible.

Bio-based polymeric materials

Arboform (Tecnaro): A bio-composite made from lignin. Fully recyclable and compostable.

Zelfo: A cellulose-based pulp material available as a board material (similar to MDF), with properties similar to that of PE. Developed, but currently not commercialized as a mouldable material.

Porcher Greenlite: A cellulose-based material, with fibres woven together to form a mat suitable for use in a similar way to carbon fibre or fibreglass matting (to be combined with a suitable bio-based resin or Acrodur®).

Södra DuraPulp: A new, paper pulp-based material currently in development. Good potential for strong but lightweight items of furniture.

Biodegradable plastics

Biodegradable plastics are not entirely relevant to sustainable furniture consumption, which is built around renewable resources, reuse and recycling. However, there may be some projects that require compostable products with a finite life, in which case designers should consider biodegradable plastic.

Biodegradable plastics are either petroleum-based polymers or biopolymers. Both require heat, moisture and, to some degree, time to decompose. Petroleum-based plastics use additives to begin this process, while biopolymers decompose naturally under the right conditions.

Manufacture: Biodegradable plastics can be injection moulded, thermoformed, compression moulded and rotational moulded. CNC machining, and water-jet and laser cutting are also possible.

Left to right:

Holz by Ben Kirkby is a prototype gas injection-moulded chair that would be manufactured using Arboform. This 'liquid wood' material can be reinforced with natural fibres, is mouldable in the same ways as conventional thermoplastics and has similar strength properties to polypropylene. The design was developed using FEA software as the first 100% organic, monobloc injection-moulded chair.

The Parupu children's chair by Swedish trio Claesson Koivisto Rune is moulded from paper pulp infused and bonded with DuraPulp, a biodegradable biopolymer derived from maize starch.

Plastics manufacturing processes

Blow moulding

Blow moulding produces largely symmetrical hollow forms, typically used for the manufacture of bottles, power-tool cases and car bumpers.

SHAPES
Hollow, thin-walled

PLASTICS
ABS, HDPE, LDPE, PET (predominantly), PC, PP, PVC

MANUFACTURING TOLERANCE
0.25–1mm (0.01–0.04in)

WALL THICKNESS (MIN–MAX)
0.4–3mm (0.02–0.1in)

MINIMUM DRAFT ANGLE
1–2°

MINIMUM RADII
2 x wall thickness

MANUFACTURING VOLUME
1000–million+

SIMILAR PROCESSES
Rotational moulding

Design guidance: Suitable for simple, largely symmetrical shape geometry with a low degree of localized detail. The ratio between the moulding's height and its depth cannot be too great. Moulding-in inserts is possible but not common.

Manufacture: There are three types of blow moulding that follow the same basic principle of inflating a molten plastic shape against the walls of a mould. To improve the gas-containment performance of bottles, a multilayer approach is applied using different plastics. Blow moulding produces hollow forms and although it is predominantly used for the manufacture of bottles, power-tool cases and car bumpers, there have also been a modest number of chair seats and backrests produced in this way.

The most recent and accomplished of these is Marcel Wanders's Sparkling Chair, which is entirely blow moulded. The legs are moulded separately from the body and, even though it could have been made more simply as a monobloc using rotational moulding, the transparent PET expresses a clear link to the visual language of plastic bottles and to the blow-moulding process.

Extrusion blow moulding (EBM) is the cheapest of the three processes and is ideal for water-carrying containers, children's furniture and toys. However, it does not give a consistent wall thickness and overall lacks the refinement of the other two injection-blow-moulding processes outlined below. An extruded blow moulding is produced when a tube of hot extruded plastic is captured top and bottom by a mating two-part split mould. Hot air is then injected through a mandrel (already inserted) at one end (which becomes the open end of the moulding), causing the extruded plastic to inflate and fill the void of the mould. Once cooled, the mould separates and the mandrel is withdrawn to reveal the finished hollow form. Because of the split mould's enclosing action, a thin 'flash' of flattened excess plastic is often left on the outside of the split line, requiring manual removal.

Stretch injection blow moulding (SIBM) and injection blow moulding (IBM) are similar processes that produce high-quality mouldings with consistent wall thicknesses, therefore cooling more evenly than extrusion blow mouldings and with less risk of distortion. SIBM and IBM mouldings are produced by inserting a hollow mandrel into a heated, previously moulded 'preform', before both are quickly inserted into an enclosed mould. Air is then injected under high pressure, inflating the preform to fill the mould void. SIBM has an additional action where the inserted mandrel lengthens to mechanically elongate the preform, prior to air injection. Because both SIBM and IBM processes start with an enclosed mould, only a very slight (if any) mould separation line is evident in the continuous wall. These processes do not result in the compression join line of EBM and are more suited to clear plastics.

Lathe, CNC routing, milling, water-jet and laser cutting

For information about CAD software and file formats, see p108

SHAPES
Metal lathe: hollow or solid, axisymmetric
Milling: hollow or solid
Routing: (primarily) flat, hollow or solid
Water-jet and laser cutting: (primarily) flat

Left to right:
The lightweight (1kg / 2.2lbs) PET Sparkling Chair by Marcel Wanders is manufactured by blow moulding.

A CNC-routed EVA foam insert for a case.

MANUFACTURING TOLERANCE
Lathe: 0.05–0.5mm (0.002–0.02in)
Routing and milling: 0.1–0.5mm (0.004–0.02in)
Water-jet cutting: 0.1–0.5mm (0.004–0.02in)
Laser cutting: 0.025–0.5mm (0.001–0.02in)

MANUFACTURING VOLUME
1–10,000m+

MANUFACTURING SPEED
Slow to moderate

UNIT COST
Moderate to high

TOOLING COST
None, unless for cutter profiles

SIMILAR PROCESSES
As above

Plastics such as HDPE and all nylons machine particularly well, but in comparison to water-jet and laser cutting, machining and CNC routing of sheet materials are the slowest of the four processes and suited to low-volume manufacturing. CNC operations are slow processes with set manufacturing costs, no matter what the volume. Without the need for tooling and up front investment, CNC-cutting technologies are accessible processes for many designers and businesses.

For short production runs and for components with re-entrant axisymmetric features and stepped axisymmetric profiles, CNC or manual lathe machining is ideal.

Plastics sheets are sometimes CNC-routed using three-axis routers but increasingly, laser and water-jet cutting are used instead because of their speed. In thin materials, CNC routing and laser cutting produce the most accurate results. Water-jet cutting is less

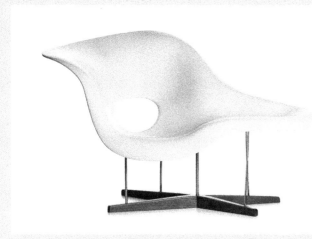

accurate in terms of producing a square-edged cut but it is quicker at cutting thick materials. However, some particular plastics such as PP are often better routed.

Plastic foams such as PUR, PS and EVA can be routed from blocks using three- or five-axis routers to produce models, patterns for moulding and compartments for equipment storage, etc. For both types of routing operations, more than one cutter type or diameter is used during the process. The minimum diameter of the cutter and slot is normally 3mm (0.1in), but smaller diameters are possible using drill bits that are part of a machine's interchangeable tool carousel set-up. It is worth noting that when routing any sort of internal angle, the minimum radius possible with a cutter is equivalent to its own radius.

Water-jet cutting is ideal for cutting thicker (50mm+ / 2in+) plastic sheet materials and can produce a reasonably good-quality cut edge. An average jet diameter is 0.5mm (0.02in) and even though it gradually widens, the difference is negligible for thin sheet, although inaccuracies do increase with sheet thickness. It is advisable to consult with a manufacturer about this detail, since different machinery and sheet thicknesses produce different results.

Laser cutting is the ideal process for cutting and engraving most thin sheet plastics because it produces perfect polished edges and is able to render ultra-fine details when etching. Laser widths can be varied between 0.1 and 1mm (0.004–0.04in) in diameter.

COMPOSITE (POLYMER MATRIX) MANUFACTURING

Polymer matrix composites are either applied to open moulds, partially injected into a closed mould or filament-wound on to a mandrel. Glass-reinforced plastic (GRP) is typically used for boat hulls, exterior seating, architectural components and details. Carbon and Kevlar fibre composites are often employed for high-performance sports equipment, fishing rods and chairs.

Manufacture: Lay-up methods (see below) of composite manufacture are defined by their labour-intensive nature, but despite this, for low-volume production and for large-scale mouldings, the advantages are clear. Tooling costs can be low for lay-up methods, with moulds being made from GRP or vacuum-form fabrications. Resin transfer moulding (RTM) uses the same thermosetting resins and reinforcing matrixes as lay-up methods but is largely a mechanized process. Filament winding is entirely mechanized, and polymer matrixes are either woven matting or chopped fibres.

Laying up

SHAPES
Thin-walled, open

PLASTICS
Polyesters, epoxies, vinyl ester, phenolics or glass, carbon and Kevlar fibres

MANUFACTURING TOLERANCE
0.6–1mm (0.02–0.04in)

WALL THICKNESS (MIN–MAX)
2–10mm (0.08–0.4in)

MINIMUM DRAFT ANGLE
2–3°

MINIMUM RADII
0.5mm (0.02in)

MANUFACTURING VOLUME
1–500m+

SIMILAR PROCESSES
Resin transfer moulding

Laying up describes the process of applying resin and reinforcing matrixes into an open mould. Although there are four distinct laying-up processes, they all share a common first stage in which the resin and reinforcing is applied.

Hand lay-up shares the common first stage but without mechanical pressure applied to the curing composite. A layer of gelcoat is first applied to a waxed mould, after which layers of resin and reinforcing fibre are applied until the desired thickness is achieved.

The vacuum-bag and pressure-bag processes compress the resin and fibres to remove any air bubbles and, by so doing, improve the performance and consistency of the final product. Autoclave

Left to right:
La Chaise by Charles and Ray Eames is made from fibreglass (GRP), stainless steel and wood.

EPP is available in several standard colours and in a wide range of densities (18–260g per litre / 2.4 –35oz per gallon), such as this example from ARPRO®.

Fold by Alexander Taylor – a laser-cut, folded and powder-coated steel light.

moulding is an advance on the vacuum- and pressure-bag processes and is used for void-free mouldings that require the maximum available performance. Through the application of heat and very high atmospheric pressures, the resin and fibre lay-up is compressed, producing parts with very high strength-to-weight ratios.

Design guidance: All laying-up methods require open moulds, but these thin-walled open shapes can be joined to others by clamping the moulds together while the resin and fibre lay-up is still wet. Very small radii and surface form are prone to damage, since they can only be formed from the polymer gelcoat, without the benefit of the strengthening fibres.

Filament winding

SHAPES
Prismatic*, hollow

PLASTICS
Polyesters, epoxies, vinyl ester, phenolics or glass, carbon and Kevlar filaments

MANUFACTURING TOLERANCE
0.1–0.6mm (0.004–0.02in)

WALL THICKNESS (MIN–MAX)
2–25mm (0.08–1in)

MINIMUM DRAFT ANGLE
n/a

MINIMUM RADII
n/a

MANUFACTURING VOLUME
1–10,000m+

SIMILAR PROCESSES
None

Filament winding is used to manufacture prismatic (*but with possible changes as it does not have to be axisymmetric), hollow profiles without inset features. The rigidity of filament windings depends on the wall thickness and types of fibres and resins used. Mandrels are either removable, reusable or part of the product and encapsulated within it. Filaments are either pre-impregnated with resin or 'wet' as a result of the resin being continuously applied to the filament.

Design guidance: Filament-wound products can be tapered or parallel-sided and asymmetrical. Profiles must have a positive form since the wound filament is always under tension. Step changes between different sectional dimensions cannot be too steep. The maximum size of a filament-wound product is dictated by the maximum bed size of machinery, which is commonly 3 x 1.5m (9ft 10in x 4ft 11in).

Resin transfer moulding (RTM)

SHAPES
Solid, open or flat

PLASTICS
Polyesters, epoxies, vinyl ester, phenolics or glass, carbon and Kevlar fibres

MANUFACTURING TOLERANCE
0.25–1mm (0.01–0.04in)

WALL THICKNESS (MIN–MAX)
1.5–13mm (0.06–0.5in)

MINIMUM DRAFT ANGLE
2–3°

MINIMUM RADII
0.5mm (0.02in)

MANUFACTURING VOLUME
10,000–100,000m+

SIMILAR PROCESSES
Press moulding

Resin transfer moulding is used for manufacturing solid shapes and panels up to a large size. A reinforcing fibre matrix is cut to size and placed in an enclosed mould. Resin is then injected into the mould void and left to cure. Tooling costs for RTM are low since moulds can be made from GRP or aluminium.

Design guidance: Complex shapes with ribs and foam inclusions are possible using RTM.

Expanded foam moulding

SHAPES
Solid, open or flat

PLASTICS
Polystyrene (EPS), polypropylene (EPP)

MANUFACTURING TOLERANCE
0.5–2mm (0.02–0.08in)

WALL THICKNESS (MIN–MAX)
3mm (0.1in)

MINIMUM DRAFT ANGLE
1–3°

MINIMUM RADII
2mm (0.08in)

MANUFACTURING VOLUME
1000–10,000+

TOOLING COST
Low

UNIT COST
Low

MOULDED-IN INSERTS
Possible

SIMILAR PROCESSES
Reaction injection moulding (RIM)

Expanded polystyrene (EPS) and expanded polypropylene (EPP) are lightweight materials manufactured from fused, low-density plastic beads. While a limited range of EPS densities are available, EPP comes in a wide range of densities (18–260g per litre; 2.4–35oz per gallon), some of which generate a skin through their contact with the mould. Tubular grain shapes are also available for manufacturing porous EPP. Expanded-foam manufacturing requires low-cost tooling due to its low-pressure requirements and the cheapness of its raw materials relative to the components' sizes.

Design guidance: Less dense EPP and EPS are appropriate for packaging and buoyancy aids, whereas the denser grades are used for their rigidity, strength and impact resistance. Some manufacturers state that it is possible to have a 0° draft angle for some components because the materials' shrinkage and flexibility make it possible to withdraw them from the mould without a draft. However, designers should stick to the 1–3° guidelines, unless advised otherwise by a manufacturer.

Manufacture: Expanded polystyrene (EPS) and expanded polypropylene (EPP) are manufactured by injecting compressed plastic beads and hot air into a heated tool. The process releases an integral foaming agent within the beads, which simultaneously increases their size and reduces their density. It is possible to mix grain densities and types within one unified moulding to give precise material performance characteristics in different areas. Moderately detailed surface patterns can be applied to EPS and EPP, although for the latter the visibility of the grain in finished mouldings can make it difficult to register such details clearly.

FABRICATION AND JOINING PROCESSES

In addition to flat-sheet fabrication, nearly all products require assembly after being moulded, cut or stamped.

SHAPES
All

PLASTICS
All structural and elastomeric plastics

MANUFACTURING VOLUME
Low

Manufacture: There are three categories of joining processes: adhesives, plastic welding and fasteners. Although different adhesives and welding processes are able to join plastics to themselves, when different plastics or completely different materials need to be joined together, designers need to decide on the most appropriate method early on – at the material-selection stage. Such strategies will differ for each project, depending on the type of stress or conditions the joints will be under, whether the means of joining can be invisible or whether the product is being designed for factory-assembly, self-assembly or disassembly. The welding of identical thermoplastics and the use of fasteners always make disassembly

and recycling more viable than if mixed plastics are welded and bonded with adhesive.

Standard fabrication includes the use of flat, line-bent or thermoformed sheet materials and profiles, and these in turn will have been dimensioned and detailed using manual or CNC machining or laser cutting. Typically, such fabrications are joined with adhesives, but this approach is more for display and point-of-sale furniture than load-bearing furniture designed for longevity. A structure of reasonable integrity can be created by cutting sheet materials so that they slot together, but because of small variations in sheet material thickness, tolerances have to be larger than would be ideal, creating a loose fit.

Adhesives

Synthetic structural adhesives are able to join both thermoplastics and thermosets. Some are better than others at coping with thermal expansion and many are not able to maintain their performance in low temperatures. Adhesives for elastomers have different characteristics than those used for structural plastics.

The advantages of adhesive joints are that they can be hidden, can be used in inaccessible areas, create air- and water-tight seals and water-resistant bonds. As with all adhesive joints, the larger the gluing surface the better the bond – particularly for butt joints. Some plastics do not bond as well as others; for instance, polypropylene can be glued together but hot-plate or nitrogen welding would form a much better joint.

There are four main groups of adhesives for joining plastics; solvent-weld cements, epoxies, cyanoacrylates (superglue) and hot-melt adhesives. Solvent-weld cements temporarily dissolve the surface of most thermoplastics, enabling components to be joined. However, such cements cannot be used for polyolefins (polypropylene and polyethylene), which instead require specialized surface treatment prior to the use of epoxy, cyanoacrylate or hot-melt adhesives.

Thermoset plastics need thermosetting glues such as epoxies, while cyanoacrylates can bond a wide range of thermoplastics and thermosets. With primer

treatments, cyanoacrylates can also create a bond between some elastomers.

Plastic welding

Most thermoplastics can be welded together, although different types of plastic can sometimes only be welded using the hot-gas process if they have very similar properties. Designers should always consult an experienced manufacturer before specifying welds between dissimilar plastics.

Friction welding

MAXIMUM MATERIAL THICKNESS
100mm (3.9in)

DISSIMILAR PLASTIC WELDS POSSIBLE?
Yes

There are two main friction-welding processes: rotary and linear. For rotary friction welding (RFW), one or both components must be symmetrical in the plane in which they are rotated (axisymmetric). The symmetrical component is rotated at high speed and then forced, in two stages, against the second component. The resulting friction and axial force heats and plasticizes both components. In linear friction welding (LFW), one component is again stationary, while the other is oscillated against it to plasticize and unify the metals. LFW is used for components that have an unsuitable geometry for rotary welding.

Hot-gas welding

This is a manual process using portable equipment that is not best suited to very thin materials or mass production.

Left to right:
Philippe Starck's Mr Impossible Chair for Kartell is injection moulded in two parts and then laser-welded together.

Part of the injection-moulding tool for the Myto Chair by Konstantin Grcic for Plank.

A test moulding of the Myto Chair.

Opposite: **Javier Mariscal's Alma Chair for Magis. Strengthening ribs on the underside of the chair blend into the backrest relief.**

Hot-plate welding

MAXIMUM MATERIAL THICKNESS
30mm (1.2in)

DISSIMILAR PLASTIC WELDS POSSIBLE?
No

This fully mechanized process is good for nearly all thermoplastics and ideal for polyolefins and elPVC. The process is particularly well suited to large components and creates impermeable joins with up to 90 per cent of the mechanical strength of the moulded material. Hot-plate welding joins two symmetrical and flat component surfaces together by positioning them on either side of a heated 'platen'. When the platen is withdrawn, the two components are quickly brought together and the bond is formed.

Laser welding

MAXIMUM MATERIAL THICKNESS
20mm (0.8in)

DISSIMILAR PLASTIC WELDS POSSIBLE?
Yes

This process for joining plastics was brought to prominence in 2008 by the launch of Philippe Starck's Mr Impossible Chair – an injection-moulded chair manufactured in two parts before being laser-welded together. Because its mating surfaces are not flat (on one plane), only a laser, following the union of the assembled components, could have achieved this result. The laser also creates a very tidy weld.

Ultrasonic welding

MAXIMUM MATERIAL THICKNESS
3mm (0.1in)

DISSIMILAR PLASTIC WELDS POSSIBLE?
Yes

Used for joining two or more thin materials (typically elPVC and polyurethanes), ultrasonic welding presses materials between a static anvil and a shaped seam or point area tool. The tool oscillates at a high frequency, creating heat, which fuses the materials

in a highly controllable process. ABS, acrylic, polycarbonate and PVC are ideal for ultrasonic welding. Polyethylene, polypropylene, polyester and nylon are too difficult to weld to any usable standard.

Fasteners

MAXIMUM MATERIAL THICKNESS
No limit (depending on available fasteners)

DISSIMILAR PLASTIC JOINS POSSIBLE?
Yes

Using rivets, snap fittings and threaded fasteners is the best way to design products for end-of-life disassembly, especially if different plastics or entirely different materials need to be joined. Also, for flat-pack, self-assembly furniture, snap fittings particularly are a quick and easy way of assembling components.

Injection moulding

Injection moulding is used to manufacture small- to medium-sized components (for example, monobloc chairs) from both thermoplastics (predominantly) and thermosets (structural plastics and elastomers). Injection-moulding tooling can be the most expensive of all plastic manufacturing processes.

SHAPES
Thin-walled, open or solid

PLASTICS
ABS, EVA, HDPE, HIPS, LDPE, PC, PE, PET, PMMA, PP, PS, PUR, PVC, TPU

MANUFACTURING TOLERANCE
0.1–1mm (0.004–0.04in)

WALL THICKNESS (MIN–MAX)
0.3–10mm (0.01–0.4in)

MINIMUM DRAFT ANGLE

1.25–3.5°

MINIMUM RADII
25 per cent of wall thickness

MANUFACTURING VOLUME
10,000–Million+

TOOLING COST
High

UNIT COST
Low

MOULDED-IN INSERTS
Possible

SIMILAR PROCESSES
Reaction injection moulding (RIM), press moulding

Design guidance: Injection moulding is suitable for the high-volume production of complex symmetrical and asymmetrical, geometric and amorphous forms with fine detail. Features such as bosses, holes and snap-fits can be moulded in. Gas-injection moulding, fillers, fibre reinforcement and foaming can be allied with IM to improve strength, mouldability, weight ratios, etc.

Manufacture: There are three main types of injection-moulding processes, all of which are quick compared to other moulding processes. The standard, injection moulding uses a reciprocating screw to inject either molten thermoplastic or thermosetting resin into an aluminium or steel tool. Thermoplastic moulding requires the tool to be cooled in order for the part to become solid enough to be ejected from a separating tool. For thermoset moulding, the tool is heated through various methods in order to assist the curing process.

Nearly all thermoplastics can be injection moulded, but the lower their melting point and the better their relative flowability, the easier they are to manufacture. Many thermoplastics have melt points up to 66°C (150°F), with nylon, PC, PET and PMMA in a higher range of up to 121°C (250°F) ; so, the relevant thermoplastics for furniture manufacturing are at worst only moderately difficult to mould.

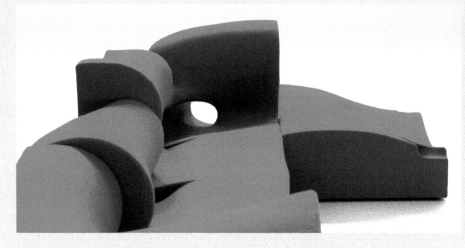

Co-moulding describes processes such as sandwich moulding and overmoulding, which mould together different plastics with various colours or properties. Sandwich moulding involves two or more injected plastic feeds meeting, but not blending, within a mould. These cooled parts may either be fused together or separated so they are movable. Overmoulding involves the insertion of a pre-moulded part into another mould so that a second phase of moulding can take place. This overmoulding action could be to add a new material of a different colour or different physical property than the first. However, overmoulding can also create parts with complex geometries that would not be possible to mould in a one-stage process.

Gas-assisted injection moulding (GIM) is a variation on standard injection moulding. Nitrogen gas is injected into the tool immediately after the injection of plastic, thereby forcing the plastic into the tool's extremities and against its walls. The internal gas pressure replaces the need for fillers and counteracts the effect of material shrinkage by pressure being maintained within the body of the part during the cooling process. This produces a lightweight part with a hollow interior and structural integrity.

GIM enables the moulding of externally thick parts that would otherwise be difficult to mould and would waste materials (because of their thickness), although thin parts are also made using the GIM process. Another significant characteristic of GIM is that components that would normally need moulding in two parts can be moulded as one, saving on tooling costs and reducing manufacturing times.

Plastic extrusion

Plastic extrusion produces long, consistently profiled lengths by forcing molten plastic through a die orifice and cooling it. Structural plastics are constricted and pulled simultaneously in order to keep the profile to shape and longitudinally straight. Extruded elastomers require the same manufacturing controls to ensure they are consistently straight, even though they are flexible. Extrusions are then converted into manageable lengths and post-processed.

SHAPES
Hollow or solid or prismatic profiles

PLASTICS
ABS, EVA, HDPE, HIPS, LDPE, PC, PE, PET, PMMA, PP, PS, PUR, PVC, TPU

MANUFACTURING TOLERANCE, PROFILE
0.5–1mm (0.02–0.04in)

MANUFACTURING TOLERANCE, PER METRE (MIN)
2mm (0.08in)

WALL THICKNESS (MIN–MAX)
0.5–12mm (0.02–0.5in)

MINIMUM DRAFT ANGLE
n/a

MINIMUM RADII
0.2mm (0.008in, should increase with component size)

MANUFACTURING VOLUME
100–1000m+

TOOLING COST
Low

UNIT COST
Low

MOULDED-IN INSERTS
Possible as 'co-extrusion' process

SIMILAR PROCESSES
None

Design guidance: Suitable for medium- to high-volume production of complex profiles in structural or elastomeric thermoplastics. To achieve an easily manufacturable and cost-efficient profile, there are a range of design guidelines. They are as follows:

The cost of tooling (die orifice) relates directly to the complexity and overall dimension (circumscribing circle diameter) of an extrusion, and it is therefore desirable to keep this dimension as small as possible. Circumscribing circle diameters for plastics can range between about 3 and 300mm (0.1–11.8in). They can be joined to each other or to different materials using a range of means, including screw ports, adhesives, threaded inserts, rivets and welding. Plastic extrusions can also be designed as male and female parts that telescope, but their ability to connect in this way is strongly dependent on the hardness of a plastic and the straightness of the extrusion.

Consistent wall thicknesses are desirable since the extruding plastic is drawn toward the larger voids. It is possible for manufacturers to counter this moulding problem but it requires a more expensive

Left to right:

Ron Arad's Misfits sofa system is reaction injection moulded (polyurethane) over a tubular steel frame.

Plastic extrusion profiles.

manufacturing set-up. Inconsistent wall thicknesses also cause extrusions to cool at different rates, making it difficult to keep them straight. Hollow profiles with internal walls should feature an outer wall that is 30 to 40 per cent thicker than the interior walls. Minimum radii for the smallest extrusions can be 0.2mm (0.008in), but this needs to increase up to 0.5–1mm (0.02–0.04in) for larger profiles. Deep, narrow (open) channels are difficult to extrude and present problems in cooling if they are more than 1:3 in proportion. Therefore, if such features are essential, two extruded sections should be joined (telescoped) together to produce the channel. Surface decoration, such as ribbing, is longitudinal and can help hide unavoidable imperfections such as heat zones.

Extrusion profile tolerances are good, but accuracies over a length are less easy to control. After extrusion, significant second-stage processing is needed to control a profile's geometry while cooling, particularly when extruding structural plastics. The speed (and therefore the cost) of extrusion is affected by the quality of surface finish required and by a profile's size and complexity. For very small profiles or those with a range of wall thicknesses, extrusion must be slowed to make the cooling process more controllable.

Although a significant proportion of plastic-extrusion manufacturing is dedicated to window and door construction, for furniture design, extrusions are mainly specified for detail components such as rigid channelling, flexible edging trims or plastic tambours. However, these extruded components are more than design footnotes and mostly are not able to be manufactured in any other way. Of course, minimum production runs for extrusions, as with all moulding technologies, dictate whether such a component will be viable; but relative to other tooling costs, dies for plastic extrusions are cheap. Set-up costs, however, mean that extrusion only begins to be viable with orders starting at 1000m+.

Co-extrusions incorporate two different unified (but not mixed) materials into the same extruded profile; these could be a fibre-reinforced inner core encapsulated by an unfilled skin, or perhaps a skinned, foamed core. Other examples could be a co-extrusion that combines a structural plastic with a thermoplastic elastomer, or an expensive UV-resistant skin co-extruded over a low-cost structural core.

Thermoforming

Thermoforming encompasses low-pressure vacuum forming and pressure forming. Both are distinct in their capabilities, but follow the same principle of forming a heated, softened sheet of thermoplastic over or into a tool. Thin plastic packaging can be formed in this way as can larger structural elements using thicker sheet materials. Although thermoforming is a labour-intensive process (because of set-up and post-processing), tooling costs are small and so for low-volume production and for some larger products (such as baths) in higher volumes, thermoforming can be a viable manufacturing process.

The term thermoforming is also loosely used to describe the process of line-bending thermoplastic sheets.

SHAPES
Thin-walled, open

PLASTICS
ABS, Acrylic Solid Surfacing, HIPS, PC, PET, PMMA, PS, PVC

MANUFACTURING TOLERANCE
0.5–1mm (0.02–0.04in)

WALL THICKNESS (MIN–MAX)
0.25–12mm (0.01–0.5in)

MINIMUM DRAFT ANGLE
2–3°

MINIMUM RADII
0.5mm (0.02in, not less than sheet thickness)

MAXIMUM DEPTH-TO-WIDTH RATIO
0.5:2

MANUFACTURING VOLUME
1–10,000m+

TOOLING COST
Low

UNIT COST
Moderate to high

MOULDED-IN INSERTS
Possible but uncommon

SIMILAR PROCESSES
Membrane pressing

Design guidance: Fabrications using thermoforms are often used for bespoke or low-volume designs, and although such an approach can be particularly labour intensive it still represents the most cost-effective option. For materials such as acrylic solid surfacing (Corian® and HI-MACS™, see p177),

the high strength and invisibility of their bonded joints and the premium value of finished products, such as moulded-in sinks or reception desks, means that thermoforming is a much more viable option than injection moulding. Solid surfacing and other acrylic thermoforms often need reinforcing, particularly vacuum-formed baths. Such strengthening is achieved by the application of GRP and encapsulated reinforcing (such as wood or steel) to the hidden side of the moulding.

Vacuum forming is the cheapest thermoforming process but because of its 'low' pressure (1 bar / 14.5psi), fine surface detailing is difficult to achieve in all but the thinnest materials. A vacuum pump removes air from beneath the sheet and the surrounding atmospheric pressure does the rest.

Pressure forming applies considerably more pressure to the surface of the sheet by pumping air into a chamber above the heated sheet while also drawing out the air from beneath with a vacuum.

Surface decoration and unwanted mould marks are the most pronounced on the mould side of the formed sheet. Thus the choice of whether a male or female mould is used depends on a design's requirements, but it is more usual to form over a male mould.

Reaction injection moulding (RIM)/foam moulding

Reaction injection moulding (RIM) and foam moulding use a two-part thermoset polyurethane resin (PUR), which expands and foams to varying degrees depending on its chemical composition. In its different forms, its uses range from prototyping to high-volume production. Although RIM is considered as a separate process to PUR foam moulding, they are essentially one and the same. The distinction lies in the material performance of the PUR resin, whose properties range from rigid, dense plastic to soft, low-density foam.

SHAPES
Thin-walled, open or solid

PLASTICS
PUR

MANUFACTURING TOLERANCE
0.1–1mm (0.004–0.04in)

WALL THICKNESS (MIN–MAX)
3–25mm (0.1–1 inch, rigid PUR as part of large thin-walled mouldings)*

MINIMUM DRAFT ANGLE
1–3°

MINIMUM RADII
0.5mm (0.02in)

MANUFACTURING VOLUME
1–10,000m+

TOOLING COST
Low

UNIT COST
Moderate

MOULDED-IN INSERTS
Possible

SIMILAR PROCESSES
Injection moulding

Design guidance: *Maximum wall thicknesses are determined by the cooled density of the PUR, i.e., the greater the density the thinner the maximum wall thickness. Bayer's most rigid PUR, Baydur 110, is ideal for large thin-walled mouldings (similar to many injection mouldings) and ideally should be specified for walls between 3 to 6mm thick (0.1–0.2in). In contrast, the company's lowest-density rigid PUR, Baydur 20, can be moulded up to 25mm (1in) thick. For large open voids with simple geometry, bulk solid mouldings can be of a much greater thickness. This applies to both structural and elastomeric PUR.

It is worth noting, however, that the geometry and surface of the moulded void always have a bearing on a design's mouldability. Therefore, it is wise to discuss a proposed moulding with a manufacturer.

A perfect surface finish is difficult to achieve because of the nature of the components' reactions and so it is usual to specify a painted finish on RIMs (a very good surface adherence is possible with the correct paints and varnishes).

RIM is typically used for the prototyping and low-to-medium-volume manufacturing of medium to large components that often have similar shape characteristics to injection mouldings, but can also be simple or complex bulk solids. Solid, microcellular polyurethane resins, such as Bayer's Baydur 110, are rigid and high density. In contrast, Baydur 20 has a low density and, although still rigid, it is less strong than Baydur 110. These less resilient but useful properties are caused by the creation of a significant volume of very small gas bubbles during the reaction process. Additionally, Baydur 20 creates a skin (a 'self-skinning foam') where it contacts the mould and, like all PURs, can take on a range of colours and surface textures.

The strength of rigid PURs can be enhanced by the inclusion of short-strand fibre reinforcement. The foam itself can also be injected into voids between walls to reinforce composite mouldings. Products of this secondary RIM process are called foam-cored composites.

Christophe Pillet's Toy Table with a rotationally moulded (LDPE) leg frame.

Foam moulding uses elastomeric PURs (elPUR) to create either open or closed cell foams that are soft and flexible, and can return to their original form. Typically, foam moulding of this kind is applied to basic mould geometries and so requires no real 'injection' pressure, since it easily expands to fill a mould's void.

Because RIM operates under much lower pressures than injection moulding, the tooling is also much cheaper. Moulds for prototyping and batch production can be made from GRP and wood, whereas for volume production, aluminium is more appropriate.

Rotational moulding (rotomoulding)

Rotational moulding (RM) creates medium-to-large, hollow, thin-walled components commonly using a limited but versatile range of thermoplastics. Blanking sections of mouldings can be machined out to create holes and, in the case of products with large open voids such as bins, two components are moulded together and then separated with a cut to create the openings. The manufacturing process involves loading a thermoplastic powder into a closed two-part (or more) aluminium mould that is then rotated on two axes within a heated oven until the plastic has melted and distributed itself evenly over the inside surface of the mould.

Tooling for rotomoulding is cheap compared to injection moulding and comparable with RIM. Cast-aluminium or fabricated-steel moulds are the most common. For prototyping with very short lead times and small production runs, it is possible to manufacture moulds from plastic composites. Carbon fibre rather than GRP is preferable, but despite the high quality of such moulds, the heating and cooling processes of production degrade this type of tooling, limiting its production runs to approximately 100.

SHAPES
Thin-walled, hollow, closed

PLASTICS
HDPE, LDPE, nylon (polyamides), PC, PE, PP, PVC, PUR

MANUFACTURING TOLERANCE
0.5–1mm (0.02–0.04in)

WALL THICKNESS (MIN–MAX)
2–15mm (0.08–0.6in)

MINIMUM DRAFT ANGLE
1–3°

MINIMUM RADII
2mm (0.08in)

MANUFACTURING VOLUME
100–10,000m+

TOOLING COST
Moderate

UNIT COST
Low to moderate

MOULDED-IN INSERTS
Possible

SIMILAR PROCESSES
Blow moulding

Design guidance: Because of the manner in which the molten plastic flows over the tool, RM lends itself to simple, curved forms without fine surface detail. As with all moulding processes, the mould's overall geometry, surface detail and radius size affects the mouldability of a design. As a general rule, rotomouldings should be no more than 1:4 in proportion. Long, thin extremities such as the legs of a monobloc chair would be impossible to rotomould with the geometry of an Air Chair (see p154); but with a generous radius into larger diameter legs and a much-enlarged void between the walls, rotomoulding becomes possible.

When designing a rotomoulded product with twin walls that largely run in parallel with each other, there must be enough space for the plastic to flow easily (although brief convergence is not such an issue). As a rough guide, any restricted void width should be a minimum of five times the thickness of the wall.

Typical wall thicknesses are between 3 and 6mm (0.1–0.2in), with a limitation on greater thicknesses created by different plastics' abilities to conduct heat through to the inside of the mould (not just if adding further layers but also in thick single-stage mouldings).

The rotational-moulding process allows for different types of plastics to be layered in the mould, whether for cost-saving purposes while maximizing physical properties, or simply for colour contrasts when a cut edge is shown. Also, inserts can easily be moulded in, as can previously moulded components, providing that they have a higher melt point than the second-stage plastic.

Polyethylenes account for about 85 per cent of all rotomoulding because of their low melt points (which require less energy) and their very good flowability. PVC and PP are used for most other thermoplastic moulding, but there is also a growing application of thermosetting plastics such as PUR to rotomoulding. Although usually more expensive than thermoplastics, thermosets present opportunities as they have broader material characteristics than thermoplastics. They also use less energy in manufacture because they require no heating, and have a quicker process turnaround because they cure in less time than it would take to cool a thermoplastic moulding.

The reinforcement of rotomouldings is possible using fibres within the plastic, but PUR foam can also be injected into a finished moulding. However, this would typically only happen when there were restrictions on a moulding's dimensions and/or weight, therefore limiting its strength (some emergency stretchers are made in this way).

Wood

Wood

The beauty and inherent diversity of wood's grain and colour make it a material like no other; it is renewable, its strength-to-weight ratio can outperform steel, it has useful elastic qualities and it feels warm to the touch. Hardwood and softwood tree species encompass a great range of material properties; within each genus, every piece of wood also has unique variances of performance and aesthetics, some useful and desirable, some not.

Wood was the original furniture-making material, yet despite this ancient lineage, wooden furniture does not have to be traditional. In fact, sourced responsibly and as a renewable resource, wood and wood fibre have significant parts to play in contemporary design and a sustainable future.

For industry and consumers, the responsible sourcing of timber has become easier through the activities of organisations such as the Forest Stewardship Council (FSC) and Friends of the Earth (FoE). But, the world is still cutting down more trees than are being replaced through planting: 20 per cent of the world's population currently uses more than 75 per cent of its timber, and it is predicted that by 2050, world timber consumption will have increased by more than 50 per cent (source: Resource Conservation Alliance).

This demand is set against a backdrop of depleted natural resources, competition for suitable land and the challenges of climate change. However, providing that there is much greater replenishment and use of fast-growing softwoods and northern hemisphere hardwoods (such as ash and birch) and provided that the exploitation of unstewarded tropical hardwoods for trivial applications continues to decline, increases in timber use may be possible to sustain in the future. Also, the potential of wood-fired power stations and the carbon-capturing abilities of trees mean that rationales for the augmented and widespread production of timber increasingly make sense. Such a shift will have to be a long-term plan, however, since the time taken for hardwood trees to grow big enough for broad use is a minimum of 30 to 60 years; and because of our collective lack of foresight, hardwood timber harvesting in Europe, at least, will need to decline from 2020 due to a lack of resources.

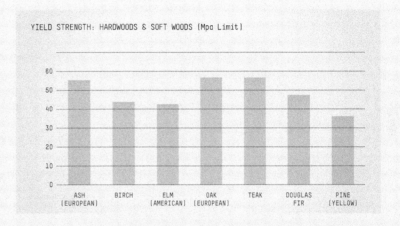

YIELD STRENGTH: HARDWOODS & SOFT WOODS (Mpa Limit)

Yield strength is the point at which a material deforms permanently under a stress or load. It is measured in megapascals (MPa).

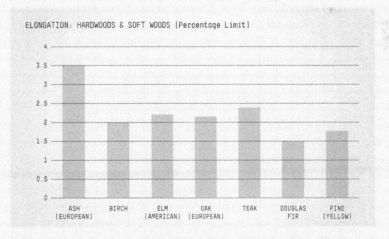

ELONGATION: HARDWOODS & SOFT WOODS (Percentage Limit)

Elongation is a measure of the point at which materials break under tension. The length of this elongation prior to breaking is expressed as a percentage of the materials' original length.

Hardwoods and softwoods

The terms 'hardwood' and 'softwood' describe botanical groupings rather than being collective descriptions of characteristics, although, with a few exceptions, most hardwoods are harder, denser and stronger than softwoods. Hardwood trees are angiosperms (broad-leaved flowering plants) and softwood trees are coniferous (cone-bearing plants with needle-shaped leaves).

Softwoods mostly grow in the northern hemisphere, while hardwoods populate both the north and south. Hardwoods are evergreen in tropical regions and deciduous in northern regions and equivalent southern latitudes. Deciduous, broad-leaved hardwoods are generally slower growing than their tropical cousins and, in all regions, softwoods are among the fastest-growing of all.

Classification

Readers should note that the strength or elasticity of a timber needed for a chair is very different to that needed for a solid wood cabinet. So while it is possible to make a chair from almost any wood, only certain species have the right characteristics for such a demanding application. Also, timber used for volume and mass production needs to be consistently straight-grained and knot-free enough to be mass processed. Some tree species are naturally like this and others can be encouraged to grow in this way by good stewardship.

BOARD MATERIALS AND ENGINEERED WOODS

Man-made boards were developed to counter the inherent instability and inconsistency of solid timbers and to enable much larger surface areas to be covered using single stable components. While the development of plywood can be traced back to the ancient Egyptians, it was not until the Industrial Revolution that laminated materials began to be used. The sophisticated production of plywood did not begin in earnest until the interwar period, when improvements in glue technologies and forming processes made possible the consistent manufacture of sheet materials and 3-D laminated forms in large volumes.

Veneered man-made boards (substrates) account for a large proportion of the materials employed by wooden furniture manufacturers and are used primarily because they can be processed at a significantly lower material and labour cost than solid wood. Also, man-made boards are easy to store and dimension, and within the construction industry their standardisation enables the systemisation of building processes. The use of urea-formaldehyde glues in sheet-material manufacture will eventually be phased out due to their contribution to VOC emissions, which damage health and the environment.

The standard sheet size for man-made boards is 1220mm x 2440mm (48 x 96.1in), but larger and smaller sizes are available to order.

Blockboard and laminboard (lumberboard)

These are similar to plywood, but instead of successive layers of veneers they are constructed from a solid wood core with a plywood outer skin. This provides much greater rigidity and stability than plywood and so is highly suitable for load-bearing surfaces such as shelves. However, their higher cost means that they are less commonly used than MDF or plywood. Because of blockboard's construction, movement in the timber substrate can show through on a veneered surface and so for the highest-quality manufacturing, laminboard is more suitable.

Blockboard's core consists of softwood or hardwood strips (typically twice the width of their thickness), laid flat and oriented in the same direction. Some of these timber strips run the length of a board, but most are shorter lengths butted together. Laminboard's core consists of many thin (typically softwood) strips of timber, laid on their edges and all oriented in the same direction.

Fibreboard

This is made from reconstituted wood fibre that is either dry-mixed with adhesive (MDF) or wet-mixed without, and pressed into sheets.

Medium density fibreboard (MDF) was introduced in the 1970s and transformed furniture and joinery construction, not least because of its stability and superior surface quality compared to plywood. MDF can be edge-moulded, although the lower density of its core means that sealing and finishing the machined edge surface is problematic and requires several more coats of sealant varnish, lacquer or paint than the board's surface. MDF also makes an excellent substrate for wood veneers and surface laminates.

Hardboards share surface characteristics with MDF but are weaker, as they are manufactured without adhesive resins. Through the combination of heat and pressure, wood fibres and naturally occurring wood resins unify to produce sheet materials with either one or two smooth surfaces.

A detail of Hans Wegner's The Chair. The backrest has been jointed and CNC routed into its final form rather than being steam bent or laminated. Such a jointing and material removal process is relatively expensive.

Using Windsor-chair-making methods, Ercol developed its Love Seat. Manufactured from elm or ash to very high tolerances by highly skilled craftspeople, the seats achieve great strength and resilience despite their minimal structure.

David Colwell's C3 Stacking Chair is made entirely from ash – both solid and steam bent – using sustainable thinned saplings from plantations.

Particle board

Various grades of wood chips or flakes are mixed with adhesives and compressed to form particle boards. Softwoods and hardwoods are used in their manufacture, as is a growing amount of waste timber, both from factory waste and recycled timber product waste. Particle boards are cheaper than plywood, blockboard or MDF, but are also weaker. They tend to be hidden within construction due to their generally unappealing surface qualities, although oriented strand board (OSB) and flakeboard are increasingly used uncovered within architecture.

Chipboards make up the largest group of particle boards and are available in a range of qualities: standard-quality single-layer chipboard has an even distribution of similarly sized wood chips throughout its thickness; and higher-quality three-layer chipboard is manufactured so that a coarse-chipped core is sandwiched between two layers of finely chipped particles. Three-layer chipboard is the most suitable for applying thin melamine foils as a veneer, but single-layer chipboard is best for surfacing with thicker, high-pressure laminates.

TEMPERATE HARDWOODS

In the following tables, the use of a wood is described as 'chairs' (which includes tables and stools) and/or 'cabinets' (which includes shelves, sideboards and other panel and frame-and-panel constructions). Each wood's primary suitability is listed first.

TYPE	CHARACTERISTICS	WORKABILITY	FINISHING	USES	WEIGHT (DRY)
Ash (American) *Fraxinus americana*	Coarse, straight-grained figure. Usable white sapwood and darker heartwood. Good for steam bending. Cost: high.	Moderate	Good	Chairs, cabinets, tool handles, baseball bats, hockey sticks, veneer.	660kg/m3 41.2lb/ft3
Ash (European) *Fraxinus excelsior*	Coarse, straight-grained figure. Usable white sapwood and darker 'olive ash' heartwood. Good for steam bending. Cost: high.	Good	Good	Chairs, cabinets, tool handles, hockey sticks, oars, veneer.	720kg/m3 45lb/ft3
Beech (American) *Fagus grandifolia*	Fine, straight-grained figure. Stronger grain figure than European ash. Good for steam bending. Cost: high.	Moderate	Good	Chairs, cabinets, countertops, turnery, tool handles, veneer.	730kg/m3 45.6lb/ft3
Beech (European) *Fagus sylvatica*	Fine, straight-grained figure. Good for steam bending. Cost: high.	Moderate	Good	Chairs, cabinets, countertops, turnery, tool handles, veneer.	710kg/m3 44lb/ft3
Birch *Betula papyrifera*	Fine, straight-grained figure, moderate strength and density. Usable white sapwood and darker heartwood. Cost: low.	Good	Good	(Low-cost) chairs, cabinets, constructional veneer or plywood, utensils.	650kg/m3 40.6lb/ft3
Cherry (American) *Prunus serotina*	Medium, straight-grained figure. Lightweight but hard. Cost: very high.	Good	Good	Cabinets, turnery, flooring, veneer, musical instruments.	570kg/m3 35.6lb/ft3
Cherry (European) *Prunus avium*	Medium, straight-grained figure. Lightweight but hard. Cost: very high.	Good	Good	Cabinets, turnery, flooring, veneer, musical instruments.	440kg/m3 27.5lb/ft3
Chestnut (American) *Castanea dentata*	Coarse, straight-grained or full figured. Cost: high.	Good	Good	Turnery, coffins, tool handles.	470kg/m3 29.3lb/ft3
Chestnut (European) *Castanea sativa*	Coarse, straight-grained or full figured. Cost: high.	Good	Good	Turnery, coffins, tool handles.	520kg/m3 32.5lb/ft3
Elm (American) *Ulmus americana*	Coarse, straight-grained or medium figured. Strong, good for steam bending, resistant to rot. Cost: high.	Good	Good	Cabinets, chairs (mainly craft), boatbuilding.	590kg/m3 36.8lb/ft3
Elm (European) *Ulmus hollandica/ Ulmus procera*	Coarse, straight-grained or medium figured. Strong, good for steam bending, resistant to rot. Cost: high.	Moderate	Good	Cabinets, chairs (mainly craft), boatbuilding, flooring, external woodwork.	570kg/m3 35.6lb/ft3
Hickory *Carya illinoensis*	Medium, straight- or irregular-grained figure. Strong, hard, good for steam bending. Cost: high.	Poor	Good	Tool handles, chairs, spoked wheels.	760kg/m3 47.4lb/ft3
Maple (Hard) (American) *Acer saccharum*	Fine, straight-grained figure, strong, dense. Cost: moderate.	Poor	Moderate	Chairs, cabinets, turnery, flooring, musical instruments, veneer.	730kg/m3 45.6lb/ft3
Maple (Soft) (American) *Acer rubrum*	Fine, straight-grained figure, moderate strength. Cost: moderate.	Moderate	Good	Chairs, cabinets, turnery, flooring, musical instruments, veneer.	650kg/m3 40.6lb/ft3

Oriented strand board (OSB) and flakeboard are intended for use in the construction industry and architectural interiors rather than for furniture manufacture. However, when sanded, stained or finished, their grain structure does offer a singular and interesting aesthetic.

Plywood

Consisting of multiple layers of constructional veneers in a range of thicknesses, most usually laid perpendicular to each other, plywood is a stable board that, although not as rigid as solid timber, does not split or warp significantly. To balance the stresses within a board, there are usually an odd number of plies (which means the board is equally stiff in each direction); but four and six plies are also used for structural applications where unequal rigidity in each direction is needed. While the majority of plywood used across the industry is manufactured from tropical hardwood, a significant and growing portion uses birch plywood and other temperate hardwood plies.

The surface faces of plywood are either as thick as the interior plies or thinner if they are decorative and high quality. There are many types and grades of plywood used by furniture manufacturers, the construction industry and boatbuilders, but for the purposes of clarity, within this section only types of furniture-appropriate plywood are described in detail.

Manufacturers use a coding system to describe the quality and type of the wood veneers used and whether the adhesives used to bond the plies are suitable for use in outdoor or damp interior applications. These environmental gradings vary between countries, but the most common are weather- and boil-proof (WBP, which includes marine ply) and moisture resistant (MR). While the WBP rating denotes a high degree of water resistance, the performance of a board is also dependent on the species and quality of wood used in construction. MR only signifies the use of moisture-resistant timber plies rather than a waterproof glue.

Manufacturers grade the quality of a board's ply cores from A to D, with A being the highest quality. Each type of board is also graded to show the quality of its

surface plies: A is the best surface available; B has small defects; BB shows more defects; and WG and X have increasing amounts of plugged knots and other surface defects. Such low-grade boards are, however, still used in furniture manufacture for upholstery carcasses. Boards either have two exterior veneers of the same quality or one face better than the other. Therefore, surface grades can be different for a single board, i.e., 'A–B' or 'B–BB'.

Drawer-side plywood has all of its ply grains running in the same direction and so produces an equivalent strength to solid timber while also being comparatively stable. As its name suggests, drawer-side ply is used for drawer construction and other applications where the majority of strength is needed in one direction.

Decorative ply has one good face of a decorative veneer, which is balanced on the back with a high-quality, although not decorative, veneer.

Flexible (bendy) ply is used for furniture, joinery and shop fitting to create tight curves and flowing forms. The construction of flexible ply is such that very tight radii can be achieved and, although its flexibility can become a weakness in one direction, sheets are rigid in the opposite direction. The most commonly available thicknesses are 3, 5, 8, 12 and 16mm (0.1, 0.2, 0.3, 0.5 and 0.6in) and the sheet sizes are 2500 x 1220mm (98.4 x 48in), 3120 x 1850mm (122.8 x 72.8in) and 2820 x 2070mm (111 x 81.5in). The flexibility of this type of plywood can be widthways ('barrel wrap') or lengthways ('column wrap'). The tightness of a bending radius depends on the sheet's thickness but, for example, it is possible to bend a 5mm-thick (0.2in) sheet around a 5mm radius (0.2in) if applied carefully with proper support.

Multi-ply is most commonly made from 1mm-thick (0.04in) birch plies. This high-cost, high-quality material is chosen for its stability (it has an odd number of veneers) and for the appearance of its edge grain. It is ideal for veneering or with an A- or B-grade surface, simply for clear finishing.

Aero-ply is also a very high-quality birch ply that is manufactured from very thin plies. Finished board thicknesses range from 0.4mm to 12mm (0.02–0.5in) thick and are comprised of a minimum of three

Left to right:

Alvar Aalto's Paimio Chair is made from laminated birch veneers.

IKEA's Ingolf pine dining chair manages to achieve a certain elegance despite the need for its components to be dimensionally larger than if they were made from a hardwood.

Stefan Diez's Houdini Chair is manufactured from birch plywood and solid timber.

Below: **'Kerfed' (repeatedly and regularly cross-cut most of the way through) MDF sheet, known as 'bendy MDF', is good for display-furniture applications; but for elements requiring greater structural integrity, flexi-ply or bendy-ply is more appropriate. Such plywoods are engineered to be particularly flexible in one direction (much more so than regular plywood) and are available with different grain orientations, enabling tight bends to be formed either across the length or width of a sheet.**

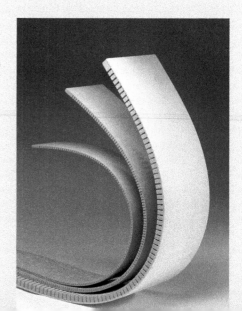

TEMPERATE HARDWOODS CONTINUED...

TYPE	CHARACTERISTICS	WORKABILITY	FINISHING	USES	WEIGHT (DRY)
Oak (American Red) *Quercus rubra*	Coarse, straight-grained figure, hard, dense. Cost: high.	Good	Good	Chairs, cabinets, joinery, flooring, veneer.	780kg/m3 48.7lb/ft3
Oak (American White) *Quercus alba*	Coarse, straight-grained or medium figured, hard, dense. Cost: high.	Good	Good	Chairs, cabinets, joinery, flooring, countertops, veneer, external woodwork.	760kg/m3 47.4lb/ft3
Oak (European) *Quercus robur*	Coarse, straight-grained or medium figured, hard, dense. Cost: high.	Good	Good	Chairs, cabinets, joinery, flooring, countertops, veneer, external woodwork.	730kg/m3 45.6lb/ft3
Sycamore (American) *Platanus occidentalis*	Fine, straight-grained figure. Cost: moderate.	Good	Good	Cabinets, joinery, flooring, veneer.	570kg/m3 35.6lb/ft3
Sycamore (European Maple) *Acer pseudoplatanus*	Fine, straight- or wavy-grained figure. Cost: moderate.	Good	Good	Cabinets, chairs (mainly craft), turnery, flooring, musical instruments, veneer.	640kg/m3 40lb/ft3
Walnut (American) *Juglans nigra*	Coarse, straight-grained or medium figured, hard, dense. Cost: very high.	Good	Good	Cabinets, chairs (mainly craft), turnery, flooring, countertops, veneer.	670kg/m3 41.8lb/ft3
Walnut (European) *Juglans regia*	Coarse, straight-grained or medium figured, hard, dense. Cost: very high.	Good	Good	Cabinets, chairs (mainly craft), turnery, flooring, gun making countertops, veneer.	670kg/m3 41.8lb/ft3

ultra-thin plies. Such plywoods tend to be used for model-making, lighting, domestic products and aircraft, but they can also be used create thicker laminations (this is an expensive approach, but for one-offs or low-volume production the numbers can make sense).

Veneers and laminates

(For formable surfacing: profile wrapping or membrane pressing see p209; for solid surfacing see p177)

Veneers, high-pressure laminates and melamine (and other plastic) foils are used for surfacing substrates to create decorative and resistant surfaces. These substrates can in some cases be metal or plastic, but low-cost timber-board materials make up the majority of the substrates.

Veneers are either constructional plies used for lamination and plywood manufacture, or alternatively they are decorative plies that cover a structural substrate. For many consumers, a veneered product seems inferior to one made from solid wood, but few can afford the latter due to the cost of the materials plus the labour and production costs of its manufacture. Veneers are, however, a very cost-efficient and more sustainable way of using

endangered or slow-growing hardwoods that are laid over lower-cost and lower-impact substrates.

The way in which a veneer is cut from a log determines its pattern and, to some degree, its performance. The most economical way to cut veneers is rotary cutting, a process by which a knife peels a veneer from a long trunk section of a tree. It is mainly used for making constructional veneers, but can also create decorative veneers such as bird's eye maple. For most decorative veneers, however, various slicing methods are used, which produce veneers that have undergone less stress in cutting and, as a consequence, are more stable. Decorative veneers are available as either natural veneer-cut effects, which can be stained, or as engineered, reconstituted veneers, often with remarkable patterning and consistency. For volume production, a much more limited selection is available as pre-veneered boards, although special orders can be commercially viable if the volume is high enough.

For the mass manufacture of furniture, either pre-veneered boards produced by specialist firms or paper-backed veneers on large rolls are used, in conjunction with easy-to-apply glue films.

High-pressure laminates (HPLs), generically known as Formica, are commonly used for work surfaces such as kitchen countertops, but their toughness also makes them suitable for flooring systems. HPLs are resistant to impact, wear, heat and chemicals, making

them the most resilient products available for surfacing furniture. They are produced by infusing layers of paper with phenolic resin and then, by the application of heat and high pressure, are transformed by the cross-linking of their layers into a unified and virtually 'bomb-proof' material. It is possible to post-form some HPLs, such as those found on radiused countertop edges, but this process requires dedicated manufacturing technologies and cannot be undertaken in a small workshop. Printed decorative surface layers and overall textures provide an endless range of product possibilities, and even though solid surfacing such as Corian® has become more fashionable, HPLs are still as versatile as ever.

Melamine foils are thinner and significantly cheaper than HPLs. They are also weaker, but this is partly due to them being less than 10 per cent of the thickness of an HPL. However, their flexibility and ease of application make these duroplastic foils cost-effective and affordable. Most domestic and contract furniture that incorporates some kind of board material surfacing uses either melamine or other foils for profile wrapping and membrane pressing. Melamine foils are able to feature some relief texture, colour and surface patterning and are manufactured in a similar way to HPLs – by infusing paper with melamine resin that is cured using heat and high pressure.

TROPICAL HARDWOODS

TYPE	CHARACTERISTICS	WORKABILITY	FINISHING	USES	WEIGHT (DRY)
Black durian *Coelostegia griffithii*	Straight-grained, feint figure. Cost: n/a. FoE rating: vulnerable*	Moderate	Good	Chairs, cabinet making, joinery.	700kg/m3 43.7lb/ft3
Idigbo *Terminalia ivorensis*	Medium coarse, straight-grained. Cost: n/a. FoE rating: vulnerable*	Moderate	Good	Chairs, cabinet making, joinery.	550kg/m3 34.3lb/ft3
Iroko *Chlorophora excelsa*	Coarse, straight-grained. High oil content, good for steam bending. Cost: high. FoE rating: lower risk*	Good	Good	Exterior and interior furniture, joinery, boatbuilding.	670kg/m3 41.8lb/ft3
Mahogany (Brazilian) *Swietana macrophylla*	Fine/medium-grained, ribbon-figured, particularly quarter-sawn. Cost: very high. FoE rating: vulnerable*	Good	Good	Cabinets, chairs, joinery, veneer.	580kg/m3 36.2lb/ft3
Obeche *Triplochiton scleroxylon*	Hard, fine-grained, relatively light. Cost: n/a. FoE rating: lower risk*	Good	Good	Joinery, cabinets, veneer.	400kg/m3 25lb/ft3
Sapele *Entandrophragma cylindricum*	Fine/medium-grained, ribbon-figured, particularly quarter-sawn. Similar to mahogany. Cost: high. FoE rating: vulnerable*	Good	Good	Cabinets, chairs, joinery, veneer.	540kg/m3 33.7lb/ft3
Teak *Tectona grandis*	Medium-grained. High oil contents. Mostly plantation timber. Cost: very high. FoE rating: vulnerable for wild teak*	Good	Good	Exterior and interior furniture, cabinets, chairs, joinery, turnery, boatbuilding.	660kg/m3 41.2lb/ft3
Utile *Entandrophragma utile*	Medium-grained, striped figured, particularly quarter-sawn. Cost: n/a. FoE rating: vulnerable*	Good	Good	Exterior and interior furniture, cabinets, chairs, joinery, boatbuilding, flooring, veneer.	670kg/m3 41.8lb/ft3
Zebra wood (Zebrano) *Astronium fraxinifolium*	Fine/medium-grained, contrasting streaked figure. Cost: very high. FoE rating: vulnerable*	Poor	Good	Cabinets, veneer, turnery.	940kg/m3 58.7lb/ft3

*FoE rating: Friends of the Earth 'At Risk' rating

Wood finishes

All planed, scraped or sanded wood needs some kind of protective coating or absorbed finish to prevent damage through staining, abrasion, moisture ingress or ultraviolet light. These finishes also enhance the wood by adding depth using lacquers or oils, or by adding colour using translucent stains or paint. Choosing an appropriate finish is mostly straightforward, but none will work to their full potential unless the moisture content of the wood is satisfactory and its surface is suitably prepared.

Oils are simple to apply, making it easy for unskilled hands to achieve consistently good results. Although oil finishes are ideal for tropical woods with a naturally high oil content, such as iroko or teak, they have become an increasingly popular finish for exterior and interior woodwork and furniture over the past decade. Although for craft production there is a burgeoning selection of organic and quick-drying oil finishes, within industry the same basic types of oil are used or prescribed for products.

For interior furniture, tung oil or Danish oil are the most suitable, since they dry to a hard finish, although they need several hours between coats. Tung oil, produces the hardest-wearing surface, is the most resistant to water and heat, but it is not suitable for food-preparation surfaces, such as kitchen countertops or chopping boards. Danish oil is good for table surfaces and can be used on countertops, although no food should be prepared directly on such a surface. For food-contact surfaces, there are several brands of non-toxic countertop and salad-bowl oils.

Wax finishes are mainly used for craft furniture and can be applied either as a stand-alone finish or as an addition to lacquer or varnish. Easy-to-apply wax finishes are mixtures of beeswax, carnauba wax and turpentine; while there is no specific advantage in using wax, its pleasing aroma and the fact that it is natural make it appealing to many people. French polish is little used in contemporary furniture manufacture due to the time-consuming nature of its application and the ease and availability of a great many other finishes that do not require such skilful application. French polish is, however, still relevant to high-quality, low-volume traditional furniture making.

In all realms of furniture production, apart from some small workshops, lacquer, varnish and paint are applied by spraying; a process that achieves the best-quality finishes using the lowest volume of materials. Quick-drying finishes are advantageous because they speed up the through-put of work and reduce the risk of dust and particles settling on a

Top, left to right:

A vast selection of decorative veneers is available, but the range of veneer types on pre-veneered boards is much more limited.

HPLs are high-pressure laminates able to withstand high temperatures and resist staining.

Melamine- and PVC-surfaced boards are ubiquitous in furniture manufacturing and, although not as tough as HPLs like Formica, they are ideal for applications such as shelving or kitchen cabinet doors.

Above, left to right:

PU varnish is ideal for most interior timber furniture.

The base of Table Layer by Gallotti & Radice is assembled from stackable wooden parts that are stained or painted.

Poul Kjaerholm's PK0 Chair is made from painted wood.

Left: The oak legs of Christine Birkhoven's Pic Table have an oiled finish.

SOFTWOODS

TYPE	CHARACTERISTICS	WORKABILITY	FINISHING	USES	WEIGHT (DRY)
Cedar (Western Red) *Thuja plicata*	Soft, fine-grained, resinous, rot resistant. Cost: high.	Good	Good	Exterior cladding, shingles, joinery.	380kg/m3 23.7lb/ft3
Douglas Fir *Pseudotsuga menziesii*	Coarse, straight-grained, resinous. Cost: low.	Good	Moderate	Construction, joinery.	532kg/m3 33.2lb/ft3
Larch *Larix decidua*	Medium figure, straight-grained, resinous. Cost: low.	Moderate	Moderate	Joinery, boatbuilding.	570kg/m3 35.5lb/ft3
Pine (Ponderosa) *Pinus ponderosa*	Coarse, straight-grained, non-resinous. Cost: low.	Moderate	Moderate	Cabinets, chairs, joinery, construction.	490kg/m3 30.5lb/ft3
Pine (Western White) *Pinus monticola*	Fine, straight-grained, feint figure, resinous. Cost: low.	Good	Good	Furniture, joinery, construction.	470kg/m3 29.3lb/ft3
Pine (Yellow) *Pinus strobus*	Soft, fine-grained, resinous. Cost: low.	Good	Good	Cabinets, chairs, joinery, musical instruments, construction.	410kg/m3 25.6lb/ft3
Redwood (European) *Pinus sylvestris*	Moderate/fine-grained, non-resinous. Cost: low.	Moderate	Good	Cabinets, chairs, joinery, construction.	510kg/m3 31.8lb/ft3
Spruce (Norway) *Picea abies*	Moderate/fine-grained, resinous. Cost: low.	Good	Good	Joinery, musical instruments, construction	460kg/m3 28.7lb/ft37
Spruce (Sitka) *Picea stichensis*	Moderate/fine-grained, non-resinous. Cost: low.	Good	Good	Joinery, musical instruments, construction	460kg/m3 28.7lb/ft3
Yew *Taxus baccata*	Hard, dense, fine/medium-grained. Contrasting sapwood. Cost: very high.	Poor	Good	Cabinets, chairs (mainly craft), turnery	680kg/m3 42.5lb/ft3

still-drying surface. For many years, industry has been using solvent-based, fast-drying lacquers, varnishes and paints, but because they contain ingredients such as nitrocellulose, which has high levels of volatile organic compounds (VOCs), there has been a legislated and cultural shift towards using water-based low-VOC finishes, many of which are almost as quick drying as their predecessors. VOCs contribute to environmental pollution and pose a risk to human health.

Wood stain is used to colour one species so it appears more like another, to match mismatched components made of the same species or to create a new colour, whether natural or not. Because stain is absorbed more readily by the more porous early-wood parts of the annual growth rings, all woods with distinct growth rings have a tendency for their grain and figure to be 'reversed' by the application of stain, i.e., the early wood becomes darker than the previously darker late-wood rings (the darker the stain, the more this effect occurs).

There are three types of wood stain: oil, spirit and water. All three have advantages and disadvantages. Oil stains dry quickly and are popular for not raising the grain, but they are not commonly used for

internal applications. Spirit stains have been favoured by industry for many decades, but because of their VOC content, they are gradually being phased out and replaced by water-based stains. Water-based stains have the disadvantage of introducing moisture to dried timber and also of raising the grain. However, their performance is continually improving and their use growing in popularity.

Wood manufacturing processes

JOINTING

Biscuit joints

SHAPES
Prismatic

MANUFACTURING TOLERANCE
0.5-1mm (0.02-0.04in)

MANUFACTURING VOLUME
1-10,000+

MANUFACTURING SPEED
Slow

UNIT COST
Moderate

TOOLING COST
None

SIMILAR PROCESSES
Dowelling, edge joints

Biscuit joints are used in cabinet construction and for strengthening edge joints between boards that would otherwise be tongue and grooved or rub jointed. Butt, edge-to-edge and mitred biscuit-joint slots are cut using a hand-held plunge saw, but it is also possible for edge-to-edge joints to be routed as slots.

Opposing slots are machined into the mating surfaces or edges of the workpieces to be joined, before compressed and snugly fitting elliptical biscuits and glue are placed into the circular slots. Then, the opposing workpiece is placed on to the biscuit and the whole assembly cramped together. The biscuit absorbs some of the glue and swells to hold fast within each slot. For edge-to-edge joints, long or continuous slots can be routed so that compressed rectangular biscuits, called Tanseli Wafers, can be inserted. These provide a greater glue surface area and therefore produce a stronger joint. Biscuit joints are available in three sizes (although all are the same thickness): no. 0 (47 x 15 x 4mm / 1.9 x 0.6 x 0.2in), no. 10 (53 x 19 x 4mm / 2.1 x 0.7 x 0.2in) and no. 20 (56 x 23 x 4mm / 2.2 x 0.9 x 0.2in).

Butt joints

SHAPES
Prismatic

MANUFACTURING TOLERANCE
0.5-0.1mm (0.02-0.04in)

MANUFACTURING VOLUME
1-10,000+

MANUFACTURING SPEED
Slow

UNIT COST
Moderate to high

TOOLING COST
None

SIMILAR PROCESSES
None

Butt joints are the simplest form of joint although they require gluing or a mechanical fixing to hold the mating surfaces together. In all butt joints that are formed between square-ended components, end grain or at least a board's end is shown. Mitred butt joints create a more elegant effect, but are more difficult to cut and machine accurately for a connecting method such as dowels or loose tongues. Square-ended butt joints are easily dowelled or machined for knock-down (KD) fittings such as cams and bolts, which also benefit from the use of dowels so that timber is braced by components that are comparatively soft while being held in place by the fittings. Butt and mitred joints can be reinforced by the addition of blocks or strips of wood that are glued to the back of previously fixed joints. This is a permanent union and so is only suitable for jointed components. If pre-assembly and invisible fixing methods are required, then the mating surfaces of mitred butt joints can be slotted to include loose tongues or biscuits, but these can be time consuming and costly to achieve.

Edge jointing

SHAPES
Prismatic

MANUFACTURING TOLERANCE
0.5-1mm (0.02-0.04in)

MANUFACTURING VOLUME
1-10,000+

MANUFACTURING SPEED
Slow to moderate

UNIT COST
Moderate to high

TOOLING COST
Biscuit joints, dowelling

Timber boards are edge-jointed to create a wider board and a more stable construction. Most timber boards used in furniture manufacture are 'through and through' or 'plain sawn' (because these are the most productive ways to convert a log). However, because these timber boards are prone to warping or cupping if used as a wide single component, they are edge-joined in such a way as to resist any dominant force of movement by alternating their growth rings so that the arcs face alternate ways (up or down for a shelf). Quarter-sawn timber boards are more expensive than 'through and through' and much less likely to cup or warp.

Edge joints achieve a high degree of strength simply by being glued and cramped, but their mechanical strength can be improved significantly by increasing the contact area of the joining surfaces using an integral tongue and groove, a loose tongue and groove, biscuits or, occasionally, dowels.

Dovetail and comb joints (including tapered finger joints)

SHAPES
Prismatic

MANUFACTURING TOLERANCE
0.3-0.5mm (0.01-0.02in)

MANUFACTURING VOLUME
1-10,000+

MANUFACTURING SPEED
Slow

UNIT COST
Moderate to high

TOOLING COST
None

SIMILAR PROCESSES
Biscuit joints

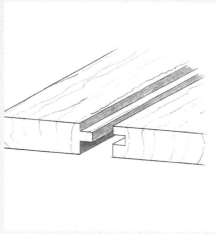

Although decorative dovetail joints are largely the preserve of craft furniture making, they can be machined using dedicated machinery or router jigs. Traditionally, dovetails were used to make drawer surrounds because no other joint could stand up to the stresses of everyday use. There are many variations of two main categories of dovetail joint: through dovetails and half-blind dovetails.

Through dovetails enable the end grain of either the pins or the tails to be viewed from either of the outside faces of the joint. The pin member should be used as a drawer front because the joint is assembled in the other direction i.e., even without gluing, the joint would be held mechanically in place.

Half-blind dovetails are where the tails do not pass all the way through the pin member and are instead held within sockets. This type of dovetail is used in drawer construction when the designer or craftsman does not want the front face of the drawer to show any visible joints, but still needs the benefit of a dovetail joint's strength. An alternative to half-blind drawer construction is to use through dovetails in the drawer front and add a false front that covers the visible joints.

Dovetail joints are labour intensive and therefore costly. Simple commercial jigs are often only able to cut half-blind dovetails, and their fixed-width 'combs' dictate the width of the boards to be jointed. More sophisticated jigs can vary the width and even the frequency of the pins and tails, and can also cut through dovetails.

Such is the perceived value of dovetails that it is not uncommon to see fake inlaid veneer dovetails on medium-cost veneered furniture.

Comb (finger) joints are similar to dovetails but instead of tapered pins and tails, the pins are all parallel-sided. This means that while an interference fit may be achieved, comb joints require gluing to ensure joint integrity.

Dowel joints

SHAPES
Prismatic

MANUFACTURING TOLERANCE
0.3–0.5mm (0.01–0.02in)

MANUFACTURING VOLUME
1–10,000+

MANUFACTURING SPEED
Fast

UNIT COST
Moderate to high

TOOLING COST
None

SIMILAR PROCESSES
Biscuit joints, edge joints

Dowelling is a quick and cost-effective way of joining small door frames and carcasses. While it is easy (by CNC or by hand) to drill the faces and edges of timber, drilling the ends of timber lengths or the edges of large boards can be difficult without a horizontal drilling machine. Designers should consider specifying biscuit jointing instead of dowelling for lower-volume applications but overall, dowelling is the best high-volume jointing method.

For craft manufacturing, dowels can be prepared by hand, but the majority of makers and industry use pre-prepared, compressed beech-wood dowels. These dowels feature longitudinal flutes that reduce friction, but their primary use is to allow excess glue to escape when the dowel is hammered in and the joint assembled. Pre-prepared dowels are usually available in diameters of 6, 8 or 10mm (0.2, 0.3 or 0.4in), but it is also possible to purchase 12mm (0.5in).

Halving joints

SHAPES
Prismatic

MANUFACTURING TOLERANCE
0.5–1mm (0.02–0.04in)

MANUFACTURING VOLUME
1–10,000+

MANUFACTURING SPEED
Slow

UNIT COST
Moderate to high

Top, left to right:
Biscuit joints can be used for butt jointing (as pictured), mitres and edge-to-edge joints.

Tongue-and-groove edge jointing.

Half-blind, machine-cut dovetailed drawer sides.

Tapered finger joints are used to end-join lengths of timber. Although not very strong, such joints enable short lengths of timber to be used in the construction of wooden countertops and timber panels.

Dowel joints are quicker to cut than mortice and tenon joints and are strong enough for most furniture frame and door constructions.

Opposite: **Von Tundra's Prairie Chair uses dowelled and glued halving joints that are not usually employed in chair construction because of their weakness compared to mortice and tenon or dowel joints.**

TOOLING COST
None

SIMILAR PROCESSES
Mortice and tenon joints

Halving joints provide moderate or little mechanical strength without being glued, dowelled or screwed. While not often appearing as major joints (mortice and tenon or dowel joints are stronger), in chair construction, if machined accurately, halving joints can be used. It would be desirable, nevertheless, for such constructions to be dowelled and to use rigid urea-formaldehyde glues rather than PVA.

Cross-halving joints are the strongest joints because they benefit from the intersecting components joint. T-halving joints and dovetailed T-halving joints are almost as strong because one member is captured by the other, whereas corner halving joints and mitred

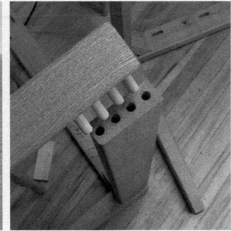

corner joints only gain minor strength from their
adjacent shoulders.

Housing joints

SHAPES
Prismatic

MANUFACTURING TOLERANCE
0.3–0.5mm (0.01–0.02in)

MANUFACTURING VOLUME
1–5000m+

MANUFACTURING SPEED
Slow

UNIT COST
High

TOOLING COST
None

SIMILAR PROCESSES
Biscuit joints, dowelling, mortice and tenon joints

Housing joints are used in the construction of
solid-wood furniture to both support and locate
shelves or uprights and to increase the surface area
and mechanical strength of two connecting boards.
Often, housing joints are employed within a
surrounding dovetailed, biscuited or dowelled frame,
since the male shelves or uprights are not usually
glued or fixed to the other female members. Housing
joints commonly join boards of the same depth and
either reveal the end of the housing 'slot' (through
housing joint), or stop the slot short of the front edge
of the frame member (stopped housing joint), which
also requires that the end of the male component is
notched so it can assemble with a flush front edge.
In traditional joinery and cabinetmaking, dovetailed
housing joints create a mechanical joint between the
male and female components. This type of joint has
the advantage of being a strong joint without the
need for visible fixings, but it is time consuming
to manufacture.

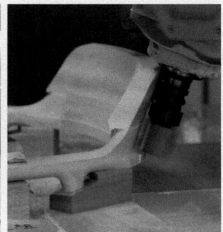

Lipping and edging

SHAPES
Prismatic

MANUFACTURING TOLERANCE
0.5–1mm (0.02–0.04in)

MANUFACTURING VOLUME
1–10,000+

MANUFACTURING SPEED
Low

UNIT COST
Moderate

TOOLING COST
None

SIMILAR PROCESSES
Biscuit joints, dowelling, edge moulding

Solid-timber lipping covers the cut and exposed edges of man-made boards and is usually employed in conjunction with a veneered board surface to give the impression of a solid-wood board. The advantages of using lipping in this way are to reduce costs by using man-made boards and to allow a radius, chamfer or bevel to be applied (features that would not be possible on the board edge or a veneer edging strip). Solid-timber lipping can also rigidify a man-made board, particularly if it is taller than the board is thick.

Lipping can be applied simply by gluing and cramping, but is more usually positioned and strengthened by biscuit joints or loose plywood tongues. It is standard practice to joint lipping so that its top surface is very slightly proud of the board. The lipping is then sanded or routed flush to visually unify the components.

Edging usually describes either veneer, HPL (Formica, etc.), melamine foil or plastic edging strips that are applied to the edge of similarly surfaced boards. However, edging also comprises plastic or thin metal edging strips of the kind found on office furniture or kitchen countertops.

Veneer or melamine edging normally has a thermoplastic glue ready-applied to the back surface, and this is either placed using dedicated edge-banding machinery or by hand with a heated tool such as an iron. HPL and plastic edging is generally attached by the use of contact adhesive, but in theory all edging can use this process.

Mortice and tenon joints

SHAPES
Prismatic

MANUFACTURING TOLERANCE
0.3–0.5mm (0.01–0.02in)

MANUFACTURING VOLUME
1–10,000+

MANUFACTURING SPEED
Slow

UNIT COST
Moderate to high

TOOLING COST
None

SIMILAR PROCESSES
Biscuit joints, dowelling, housing joints

Mortice and tenon joints have superior strength compared to all other framing joints, due to the straightforward mechanics of their connection and also because of the large interior surface area of the joint. When combined with glue, it produces a union as strong as the wood itself. Mortice and tenon joints were developed over centuries through structural necessity since glues were fundamentally weak. Now that glue technologies have advanced so greatly, mortice and tenon joints are, in many applications, over-engineered solutions. Dowels, and in some cases biscuits, can perform as well as stub or through tenons, but consumers and designers still appreciate the surety and aesthetics of apparent construction methods, which through tenons, wedged tenons and loose-wedged tenons provide.

There are many types of mortice and tenon joints, but these can be usefully categorized into three main areas: through tenons, stub tenons and haunched tenons. Usually, when a tenon member connects to the edge of a mortice member, the tenon's thickness is equal to one third of the mortice member's thickness. However, if a tenon member connects to the face of a mortice member then this general rule does not apply. Instead, the tenon has the same thickness as the tenon member itself and is probably divided up into two or three tenon pins.

Through tenons pass right through a mortice member and are either trimmed flush or left protruding with a perpendicular wedge hammered through a hole in the tenon to keep the joint together.

Left to right:
Solid-timber lipping is tougher than a veneered edge and enables radii, chamfers and decorative mouldings to be added.

Machine-cut mortices and tenons sometimes feature rounded edges if the mortice is cut with a router cutter or slot mortice bit. However, morticing machines with square hollow chisels produce square mortice edges.

CNC routing the backrest of a Hiroshima Chair (see pp130–31).

A wide range of decorative and functional profile cutters are available, and specialist tool manufacturers offer a bespoke cutter service.

For low-volume production, wooden spindles and discs can be produced manually, but for moderate- to high-unit production CNC turning becomes increasingly viable.

Traditionally, this joint is unglued and featured on furniture intended for disassembly. However, such wedges can also be a decorative addition for a permanent glued joint.

Stub tenons do not pass right through a mortice member, but typically run two-thirds of the potential depth. Such tenons are used for either the mortice member's edge or face.

Haunched tenons are used in frame construction so that the mortice does not become an open slot at the end of the mortice member. Such tenons are, therefore, only applied to mortices on the edges of mortice members. The haunch (removed section of the tenon) simply stops the tenon being the full width of the tenon member.

MACHINING

ROUTING, WATER-JET AND LASER CUTTING
For information about CAD software and file formats, see p108

SHAPES
Routing (primarailly) flat. hollow or solid; water-jet and laser cutting: (primarilly) flat

MANUFACTURING TOLERANCE
Routing profile: 0.1–0.5mm (0.04–0.02in); water-jet-cutting profile: 0.1–0.5mm (0.004–0.02in); laser-cutting profile: 0.025–0.5mm (0.001–0.02in)

MANUFACTURING VOLUME
1–10,000

MANUFACTURING SPEED
Slow to moderate

UNIT COST
Moderate to high

TOOLING COST
None

SIMILAR PROCESSES
As above

In addition to CNC turning (see below), wood is more commonly routed from sheets using three-axis routers or from blocks using five-axis routers. For both types of routing operations, more than one cutter type or diameter is used during the process. The minimum diameter cutter and slot would normally be 3mm (0.1in), but smaller diameter holes are possible using drill bits that are part of a machine's interchangeable tool carousel set-up. It is worth noting that when routing any sort of internal angle, the minimum radius possible with a cutter is equivalent to its own radius.

The CNC routing of timber sheet materials is suited to low- to medium-volume manufacturing because it can be a slow operation with set manufacturing costs, no matter what the volume. However, without the need for tooling and upfront investment, CNC is an attractive and accessible process for many designers and businesses. More complex five-axis routing has the same characteristics, but for the manufacture of solid-timber components with complex geometries, it is the only viable volume- or mass-production process (the only alternative would be to return to a combination of hand skills and machining, or to use a different material and process).

Water-jet cutting scores man-made sheet materials without them becoming particularly wet. An average jet diameter is 0.5mm (0.02in) and even though it gradually widens, the difference is negligible for thin sheets, although inaccuracies do increase with sheet thickness. It is advisable to consult with a manufacturer about this detail, since different machinery and different sheet thicknesses produce different results. Unless you require very narrow slots, CNC routing is a better, although slightly more expensive, solution for furniture manufacturing.

Laser cutting wood is a minor activity, mainly restricted to decorative fretwork and engraving where the detailing is too fine for any other cutting method, or where the burnt edge is a desired aesthetic. Laser widths can vary between 0.1 and 1mm (0.004–0.04in) in diameter.

PROFILING (MOULDING)

SHAPES
Prismatic

MANUFACTURING TOLERANCE
0.3–0.5mm (0.01–0.02in)

MANUFACTURING VOLUME
1–10,000+

MANUFACTURING SPEED
Moderate to high

UNIT COST
Low to moderate

TOOLING COST
Low

SIMILAR PROCESSES
Edge joints

Decorative and functional timber profiles (mouldings) are manufactured either by routing or spindle-moulding. A great array of tool profiles are available to machine these, but should a designer specify an original profile with a specific set of dimensions, manufacturers either approximate a match or commission cutters to specification. Despite the ease of commissioning bespoke router cutters or spindle-moulder profile cutters, manufacturers and clients often opt for the easier solution and approximate a match. To avoid such circumstances and the potential degradation of a design, it is wise to specify profile and dimension combinations that already exist, or clearly state the need and justification for tooling from the outset of the project.

The largest single-moulding profiles tend to be for cornices or architraves (casings), but in fact most large-scale mouldings are composites of two or more moulded profiles. Not only does this approach make it easier for smaller-scale manufacturers to machine to specification, but it also makes sourcing suitable timber stock easier.

TURNING

SHAPES
Prismatic, axisymmetric

MANUFACTURING TOLERANCE
0.5–1mm (0.02–0.04in)

MANUFACTURING VOLUME
1–10,000+

MANUFACTURING SPEED
Low

UNIT COST
High

TOOLING COST
Low

SIMILAR PROCESSES
CNC routing

Woodturning can either be a manual, semi-automated or CNC operation. It should be commissioned from a specialist manufacturer who is experienced in choosing suitable timber stock and can review and advise on design details prior to a contract.

Small production runs are usually carried out by hand unless a high degree of accuracy is required, but for larger volumes, manufacturers either use a copy lathe to mimic a pre-turned pattern or create a cutting-knife template. This latter option is becoming less common, though, as CNC equipment becomes more widely available.

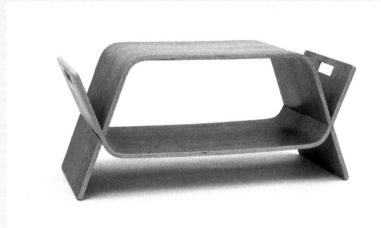

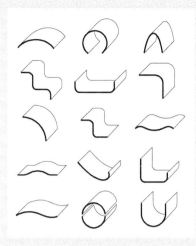

FORMING

Lamination and veneering

SHAPES
Thin-walled

MANUFACTURING TOLERANCE
1–2mm (0.04–0.08in)

MANUFACTURING VOLUME
1–10,000+

MANUFACTURING SPEED
Slow

UNIT COST
Moderate to high

TOOLING COST
Moderate

SIMILAR PROCESSES
Membrane pressing

Laminations are composites, made from thin layers of wood and rigid glue. Plywood is a lamination although because its purpose is normally to be flat and stable, its constructional veneer plies are usually layered with alternate grain directions. Structural laminations with shallow curves can be laminated in the same way, but in order to achieve relatively tight radii and flexible, spring-like qualities, they usually have their plies' grain orientated the same way. Flexible laminations of this kind, however, have a limited range of stress and elongation; if they are over-stressed, their plies and glue rupture, causing de-lamination.

Standard structural veneers are usually made of beech, although birch is also widely used. Decorative veneers and other surface laminates can be part of the initial forming process, although in some applications surface veneers can be vacuum pressed over pre-moulded parts prior to trimming. However, non-standard constructional veneers such as 3-D veneers (see pp138-39) are engineered to be much more pliable than regular veneers so that it is possible to create radii and forms that were previously only possible in plastic.

Standard constructional veneers are produced in three thicknesses: 1.1, 1.5 and 2.3mm (0.04, 0.06 and

0.09in). Their thickness determines the minimum radius that is achievable by their lamination and also the number of plies necessary to create a component thickness. The material and labour cost invested in the number of plies means that there is an even greater need than normal for laminated components to be dimensionally efficient. For high manufacturing volumes, wood lamination is an expensive process compared to injection moulding because of the set labour costs associated with gluing and setting up the plies.

For batch production, male and female formers can be used to create laminations; however, for batch and volume production, vacuum presses that also apply heat are the most suitable technology. For the mass manufacture of laminated components, two-part aluminium moulds are used, which employ either conducted heat or radio-frequency heating to speed up the drying process.

Many furniture components are cut from sections of longer laminations with the same profile. Others, such as one-piece chair shells are moulded individually. All mouldings are manufactured with excess material at their extremities and so require trimming. This operation can be difficult to conduct manually because of problems associated with safely supporting and cutting workpieces, but trimming is made significantly easier by the use of multi-axis CNC-routing technology that drills, trims and separates components.

Profiles with two or more internal angles of 90° and less (which encapsulate the mould) are difficult to manufacture with a low-tech former approach and more so with a vacuum press, since it is hard to exert enough sideways force to consistently or effectively compress the plies and glue (a small amount of spring-back is of course needed to remove such laminations from a mould, or vice versa). However, specialist manufacturers are able to achieve such profiles by using moulds with multiple parts and side actions to apply consistent pressure all around the lamination. Such complex tooling is comparatively expensive and so, where possible, fabrications of two or more laminations should be considered as an alternative.

Compound curves become more difficult to achieve the more pronounced their form and the rate of transition between their planes. Forming compound

Constructional veneers are thicker than decorative veneers and can be laminated into flat sheets of 3-D forms. A minimum internal radius is largely dependent on the thickness of the veneers used.

A wide range of laminated furniture components are available from manufacturers such as SPA Laminates. Components are cut from larger, wider laminations of the same profile.

The RU chair by Shane Schneck is assembled from seven laminated components.

Table, Bench, Chair by Sam Hecht for Established & Sons. The chair frames are steam-bent beech, joined and morticed through a laminated block of beech.

curves externally around a male shape can be easy, but such curves need serious pressure if they form a localized recess. Laminated chair shells often feature such compound surface transitions between the lumbar and thoracic regions, but these are manufactured industrially using significant moulding pressure. To save on materials, increase strength and produce more dynamic laminations, it is possible to manufacture components of varying thickness by laying-in localized, smaller pieces of structural veneer. Such an approach requires high ranges of pressure to unify the areas of transition and so is not necessarily possible for all manufacturers.

Veneering is also a type of lamination but is generally thought of as a separate process. Decorative veneers are thinner than constructional veneers and tend to cover flat man-made timber-board substrates (known as groundwork), either in the production of ready-made sheet products or applied to specific components as part of a manufacturing job. Veneers can also be put on curved, laminated components using various vacuum-bag processes (these need to be supported by a former). Traditionally, veneers were

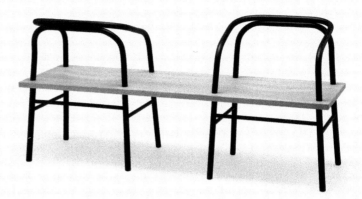

added as a craft process using heated animal-based glues but, in the present day, traditional, paper-backed and engineered veneers are applied using thermoplastic glue films, urea-formaldehyde adhesives and highly efficient vacuum technologies.

Steam bending

SHAPES
Prismatic

MANUFACTURING TOLERANCE
1–2mm (0.04–0.08in)

MANUFACTURING VOLUME
1–10,000+

MANUFACTURING SPEED
Slow

UNIT COST
Moderate to high

TOOLING COST
Moderate

SIMILAR PROCESSES
Lamination

For furniture manufacture, beech and ash are the most commonly steam-bent woods, but elm, birch, iroko and hickory are also well suited to bending. The bending process has been used by boatbuilders, tool makers and musical-instrument makers across the globe for centuries, but it became a truly industrialized process in the 1850s through the activities of Michael Thonet (see p14).

Although wood is naturally flexible, in order to plasticize it sufficiently for its fibres to be stretched and compressed into permanent bends, it either has to be worked green (although this is a craft process with significant limitations) or soaked and then steamed under low or high pressure. Low-pressure steaming is a low-tech craft process, whereas high-pressure steaming increases the throughput of materials and is a high-volume, industrialized process. However, although bends on one plane or axis can be formed en masse in hydraulic bending machines, forming jigs for compound curves, such as the backrest and back legs of a Thonet No. 14 chair (see p14), are easier to prepare and bend by hand one at a time.

Hydraulic bending either creates open bends, such as the Thonet backrest, or closed 'circle' bends (not necessarily circular) that form the same chair's seat or leg frame. Because the steamed and bent components need to be dried while still being held in forming jigs, tooling costs are moderately high, because to sustain continuous manufacturing a large number of jigs will be occupied in drying kilns for up to 48 hours.

Formable surfacing: profile wrapping and membrane pressing

SHAPES
Bulk solids, flat

MANUFACTURING TOLERANCE
0.3–0.5mm (0.01–0.02in)

MANUFACTURING VOLUME
100–10,000+

MANUFACTURING SPEED
Moderate

UNIT COST
Moderate to high

TOOLING COST
None

SIMILAR PROCESSES
Lamination

Profile wrapping applies real veneers, and melamine and other plastic foils to the glued surface of linear substrates, including metal or plastic extrusions and timber or MDF profiles. It creates finishes that are impossible to achieve in any other way. Using the process, extruded plastic and metal windows can receive a woodgrain-effect wrapping, whereas moulded lengths of MDF can receive the same vinyl effect or real veneer, becoming cheaper and more stable than a solid-wood moulding. Depending on the substrate and wrapping type, products profiled in this way can be specified for interior or exterior applications.

Membrane pressing is a process in which board materials, used in the production of panel-based fitted furniture, are encapsulated with thermoplastic vinyl and other plastic foils as an alternative to painted or lacquered finishes and high-pressure laminate surfacing.

Boards with a pre-laminated melamine or vinyl back face are used as a substrate (invariably MDF); these are dimensioned and edge- or surface-moulded by CNC routing to become doors, display panels, textured wall cladding, etc. The faces and edges are then sprayed with a thermoplastic adhesive (typically tPUR) before being laid on the vacuum-forming bed of a membrane-pressing machine. A thin membrane of thermoplastic is tensioned above the bed and heated before an elastic 'bladder' is sucked down on to the membrane, components and the surrounding bed, encapsulating the face and edges of each component. Once cooled, the surrounding excess is separated and the completed components trimmed. The surfacing membranes can feature an almost endless range of colours, textures or imagery, and although historically PVCs have predominantly been favoured, less controversial materials such as acrylic and polyester membranes are becoming more widely used.

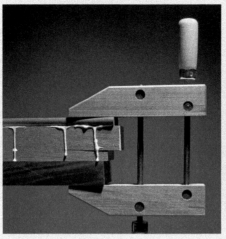

WOOD ASSEMBLY

Adhesives

A broad range of woodworking adhesives are available for a variety of performance requirements and environments. Some craftspeople still use the animal-based glues that were universal until the 1920s, but now a choice exists between PVA, urea-formaldehyde, resorcinol-resin and contact or hot-melt adhesives.

Hot-melt adhesives (HMAs) are only used for manufacturing in the form of glue films for bonding veneers or structural laminations. In glue-stick form, hot melts are a useful and quick way of making test rigs or simple jigs but they are not suitable for product manufacture.

Polyvinyl acetate (PVA) is the most widely used woodworking glue; it is cheap, non-toxic and, in some forms, water resistant. Aliphatic resin is a form of PVA that is more thixotropic and so is easier to apply and handle in certain applications. It is also possible to sand this form of PVA, which is better at resisting heat and moisture, although such conditions are often more suited to resorcinol-resin and urea-formaldehyde adhesives. PVA is softer and more flexible than aliphatic resin, but neither is completely rigid. As a consequence, PVAs cannot be used for structural laminations such as chair components since they are more flexible than the plies themselves, causing spring-back or catastrophic failure. PVAs can, however, be used for applying decorative veneers from batch to volume production.

Resorcinol-resin adhesive is a form of urea-formaldehyde adhesive with outstanding performance; it is the most rigid and stable of all woodworking adhesives and resists immersion in water, boiling and moderately high heat. It is, therefore, the most suitable adhesive for demanding furniture and architectural applications, not least in outdoor environments.

Urea-formaldehyde adhesives are rigid, strong and ideal for wood lamination. Some woodworkers use these adhesives exclusively for carcass and frame construction, although for most of those applications PVAs will in fact suffice. Urea-formaldehyde adhesives are good for applying decorative veneers.

Contact adhesives are used mainly for the application of high-pressure laminate (HPL) to man-made timber boards, particularly in countertop manufacture. Contact adhesives can bond most materials together but because they are not rigid, they work best over a proportionally large surface area.

Furniture fixings and fittings

Whenever possible, in order to save time and money, designers specify off-the-shelf fixings and fittings. If there really is no product to suit a task and it is not possible to change a design to accommodate an existing fixing or fitting, a designer may have to start from scratch. In this situation, at the very least, the designer needs to become fully conversant with all of the parallel products that are available so that their designs benefit from the accrued knowledge of the past. Special orders from component manufacturers or post-processing adaptations from others can broaden the functional and aesthetic range of products, but the additional costs and the need for high volumes to justify any new tooling for a project mean that for most jobs off-the-shelf is best.

Drawer runners

As well as supporting drawers, drawer runners extend work surfaces, cabinet baskets and keyboard shelves. Drawers can be mounted in four different ways: groove running, side fixing, bottom fixing and concealed fixing. The most commonly used types are side fixing and bottom fixing and, apart from the aesthetics of where they fix, there is little difference in performance between them (although soft-closure attachments may not be available for all).

The amount that a drawer can extend depends on the choice between single-extension or full-extension runners. Single-extension runners open to approximately 75 per cent of their depth and achieve

Left to right:

Membrane-pressed or thermo-foiled cabinet doors.

Various wood adhesives should be considered: PVA, urea-formaldehyde, resorcinol-resin, contact adhesives and hot-melt adhesives.

A wide array of castors, wheels, feet and glides are available, even if their aesthetic range can be limited – this example from Blickle comes with a rubber tread.

The ball-bearing action on full-extension runners.

A range of cabinet hinges is available to provide different angles of door opening – this is a 100° cranked hinge.

For flat-pack furniture, 'knock-down' fittings are the perfect assembly solution.

their sliding action with a single plastic roller wheel for loads up to about 30kg (66.1lb). They are low-cost, highly functional fittings. Full-extension ball-bearing runners are medium-to-high cost, precision-engineered fittings capable of loads up to 160kg (352.7lb). As their name suggests, full extension telescopic runners open a drawer to its full depth in relation to the cabinet.

Hinges

The ways in which doors are hung on cabinets and table flaps or bureau fronts compact away are largely dependent on the types of hinges used. Although there are variations of each, there are seven main types of hinges used as furniture fittings. Cabinet doors can either be in-set (set flush within a cabinet frame) or lay-on or overlapping (a door that overlaps the cabinet or frame).

Butt hinge: This standard domestic door hinge is recessed flush into the door and frame. It is well suited to cupboards and boxes. Most often, they are used for in-set doors, but they can be used for lay-on or overlapping doors.

Centre hinge: Mainly used for lightweight cabinet doors, centre hinges can also be used for flaps. They are recessed into the top and bottom edge of a door and the facing surfaces of its frame.

(Concealed) cabinet hinge: The ubiquitous cabinet hinge is used for fitted kitchen cabinets and most flat-pack panel-based furniture. Many variations are offered for easy fitting and adjustment. They are available as 95°, 110°, 125°, 155°, 170° and 177° openers. Cabinet hinges are designed to avoid hitting other doors on closely abutting cabinets and to allow easy cupboard access.

Flush flap hinge: A moderate-strength, flush-recessed hinge, this is used for mounting lay-on or overlapping flaps such as a bureau front.

Flush hinges: Light- to medium-duty hinges used for in-set doors that do not need to be recessed.

(Self-supporting) table hinges: Strong, flush-recessed hinges used for mounting in-set table flaps. The open table flap and the leverage stress is supported by the hinge, not the flap or connecting component's edge.

Soss hinges: Used for concertina and bi-fold doors. They are edge-mounted within recesses to in-set and butting doors. Cylinder hinges function in the same way for lighter-duty applications.

Stays

Stays are used to support fold-down flaps, such as bureau fronts, or for limiting the opening extent of vertically hung doors. There are three basic types: door stays, fall-flap stays and lift-up locking stays.

Door stays: Used for cupboard and cabinet doors to limit how far they open in order to stop the door hitting an obstruction or the hinges tearing out.

Fall-flap stays: Support and limit the opening of fold-down flaps such as on bureaus and cabinets. The stay is either in two halves that pivot at its joint or a single arm that slides and pivots through a bracket on the cabinet frame.

Lift-up locking stays: Used, for example, in high kitchen cabinets with top-mounted hinges. When the door is opened fully, it is held in place by the arm locking, which can easily be released. Gas struts are also used for this purpose.

Knock-down fixings

For the assembly of flat-pack furniture, or for the assemblage of larger constructions' sub-assemblies, knock-down fittings (the generally accepted catch-all name, despite it referring to the latter) are the perfect solution. While the preparation of the components' holes, slots and rebates requires specialist machinery, little more than two screwdrivers and a hammer are needed for assembly. For flat-pack furniture, the cost to the consumer is reduced because storage and transportation are optimized and little or no factory pre-assembly is required.

Self-assembly

Cam and bolt systems enable two panels to be fixed together by the insertion of the bolt head through a hole in the horizontal board and into the cam or housing. The cam or housing is then rotated with a screwdriver, drawing the workpieces together.

Corner plates are widely used to fix the legs of flat-pack tables. The system obviates the need for tenons or dowels and simply requires a lateral and perpendicular hole in the leg and two fine grooves in the frame.

Dowels tend to be used dry in flat-pack furniture and are typically used in conjunction with cam-and-bolt systems or screw connectors.

Panel connectors are mainly used for connecting kitchen countertops.

Knock-down screw connectors are deep and coarse-threaded chipboard screws, usually with hex-key socket heads.

Threaded inserts (screw sockets) are a deep socket nuts with a coarse timber thread on their outside and a fine machine-screw thread on their inside. They are screwed into a pre-drilled workpiece hole to receive fixings or attachments.

Tee nuts are top-hat-shaped barrels with spikes on their rim and a fine machine-screw thread on their inside. The rim is drawn into the wood as a bolt fixing is tightened from the other side of a workpiece.

Misc

Upholstery, structural fabrics and weaving

A designer's approach to upholstery need not be traditional; furniture such as Inga Sempé's Ruché Sofa deconstructs the idea of what upholstery should be, and even though it is more of a padded bench than a lounging day bed, Sempé has successfully circumvented, or at least simplified, the complex fabrication processes that can constitute upholstery. However, rejecting more traditional approaches as a starting point would seriously limit a designer's options, and so in order to gain a professional repertoire with breadth, a good knowledge of 'what lies beneath' is required. To achieve an imagined result in terms of form, detailing and comfort, designers must familiarize themselves with the materials available and each stage of the different fabrication processes so that they can 'reverse engineer' their ideas, and design from the inside out.

Upholstery can be a relatively slow, labour-intensive process requiring skilled craftspeople. It is both a low-volume craft process and a high-volume mass-manufacturing process. The degree to which a design is hand crafted depends on its designer's attitude; what could be considered as the traditional approach of a beech frame with springs, padding and a pattern-cut cover sewn directly over the assembly is only one option. By specifying moulded PUR foam, designers can industrialize the manufacture of upholstered furniture, but such an approach is not always relevant.

Inga Sempé's Ruché is certainly on the periphery of 'upholstery' but it does follow the age-old approach of loose cushions on a frame. Lucian Ercolani's elemental Studio Couch for Ercol follows just such a concept, although it is likely that Ercol simply wished to continue doing what they did best as much as they were following an older tradition. The couch's backrest cushions lean against a one-piece wooden backrest and the seat cushions are supported by interwoven webbing straps. In contrast, Jasper Morrison's Place Sofa system for Vitra uses a semi-traditional approach in its combination of a wooden frame and a tubular-steel backrest support. The reason why these two framing materials are combined is due to cost and efficiency of manufacture – two guiding principles that lead almost all design in its development. The surrounding upholstery combines particulate

polyurethane foam rods and feathers, resulting in lightweight, voluminous cushioning. The covers are not removable, but an approach to upholstery such as Place's would make this possible with few if any visual changes.

Of course, upholstery can mean any type of fabric covering or cushioning, and so Louise Campbell's Prince Chair could certainly be classified this way. The chair's laser-cut steel shell is cushioned by water-jet-cut neoprene foam, which was pre-laminated with felt. Designers who experiment with alternative materials for upholstering furniture should be aware of the principles behind their country's fire safety regulations in this area before starting the design

Typically unconventional, Hella Jongerius's The Worker Armchair uses contrasting fabrics and stitching details to create a singular aesthetic.

Opposite: **Jasper Morrison's Place Sofa for Vitra uses a wooden frame with a tubular-steel backrest support. The upholstery combines polyurethane foam rods and feathers.**

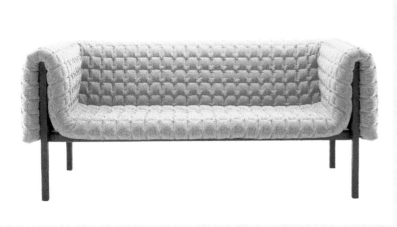

Above, left to right:
Inga Sempé's Ruché Sofa for Ligne Roset has a simple beech frame with a separate quilted cover.

The seat shell of Louise Campbell's Prince Chair is made from laser-cut steel covered with water-jet-cut neoprene foam.

Left: **Lucian Ercolani's Studio Couch for Ercol supports the backrest cushion with an additional spindle frame and the seat cushion with interwoven webbing straps.**

process. Flammability ratings for foam, padding and fabrics must conform to these regulations for products to be sold to the public. A failure to do so could lead to prosecution for negligence, although the accused is much more likely to be the owner of a business that sells furniture than a designer. Businesses are well aware of this and so employ technologists to assess the risk of new or proposed products, but, regardless of this, designers who wish their concepts to be manufactured should go some way toward pre-empting negative feedback. It is interesting to note, however, that products are nearly always the result of collaboration between designers and manufacturing engineers or technologists, so designers will have received good guidance. Regulations for domestic furniture are set at one level, but because contract furniture environs can range from low (such as schools) to high risk (such as prisons), their regulations are more complex, or at least relate to a specific set of risks.

Fire regulations for domestic furniture in all countries should consider the following (shown here are the UK fire safety regulation categories):

_____ Filling materials must meet specified ignition requirements
_____ Upholstery composites must be cigarette resistant
_____ Covers must be match resistant
_____ A permanent label must be fitted to every item of new furniture (with the exception of mattresses and bed bases)

_____ A display label must be fitted to every item of new furniture at the point of sale (with the exception of mattresses, bed bases, pillows, scatter cushions, seat pads, loose covers sold separately from the furniture and stretch covers)
_____ The primary supplier of domestic upholstered furniture in the UK must maintain records for five years to prove compliance.

Design

As with all design processes related to a manufacturing method, almost any imagined upholstered furniture detail is possible but the cost of achieving it may be too high – whether due to it being impractical for a certain application, too expensive or because it creates a loss of comfort or ergonomics. For example, a component cannot be padded sufficiently for comfort yet still achieve a specified thinness; or a complex form upholstered in a non-elastic fabric requires more seams than desired for it to be covered closely. Convex surfaces are easy to cover, whereas concave surfaces need both a system of drawing in and holding the fabric, or a combination of pattern cutting and localized rigidification. However, if a removable cover is the goal, such design details will be much less easy to attain. Loose seat cushions that weigh down and hold a sofa or chair cover into the seating recess would be

one solution to this problem. But if a tight-fitting cover was desired without cushions, a different approach would be necessary, such as rigidification and/or tie-in straps to connect the internal extremities of the cover, under tension, to the chair.

No matter what the goal, working with an experienced manufacturer or craftsperson is essential. Designers should be mindful, however, that producers who only use traditional techniques are often resistant or unable to manufacture an innovative design to a demanding specification.

Techniques

There is rarely only one way to manufacture components, and so designers who are committed to working with a manufacturer or are restricted by a client's arrangements, should be prepared to adopt different techniques and approaches. Manufacturers' methods are dictated by their set-up, experience, preferred practice and how the project is financed.

Framing timber or steel is predominantly used for upholstery framing, each with its own advantages. Hardwood framing is the oldest and most widely used solution for providing structure to support upholstery, and also for offering a strong and tough fixing frame in which pins and staples stay fast. Beech is the most widely used hardwood, but oak, alder and birch are increasingly used as lower-cost alternatives.

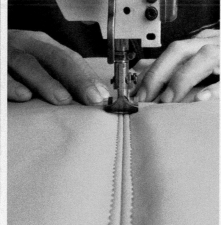

Above, left to right:

Upholstery is a relatively slow and labour-intensive process, and requires skilled craftspeople.

A double-stitched seam.

Right: **The Apollo Chair by Patrick Norguet is an upholstered plywood lamination on a steel base.**

Softwoods are also used for framing but because they are more prone to splitting and less dense, the frames are more likely to break and the fixings more likely to become loose. Softwood is, therefore, the preserve of low-cost furniture with a typically short life expectancy.

Wood laminations can be used to form the substructure to backrests, seat pans, armrests and sometimes sprung slats. Framing for non-linear furniture forms can be created through the use of such laminations, but usually (unless staples and pin fixings are required) steel tubing with different profiles is a more cost-effective solution. Such tubing arrangements can also include attached laminated or plywood panels.

Stitching: there are three main types of stitching used for upholstery: lockstitches, overlock (serge) stitches and chainstitch.

Lockstitches are used for joining and decorative seams. They are sewn using two threads, either as one straight or zigzag stitch line or in pairs as parallel stitch lines (in one process, using a machine with two needles). Because decorative seams can feature a low frequency of stitches, the seam can often separate easily and cause the stitch to break. To counter this problem a reinforcing seam tape can be applied to the back of the seam.

Overlock stitches are crucial in finishing the edges of fabric to stop fraying and to create a finished aesthetic. Overlock stitches are sewn in a high-density band that parallels the edge of fabric.

Chainstitches were the earliest form of mechanized stitching, but because they are formed from only one thread, they unravel easily if the thread breaks. Double chainstitching is more commonly used because of its increased reliability.

Materials

As well as the obvious choices of colour, pattern and texture, upholstery fabrics are also specified in relation to the amount and type of wear they will endure. Their durability and suitability for different environments is measured by submitting them to abrasion testing. There are two slightly different testing systems in Europe (Martindale) and the US (Wyzenbeek), which both involve rubbing a mesh or gauze repeatedly over a fabric sample. The amount of time taken in these tests for the fabric to have noticeable wear is assigned a value; the greater the number the tougher the fabric. The values for light-to heavy use range between:

Domestic (light to heavy): (Martindale) 9000–30,000/(Wyzenbeek) 6000–15,000

Contract (medium to heavy): (Martindale) 20,000–40,000/(Wyzenbeek) 15,000–30,000

Fabric and leather for upholstery are available in set sizes and, although designers will not usually consider this kind of detail at the initial design stage, it is advantageous when planning stitching details to know that most rolls of fabric are 1.4m (4ft 7in) wide and that leather cow hides are on average 3.8m² (40.1ft²).

Apart from adherents to traditional upholstery techniques and materials, the majority of upholstery padding is made up of polyurethane (PUR) foams and polyester (Dacron) fleeces (known as 'batting' or 'wadding'), which are used between foams and fabric to soften edges and to aid the upholstering process.

Upholstery foam is either 'converted', i.e., cut from large blocks into sheets of different grades and thicknesses, or moulded (RIM) into forms that are directly upholstered. RIM mouldings often contain rigidifying armatures and encapsulate fixing bosses or threaded inserts.

The weight of upholstery foam is relative to its density, which is measured in kg per m³. Its hardness or softness is measured by the force (Newtons) needed to depress its surface; for upholstery foams this ranges from 70 to 180N.

Polyurethane block foam is available in a range of densities, thicknesses and colours. There is no agreed colour-coding system related to density or performance. Available densities: 18-65kg/m³ (1.12-4.06lb/ft³).

Reconstituted polyurethane foam (chipfoam) is normally used as a substrate and covered with PU block foam. Available densities: 18–240kg/m³ (1.1–15lb/ft³).

Cold cure foam (PUR) is used for moulding during the RIM process. Available densities: 40–400kg/m³ (2.5–25lb/ft³).

Latex foam is the most durable upholstery foam available, although compared to PUR it has a high cost. Available in three densities: soft, medium and hard.

Structural textiles

Woven textiles can be flexible or rigid and use thread, encapsulated wire or various organic fibres such as rattan for their construction. The more rigid the strands, the less need there is for tension or framing to support the weave. However, thin-stranded, open weaves such as a cane-woven seat, work very well under tension to provide elastic, comfortable cushioning with free air movement, using a minimum of materials. Nearly all structural textiles applied to furniture are industrially produced, pre-woven sheet products that, with varying degrees of handwork, are tension-fitted to frames. A smaller-sized craft industry weaves and applies single strands to furniture by hand.

Structural textiles can be divided into two main categories: flexible, encapsulated open weaves and semi-rigid open and closed weaves.

Flexible open-weave polyester textiles that are encapsulated in PVC are used in a variety of applications that demand strength plus free-draining, sun-screening and wind-dissipating characteristics. They are machine-made, mass-manufactured products, the leading brands of which – Textilene® and Phifertex® – are produced in a range of performance grades, particularly for use as structural slings for outdoor applications. All Textilene®-type textiles block out between 45 and 95 per cent of sunlight depending on the weave size, have high-tensile strength properties and are extremely durable in outdoor environments by being resistant to the UV degradation of performance, colour fading and mould growth.

Semi-rigid open and closed weaves include rattan and rush weaves, plus Lloyd Loom's wire and paper weaving material and similar plastic-coated wire materials. Traditional wicker furniture-making techniques were developed and industrialized in the 1920s by Lloyd Loom, whose unique process created the weave material from woven twisted paper and galvanized wire. This material is then applied by hand to a steam-bent beech-wood frame. While they still manufacture interior furniture with the same materials, the company and many of its competitors have also developed a weatherproof and UV-resistant plastic-coated cord that is woven and applied in exactly the same way.

The majority of natural cane weaves are made from the many species of rattan that grow in South-East Asia. Rattan creepers are split into various widths of cane and are also used in their original thick vine state to create the forms of furniture after being steamed and formed.

Rattan canes and other species of organic weave materials are either converted into flexible woven sheets on rolls, or used as individual canes that are applied directly to furniture, baskets, etc., as part of a pure craft process.

Concrete

Ever since Willi Guhl's extraordinary Loop Chair made from Eternit was launched in 1955, fibre cement and high-performance concrete have held a special fascination for designers. Yet, it could be argued that little progress, in furniture design at least, has been made until recent years, particularly 2009, when Rainer Mutsch's award-winning Linea seating system engendered a resurgence of interest in Eternit. Linea used a cellulose fibre and cement composite that is soft and pliable when freshly made, but requires working quickly by drape moulding over formers.

Concrete Canvas (CC) is a flexible cement-impregnated fabric that hardens on hydration to form a thin, durable waterproof and fireproof concrete layer. CC is available in three different thicknesses, 5, 8 and 13mm (0.2, 0.3 and 0.5in). Its launch in 2010 received significant press and attention from

Top, left to right:

A single leather cow hide covers on average 3.8m² (40.1ft²) and so when designing in leather, the consideration given to wastage in relation to the hide shape and pattern cutting is often paramount.

The Longframe Lounger was created by Alberto Meda in 1993. The structural textile sling is made from PVC-coated woven polyester fabric (Textilene® is the most well-known of such materials), and ideal for exterior applications such as seating.

Lloyd Loom furniture has been using the same woven materials and techniques to manufacture its furniture since the 1920s.

designers, not least because it can be worked anywhere – unlike Eternit's fibre cement. Perhaps the most interesting and productive experiment with this material is Florian Schmid's Stitching Concrete seating. As an exterior material, however, Concrete Canvas is limited by its surface tendency to grow algae. Some might consider such 'degrading' an aesthetic plus, however.

TAKTL's ultra-high performance concrete (UHPC) was unveiled in 2011, and although it does not have the 'craft' accessibility of Concrete Canvas, it lends itself much better to longevity and volume production because of its high compressive, tensile and flexural strength, its superior surface finish and its ability to receive pigmentation. The Bevel Bench by Forms + Surfaces is assembled from two repeated TAKTL UHPC components that are bolted together. The bench's weight means that it does not require a ground anchor system.

Index

Panton Chair (polyproplylene
version), Verner Panton, 1969

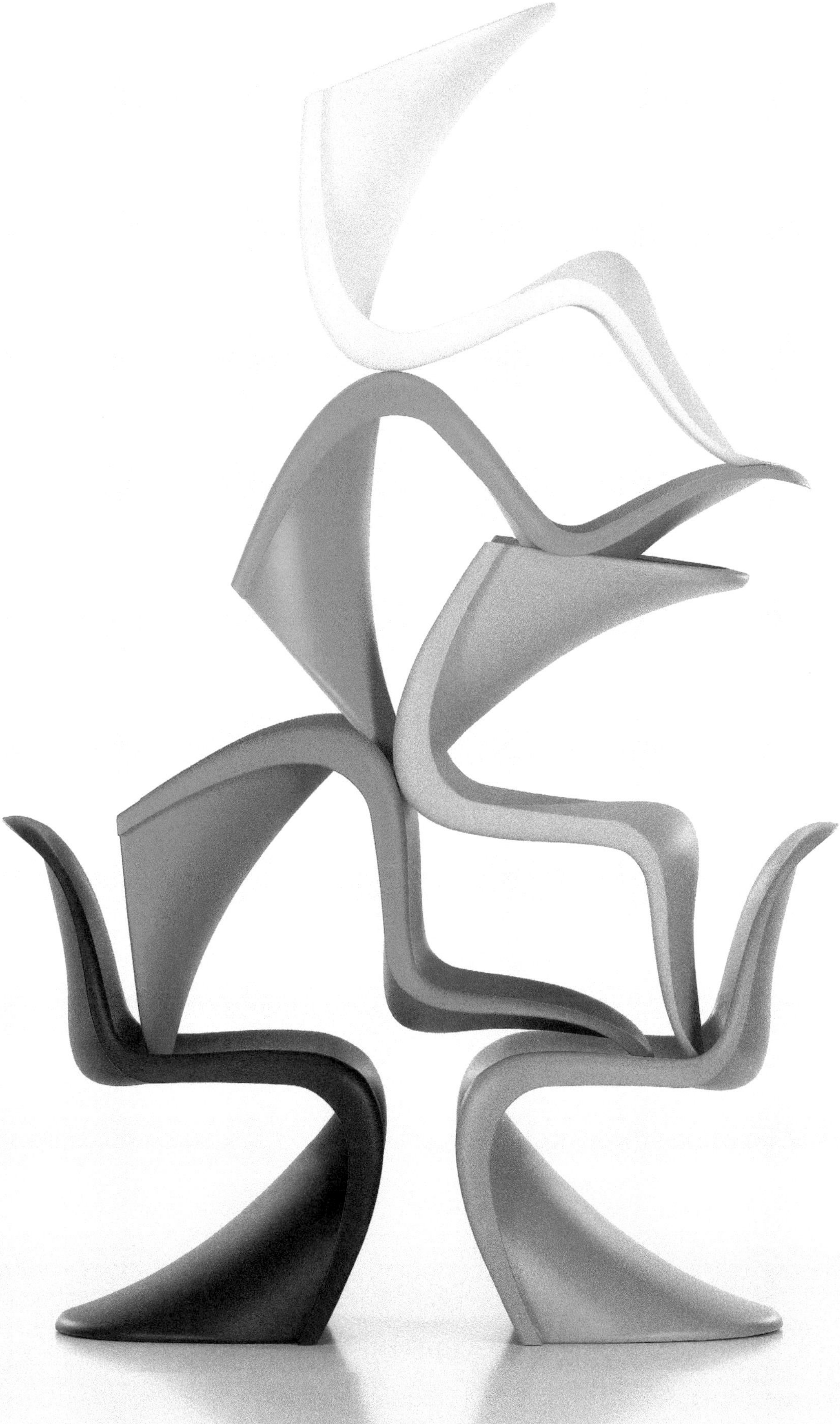

Picture credits

6   (t) Courtesy of Herman Miller, Inc; (b) 606 Universal Shelving System

7   © Vitra

10   (tl) Alessandro Paderni; (tr) Maarten de Ceulaer for Nilufar, images: courtesy of Nilufar, www.nilufar.com, www.maartendeceulaer.com

12   Wittman

15   (l) © Thonet GMBH, Germany; (r) V&A Picture Library, courtesy of the Trustees of the Victoria & Albert Museum, London. © ARS, NY and DACS, London 2012

16   Wittman

17   (l) digital image, The Museum of Modern Art, New York/Scala, Florence © DACS 2012; (r) digital Image Museum Associates/LACMA/Art Resource NY/Scala, Florence © DACS 2012

19   (t) Aram Designs Limited holds the worldwide licence for Eileen Gray designs (b) Thonet.de

21   (tl) Crafts Study Centre, University College for the Creative Arts; (tr) digital image, The Museum of Modern Art, New York/Scala, Florence (b) Design Council Slide Collection at Manchester Metropolitan University

22   Design Council / University of Brighton Design Archives www.brighton.ac.uk/designarchives

23   (t) courtesy of Herman Miller, Inc; (bl) Dansk Møbelkunst – www.dmk.dk; (br) Onecollection A/S, www.onecollection.com

26   © Vitra

30   (l) image courtesy of The Advertising Archives; (r) © Gae Aulenti, Photo: Collection Centre Pompidou, Dist. RMN

31   (l) STARCK; (r) Cassina I Maestri Collection

32   Alberto Meda

34   IKEA

36   © Studio Bouroullec

37   (b) © Stefan Diez Office, photo: Wilkhahn

39–41   all images © Vitra

42   606 Universal Shelving System

43   www.hille.co.uk

44–5   courtesy of Herman Miller, Inc

46   Tripp Trapp, design: Peter Opsvik, manufacturer and photo: Stokke

47   © Foster + Partners

49   © Collection Centre Pompidou, Dist. RMN/ Jean-Claude Planchet

50   © Sellex

51   courtesy of Herman Miller, Inc

52   Imprint chair (Foersom & Hiort-Lorenzen)

54   Current range from Knoll, Inc.

56   © Stefan Diez Office, Photo: Ingmar Kurth

58-9   Michel Bonvin: www.michelbonvin.com

61   courtesy of Nilufar, www.nilufar.com, www.maartendeceulaer.com

62   © Vitra

63   photo: Alessandro Paderni

64   Cork Stools, Jasper Morrison, ·MOOOI, www.moooi.com

65   (tr & b) © Frank

67   Marcel Wanders, photo: Cappellini

68   (l) photo: David Sykes

71   (r) Alessandro Paderni

72   (t) Design by Peter Marigold, produced by Movisi

73   Sumo by Xavier Lust © Cerruti Baleri, photo: Ezio Manliucca

75   (t) © Ronan & Erwan Bouroullec – 2004

76   (t) Sebastian Bergne for Vitra, photo © Vitra

78   (t & b) design: Shin & Tomoko Azumi

81   Carbon Chair, Bertjan Pot and Marcel Wanders, 2004

83   © Paul Tahon and R & E Bouroullec

92   © Ett la Benn, photo Yves Sucksdorff

93   (t) 606 Universal Shelving System; (bl) © Beat Brogle; (br) Manel Saez (design director), Lachezar Tsvetanov (senior designer), Yuji Fujimura (industrial designer), Humanscale

95   image © Henry Dreyfuss Associates

96-97   © Pierandrei Associati (Alessandro Pierndrei, Fabrizio Pierandrei, Stefano Anfossi), Manufacturer: Tecno Spa

103   (b) courtesy of Herman Miller, Inc

104   courtesy of Herman Miller, Inc

105   © Paul Tahon and R & E Bouroullec

106   (tr) Foster + Partners

109   www.exchange3d.com

107   (b) courtesy of Herman Miller, Inc

110   © Morgane Le Gall

111   (b) Photo: Blu Dot

112   © Stefan Diez Office, photo: Ingmar Kurth

113-4   (all) © Stefan Diez Office

115   photography: Plank

118-9   © Paul Tahon and Ronan Bouroullec

128-9   courtesy of Herman Miller, Inc

132-3   photography: Miro Zagnoli and Francisco Gomez

150   photo: Lennart Durehed

151   (t) Getty Images; (b) photo: Michael Roberto

152   courtesy of Herman Miller, Inc

154   (r) photo: Walter Gumiero/Magis

158   © Sellex

159   (r) Sarah Fisher, Matters of Style, www.mattersofstyleblog.com

160 (l) Carl Moore Antique Inc./Houston, TX; (m) © Morgane Le Gall; (r) producer: MUJI Ryohin Keikaku Co., Ltd (Japan), Designer: KGID Konstantin Grcic Industrial Design (Germany), Manufacturer: THONET GmbH (Germany)

161 (l) IKEA; (r) © DACS 2011

163 (l) IKEA; (r) © Vitra

164 (r) courtesy of Tom Dixon, www.tomdixon.net

165 (m) © iStockphoto/ribeirorocha

167 (l) & (r) © Stefan Diez Office, photo: Wilkhahn

168 (r) Mircea BEZERGHEANU/Shutterstock

169 James Michael Shaw

170 (l) courtesy of Herman Miller; (m) photo: Tom Vack

172 (l) © iStockphoto/KristinaGreke

173 © iStockphoto/dlewis33

174 courtesy Claessn Koivisto Rune

176 (r) courtesy of Karim Rashid Inc

178 (m) photo: Gareth Neal, www.garethneal.co.uk; (r) Alberto Meda

179 (r) STARCK

180 courtesy of Ocean Kayak

181 (tl) courtesy of Tom Dixon www.tomdixon.net; (tm) Marcel Wanders, photo: Magis; (bm) Movisi GmbH, www.movisi.com

183 (bl, m & r) photos by Ikunori Yamamoto;

184 (r) courtesy Claesson Koivisto Rune

185 (l) Marcel Wanders, photo: Magis; (r) Condor Cases Ltd.

186 (l) © Vitra

187 Fold/Fold Corten by Alexander Taylor for Established & Sons, photographer: Peter Guenzel

188 (l) STARCK

190 (r) Jim Barber/Shutterstock

192 studio Christophe Pillet

194 photo: James Merrell

196 (l) Dansk Møbelkunst – www.dmk.dk; (m) courtesy Ercol; (r) courtesy David Colwell

198 (l) digital image, The Museum of Modern Art, New York/Scala, Florence; (m) IKA; (r) © Stefan Diez Office, photo: Ingmar Kurth; (b) Neat Concepts Ltd

201 (tl) © iStockphoto/Branislav; (tm) Needs Plastics Ltd; (tr) © iStockphoto/heidijpix (bl) courtesy Christian Vivanco; (br) courtesy Republic of Fritz Hansen; (main) photo Philipp Hänger

204 (m) illustration by Mario Rodriguez, from Fine Woodworking Magazine, © The Taunton Press, 2003; (r) © iStockphoto/acsinger

205 (tl & tr) photo Matthias Wende; (b) Dan Anderson & Chris Held

206 (l) David Bailey Furniture Systems; (m) mortises and tenons made with the Leigh FMT Pro Mortise & Tenon Jig – photo courtesy of Leigh Industries Ltd

207 (l) © iStockphoto/Branislav; (m) Marijus Auruskevicius/Shutterstock.com

208 (l) John Gree www.johngreendesigns.co.uk; (r) courtesy of Spa Laminates

210 (l) Lenetstan/Shutterstock.com

211 (all but tr) Hettich UK, www.hettich.com; (tr) © iStockphoto/lleerogers

212 photo credit: Marc Eggimann

213 © Vitra

214 (tl) courtesy Ligne Roset; (tr) Photo: HAY; (b) courtesy Ercol

215 (tl) © iStockphoto/sarasang; (tr) Nikoner/Shutterstock.com; (b) Artifort/Patrick Norguet

216 (l) © iStockphoto/Elenathewise; (m) Alberto Meda; (r) courtesy Lloyd Loom

217 (tl) Shawn Place

221 © Vitra

224 courtesy Ligne Roset

Acknowledgements

For their support and guidance in writing this book, the author would like to thank:

Editors; John Parton, John Jervis and Susan George, plus Ruth Jindal, Levent Çaglar (FIRA), Anthony Eland and Nicki Theokritoff.

Ruché Sofa, Inga Sempé for
Ligne Roset, 2010

UNWINDING

SUPER MASSAGE FOR STRESS CONTROL

GORDON INKELES

Weidenfeld & Nicolson, New York

SUPER MASSAGE
FOR STRESS CONTROL

Library of Congress Cataloging-in-Publication Data

Inkeles, Gordon.
Unwinding: super massage for stress control / First edition
1st ed.
p. cm.
ISBN 1-555-84050-7.
ISBN 1-555-84148-1 (pbk.).
1. Massage—Therapeutic use.
2. Stress (Psychology)—
Prevention.
I. Title.
M721.I563 1987
613.7′9—dc 19
87-22491 CIP

Acknowledgments

I am grateful to Lee Wakefield, who said "everyone you meet is looking for a way to *unwind*," and to Iris Schencke, who simply said "yes."

I particularly want to acknowledge the following models in these pages: Ringit Gurlich, Chris Tesser, Yvonne Armstrong, Lars Tragardh, Laura McCauley, Alex Bratenahl, Joseph James, Claire Iris, David Mohrmann . . . and Little. And special thanks to Margaret Brown, to the Bourassa and Knapp families, who offered their homes for photography, to my editor, Susan Victor, to designer Tarané Saylor, and to my grip, Scott Harrison, who did all the photo processing.

Always consult a doctor if you are in doubt about a medical condition, and observe the cautions given in the book.

Published by Weidenfeld & Nicolson, New York
A Division of Wheatland Corporation
10 East 53rd Street
New York, NY 10022

Published in Canada by General Publishing Company, Ltd.

Designed and produced by Jon Goodchild/Triad.
Photographed by Gordon Inkeles
Illustrations by Sigga Bjornsson

Manufactured in the United States of America

Unwinding was photographed with a motorized Nikon F-3 using focal lengths of 35 to 180 mm. With the exception of the Insomnia chapter, which was shot in San Francisco, all of the pictures were taken in the natural winter light of Humboldt County, California.

BOMC offers recordings and compact discs, cassettes and records. For information and catalog write to BOMR, Camp Hill, PA 17012.

To my mother,
Alice Taft Inkeles

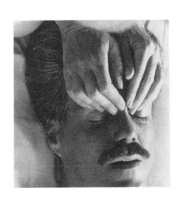 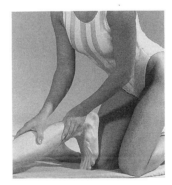

Other books by Gordon Inkeles

The Art of Sensual Massage

The New Massage

Massage and Peaceful Pregnancy

Contents

Preface

This is a book for hardworking people who want to remain relaxed and healthy. What follows is not a complete health plan but it is, perhaps, the missing element in the plan you've been practicing. Have you tried exercising, diets, and self-improvement programs only to find that stress remains a major problem in your life? The smug Puritan may insist, "There's no gain without pain," but in massage we have another idea: you should be able to be busy and productive without suffering from constant stress. And without hurting.

This is not a self-help program. When dealing with stress, almost any kind of self-help is futile because *most seriously stressed individuals cannot help themselves relax.* Exercise, meditation, and hobbies too often become obsessive and competitive, transforming what should have been a relaxing experience into a stressful ordeal. Thinking rationally about stress (or trying hard not to think about it) just makes it worse. Help has to come from outside, from other people.

Massage is drugless stress control. To the executive it means quick energy boosts and a way to cut through fatigue, to the athlete it offers sensational muscle recovery rates after exercise, to the insomniac it brings peace, and to the lover, a new way of touching. It can also provide a simple but amazingly effective facial. Taken regularly, massage can change one's life.

All of the techniques in this book are easy to learn and they all work in minutes. My hope is that you will now open the book to any page and try massage on a willing partner. The results? In minutes you will see stress-induced pain vanish as pure pleasure takes its place. That's one of the things human hands can do; ease pain. But that's only the beginning.

January 1988
Miranda, California

Introduction

There are the continually wearied, wakeful, and nervous business or professional men with numerous and varying ailments, who have learned by experience that "the labor they delight in physics pain," and who find more relief in work than in rest. Mas-sage will sometimes put such on a higher plane of existence and give them a zest for work which they have not derived from any other source.
—Douglas Graham, M.D.,
A Treatise on Massage

The Seduction of Stress

Have you resigned yourself to living with stress? Do you experience daily soreness around the neck and shoulders, aching feet, headaches, lower back problems? Do you have trouble falling asleep? Does exercise leave your body aching for hours? You're not alone. Nonspecific aches and pains are now one of the main complaints in hospital emergency rooms all over the country. Perhaps you've checked with a doctor and discovered that nothing's seriously wrong with you — you're just under a lot of pressure. But isn't every successful individual under a lot of pressure and in a hurry? Must one, then, simply find a way to live with nonspecific pain?

If you accept high stress levels as inevitable, you adjust to various stresses rather than avoiding them; you take pride in the ability to squeeze that extra ounce of effort out, no matter what the cost to the nervous system. And if stress is inevitable, so is pain.

Of course, days with no stress whatsoever would be relentlessly dull — a stimulating life should help you stay healthy into your seventies and eighties. But to remain productive, happy and relaxed in the modern world you need an effective way of controlling stress; you need to find a way to unwind. You can't afford to fool around with drugs; the side effects are too costly. You've had it with toothless self-help programs; you want to feel better right now, not three months from now. You're committed to your career — imagine how much you could accomplish if you were able to work hard without hurting.

Unwinding with Super Massage

Forget the thirty-day program or the regimen of costly therapy—overstressed people deserve a much quicker solution. The techniques in this book work in *minutes*, not days, weeks, or months.

Practiced everywhere on earth since Biblical times, massage is the most ancient form of stress control; it is the original medical tool. The Super Massage program is designed to cut through stress and bring relaxation fast. As you begin to use it, you will learn to recognize the warning signs of excessive stress and take action. On every part of the body you can do things with massage that your partner simply cannot do for himself. High stress levels are accompanied by ominous chemical changes inside the body. These too are reversible with Super Massage. Many of the techniques described in this book are designed to penetrate deep within the body and reach hidden sources of stress. You'll also learn to analyze the chemistry of fatigue and purge the body of acidic irritants that keep the muscles perpetually tensed.

At the heart of the Super Massage program is the amazing fluid release effect, a massage technique that alters, in minutes, the chemistry of

fatigue and stress. The fluid release effect adapts a technique that is employed by Olympic trainers, allowing stressed parts of the body to be super oxygenated while irritating acidic wastes are pressed out of the tissues.

The results simply have to be experienced to be believed: nagging aches and pains disappear, fatigue vanishes, and a sense of well-being takes its place. After fifteen minutes of fluid release massage, muscle recovery rates double and work output increases by more than 100 percent.[*] Massive increases in red and white blood cells are noted in the massaged areas, and oxygen levels also jump. Perhaps most significantly, irritating acidic wastes that would normally linger in the tissues for days, even weeks, are dispersed in minutes.[†] There is, simply, no way outside of massage to duplicate these astonishing effects.

Massage allows people to feel instead of think. It immediately brings relaxation to tensed muscles, reversing the

tendency of stress to create more stress. It eases pain without resorting to drugs. It calms the nerves and stimulates circulation. And it works every time.

Super Massage techniques feel very good and that, too, is part of the program. In

massage, pleasure itself is therapeutic. The astonishing changes that occur during Super Massage—spectacular muscle recovery rates and extended endurance—have been documented by scientists only recently but the techniques have been tested for thousands of years.

[*]Douglas Graham, M.D., *Massage: Manual Treatment, Remedial Movements* (Philadelphia: Lippincott, 1913), p.83.

[†]Hermann Bucholtz, *Therapeutic Exercise and Massage* (Philadelphia and New York: Lea & Febiger, 1920), p. 122.

Modern scientists have provided the evidence that the ancients took for granted. A hundred years ago massage enjoyed a renaissance as an accepted medical treatment for rheumatism, gout, sprains, nervous tension, fatigue, and a number of other afflictions. At the turn of the century the medical community looked on with great interest when a Dutch physician named Metzger chose to massage the chronically aching joints of Denmark's sickly prince. His highness's renewed interest in skiing, just one week after the massage began, brought eager students to Amsterdam from all over Europe (among them, the prince's personal physician) to study Metzger's methods. At the same time, scientists became intensely interested in the remarkable powers of massage. Embraced by healers for centuries, the practice would finally be tested in the laboratory.

First, the experimenters tried to find out what actually happened inside the body during massage. In Philadelphia, Dr. Weir-Mitchell injected the thigh muscles of two rabbits with India ink, then let them run around as usual. One rabbit was massaged regularly, the other not at all. After two weeks the India ink in the rabbit that was not massaged had spread to surrounding tissues, staining them a deep black. But in the rabbit that was massaged there was no trace of India ink anywhere in the body! Urinalysis of human subjects confirmed the findings: a higher concentration of toxins was expelled from the body up to one full week after a single massage.*

But there were even more dramatic changes ahead. Dr. Weir-Mitchell had written a book called *Fat and Blood* in which he examined the chemistry of fatigue and speculated on its causes. Portions of the body, he said, become stagnant either through disuse or constant tension, then diseased. Stagnant tissues, packed with irritating wastes, became tense and tended to remain that way, resisting the effects of exercise and various drugs.

*Dr. Emil A.G. Kleen, *Massage and Medical Gymnastics* (London: J.A. Churchill, 1918), p. 69.

Unwinding with Super Massage (cont'd)

Would massage help? The experimenters noted an elevated red and white corpuscle count immediately after massage, which meant that fresh oxygen was being pumped into the tissues. In oxygenated parts of the body, trapped gasses, acids, and toxins that kept muscles tense began to burn off, leaving stagnant tissues refreshed after a single massage. During the stroking, wastes that didn't combust were squeezed out of the muscles and finally eliminated from the body as surely as the India ink in the massaged rabbit's thigh. Acidic irritants and toxins that usually lingered for days actually vanished in minutes.

But the most amazing data of all emerged from studies of fatigued muscles, which were conducted almost simultaneously in Italy, Germany, and the United States. Normally, muscle recovery rates five minutes after exercise are about 20 percent. But when five minutes of massage was substituted for the five minutes of rest, muscle recovery rates greater than 100 percent were recorded.*

Douglas Graham, the great American physician who devoted his life to massage, immediately began testing the new findings on his patients. He found that just five minutes of massage would restore a specific muscle group as well as two hours of sleep; ten minutes of massage had the same effect as a whole night's rest!† One didn't have to endure fatigue all day long; there was an alternative.

With the discovery of antibiotics and modern pain-killers, however, massage abruptly lost favor in medical circles. The evidence was in: massage could alter the chemistry of fatigue; it could relieve pain and relax tensed muscles in minutes. But now there were pills that seemed to do the same thing even faster. Overworked doctors welcomed a deluge of "mira-

cle drugs," overlooking, for the time being, their ominous side effects. It became more cost effective to knock out the whole central nervous system to cure a headache than to massage a patient for five minutes. A few Olympic-class athletes continued to use massage as a kind of secret weapon (most notably, runners Waldemar Cierpinski and Alberto Salazar, world record holder in the marathon from 1969 to 1982). But for most people massage became a rare luxury to be sampled only by the rich and powerful.

In fact, some of the most pressured characters in history— Julius Caesar, Cleopatra, Louis XV, Ulysses S. Grant, Ivan the Terrible, Indira Gandhi, Bob Hope, Marlene Dietrich, and Henry Kissinger, to name just a few— seldom left home without a masseur. They understood that massage can make the extraordinary physical and emotional strains of leadership bearable. A good masseur can relax almost anyone. Now you can, too.

---

*Professor J.B. Zabludowski, "Über die physiologische Bedeutung der Massage," *Centralblatt für die Med. Wissenschaften*, April 7, 1883 (in Graham, *Massage: Manual Treatment, Remedial Movements*, p.82). Professor Maggioria, *Archives Italiene de Biologie* (University of Turin), Tome XVL, fasc. ii-iii (in Graham, *Massage: Manual Treatment, Remedial Movements*, p.85). *American Journal of the Sciences*, May 1894 (in Graham, *Massage: Manual Treatment, Remedial Movements*, p.93). W.S. Playfair, M.D., *Nerve Prostration and Hysteria* (London: King's College), p.85 (in Graham, *Massage: Manual Treatment, Remedial Movements*, p. 118).

†Harvey Kellogg, M.D., *A Practical Manual for the Nurse, the Student, and the Practitioner* (Battle Creek, Michigan: Modern Medicine Publishing Co., 1929), p. 273.

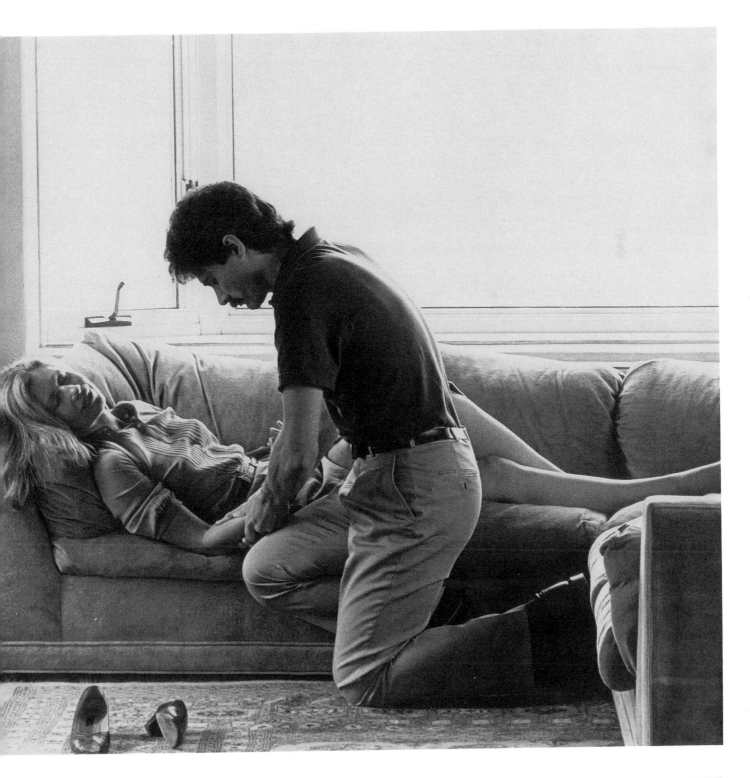

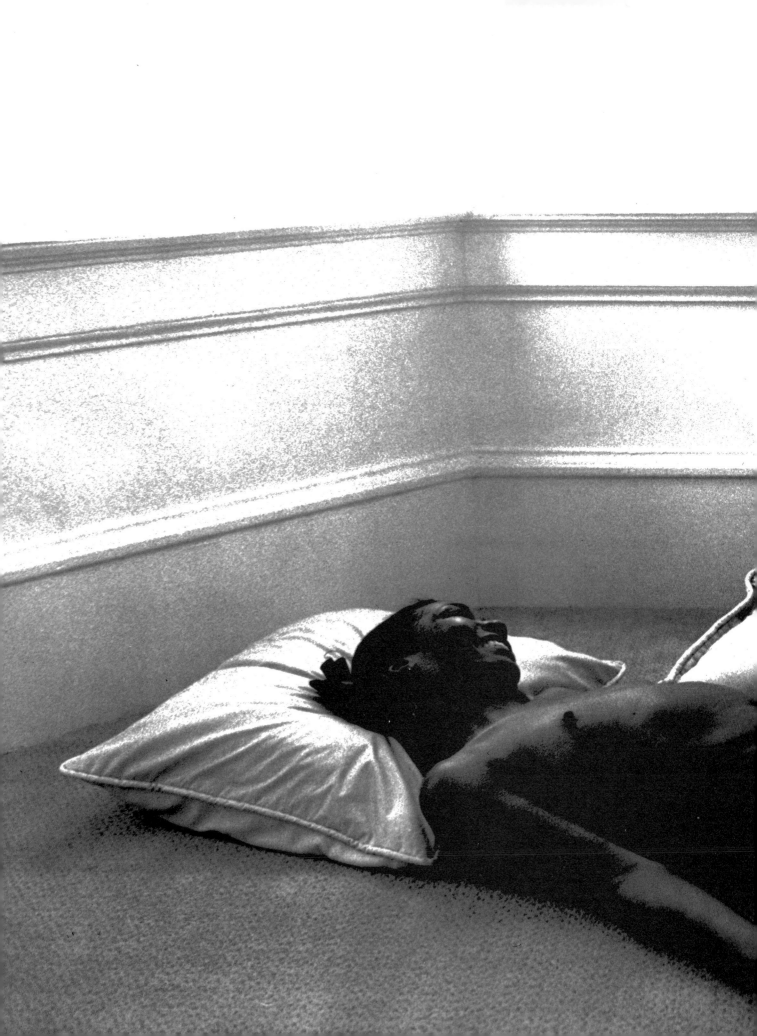

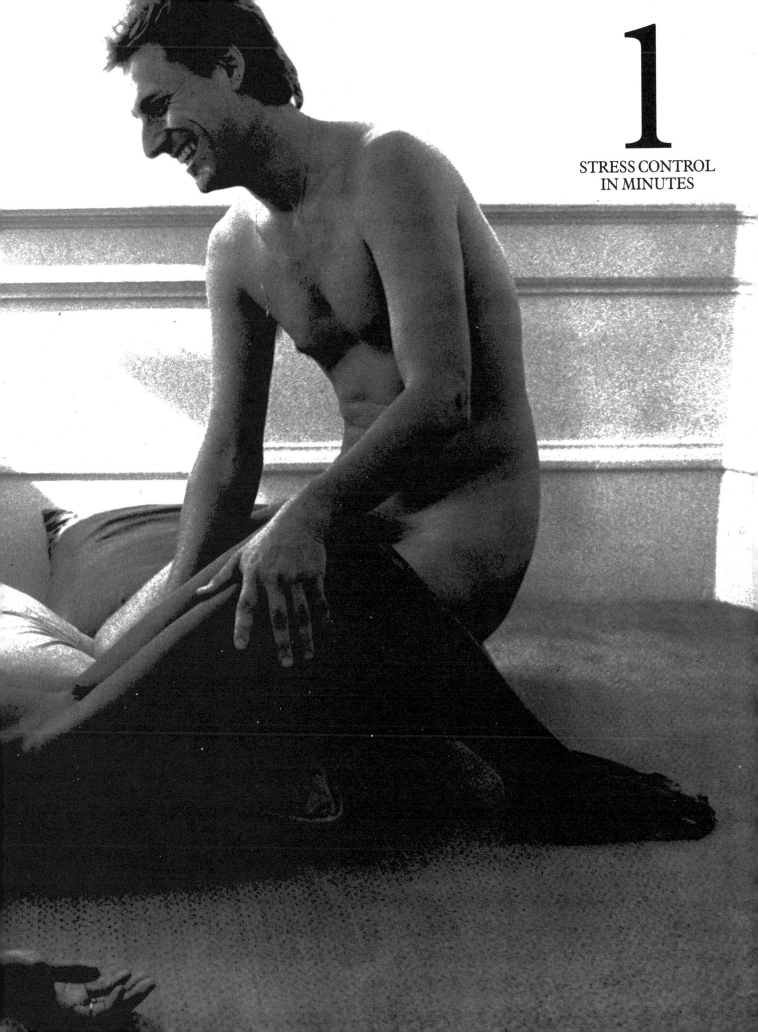

1

STRESS CONTROL
IN MINUTES

1.
Inside the Body:
The Power of
Super Massage

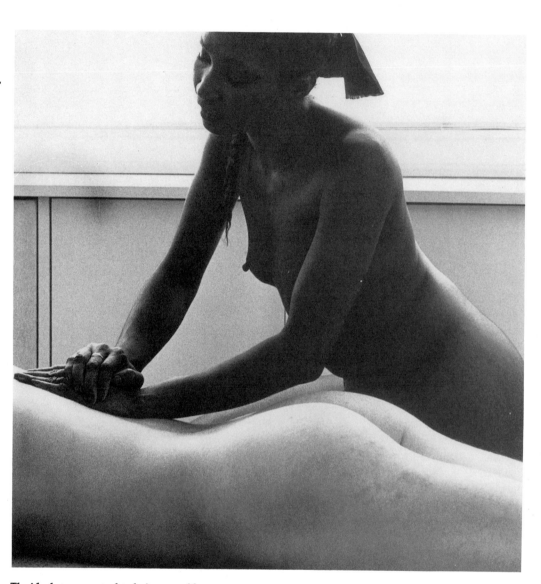

The ideal stress-control technique would:

- ☞ Remove acidic irritants from the tissues.
- ☞ Oxygenate the whole area.
- ☞ Not speed up the heart
- ☞ Not depend on a drug.
- ☞ Work in less than five minutes.

The Amazing Fluid Release Effect: How You Can Use It to Control Stress

Reach down to man's most atavistic levels, and release the automatic tensions that make him a slave to his own boredom and to the world around him.
—Colin Wilson, *The Mind Parasites*

It's tempting to conclude that stressed people are suffering from purely psychological problems. Can one then explain, rationally, to the stressed individual that constant nervousness, snappish behavior, and trouble concentrating are destructive? Probably not. Medical research has determined that stress is often caused by biological agents deep within the body. That's why you can't control the wild mood swings and mysterious ailments with rational thinking, positive thinking, or any other kind of thinking. You have to go directly to the body.

Where does stress begin? Every muscle, skin, and nerve cell requires a constant supply of oxygen and nutrients in order to function properly. Cells are literally bathed in blood-soluble nutrients every moment of the day and night. Inside the cells these nutrients combine with oxy-

INSTANT BENEFITS:

Circulation

Interior oxygen level boosted
Heart rested
Blood pressure lowered
Vascular and lymphatic toning

Muscles

Muscles recover from fatigue more than 300 percent faster!
Increased endurance

Nerves and brain

Immediate relaxation
Wrinkle and worry lines recede
Relief from cramps
Diminished anxiety and nervous tension

Skin and hair

Removes dead skin
Moisturizes the hair

gen and then combust to produce life-sustaining energy. Stress is created when the exhaust gasses, toxins, and wastes produced by combustion remain within the cell. Deep within the body chemical concentrations that trigger stress must be released from the cells before real relaxation is possible. When stress is viewed as a *chemical* phenomenon rather than a purely mental one, the tremendous potential of fluid release massage becomes clear.

We all agree that stressed people can become terribly irritating; however, their tendency to attack others is mirrored within. The stressed individual is under relentless attack from inside his own body by powerful acids and poisons. Normally, most toxins are expelled from internal tissues via the intricate capillary and lymphatic systems whose vessels are no more than a fraction of a centimeter in diameter. But when the body reacts to a stressful situation, the entire vascular and lymphatic system abruptly contracts. At the same time, the blood supply to interior tissues is sharply reduced. As the oxygen rate declines, nearby muscles tighten, pressing hard against the interior lymph and blood vessels.

Fluid Release Effect (cont'd)

During the massive vaso-constriction that follows, major blood vessels are often visibly contracted. Smaller ones sometimes close down altogether, blocking nearly all waste dispersal from the surrounding tissues. Irritating acidic wastes then begin to accumulate in the tissues, and the classic vicious cycle of stress is complete: the wastes produce tension, the tension produces more vaso-constriction, which in turn causes more acidic wastes to collect in the tissues. Relaxation becomes difficult because the muscles, constantly irritated from within, will not let go. In the end, the stressed individual is poisoned by his own wastes.

Vigorous exercise, the holy grail of the overstressed, can easily make the whole situation worse. Blood circulation is temporarily boosted, only to have large quantities of a new irritating waste, called lactic acid, pumped into the tissues. One must do less to be free of stress, not more.

The amazing massage technique called the fluid release effect, developed and widely tested (most recently on Olympic athletes), actually counters the effects of stress. In fluid release massage we concentrate on opening the intricate capillary and lymphatic systems that wastes

must pass through to get out of the body. Masseurs deal with stress as a physical problem and seek to restore tranquility by creating gentle changes inside the body. During fluid release massage an intense cleansing process begins at the cellular level.

Recently, a team of scientists set out to analyze the effects of various strokes by measuring the precise chemical content of wastes expelled from the body before and after a massage. After dozens of chemicals had been monitored, two dramatic changes in body chemistry, indicating

how extraordinarily powerful massage could be as a stress control agent, emerged. The scientists found that when tensed muscles relaxed their grip on the fragile lymphatic vessels, adrenaline, perhaps the most stressful chemical of all, was suddenly expelled from the body at a rate 50 percent faster than normal. Expulsion of histamine, the nasty stuff that cold and allergy remedies try so hard to vanquish, was accelerated by a phenomenal 129 percent![*] Fluid release massage, it turned out, had a selective tranquilizing effect that no

drug could match; somehow, *just the chemicals that actually cause stress were pressed out of the tissues and expelled from the body.*

As wastes are pressed out of the cells, the capillary and venous systems are opened and, simultaneously, great quantities of oxygen and nutrients are pumped into the tissues. The result? Your partner will rise from the massage feeling refreshed, calm, and curiously energized.

[*]W. Kurz and G. Wittlinger, *Angiology* 10 (1978), pp. 764–72.

Benefits to Circulation

After five minutes of Super Massage, the oxygen content of all massaged tissues has increased from 10 to 15 percent. Saturating the tissues with oxygen-rich blood provides a kind of natural analgesic—everything that hurts, hurts less. Inside the body even more dramatic changes are taking place. Massage cannot manufacture blood cells, but it can direct existing quantities to a specific area.

Repeating a simple circulation movement for five minutes boosts the white blood cell count in the massaged area by 85 percent. At the same time it increases local blood flow without straining your partner's heart and circulatory system. In fact, while you massage, your partner's pulse rate will actually decline as the heart pumps more slowly.

When you give a Super Massage, your hands take over some of the work that is usually done by your partner's heart. The vascular system is toned, blood pressure drops, and the heart is rested. Again, these effects cannot be reproduced, all at once, outside of massage.

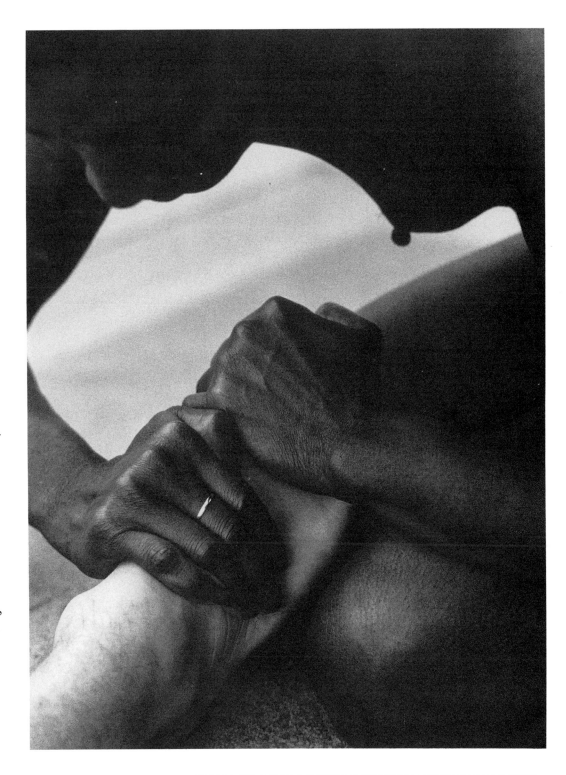

Benefits to Muscles

Recently, professional athletes and trainers have become fascinated with the astonishing muscle recovery rates that have been recorded after just a few minutes of fluid release massage. Although the original experiments were done by medical people at the turn of the century, their results were ignored for decades by an antitactile society.

Athletes became seriously interested in fluid release massage when they realized it offers a way to dramatically reduce muscle fatigue. In sports where extended muscle endurance is required, massage is now considered indispensable. Cyclists competing in endurance races like the Tour de France and the Giro de Italia, which call for sprints of more than one hundred miles a day, simply cannot compete without massage. *Runner's World* author Ray Hosler emphasizes just how crucial massage becomes in cycle marathons where "the legs take incredible punishment and the buildup of lactic acid is inordinate. Were a professional to be without his daily leg massage, he would soon find himself slipping in the standings." Recently, Alberto Salazar

revealed his secret: a twice-weekly massage session which permitted him to commit to a phenomenal seventeen-week training schedule with no breaks! Salazar is convinced that he couldn't have achieved his world records without the massage.*

What, precisely, can fluid release techniques do for fatigued muscles? Normally, the muscle recovery rate after exercise is slightly less than 20 percent. An individual capable of doing a hundred sit-ups has recovered enough

energy, after five minutes of rest, to do no more than twenty additional sit-ups (a 20 percent recovery rate). But if we completely eliminate the rest period and substitute five minutes of fluid release massage, the muscle recovery rates increase to between 75 percent and 125 percent! It was this astonishing performance jump that attracted the interest of U.S. Olympic trainers, who now follow the

example of the East Germans and include massage in almost all sports training. But the full ramifications of the amazing muscle recovery rates after Super Massage extend far beyond athletics. Who can say what any of us would be capable of if we could work three times as hard before getting tired?

---

*Ray Hosler, *Runner's World Massage Book* (Mountain View, California: Runner's World Books, 1982), p. 186.

Benefits to the Nerves and Brain

The first step in controlling wrinkles is to soothe the nerves that supply the facial muscles. The same acids that clog muscle cells deposit microscopic debris on the nerves.*

Nerve debris interferes with electrical transmission, creating a disturbance that is communicated directly to the muscles. Probably the most mood-sensitive part of the body is the area around the mouth and eyes, where the tiny muscles of expression are shaped. Here, nervous tension simply cannot be hidden; the skin wrinkles visibly with every mood change. Relax the nerves that supply the face and your partner's expression is transformed, sometimes while you're massaging. Suddenly the face appears more natural and composed, as though unnecessary lines have been eliminated. They have. Very often, fully half of the visible wrinkles are nothing more than "tension tracks" that

disappear without a trace after five minutes of Super Massage.

On other parts of the body deeper nerves are more pressure-sensitive. Light to moderate pressures during massage are stimulating; heavy pressures have a sedative effect. A woman's nerves are more sensitive to touch than a man's.

Cramped muscles can sometimes be traced to irritated nerves. Direct pressure, with compression strokes (see p. 50), on the nerves that supply the cramped muscle will sometimes relieve the cramp.

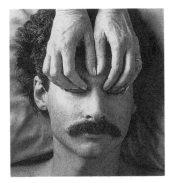

Although the brain itself cannot feel, it can be massaged indirectly via the nerves. Soothe the nerves and your partner's anxieties begin to vanish. Again, in massage we deal with emotional or mental problems as physical events. Relax the body, remove the sources of stress, and you transform your partner's outlook. After ten minutes of Super Massage chronically worried individuals often have trouble remembering what they were worried about.

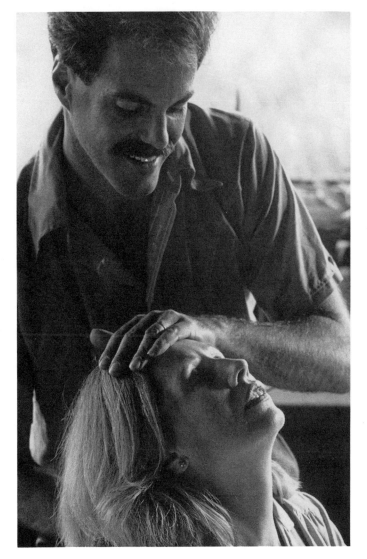

---

*"…the peculiar calm, soothing, restful, light feeling that is the most frequent result of massage cannot be understood until experienced. It doubtless arises to a great extent from the pressure of natural worn-out *debris* being speedily removed from off terminal nerve-filaments."
From Graham, *A Treatise on Massage*, p. 111.

Benefits to the Skin and Hair

Massage breaks loose dead, brittle skin cells, exposing the living tissue below. When the subcutaneous tissues are super oxygenated, the skin becomes smoother, more supple.

Unfortunately for the makers of various gooey "miracle" ointments, hair is nourished only from within the scalp. Scalp massage (see p. 87) stimulates the surface blood vessels and the sebaceous glands, which will secrete various oils while you work. After four minutes of scalp massage, the hair appears glossy and moisturized.

Relaxation in Minutes

Most of the solutions that follow, for headaches, insomnia, back pain, and other ailments, require that you spend only a few minutes massaging a single part of the body. In minutes the astonishing fluid release effect begins working spectacular changes inside your partner's body (see chart). Most people you massage will probably have no idea how effective massage can be in controlling stress. You can cite scientific experiments to prove its power, you can point to recent athletic success stories, celebrity beauty treatments, or the new wave of in-house corporate massage but, ultimately, your partner must actually experience a massage to believe in it.

This book is meant to be used. See it as a tool; lay it open flat beside you while you're doing massage. Get familiar with the four basic strokes (see p. 32) but don't worry if you can't do them perfectly. Throughout the book you'll find detailed instructions for adapting each one of them to specific parts of the body. Once you've read this chapter, simply find out what's bothering your partner, turn to the appropriate chapter, and start massaging.

To be successful, the fluid release effect requires many repetitions of the "essential

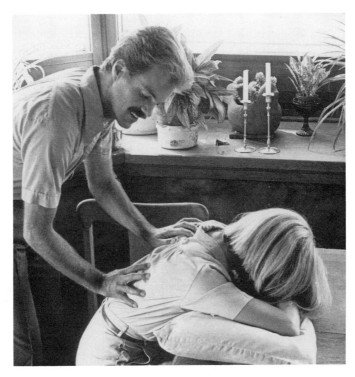

strokes," which appear at the beginning of each chapter. They're easy to learn — nearly all are variations of the four basic strokes. Don't hesitate to repeat simple movements dozens, even hundreds of times each. Repetition is far more important than variety in massage.

Once you've completed the essential movements, try a few of the general strokes which are included in each chapter. There's no need to fit them all into one massage — save a few for next time. Whether you do a three-minute headache massage or a ten-minute erotic session, your stroking should be focused and consistent for the entire period.

Expect some resistance before a first massage. People take their tensions so seriously that a possible quick fix may appear frivolous. But, as every masseur knows, it happens all the time. Using your own hands and a bottle of warm oil, you can relieve stress without help from special equipment, pills, or extended treatment schedules.

Results come in five minutes, not five weeks or five months. Get started quickly and minimize conversation — the message is the massage. Finally, don't be afraid of a nervous partner. In a tense situation, the massage itself becomes an ice breaker because, as you begin, the last thing your partner expects is about to occur: pain disappears and pleasure takes its place.

After five minutes of super massage:

Acidic irritants and wastes are removed from the muscles.
Pain is controlled — the nerves are soothed.
Cramped tendons and ligaments are stretched.
Local circulation is boosted without speeding up the heart.
The oxygen content of the tissues is increased.

Which means that:

Headaches disappear without pills.
Facial wrinkles are smoothed.
Tension vanishes and relaxation takes its place.
Feelings of depression are replaced by a positive, optimistic outlook.
Digestion, circulation, skin quality, muscle tone, and sleep are enhanced.
Endurance increases.

2.
Learn
Super Massage
in One
Evening

A basic stress-control sequence

☛ Stroking super-oxygenates the tissues.

☛ Kneading squeezes wastes out
of the tissues.

☛ Friction lubricates the joints and
reaches internal organs.

☛ Percussion soothes the nerves and
boosts circulation to a large area.

☛ Stroking again clears all wastes and
bring in super-oxygenated blood.

When Should You Do Super Massage?

In classic full body massage your partner needs to relax the entire body before you massage any part of it. When all distractions have been removed, he will lie down on a comfortable, warm surface without clothes, jewelry, or thoughts of this world. Only then does the actual massage begin, and it can last for an hour or more. However, if long sessions with complete nudity and total relaxation become a prerequisite for every massage, your opportunities to help people will decline. Stressed individuals, in particular, will usually find a reason to avoid massage if a lengthy preparation is involved. Don't give them an out.

When your partner is suffering from a single stress-induced problem, a time-consuming full body massage may not be necessary. After just a few minutes of Super Massage directed to a single part of the body, amazing changes can occur. You may want to tell your partner that before you begin.

The continual work done by the body to support the head, arms, hands, and fingers is so fatiguing that nearby muscles are often kept in a state of tension all day long. After a while sufferers resign themselves to hours of neck, shoulder, or lower back pain every

day. As modern life becomes more automated and less physical, this low-level pain, known as background tension, is becoming a fact of life in many professions. Unfortunately, even an hour of vigorous exercise may not be enough to offset the effects of eight hours spent sitting at a desk or standing behind a counter. What, then, is the answer? Will the coffee break be replaced by an aspirin or Valium break? Must we graduate to stronger drugs to cope with increased job demands?

Enter Super Massage and the three-minute stress-reduction program.

Your first concern in preparing your partner for Super Massage should be to completely *relax the entire area that you plan to massage.* The head, for example, is a particularly heavy object that must be carried by the shoulder muscles all day long. Finding a different way to support your partner's head immediately relaxes the shoulders. Only then, as the background tension is relieved around the massage area, does truly effective neck massage become possible. The same principle applies to other supported body parts: you must take over the support before real massage can begin. Throughout the book you will find hints on how to support the head, arms, legs, and feet while you massage them.

Don't massage if:

There is an infection or fever.
There are extensive skin eruptions or bruises.
There is intense pain that shoots down a leg or interferes with sleep.
A doctor has advised against it.

Avoid massaging areas if:

Skin is bruised, cut, or erupted.
Joints are inflamed.
Veins are sensitive.
There is a tumor.
There is a painful reaction.

Quick Set-Ups at Home or at Work

Massaging on the job means compromising. You must allow for interruptions, you must work around restrictive clothes, and you must be prepared to stop in minutes when you might be tempted to go on for half an hour or more. Nevertheless, the benefits to your partner are so great that you simply cannot afford to make excessive demands. With a little ingenuity you can transform your partner's work experience and introduce massage as an aid to productivity.

It does make sense to reduce unnecessary distractions. You may want to present massage as a kind of "break" in which one takes a few minutes off from the usual demands of business. Phone calls, meetings, and appointments are simply put on hold for a few minutes. Give your partner some idea of how much time you will need. Allow him at lease a minute or two of relaxation afterward for the massage to sink in.

Don't allow your partner's anxieties to become your own. Remain calm and proceed in an orderly fashion. Remember, *continual* stress is most dangerous. Before you lay hands on your partner, it's useful to do whatever you can to break the pattern of relentless stress. Unplug the phone (or turn on the answer-

ing machine), turn off an intercom, or just close the office door. Dimming the lights makes it easier for your partner to close his eyes and drift off. The idea is to create a space in the busy day for relaxation. Then say a few words about releasing tension—give your partner "permission" to relax for a while. Don't be discouraged if your partner seems too busy for massage or actually ridicules your efforts. (See the hints for massaging stress addicts on p. 99.)

Try to simplify all preparations. If you're planning to use oil, have the squeeze bottle filled and scented. Bring your own pillow if your partner isn't likely to have one handy. Lay out towels and other accessories nearby. Don't move furniture or equipment unless it's absolutely necessary to do so.

You can do things for your partner at home that are difficult in a less intimate setting. You don't have to work around (or through) layers of clothes. Interruptions disappear, along with the usual on-the-job demands to get involved with stressful activities the moment a Super Massage is completed. Once nudity becomes possible, the full range of massage movements can be focused on every part of the body. And afterward, while the effects of your massage soak in, your partner can relax and do absolutely nothing.

All that's needed to massage at home is a warm, quiet place large enough for the two of you. But if you're going to work with a nude partner, you do need to pay special attention to the temperature of the massage surface. A few simple preparations will make the difference between an unforgettable experience and an unpleasant one for your partner. The normal reduction in all metabolic functions that occurs when the body is at rest is accelerated during massage. In the midst of an energetic fluid release sequence, you may feel perfectly comfortable while your naked partner could be on the verge of shivering. Unless you warm the body first, massaging chilled muscles has little effect; cold muscles will remain contracted, spreading tension throughout the body. People simply cannot relax when chilled, so a cold massage surface is never acceptable.

Unless you live in the tropics, the area where you massage should be warmer than normal room temperature—at least 75 degrees Fahrenheit. The best way to insure your partner's comfort is to set up an electric heater close to the

massage surface. If you're working on the floor, the room temperature will probably have to be considerably higher than usual. While any heater will do the job, an oil-filled electric radiator is best for warming a massage area. They're fast, clean, safe, and utterly silent. Most models have thermostats and wheels. While your partner takes a hot bath or shower — always a good idea before extended massage — bring the room up to a comfortable temperature.

Trust is particularly important in all massage, the more so if your partner is nude. From the moment she lies down in front of you, eyes closed and totally naked, an implicit understanding, that you are going to be very careful with her body, exists. Above all she must trust you not to do anything that would be painful. Pain has no place in massage. One ill-advised finger poke or overtwisted joint can shatter an hour of peace and relaxation. It also violates the unspoken contract between a masseur and his partner: *I will never hurt you, I will only give you pleasure.*

If it's a first massage, your partner may have no idea what to expect. Anything you can do to create a relaxed atmosphere in your massage area will help her begin to unwind and surrender to the more subtle effects. Low lights and soft music help create the right mood.

Find a firm but cushioned surface for massage, one that will permit you to press down hard on the more intense back movements without losing control. Four inches of

foam rubber is ideal; a few thick blankets covered with a sheet will do almost as well. Avoid waterbeds and very soft mattresses.

If you're working on several parts of the body, you'll need room to move around your partner during the massage. Put everything you need within reach before you begin. Hesitation (while you move a chair or search for your glasses) spoils the mood. You should remain invisible during massage so that what your partner actually experiences is purely tactile.

Finally, lay out your towels and place a bottle of heated oil near the part of the body you plan to massage first. To warm your hands, hold them tightly under your armpits for a minute or two, or cover them with a hot towel. You may want to say a few words to help with the transition between normal reality, where all the senses are used, and massage, where nearly everything that is experienced is simply felt. Something complimentary about your partner works well. If you must speak during a massage, your tone is generally more important than what is actually said.

Oiling

All massage strokes, except percussion and friction movements, work better if you lubricate your partner's skin first with a light vegetable oil. "Commercial" massage oils are often nothing more than ordinary vegetable oil which has been renamed, overpackaged, and over-scented. You can save time and money by scenting a small bottle of ordinary coconut, sesame, or saf-flower oil with a few drops of fresh lemon juice. Olive, corn, and peanut oils are too thick for massage. Lemon scent is generally pleasing and has practical benefits for both the masseur and his partner. The skin's natural acidity, under daily attack from soaps (the hands are almost always the first part of the body to wrinkle), is restored by lemon juice. Many other essences and perfumes can be used — the most important consideration in choosing a scent, however, is to please your partner. Some people prefer bringing their own scent for the oil to a massage.

If you'd like to try something exotic, one commercial massage oil, called Monoi Tiare from Tahiti, stands out from all the rest. It's sultry floral scent unmistakably evokes the enchanted islands of the South Pacific. Once a rare and much sought-after prize,

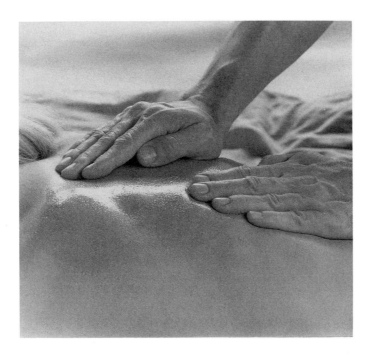

this exquisite oil is now available in most parts of the United States. Check for it at your local bath shop.

You can put your oil in a simple bowl or, to avoid spills, use a plastic squeeze bottle. To please your partner the oil should be heated first. Place the container in a cup of hot water until the oil is close to body temperature. Choosing the right temperature and the right scent (for your partner) is very important because oiling often marks the beginning of a Super Massage. You oil first, then you massage. If it's your partner's first massage, remember that with oiling you're establishing the

initial contact. Avoid an impersonal, casual, or mechanistic approach. Oiling should be a deliberate part of the massage itself.

Always add oil to your own hands first, then transfer it to your partner's body. Spread the oil slowly, with even, circular movements, using the whole surface of your hands. Avoid jerky, scrubbing motions. Add just enough oil to permit your hands to move smoothly without pulling at the skin. Too much oil makes for a sloppy massage. Use extra oil carefully. Body hair requires a few additional drops; add a bit more if skin begins catching at your hands

during an extended kneading or circulation movement. Be careful not to break contact with your partner when adding oil. On the fleshier parts of the body simply turn one hand over, maintain contact with the backs of your fingers, and add oil to the upraised palm. If you must remove both hands for a moment, press a knee or the side of an arm against your partner so that some body contact is maintained.

After the massage, oil comes off easily with a light towel or with rubbing alcohol. Alcohol must be used cold, which limits its effectiveness in massage. Some people crave the exhilarating shock, others feel it shatters the calm mood you've just established.

Oiling provides a unique sensual experience that you can return to again and again during a massage. Combine it with various movements so the oiling blends with the massage or during high-volume fluid release techniques that require many repetitions of the same movement. Add more oil without breaking the rhythm. Take your time when oiling. Think about what your partner is feeling. Let your partner savor the deliciously warm scented oil as it spreads slowly across the body.

Repetition and Relaxation

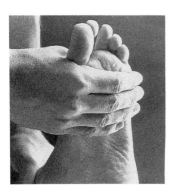 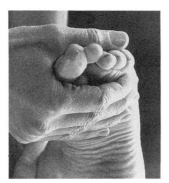 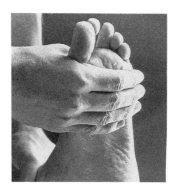 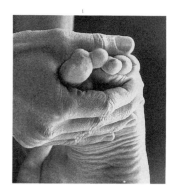

In an ordinary full-body massage most movements will be repeated three or four times. If one maintains a steady rhythm, it takes an hour or more to cover the whole body from head to foot. During a Super Massage, however, you concentrate all of your attention on a single stressed area. Rather than repeat a hundred movements three or four times, you repeat three or four movements a hundred times each. Don't be frightened by the big numbers—almost every sport routinely calls for much greater repetition. A bicyclist who pedals three or four hundred times is just warming up; so is the serious swimmer or runner after the first couple of laps. Actually, the repetition you're called upon to do during a Super Massage is much less strenuous. It doesn't require great strength

or speed, and you're not expected to compete against yesterday's score. Just relax, focus on your stroking, and keep going. You can do it easily without breathing hard.

If you're counting to yourself while stroking, remember that your partner definitely isn't. Whenever something feels good, people never count—they just want more. After the first fifty repetitions you will begin to feel tensed muscles relax under your hands as the amazing fluid release effect starts working. Add another two hundred strokes, and it will still be working the next morning.

Your stroking frequencies can vary greatly. Large-area strokes like the magnificent full body circulation movement, which takes close to a full minute to move from the feet to the head and back, simply cannot be rushed. Throughout the book, however, you will focus on the workhorse strokes of the fluid release effect, local kneading, and friction variations, which are most effective when repeated about fifty times per minute on a single spot. Again, don't be put off by the large numbers. Ordinary walking continues for hours at comparable frequencies without causing noticeable fatigue. Remember that irregular bursts of speed can destroy the hypnotic mood you're working to create. On the faster strokes, find a frequency that you can maintain easily and stay with it.

When you massage a single limb, hand, or foot, it's always best to spend some time on the other one as well. You may be working on a specific complaint that occurs on only one side of the body, say, a cramp in the left leg. The cramped area will be tight as a drum, especially when compared to the same area on the other leg. Nevertheless, after a complete fluid release sequence the cramp will probably yield, leaving the left leg so profoundly relaxed that the right leg will begin to feel tense by comparison. This is not to say that you must automatically double the amount of time spent massaging each part of the body. If you do nothing at all, the massaged limb will feel lighter and more energetic than the nonmassaged one for hours, even days afterward. Just a minute or two spent on the opposite limb will add balance to your massage.

Get feedback on frequency and pressure preferences from your partner. Some people like raw speed while others prefer slower, more penetrating strokes. If it's a first massage, you may have to experiment for a few minutes while your partner sorts through the new sensations. (When she moans with pleasure you're doing something right—keep doing it.) Whatever stroke you do it's important to ask yourself, "What is my partner *feeling* right now?" You create feelings with your hands during every stroke, and those feelings are the only true measure of any massage.

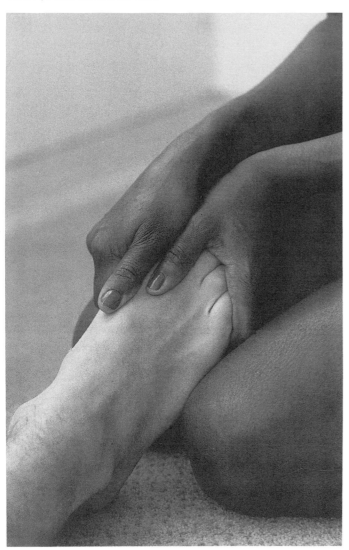

Do

Ask about painful areas before massage. Stay away from bruises and any place where the skin is broken.

Remove jewelry from the entire massage area.

Warm your hands before you start.

Use heated oil in a plastic squeeze bottle.

Create a quiet, peaceful atmosphere in the room.

Insist on no interruptions while massaging. Phone calls and appointments must wait. Children and pets should be cared for by somebody else.

Be scrupulous about your personal hygiene.

Support the entire area to be massaged with a part of your body or a pillow.

Maintain the same rhythm throughout. All strokes move at the same speed.

Keep your fingers together.

Keep all movements smooth and even—avoid abrupt transitions.

Don't

Rush or affect an ultra efficient manner. A good masseur should be invisible.

Comment on how tense your partner seems to be.

Hurt your partner. One moment of pain can ruin the entire massage.

Break contact. If you forget what to do next, continue with what you were doing.

Massage while your partner does something else.

Encourage conversation. Complaining doesn't let off steam, it usually brings on more stress. Try silence or quiet music.

Massage next to an open window on a cool day.

Compete with pain pills or tranquilizers. You will be blamed when the pills fail.

"Dig in" to soft tissues with your thumbs.

Interrupt the massage or pause between movements.

Comment on the time or wear a watch.

Four Easy-to-Learn Basic Movements:
Friction

Friction is the most versatile but the most misused massage stroke. Under the right circumstances a few minutes of deep friction can reach deep inside your partner's body to provide quick relief from nagging pain. Here is a stroke that requires no oil or special preparation and can be done in almost any setting, clothed or unclothed. It's ideal for onsite stress reduction. Use it in the home, on the sports field, or at the office but not while your partner drives a car or makes a phone call. Leave that kind of friction to Hollywood.

For quick results no stroke can compete with friction because moments after you begin, the effects are registered deep within your partner's body. Friction is also a kind of natural anesthetic. Every mammal understands that rubbing a sensitive spot will bring relief. Think of friction as educated rubbing. Specialized friction movements stimulate, soothe, and warm your partner's body. Some stimulate just the skin and surface organs; others will penetrate deep within the dense tissues around joints.

Friction is easy to learn. A part of the hand, with fingers held together, ranging from the fingertips to the whole

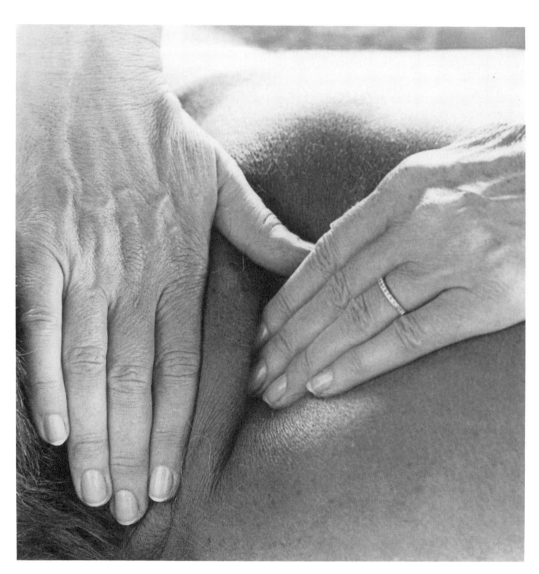

surface, is rotated against a specific spot on your partner's body. But, unlike other massage movements that glide across the surface of the body, friction will press down against the skin until you can feel the muscles within. You grip the skin while rotating your fingertips, palm, or

hand on interior muscles. Since you sometimes have to rotate fairly hard, it's easy to shake your partner's entire body during the more intense friction variations. To avoid doing this, every friction stroke must be anchored, a process that limits outward movement from the immediate massage area.

Basic Friction

Use one hand to anchor, the other to apply friction. When anchoring concentrate on what your partner will actually feel. Do you want the entire leg to flop around while you massage a knee? In order to control excessive movement while you massage, the anchor hand should press down and hold the tissues near a friction site steady. As a stroke moves, so does the anchor hand. Often the thumb is held out to control a larger area. Always anchor first, then begin friction. On fleshy parts of the body you can push a fold of flesh toward the massage site with your anchor hand, making it easier for friction to work without pulling the skin. Remember that the fingers should be held together during all friction strokes lest the deep, penetrating effects dissipate. You can sometimes feel the outline of muscles and internal organs gliding beneath your fingers.

Generally, three kinds of friction movements are used: one for thick tissues like the thighs and larger muscles; another for "hard" body areas, like the chest and feet, with large bones near the surface; and a third for the muscles of the face. Simple full hand friction for the outside of your partner's thigh will get you started with a multipurpose stroke that travels well.

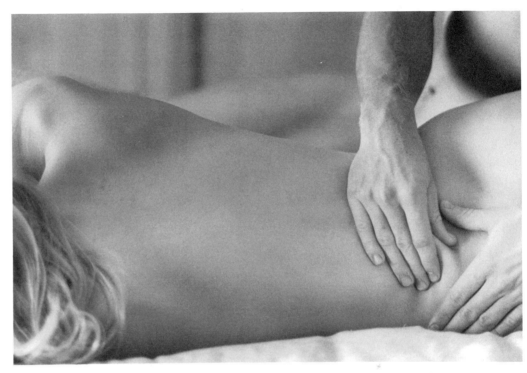

First, look for a way to anchor the stroke. If you're right-handed, open the thumb of your left hand and press down on the top of your partner's back as shown. At the same time press in toward the friction site until you are actually pushing a fold of flesh ahead of your hand. This important step relieves skin tension over the friction area. If you're left-handed, simply reverse the process. Once you've established a firm anchor, you're ready to move in with the friction hand and begin.

Use as much of the hand as possible; never "dig in" to your partner's body. Here on the back you will be able to use the whole surface of your hand from fingertips to the base of the palm. Massaging around the hands, feet, and face, you'll use just the fingertips. Press down on your partner's back, allowing your hand to bend to conform to the shape of the muscles. Use a speed that you will be comfortable maintaining for several minutes. Rotate your hand while you press. You will feel the muscles of the back rippling beneath your fingertips. Use even pressure. You may need to reposition the anchor hand from time to

time, but don't break contact with your friction hand or stop massaging to do this. Keep rotating your friction hand. You can do friction with your fingertips, the flat part of the fist, or the whole hand. Whatever method you choose, remember that interruptions are particularly distracting for your partner. Think of what she's feeling and let the feeling go on.

Kneading

If you had to settle for a single massage technique, simply learning to knead would provide a powerful tool that can be used on every part of your partner's body. Repeated kneading presses toxins out of the tissues like squeezing liquid from a sponge—it is the most important element of the fluid release effect. A thoroughly kneaded part of the body is transformed for hours, even days. Sluggish, fatigued muscles suddenly feel light and energetic, as though they had been rested overnight. The nerves are soothed and the joints work more smoothly.

Kneading is the ideal stroke to use on skeptics. Your partner doesn't have to wait to see if it works—the effects are immediate and very dramatic. In fact, a well-kneaded part of the body feels great almost from the moment you begin massage. Repeat the movement for five minutes across the bottom of a fatigued neck and you will convert almost anyone to the joys of massage.

Repetitious kneading creates a deeply hypnotic mood while it cleanses the tissues. As tension is surrendered, knotted muscles will soften under your hands, bringing forth the self-satisfied moans that every masseur knows so well. But to work properly the

kneading stroke must be consistent. Any abrupt change or hesitation will break the mood and distract your partner. Learning to control your thumbs will give you the confidence to knead a single set of muscles hundreds of times without thinking about what you're doing. Know your thumbs before you begin kneading.

Learning to knead is a two-step process: first, learn to rotate your hands in opposing circles, then add proper thumb technique. The best place to learn kneading is on the flat, fleshy outer side of your partner's thigh.

Basic Kneading

1. Start by holding your thumb flat against your forefinger and simply rotate one hand on the thigh. Keep your fingers pressed together and try to make contact with the whole surface of your hand; this may mean bending your hand slightly to conform to the shape of your partner's thigh while you circle. When you can circle effortlessly, you're ready to try it with both hands.

Do exactly the same thing with the other hand, moving in the same direction, but circle in opposition. When your first hand is at the top of a circle, your second hand will be at the bottom. Try this for a few minutes. Go ahead and lean into the stroke as you develop a gentle rhythm, using your entire arm.

2. Now add thumb technique. On every circle, simply pick up a fold of flesh with each hand between your thumb and fingers. When one thumb is wide open, the other one is picking up flesh. The thumbs are also used to direct kneading to a specific area. You can in fact focus both thumbs on the same spot. As you circle, each thumb will pick up the same fold of flesh again and again.

Once you learn how to knead, it's easy to go on for a long time almost anywhere on the body. Kneading variations include thumb and fingertip strokes for smaller parts of the body, as well as the full hand stroke shown here. As you knead you can sometimes actually feel tensed muscles soften beneath your fingertips. Keep going—what you're doing is working.

Percussion

Need a quick massage solution to on-the-job stress? Percussion movements work right through clothes and they're effective in almost any setting. A five-minute percussion break will leave your partner feeling energized, relaxed, and smiling.

If this is a first massage, your partner is probably nervous about being touched. He may be wondering how to act or what he's supposed to feel. If you're working with complete nudity, he may stiffen or start fidgeting as you begin preparing to do massage. Stress addicts (see p. 97) show fear more aggressively by arguing with you about technique, scheduling, decor, or anything else that comes to mind. Nevertheless, what most people want out of life is simply to have a good time, and that, on the most fundamental level, is exactly what massage is all about.

Ask your partner if she has ever had a full body massage. How many other experiences in life offer one uninterrupted physical pleasure for an hour or more? By saying a few words about the benefits of massage, you effectively give your partner "permission" to relax. Let the conversation end when you start massaging, because whatever you've been talking about won't seem very important after a few minutes of percussion.

Percussion (cont'd)

Percussion movements provide a good way to neutralize all kinds of elaborate defenses and get right into Super Massage. After two or three passes up and down the back, nervous conversation stops, fears evaporate, and things settle down quickly. The impact created during percussion—penetrating waves of pleasure that carry right through the whole body—is so overwhelming that most people will simply surrender to the feeling. And there's no other feeling anything like it.

Moments after you begin, things start happening fast inside the body. Deep arterial circulation is boosted, supplying the tissues with fresh oxygen and nutrients. Percussion movements reach where no other massage stroke can go. Through a combination of deep, penetrating vibration and direct pressure to various nerves, the effects of massage are transmitted to the heart, lungs, and other organs beneath the rib cage. At the same time dead skin is loosened on the surface of the body and subcutaneous muscles are toned. After a few minutes of percussion the effects sometimes become visible as your partner begins smiling to herself.

Basic Percussion

From the thickly muscled back to the delicate structures around the eyes and mouth, the amount of pressure you use will vary enormously. In most percussion strokes the contact hand—the hand that actually guides the stroke across the skin—bends to

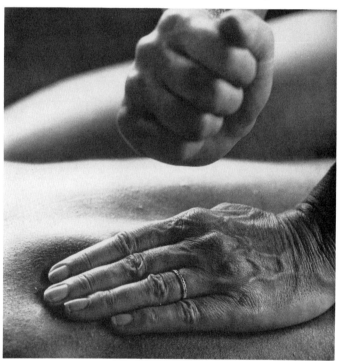

conform to the shape of your partner's body. Strike the back of the contact hand about fifty times per minute with your other hand, the percussion hand. As you strike the contact hand, slowly move it around the area you want to massage. Every "blow" must be cushioned to control pressure on

interior tissues. To regulate the force and create a more pleasing effect, the percussion hand should break at the wrist just before reaching the contact hand. Tap your partner with the side of your hand instead of pounding on her with your whole arm. Even when you apply percussion with both hands, the stroke

must still break at the wrist to be effective.

The notion that percussion movements must be painful in order to work is old and false. You don't relax tensed muscles by causing pain. In fact, pain will cause the muscles to tighten and eventually

go into spasm. *Never do anything in a massage that will hurt your partner.* One moment of pain can shatter the trust between the two of you and destroy an experience of uninterrupted pleasure.

When you're learning a percussion movement ask your partner what feels good and what doesn't. After a few dozen Super Massages you'll begin to get a sense of how much pressure different body types require. Most people want extra pressure on the heavily muscled sides of the legs and the upper back.

Percussion variations range from a vigorous pounding movement with the full hand or elbow on powerful back muscles to a tiny pinky snap, which can be used to tone delicate facial tissue. Good percussion technique, like all massage strokes, depends more on timing and control than strength or endurance. Don't rush. A steady, predictable rhythm is far more important than speed. Percussion should feel like a light rain, not a thunderstorm.

Stroking

Stroking is the easiest massage movement to learn — you'll be doing it well after a couple of tries. Some variations cover large areas of the body with a single stroke, allowing your partner the luxury of experiencing relaxation as a separate sensation that travels up a limb or across the back.

Does your partner fear relaxation on the grounds that it could undermine efficiency and drive? Are tension headaches, poor digestion, chronically aching muscles, or recurring rashes already a fact of life? Are you anxious to help but wondering where to start? Here's how to provide fast relief from the condition that seems to precede most other stress-induced problems. Stroking is the first step in reversing the dangerous pressures on the circulatory and nervous systems created by the vasoconstriction effect. With just a few dozen repetitions you can cut through stress by flooding congested tissues with fresh oxygen and nutrients.

During stroking movements you take over part of the work that is usually done by your partner's heart. After just one minute of stroking, blood circulation is significantly accelerated — your partner experiences a warm rush

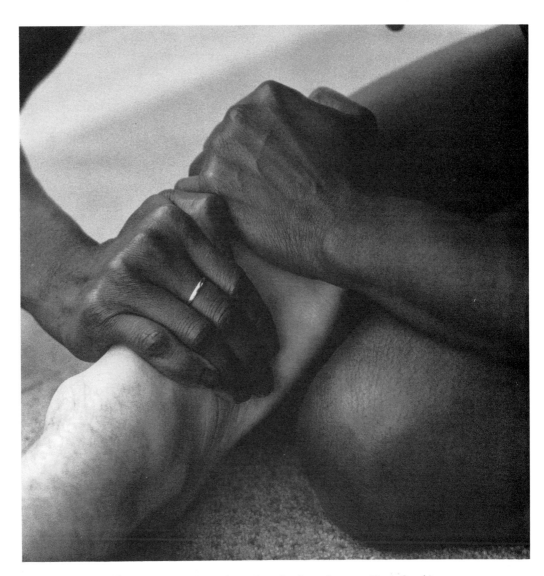

spreading outward from your hands. A stroking variation is particularly effective on the limbs, where high stress levels plus constant muscle tension tend to cut off proper blood flow. Use it on desk-

bound people to begin and end a Super Massage. Starting on the feet and ending at the waist, you can warm the entire leg as though your partner were exercising hard. Actually, he's completely relaxed and the heart rate is lower than usual.

Basic Stroking

Work toward the heart in all stroking movements. Press down with the whole flat surface of your hands as you move up toward the heart. Some stroking movements that begin on the lower part of the body will extend past the heart all the way to the

Stroking (cont'd)

shoulders. Moving away from the heart, on the return part of the movement, light contact is sufficient. As you push forward with the full flat surface of your hands, hundreds of tiny intravenous valves are forced open, causing blood pressure in the major veins to decrease. Blood is then sucked into the temporary vacuum from the arteries and fresh oxygen floods the tissues. The blood pressure and heart rate decrease while circulation through the tissues is speeded up. This is the beginning of the fluid release effect that is unique to massage (see p. 17). With it you can begin to reverse the effects of accumulated tension and stress in a few minutes.

Stroking variations include back pressing, compression, and full body stroking. Generally, your fingers should be kept together when doing massage, but during stroking it's particularly important to make as much contact as possible. As your partner develops the exquisite sensual awareness that comes with repeated massage he will immediately notice the difference if your fingers drift apart — a smooth, sinuous movement becomes suddenly jagged and dissonant.

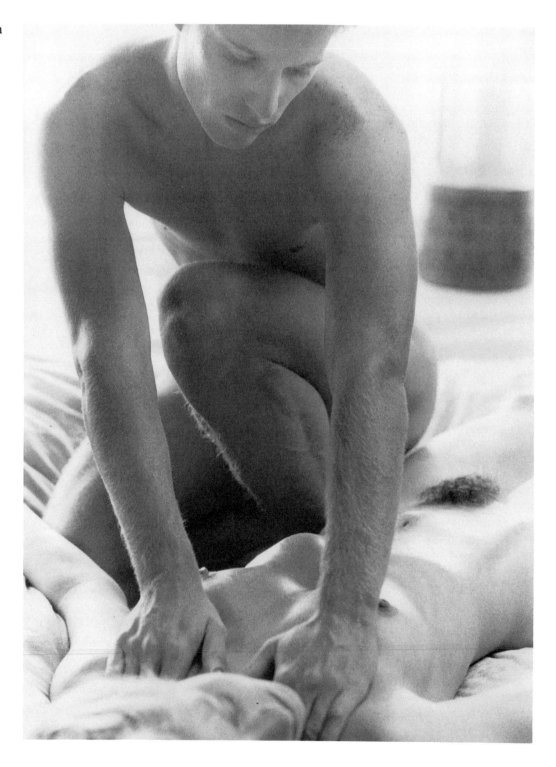

Basic Stress Control

Since every individual's body reacts differently to stress, each chapter offers several approaches to relaxing tension. One stiff neck may respond to a combination of kneading, friction, and stroking, while another will simply require a single percussion stroke repeated for several minutes. However, masseurs prefer certain movements for specific parts of the body, and these are indicated in the "essential strokes" charts at the beginning of each chapter.

Choose these strokes to create a basic but effective stress-relief sequence, and as you learn more about your partner's special needs, use the general strokes in each chapter to extend the massage. One minute spent repeating each of the movements shown on the Basic Stress-Control Sequence chart will give you a powerful five-minute massage. Shorten each of the strokes or skip the final stroking repetition when doing three- and four-minute massages.

If you have the privacy and the time, find a comfortable, warm place and massage your partner in the nude. If not, use oil where you can and give special emphasis to the percussion and friction movements that work right through clothes in virtually any setting.

If your partner is suffering from a localized problem like a headache or neck and shoulder pain, it's not necessary to read the entire book — just turn to the appropriate section and start massaging. Don't worry if your technique isn't perfect at first. Your partner will enjoy being touched and you can learn as you go.

3.
Three-Minute Relief from Headaches

Three essential strokes
One minute each, fifty repetitions

☛ Brain circulation
☛ Kneading the neck and shoulders
☛ Deep friction

What Causes Headaches?

The brain itself feels nothing: it simply registers feelings that originate elsewhere. But the entire organ is supplied by tiny blood vessels, many less than a thirty-second of an inch in diameter, which are exquisitely sensitive to mood changes. Under stress they contract sharply (the effect is even more pronounced here than elsewhere in the body), cutting back the vital oxygen supply to interior tissues. Nasty things begin to happen near the surface of the skull when the brain is starved for oxygen.

The first sign of tension within is usually transmitted directly to the face via large nerves from the center of the brain. Tiny muscles of expression are immediately pulled taut, turning smiles into grimaces. As smiling becomes a chore, tenacious little wrinkles begin to appear out of nowhere at the corners of the eyes and mouth. The jaws tighten from just below the ears and the mouth begins to feel dry. Tension spreads rapidly to the muscles of the neck and upper back. The head begins to turn awkwardly, the shoulders appear hunched, and finally the spine itself is twisted out of shape. Eventually the chin tilts forward and the posture of the head, even the whole body, is affected. With no

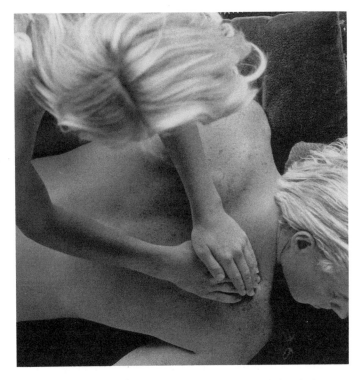

relief, major muscles of the neck and back, strong enough to bend the spine, clamp down on the blood vessels that supply the brain. This, of course, is the classic vicious circle of vasoconstriction; decreased circulation creates muscle tension which in turn further inhibits circulation. If nothing is done to relieve the pressure, the body will finally try to slow things down by sending an unmistakable message: a nasty headache.

Once a headache begins, it's difficult to think clearly about where it came from. Perfectly calm individuals can suffer for no apparent reason and, of course, shattering migraines, caused, perhaps, by chemical imbalances deep within the brain, can wreck an entire day. Exceptional headaches which require specialized medical attention may have little to do with muscle tension or circulation. Nevertheless, the garden variety blinding headache with shooting pain behind the eyes and a stiff neck is probably brought on by too much stress. And since the worst headaches can be so intense, panic and opiate gulping takes over at the first sign of pain. Once the more stupefying antiheadache drugs become part of the picture, massage has little chance. After a while, it simply hurts whenever you're not taking a pill.

Every masseur who knows where to look for the real source of a headache has seen throbbing pain vanish with just a few minutes of directed friction and kneading. The strokes that follow offer a drug-free method of headache control that works in minutes.

Do

Be sure the head and torso are supported.
Include the whole upper back in your massage.
Be sure your partner's eyes are closed.
Warm your hands first.

Don't

Massage while your partner does something else.
"Dig in" under the vertebrae and bony parts of the shoulders.
Put pressure directly on the spine.
Massage under a bright overhead light.

The Massage Solution

If you can reverse the vaso-constriction effect at its source, many stress-induced headaches will disappear as quickly as they appeared. Masseurs seek to release afflicted nerves and blood vessels from the iron grip of overtensed muscles. Relaxing the muscles allows constricted blood vessels to open up and permits large quantities of oxygen to be pumped directly into the brain. The question is: which tensed muscles do you relax?

Facial massage, by itself (see p. 85), is not generally effective against headaches. Only if throbbing frontal headaches centered just behind the eyes have been torturing your partner should you focus the massage on the face itself. Complete instructions are included in Chapter 7. In fact, many headaches are caused by tension in the most unlikely parts of the body. If your partner wonders exactly what you're doing under his shoulder blades or at the base of the jaw, simply ask him to repeat the question in three minutes. In just three minutes, working from the base of the neck, you can triple the oxygen content of the brain. In another minute or two, you can further relieve pressures on certain crucial nerves in the upper back until

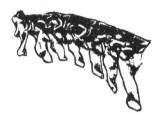

Do these vertebrae bend easily?

local muscle tension completely vanishes. This not only gets rid of your partner's headache, it completely transforms a bad mood.

Nothing like oxygen for an irritable brain.

A Simple Tension Test

Generally, men and women experience tension in different parts of the body. Men usually complain of tightness and pain in the lower back, while women are annoyed by pervasive tension in the neck and shoulders.

Ideally, while you're stroking, your partner will simply surrender to the pleasure of massage. But if the muscles are near spasm, any kind of relaxation becomes virtually impossible. Remember: *never comment on how tense your partner seems to be* — that only

makes things worse. Watch for the nonverbal cues that indicate exactly where tension originates. On this part of the body pay close attention to the way your partner's head is carried. The head is a heavy object that must be supported all day long by the muscles of the upper back and neck. If those muscles are near spasm, your partner will find it difficult to allow her head to relax. Use this test: does the head fall back when you lift the neck? If your partner "helps" you by lifting the entire head when you raise the neck, you've located tension around the neck and shoulders. Work on the neck and shoulders for a few minutes until you feel tightened muscles begin to soften.

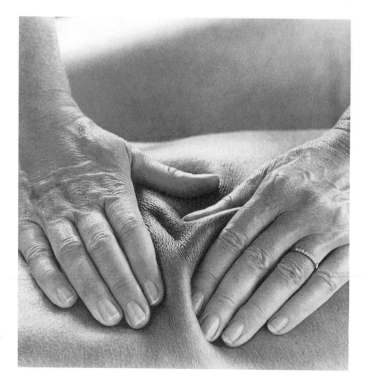

Quick headache relief
- ☛ Oxygenate the brain.
- ☛ Lift and knead the neck.
- ☛ Press the forehead for a full minute.
- ☛ Liberate the shoulder blades.
- ☛ Percussion for the heart and lungs.
- ☛ Deep friction along the spine.
- ☛ Compression.
- ☛ Elbow pounding.

Lifting the Neck

An effective neck lift allows the head to fall back in a graceful arc, reversing some of the pressures at the top of the spine. More importantly, as you lift, the muscles of the upper back are no longer required to support a heavy object that tends to lean slightly forward most of the day—your partner's head. Suddenly it falls back luxuriously beneath your hands, providing welcome relief to the whole upper back, flexing the neck, and opening all the vertebrae within. A well-executed neck lift feels as liberating as it looks.

Be sure you're well balanced and comfortable before trying any lift. Again, if your partner's eyes are open, she's not completely relaxed. Begin by cupping one hand across her eyes while pressing the fingertips of your other hand against the center of her forehead, one of the most sensitive parts of the body. Holding both hands in position for ten seconds permits your partner to close her eyes and concentrate on pure sensation. After your silent count to ten you may want to continue for a moment or two and say a few reassuring words: it's OK for her to keep her eyes closed; darkness makes the experience even more enjoyable.

When her eyes remain closed and her breathing becomes

more regular, you're both ready for the lift. Clasp your fingers basket style (as shown) just beneath your partner's neck and lift straight up. Be careful not to press inward against the large blood vessels on the sides of the neck. The real pressure in this stroke should be right across your fingertips. Lift until you feel resistance, then hold your partner's neck up at the point of tension for a silent count of five before lowering it. Don't force the neck; some will bend further than others. When your partner's head falls all the way back *without resistance*, her whole upper body is close to true relaxation. Once the lift begins,

your partner is likely to ask for more, so be ready to continue for a while. Lift and lower the neck at the same speed, avoiding sudden, jerky movements. Maintain the same even rhythm with each lift.

Boosting Circulation in the Brain

With this simple circulation stroke you can begin to counter the effects of vaso-constriction inside the brain. During each stroke you're in close contact with the blood vessels that supply the brain. And each stroke pushes blood into the head, increasing both the circulation rate and blood volume, *without speeding up the heart.* Here again, there is no other way to do this outside of massage.

Before you begin oiling, move your partner's hair out of the way so the movement can be easily extended to the neck. Most upper back strokes work as well on the back of the neck. Cup your hands slightly to avoid putting direct pressure on your partner's spine. Otherwise, make contact with the full surface of both hands, from fingertips to the base of the palm, throughout. Use moderate pressure.

The stroke begins at the center of the back, on both sides of the spine, and continues up to the base of the skull. Stay off the spine itself. Hold your hands flat, finger-tips facing up. Push up to the neck with one hand while your other hand remains in place. Apply pressure with the hand that's moving up the spine—the other hand should simply rest in place. Be ready to add extra oil if the skin soaks up the first few drops you use. At the top of the stroke allow your fingers to form themselves to the shape of your partner's shoulders. As one hand is lifted at the top of the neck, immediately begin moving up with the other so that what your partner feels is a single, smooth, uninterrupted motion—as regular as a heartbeat.

The complete stroke starts at the middle of the back, travels to the shoulder tops, then returns to the starting point. After the second or third repetition, increase the speed (but not the pressure). In a half a minute you can be moving two or three times faster than your starting rate. Now you're aiming directly for the head with a variation, called "fast stroking," which simply allows you to concentrate on increasing the blood volume in a selected part of the body.

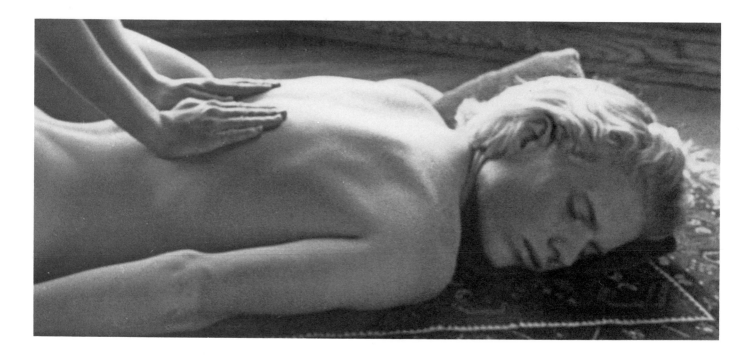

Fingertip Kneading the Neck and Shoulders

Extending from shoulder to shoulder and up onto the neck, the massive trapezius muscle dominates the upper back. Relax it in stages with a kneading stroke that can be done with the fingertips on the neck or using the whole hand on the fleshy parts of the upper back.

Remember that correct use of the thumb is always the key to effective kneading. On the upper back and neck, whether the whole hand is used or just the fingertips, each thumb must pick up a fold of flesh every time you knead.

You only need to do this stroke from one side of the body. Get comfortable next to your partner's upper arm and begin kneading one shoulder, moving across the top of the back to the opposite shoulder. Your partner should be facing you if you plan to extend your kneading to the neck itself. If he's facing away from you the possibilities for neck massage are limited because exposed blood vessels on the side of the neck make kneading difficult.

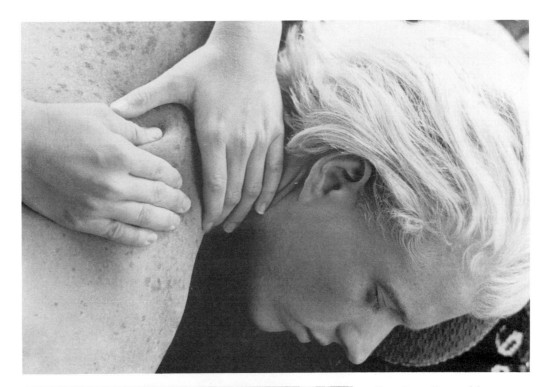

Start kneading at thirty strokes a minute (a complete stroke every two seconds). Then keep going for a full minute or more. Extended kneading is the ideal stroke for fatigued muscles.

Liberating the Shoulder Blades

As tension spreads downward from the head, major muscle groups of the upper back begin to freeze. Just as muscle tension in the neck limits the mobility of the head, tension across the top of the back begins to affect the entire upper torso. Once the back tightens up, the neck and head become even more tense. This is a typical headache syndrome, with tension from the back and head reinforcing each other. Some of the most intense headaches are caused by pressure to large nerves just below the shoulder. Look carefully at your partner's shoulders. Do they seem tight, hunched forward, or permanently elevated? Do they move freely or are they frozen in a single position?

Get comfortable next to your partner's shoulder and use this simple, very satisfying, two-step process for liberating the shoulders. First, try a series of fingertip kneading strokes from the neck down onto the center of the upper back. Then, once the muscles have been relaxed, rotate the massive bony framework of the shoulders. When you do all the work in moving your partner's body, the stroke becomes a "passive exercise." Repeated many times at a constant frequency, this kneading-rotating combination will melt the large trapezius muscle and relax the entire upper back.

Rotating the Scapula

The large, visible scapula that stands out from the back moves independently from the rib cage. By anchoring just below the rounded top of the arm with one hand and pressing down from above with the other (as shown), you can lift and turn the whole scapula. Lift from a low angle. Initially, the range of rotation will depend on just how tight your partner is feeling. Rotate slowly, keeping a firm grip on both surfaces. You'll feel an irregular sort of circle begin to emerge as you turn. Work just inside the point where you feel tension. Gradually, as you turn, the circle will become wider.

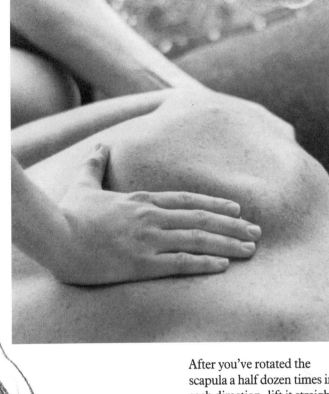

After you've rotated the scapula a half dozen times in each direction, lift it straight up with your bottom hand and apply friction under the bony protrusion with the thumb side of your top hand. Press in under the bone and let your hand follow the shape of the depression. When you're through, lower the shoulder slowly. Remember: *every motion, no matter how insignificant, is felt and becomes a part of your massage.* Make each one count.

Compression

Deep Friction

Is your partner's headache accompanied by a stiff neck? Pressure on nerves that begin in the middle of the back may be the cause of both problems. Start by relaxing the upper back, and the neck pain will often disappear along with the headache. Compression strokes, useful on any fleshy part of the body, work best over thicker muscles, where you can bear down as the hands are rotated. This is a particularly easy movement to learn because, as the stroke travels, the initial hand-over-hand position remains the same.

Oil the entire area you plan to massage, then, with your fingers held together, press down with one hand over the other (as shown). Keep your fingers together and make certain that your bottom hand maintains full contact from the fingertips to the base of the palm throughout the movement. Begin a series of tight circles that will slowly move back and forth across the massage area. Let your fingertips bend over the shoulders and around the sides of your partner's body. After plenty of repetition, compression strokes begin to spread a warm, penetrating feeling that is so pleasant, your partner may not want you to stop.

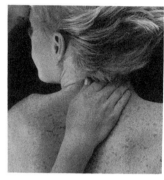

The spinal nerves link the brain with every part of the body. Vertical rows of muscles that hold the spine erect are the first to pick up tension when the nerves are irritated. Soothe those muscles and you reach deep within the spine to the body's major nerves. A more direct connection to the brain cannot be found anywhere in the body.

Locate the ridge of raised muscles that run parallel to each side of the spine. On the lower back these muscles can actually pull the spine slightly out of alignment, causing truly alarming pain. At the top of the back, thick, bony structures keep things in place, but excessively tense muscles next to the spine can still cause terrible discomfort.

This is the source of several remote problems, most commonly stiff necks and headaches.

Anchor your friction movement above or below your working hand. This stroke will take you very close to the spine, but you should avoid pressing directly on sensitive vertebrae. Push down with the fingertips of your friction hand and circle on the muscles. Move up and down the side of the spine from mid-back (not below the bottom ribs) to the base of the neck. Spend extra time on the back of the neck—five strokes for every one you did near the spine. Much of the tension you felt along the spine has been concentrated here. Anchor against the front of your partner's forehead. Feel for the thick neck muscles and rotate your hands on the hardest spots. Again, avoid pressing on the spine itself.

Elbow Pounding

Is your partner beset by minor aches and pains? Here is a way to make something powerful and very pleasant happen that may release him from his worries. With elbow pounding you can sometimes completely replace low-level irritations and nagging pains with the overwhelming feeling of the stroke itself. At the very least, this movement will relax the large muscles of the middle back, the hidden source of many headaches. Don't try to resist elbow pounding; the effects are immediate and overpowering. Intense vibrations spread from the point of contact and can carry right through your partner's body. No massage stroke uses more pressure and no stroke penetrates more deeply. Even so, one doesn't simply pound away with complete abandon. The stroke works best if it's carefully controlled so that the percussion effect can be aimed effectively.

During elbow pounding, as in all percussion movements, (see page 35), the actual "blow" is cushioned by part of your own body. Here, you simply place your elbow against the muscle, bend the hand back, and pound against the base of the palm with the other hand (as shown). Find the two muscu-

lar ridges that run parallel to the spine. If your partner is suffering from a headache, most likely at least one of the ridges will be raised and obviously tight. During the stroke, let your elbow ride along each ridge from the midback, just above the bottom of the rib cage, all the

way up to the base of the neck. Stay off the neck itself. This is a powerful stroke — don't overdo it. Avoid "digging in" to the muscles with your elbow. Again, ride along the surface, letting the elbow push into the muscle only at the moment of the blow. Half of your arm absorbs the blow so what your partner actually

feels is a generous vibration that begins near the spine and penetrates deep within. Here on the upper back, elbow pounding travels well as long as you confine it to major muscles and avoid the spine itself. Make at least three complete passes over each area you pound.

4.
Three-Minute Relief from Neck and Shoulder Pain

Three essential strokes
One minute each, fifty repetitions

☛ Circulation (stroking)
☛ Fingertip kneading
☛ Deep friction

Relaxing the Neck and Shoulders

Neck and shoulder pain, once practically the exclusive complaint of women, now shows up nearly as often in men. When dealing with work-related stress, many of the serious neck and shoulder problems you will encounter will come from people who operate typewriters and computers. Since a woman's shoulder muscles are often disproportionately smaller than a man's, the effort of supporting the head, a heavy object, for hours in the fixed positions required by office work can generate severe tensions. However, computer work is so demanding on the neck and shoulder muscles of *any* operator that, eventually, certain aches and pains are simply taken for granted.

Away from the office, we experiment with various exercises and drugs, and when they fail, resign ourselves to perpetually tense shoulders and aching necks. Constant stress then takes its inevitable

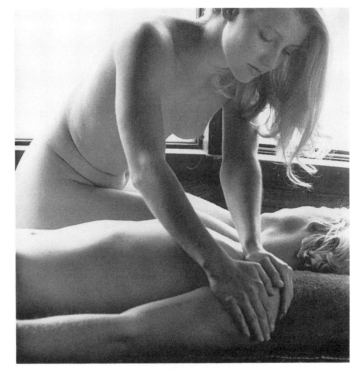

toll; bad moods last longer, irritable behavior becomes the rule, and, eventually, major personality changes are established.

The massage solution to aches and pains in the neck and shoulders calls for many repetitions of a few simple movements. A single fingertip kneading stroke, for example, can easily be repeated more than one hundred times in only three minutes. Whether your partner is male or female, you can begin to change fixed patterns of tension in the neck and shoulders with your first Super Massage.

Rotating and Pulling the Head

Does your partner have a noisy neck? When the head is turned from side to side do you sometimes hear grinding or popping sounds? Interior stiffness almost anywhere in the body can eventually lead to the kind of chronic aches that make it impossible to escape from pain. Use the following movement—a simple passive exercise—to restore the natural mobility of the neck. It will stretch out stiff ligaments, flex the cervical vertebrae, and leave your partner smiling.

When rotating and pulling various parts of the body, you will find natural "handles" just about everywhere you want them to be. The head, for example, can be grasped at the base of the skull and beneath the chin (as shown). Supported at both points, it rotates evenly.

Slowly turn your partner's chin toward one shoulder until you feel resistance, then stop—the moment you reach the point of tension, it's time to begin rotation. There's no need to lift the head more than an inch or two. Simply pull straight back under the chin and the base of the skull, then turn the head slowly

from one shoulder to the other. A flexible neck permits the head to turn almost all the way across, but, of course, stiffness will limit the arc. Never force the head past the point of tension, and try not to call attention to tensed muscles. Super Massage, not talk, will loosen the stiffness. At the far side of each rotation, pause for a moment, then bring your partner's head back to the starting point. Keep the arc smooth and even. During this movement it is particularly important to avoid short, jerky motions. After ten rotations, the point of tension begins to recede gradually as the neck becomes more supple.

Circulation for the Upper Back

Start relaxing the neck and shoulders from far below. Two clearly visible vertical ridges of muscles run parallel to each side of the spine, helping to hold it in place. Trace these muscles with a series of long circulation strokes that will turn across the shoulders and descend to a starting point just above the beginning of the rib cage.

Sit comfortably near your partner's waist. Some people appreciate a small pillow under the head and beneath the ankles. Begin by pressing the base of your palms against the muscles near the middle of the back (as shown). With your hands in place press all of your fingers forward until they lay flat on either side of the spine. If your hands are significantly wider than the spinal muscles, let your fingers ride on the outside of the muscles. Never press directly on the spine itself.

As you push up along the spine, distribute pressures equally from the base of the palms to your fingertips.

Turn at the base of the neck and move out to the shoulders, letting your fingers mold themselves to the contour of your partner's body. Turn again at the outside of the shoulders and begin your descent along the sides of the back, fingers pointing toward the massage surface. Turn a final time at the middle of the back and return to the starting position. Practice this stroke a few times until the various turns flow into each other and the entire stroke becomes a single, smooth, uninterrupted movement.

What your partner feels is a wave of sensation flowing up the center of the back and down his sides. Usually, by the fourth or fifth repetition you will feel the spinal muscles begin to soften. If they're still tense, continue, even if it means extending the entire massage session, until you feel a change. Your partner will appreciate the extra consideration.

Fingertip Kneading the Spine

Whether you're massaging around the top or bottom of the back, it's crucial to relax the long muscles that run parallel to the spine. Any pressure on the spine itself will create tension throughout the whole neck and shoulder area. This basic fingertip kneading stroke travels so well that you can find ways to use it on nearly every part of the body. It's especially good on hard-to-reach spots where full hand kneading becomes difficult.

This stroke moves exactly the same way as full hand kneading but the contact is more specific. Grasping a small fold of flesh with your fingertips permits you to direct the kneading effect to a single set of muscles, while excluding the surrounding tissue. The spinal muscles, for example, can be kneaded with your fingertips while the spine and rib cage remain unaffected.

Get comfortable and reach across to the opposite side of your partner's spine. You can knead both sides of the spine without changing position. While moving the hands in opposing circles, pick up a fold of flesh between the fingers and thumb of one hand while the other hand is open wide (as shown). As you move up and down the spinal muscles, first one hand then the other will pick up a fold of flesh. Begin fingertip kneading just above the bottom of the rib cage and move up toward the neck along the long muscles that run parallel to the spine. Knead the side

of the neck and the shoulders before moving back down the same side of the spine. Massage one side of the spine at least three times, then do the other. After a few repetitions you can often feel tension melt as the spinal muscles become relaxed and supple.

Real relaxation for the neck and shoulders is now within reach.

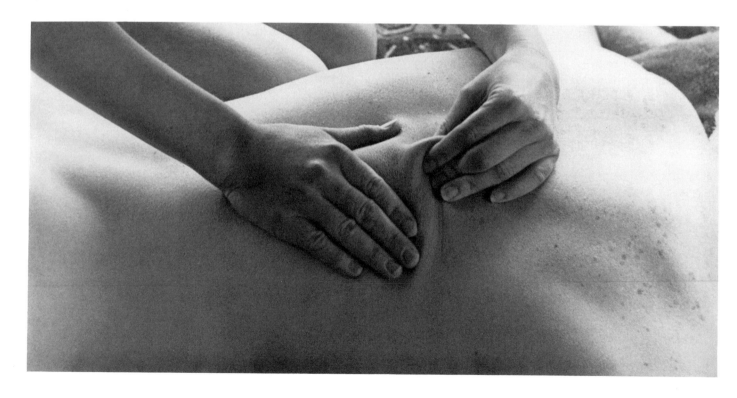

Deep Friction

Happily, neck and shoulder fatigue can disappear remarkably fast. Even after days of discomfort, headaches and assorted aches and pains will vanish in minutes with the right massage treatment. Most fatigued backs long for several minutes of uninterrupted deep friction. Here is a way to extend the friction strokes from the headache chapter to include the whole of the upper back. When spreading friction across the upper back, stay off the spine, shoulder blades, and bony shoulder tops. Large, powerful muscles of the upper back will accept pressure from the whole surface of your hand (from the fingertips to the base of the palm). Deep friction strokes on this part of the body require more pressure than most massage movements. Be sure your partner is comfortable and well cushioned.

Kneel or sit cross-legged on a small pillow below your partner's shoulder. Give equal attention to both sides of the spine during upper-back friction strokes. If your partner's neck is so stiff that the head doesn't turn easily, you may want to support the shoulders from below with a couple of small pillows.

Anchor the stroke above or below the massage area, using the whole surface of one

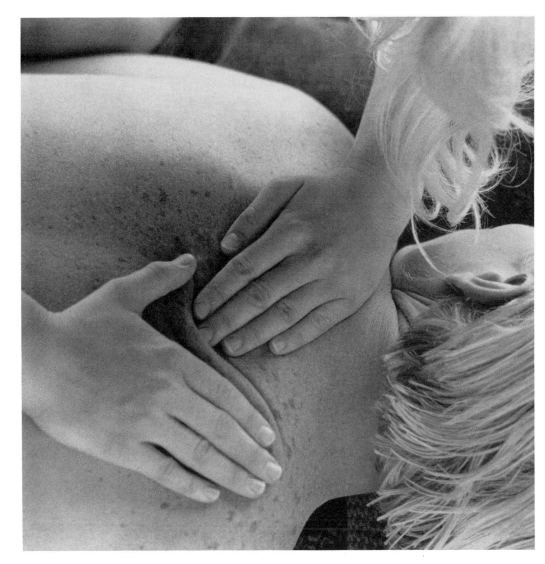

hand. Keep the thumb and forefinger spread wide for best control. When repositioning of the anchor hand becomes awkward, keep it in place and press under it with your friction hand. Open the thumb and forefinger (as shown) and push a fold of flesh under the forefinger with your friction hand. Locate the muscles you want to massage with the fingertips of your friction hand, then lower your whole hand onto your partner's body. With your fingers pressed together, push down and rotate on the muscular tissue below. Let your hand form itself to the changing shape of your partner's body as the stroke travels from one part of the back to another. Do one side of the spine thoroughly, then the other.

Pounding

If your partner moans and groans with pleasure throughout a friction movement, you can intensify the feeling, without changing your position, with pounding, a delightful percussion variation. Vibrations from this stroke will penetrate deep within, in some cases *right through* your partner's body. Percussion strokes have a way of taking over and creating a reality of their own. Let it happen.

Provide a cushion for your pounding stroke by striking the back of one hand with the other. It's best to pound on the back of the fingers (as shown) and let the vibration carry through to your partner's body. Move the contact hand, as you pound, to focus the stroke on the heavily muscled parts of the upper back. Again, stay off the spine itself, and the neck.

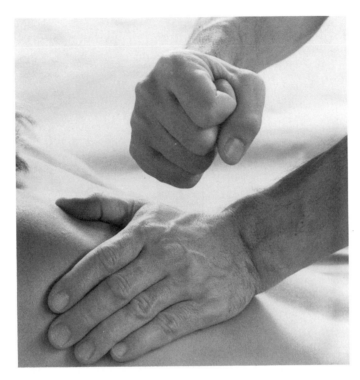

Remember that the key to effective percussion is restraint; all the "blows" should be cushioned and carefully directed. You want a light rain, not a thunderstorm.

One simple rule in massage is to do big things on the big parts of the body and save the little things for little parts of the body.

Since the back is the very largest part of the body, it fairly cries out for a luxurious stroke like the forearm press. The moment you begin, your partner feels a languid warmth spreading slowly across the whole upper torso; just right after deep, penetrating friction sequences.

The forearm press is easier to do if you reach across your partner's spine and massage the opposite side of his back. Keep the flat part of your clenched fist down and in contact at all times. The two main points of contact are on the flat part of the knuckles and against the fleshy inner forearm. On curved parts of the body, such as the sides, bend your knuckles and keep the forearm down on the flat part of the back as you rotate. Generally, the whole forearm and hand will rotate as one. As the forearm press moves up and down the back, lean into it to avoid breaking contact at any point.

Circling slowly with your contact hand, covering the back from the bottom of the rib cage to the shoulders, continue up and down the back at the same speed for a full minute or two.

Compression

If your partner has a stiff neck *and* seems nervous, try several minutes of compression on the upper back. Compression strokes are one of the quickest antidotes to nervous tension. (More on that in Chapter 8.) They are easy to do and will work with little preparation in almost any setting. The penetrating, immensely soothing motion has a hypnotic effect that calms jangled nerves.

Effective almost anywhere on the body, compression movements are especially useful on the fleshy parts of the back. Simply place one open hand on top of the other, press down, and rotate in small circles. As you rotate, let your fingers curl around the edges of your partner's body, maintaining full contact from the fingertips to the base of the palm. Large muscle groups will accept plenty of pressure—check with your partner to see what feels good. Intense movements, like compression and friction, must stay off bony protrusions around the spine and shoulder blades, and avoid the sides of the neck. Cover the whole fleshy surface on one side of the spine with compression, then do the other side. Repeat the movement at least three times.

Rolling

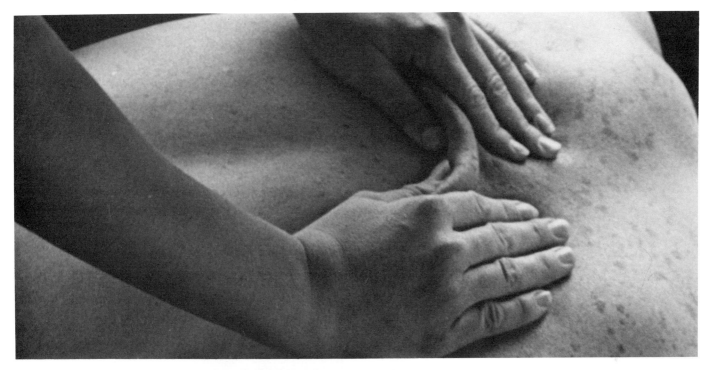

Here is a pleasing variation of the popular fingertip kneading stroke. Rolling allows you to amplify the plucking part of kneading during which the thumb and forefinger grasp a tiny fold of flesh. Typically, when you are fingertip kneading the upper back, only the tips of the fingers can be used to pick up flesh, but with this variation you can fold the flesh over the

whole length of your forefingers. It's sometimes surprising just how large an area you can roll. Even on well-muscled backs, your forefingers will disappear beneath the long fold of flesh.

Put your hands down on your partner's back palm side down. Move in to the area you want to roll until your fingertips are nearly facing each other on opposite sides of the spine. Push down with your fingers until a small fold

of flesh appears above your thumbs. Then use your thumbs to fold it back over the forefingers (as shown). Once you've grasped the fold of flesh, push forward with both forefingers while pulling back with the thumbs. You're ready to roll—use both thumbs at once.

5.
Three-Minute Relief from Lower Back Pain

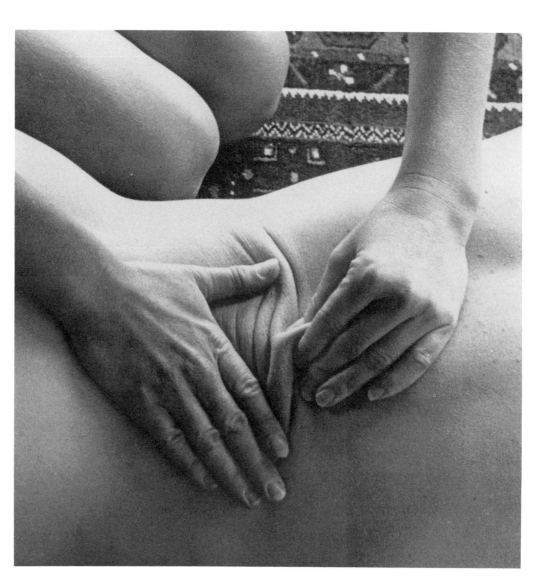

Three essential strokes
One minute each, fifty repetitions

☛ Back stretching
☛ Kneading the side of the back
☛ Hip friction

How to Avoid Lower Back Pain

This part of the book is mainly (but not exclusively) for men. In Chapter 3 we saw how women tend to experience tension in the neck and shoulders—men are most sensitive around the lower back. Sudden cramps next to the spine can bend the whole body to one side, making standing up a painful ordeal. Panic takes over quickly—how do you adjust to pain that doubles you over? This close to the spine, however, immobilizing pain can be caused by nothing more serious than a local muscle spasm. Nevertheless, to be certain there's no structural damage, whenever severe pain occurs in the lower back, your partner should be checked by a doctor before beginning massage.

Most lower back pain arrives so suddenly and is so intense that your partner may fear the worst: the dreaded slipped disc. But powerful back

muscles pulling hard on the bottom of the spine can cause almost as much discomfort without doing any permanent damage. The moment the spine is bent past a certain point, intense pressure builds on the nerves of the lower back. Pain so excruciating that your partner may have difficulty standing up straight can follow. If the source of the pain is muscular (most lower back complaints are), use Super Massage to straighten up the back in just three minutes.

Look carefully at the muscles of your partner's back. Don't be intimidated by a rock-hard ridge on one side of the spine—you've probably found the problem. The tension will yield, gradually, to a combination of passive exercise and massage. When cramped muscles contract so fiercely that they refuse to expand, the immediate problem is lack of oxygen. However, before you can oxygenate the tissues, it's important to begin as you would with any cramped muscles: stretch out the whole lower back.

Quick Relief from Cramps: Back Stretching

Kneading the Side of the Back and the Buttocks

Back stretching is Super Massage at its very best. By providing fast, drugless pain relief, this single movement can eliminate hours, days, or even weeks of suffering. Since most lower back cramps are stress induced, the initial muscle spasm has a nasty habit of striking at the most inconvenient times: just before a board meeting, during a tense negotiation, or while packing for a much needed holiday. Happily, back stretching requires no special preparation or equipment. In the office, at home, or at play—wherever pain strikes—you will be ready to help.

Whenever you're working on a cramp, be gentle—forcing the issue will cause more pain. Pull down on the cramped lower back muscles by pressing your partner's knees against her chest. This simple movement has a curious side effect: as the muscles on the backs of the legs are pulled tight, the long muscles that run parallel to the spine are stretched out.

Support your partner's legs with both hands as you lift until her knees are straight up. Then flex the knees and press forward on her shins with the fleshy part of your forearm (as shown). It's important to move slowly and deliberately throughout this

sequence. Avoid sudden, jerky movements when you lift, press, and lower the leg. An unhurried, consistent rhythm works best. Press to the point of tension, hold for a silent count of ten, then lower the legs to the starting position. Remember: as you press down on the knees, you're stretching out cramped muscles in the lower back. If you're not sure where to stop, get some feedback from your partner. (Moaning and smiling means you've got it just right—keep going.) As the muscles of the lower back begin to relax, the point of tension will gradually recede. Release your partner from the cramp, and the pain will vanish as quickly as it appeared. Repeat the movement at least three times.

A perennial favorite of masseurs, the side and the buttocks offer the best opportunity for kneading anywhere in the body. Most kneading strokes must work around bony structures or stay within a single small area. On the buttocks, however, you're finally free of bony obstacles and major surface blood vessels, so there's no reason to limit the stroke to your fingertips. Reach across your partner's body, open up your hands on the side, and knead.

The large gluteal muscles in the buttocks receive almost no benefit from ordinary walking or running; you have to actually climb something before the muscles begin to tighten. Thus, the alarming pear-shaped figure that mysteriously plagues so many committed runners. To be sure, your partner may have significant cosmetic reasons for toning the buttocks, but for highly stressed individuals who live on the threshold of excruciating back cramps, the benefits to the lower back are far more important. The gluteals begin well above the

lowest part of the spine. If they're kept well toned, the whole lower back is more likely to be properly stabilized.

Kneading the buttocks also feels very good. Your partner will usually remind you of that after the first few strokes.

Use the whole flat surface of your hands. For once, you can pick up a generous fold of flesh with your thumbs on each kneading rotation. Squeeze gently. The buttocks can be kneaded separately or combined with a general stroke that includes the whole side of the back (as shown). Start kneading just below the lower ribs and work your way down to the buttocks. On the outside of the thigh, where the gluteals end, reverse the stroke and return to the starting position.

Hip Friction

Once the side and buttocks have been well kneaded, it's easy to reach the deep-set joint at the top of the leg with a penetrating friction movement. Anchor above the joint, opening your thumb wide (as shown). Push inward and down with the top half of the fingers. When you can feel the joint, begin to rotate your hand slowly, spreading friction with the top half of your fingers. Hip friction becomes awkward on the near side of the body. It's best to move to the other side and reach across to massage the opposite hip.

Remember: whenever you change sides, do so quietly while maintaining contact with a single hand or even a fingertip. Throughout every massage, continuous physical contact is crucial. Breaking it interrupts the hypnotic mood you've been working to create, and your partner goes from feeling pampered to feeling abandoned.

Hip friction can also work nicely around the small of the back, where the nerves that supply the legs emerge. Use less pressure here, more speed.

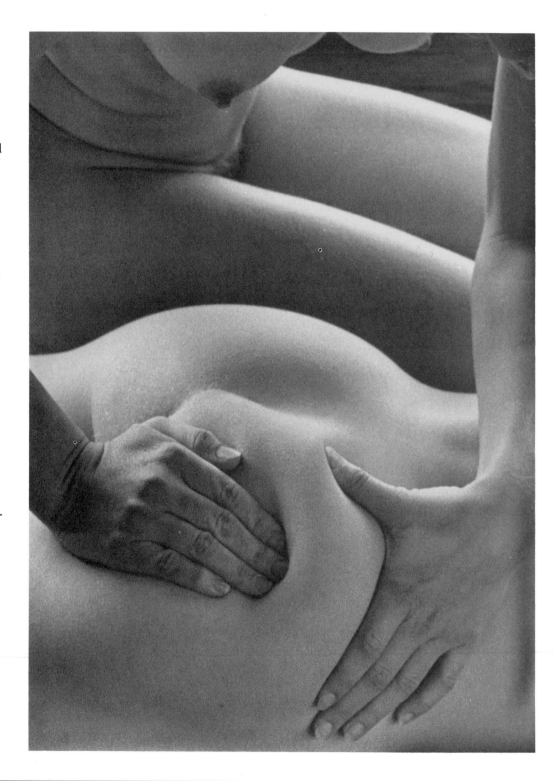

Compression

High Intensity Compression

Compression is even easier to do on the lower back than it was on the bonier neck and shoulders. And it feels just as good.

During this stroke keep the whole side of your leg in contact with your partner's body. A comfortable starting position allows plenty of room to reach the far side of the back and makes it easy to maintain contact if you need to reposition your hands. Oil the whole lower back area, put one open hand over the other, and begin circling. Turn your hands in small circles, use moderate pressures, and cover the whole area from the thigh to the bottom of the rib cage. On this part of the body, compression strokes are enhanced by maintaining full contact from the fingertips to the base of the palm. As your hands turn, push down so that pressures to your contact hand are distributed evenly. (Don't "dig in" with your fingertips.) The heavily muscled parts of the lower back and the buttocks, where the most debilitating cramps originate, will accept deep pressures. Ease up a bit just below the lower ribs, where you're directly over internal organs.

Once you get started, it's easy to continue with compression for a long time. At times, this simple movement feels just as good to your partner as the more complex kneading and percussion strokes.

If the lower back is so tense that ordinary compression movements seem to glide ineffectually over the surface (or if you're much smaller than your partner), use this stroke to intensify the penetrating effect. Heavily muscled types always seem to appreciate the extra pressure.

Make a fist with one hand and press the flat part of your knuckle against your partner's back. Grasp the contact hand around the wrist, then begin turning while pressing down with both hands (as shown). Lean into the movement when massaging thicker muscles, but avoid "digging in" with the tips of your knuckles or the bottom of the palm. Like other strokes that require extra effort, high intensity compression is more effective if you reach across the back to massage the opposite side of your partner's body. Circle slowly.

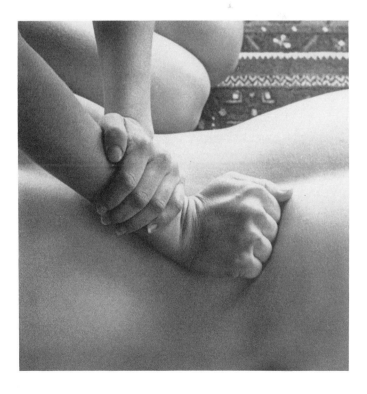

A Half Body Lift

This is one of the rare massage strokes in which physical strength matters. If your partner is much bigger than you, skip the half body lift and instead try one of the back flexes described in Chapter 10. The lift is, however, much easier to do than it looks.

To practice it, prop up your partner's head and shoulders on a pillow—that way if you let go suddenly, the trip down will be a pleasant one. Practice until you can move from the initial lifting position behind the neck to the full upright position without hesitation. As always, pay close attention to how your partner is actually feeling. Try to emphasize the lifting sensation, not the mechanics.

The lower back lift is an effective passive exercise for the massive sacroiliac joint where the bottom of the spine meets the hips. Pressures generated during stress tend to tighten up the muscles and tendons around this joint. Here's a way to reverse those destructive forces.

During the half body lift it's helpful to have a medium-sized flat pillow for your knees. Get comfortable, then stretch your hands under your partner's armpits, clasping your fingers around the back of the neck. Let your fingers meet at the center of the neck, lacing them together if possible (as shown). As you lift, put your front foot squarely on the ground, forming a kind of stabilizing tripod, and be sure not to push forward on the neck—this is massage, not wrestling. All the real pressure is exerted just below your partner's shoulders. Avoiding sudden, jerky movements, pull up slowly until you feel resistance. As always, the point of tension will vary—never force your partner past it. Hold steady at the point of tension for a silent count of ten, then lower your partner slowly to the massage surface. Take a deep breath and try another half body lift. Moving at the same measured speed, repeat the lift at least three times.

Deep Plucking

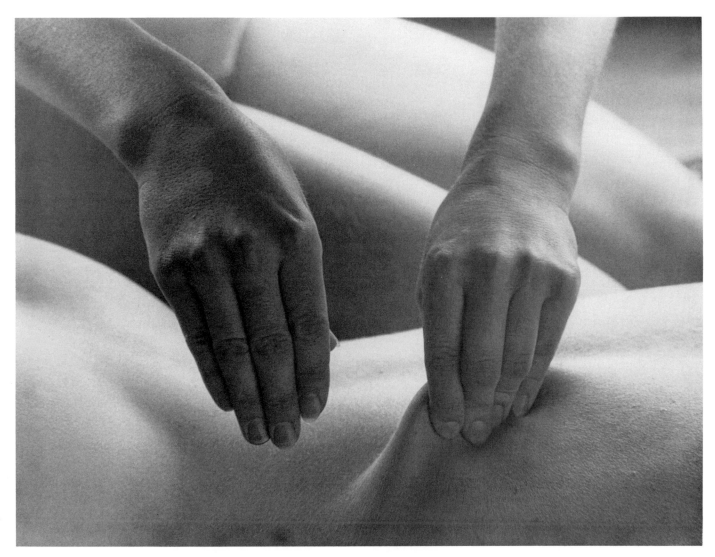

Plucking was supposedly the favorite stroke of Julius Caesar, who used massage to unwind when he wasn't busy conquering the world. From the moment it begins, this unique percussion stroke has a way of commanding one's full attention. Have you been struggling to convince a very self-absorbed individual to find time for massage? Are you trying to find a way around the rush reflex (see p. 98)? Start with a minute or two of deep plucking and your partner should settle down fast.

(see p. 98)

Push down gently into the soft tissue of the lower back or buttocks to pick up a fold of flesh between your thumb and four fingers (as shown). Lift and then release it. As you release one fold, lift the next with your other hand. By alternating hands like this you can move slowly across an entire fleshy part of the body, plucking as you go. Avoid pinching your partner — the ideal effect is a gentle squeezing. Pluck on the muscular ridges along the spine and below the ribs, but stay off the bony rib cage itself. Plucking works best where the flesh rises easily.

70   Three-Minute Relief from Lower Back Pain

A Full Body Sweep

The luxurious body sweep spreads sensation from the center of your partner's body outward toward the extremities. The stroke begins and ends on the lower back.

Touch your partner's body with your knees — it's easier to reach forward if you sit close to your partner. Press down on the small of the back with the full surface of both forearms. Make a fist with both hands and bend them in against the body (as shown). Every bit of contact during a forearm sweep will magnify the sensation. Maintaining

contact from the elbow to the surface of your fist, move your top arm up to the shoulders while the lower arm descends to the knees. Naturally, the precise finishing point for each arm will depend on the size relationship between you and your partner. Move the arms at the same speed, stopping

only at the furthest extremity and the starting point for a few moments.

Sweep the whole back of the body three times.

6.
Three-Minute Relief from Sore Feet

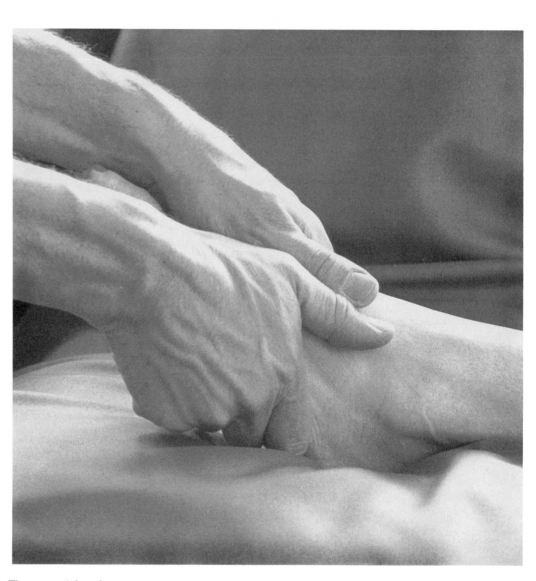

Three essential strokes
One minute each, fifty repetitions

☛ Circulation
☛ Fast stroking the calf
☛ Multiple joint stretching

Complete Peace for the Feet

Most adults haven't been touched on the foot by another person since childhood. Feet, we are led to believe, require little care and are quite incapable of experiencing pleasurable sensations — they either hurt or feel nothing at all. You bind and gag the feet in tight leather shoes, then you step on things; you kick things. Fitness plans usually emphasize the upper part of the body: the face, biceps, waistline, perhaps the hips and legs, while the feet are taken for granted. It's assumed they will perform on demand — nothing complicated is supposed to happen below the ankles.

We usually think of stress as a complex mental state that originates at the very top of the body. In fact, since the feet are richly supplied with nerves from the lower spine, pain that originates, say, in the arch, will travel quickly. Sore feet will sour a good mood in minutes and make pills that knock out the whole central nervous system tempting. If you want to control stress, the importance of relaxing the feet cannot be overemphasized.

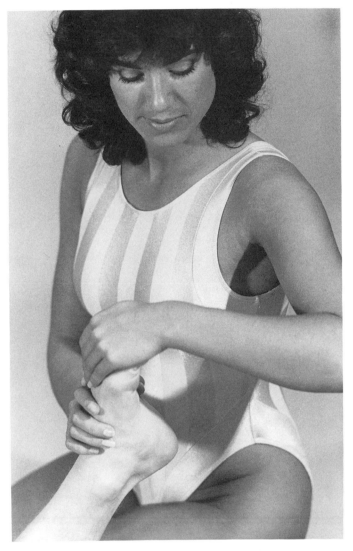

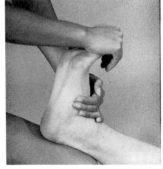

A foot massage is **an excellent** introduction to the powers of massage. Highly stressed types who would not normally sit still for a massage will always let you fool around with their feet for a few minutes (if only to get rid of pain and restore the feet to their "normal" deadened state). Once you've relaxed and reinvigorated the feet, you'll have a convert who's anxious to test Super Massage on other parts of the body.

A decent foot massage requires some real effort — expect to work up a sweat before you're through.

Circulation

Massaging the top of the foot where the venous system becomes clearly visible, you can see another important element of the fluid release effect at work. Stroking toward the heart accelerates circulation while the heart slows down. This of course is the very opposite of what happens during stress. If your partner is suffering from the effects of vasoconstriction (pale skin, shallow breathing, snappish behavior), try beginning your massage on the feet, the furthest spot in the body from the heart.

Kneel just below your partner's feet, resting the foot you plan to massage against your knee. Wrap your hands around the top of the foot, with the fingers facing in opposite directions (as shown). Keeping your fingers and thumb pressed together, press forward with both hands at once. End the stroke above the ankle or, if you can reach comfortably, halfway up the calf. Maintain contact with the sides of your partner's foot as you return to the starting position. Foot circulation feels especially good at high speeds. Start slowly to establish the form of the stroke (every foot is different), then, smoothly, build

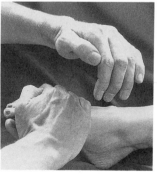

up speed. At faster speeds it feels good to press forward with one hand at a time. Take care not to slap at the foot — whatever the speed, keep your rhythm consistent.

Rotating the Top of the Foot

The feet bend in several places besides the obvious one at the ankles. Notice the clear separation of movement when you rotate a foot at the ankle: the leg remains perfectly still while the foot turns. Near the toes, structures become less flexible, but the joints are mobile enough to stretch nearby muscles, tendons, and ligaments. Here again, you can do things on the bottom of the foot that your partner simply cannot do for himself. During this stroke the top half of the foot will rotate while the bottom half remains still.

To get started, rest your partner's foot on or just above your knee and fold one hand over the top of the toes. Anchor the stroke with your other hand just below the ankle (as shown). Try to isolate most of the movement above the anchor hand.

Determining the point of tension by gently rocking the top of the foot from side to side provides a sense of how much movement is possible. The greatest range of movement is either straight up or straight down, but the whole top of the foot will rotate in an irregular arc. Make at least three complete revolutions in each direction.

Then, using just your thumb and forefinger, grasp the sides of each toe and rotate slowly. Don't rush the toes. It's probably been a long time since your partner has been touched here by another human being.

Fast Stroking the Calf

Since the muscles and tendons that operate the foot descend from the calf, a decent foot massage should start just below the knee. Beginning on the midcalf, the powerful Achilles tendon wraps around the heel, extending all the way to the bottom of the foot. It is the body's largest and most unpredictable tendon. Any tendon can tear unexpectedly, but when the Achilles gives way, proper walking becomes impossible. High-heeled shoes tend to shorten it, while competitive sports stretch it to the limit. Sports masseurs are careful to keep the tendon supple, even if that means spending an extra five minutes a day on the back of the leg. But it doesn't take a rigorous workout to tighten up a tendon—stress can have much the same effect. When exercising, stressed individuals often make the dangerous mistake of skipping a warm-up. If something breaks, it's likely to be the Achilles tendon.

A variety of friction and fingertip kneading strokes work well on this tendon. But if you have time for only one movement, a fast hand-over-hand pulling stroke will warm the whole area and leave it feeling invigorated.

With your partner lying on his back, support the leg just above the knee with a small pillow or simply lift it straight up (as shown). Either way, it's easy to pull back from the bottom of the knee to the ankle, using the whole surface of your hands. Start slowly and build up speed. One hand should be up near the back of the knee while the other pulls down to the ankle. What your partner feels is a single, uninterrupted wave of sensation cascading down the leg. Keep it up for a full minute.

Finish the movement by pulling both hands down the foot all the way to the toes. Then do the same thing on the other leg.

Thumb Kneading the Bottom of the Foot

The bottom of the foot will accept more pressure than almost any other part of the body. One can bear down against the arch with the heel of one hand or, better yet, the thumbs can be brought to bear directly. This is a fingertip kneading variation, a stroke that is usually reserved for the more delicate parts of the body. Here on the bottom of the feet, however, the powerful muscles of the arch fairly cry out for plenty of pressure. Give it to them with your thumbs.

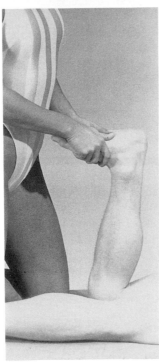

Raise the bottom half of your partner's leg by bending it at the knee. Kneel at the toes or behind the heel when massaging the bottom of the foot. Wrap your hands around the top of the foot, keeping your thumbs parallel on the bottom of the foot. Keep a firm grip on the foot throughout this movement. Pressing down hard, rotate your thumbs on the tough bottom of the foot. Each thumb rotates in an independent circle, just as each hand worked in an independent circle during the full hand kneading strokes (see p. 34). And, again, the circles are in opposition—one thumb is up while the other is down. Moving slowly, cover the whole bottom of the foot from heel to toes. Then return to the starting position. Repeat the stroke three times, then do the other foot.

Deep Compression

Lubricating the Ankle

Your partner may be delighted to discover that the usual pressures on the bottom of the foot can be reversed. If thumb kneading was appreciated, you can amplify the same sensation with this stroke. Lean into a deep compression movement and bear down on the arch with your whole arm.

All that pressure requires a bit of extra control. Avoid bending the foot too far back by kneeling close enough to support it with the front of your knee or a small pillow while anchoring just above the ankle (as shown). Put pressure on the bottom of the foot with the whole flat part of your knuckle and, space permitting, the fleshy base of the palm. Press down hard with your closed fist and begin rotating. Start on the arch, moving up onto the ball of the foot and down to the thick surface of the heel. Stay on the bottom of the foot with this movement. Avoid "digging in" with the sharp part of your knuckles. Turn your hand in small circles, always making as much contact as possible.

No joint anywhere on the body is subjected to greater stress than the ankle. When you exercise, particularly when you run, the ankle is literally pounded from above by the whole weight of the body; nevertheless it must lift and turn without complaint. Stiffness here can lead to all kinds of nasty injuries, the least of which is the well-known sprained ankle. Happily, though, it's easy to isolate the foot from the destructive effects of stress that originates elsewhere in the body. Have your partner lie down on her back, then support the leg with a small pillow under the knee. That takes care of the leg, now you can take care of her ankle.

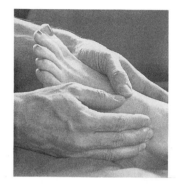

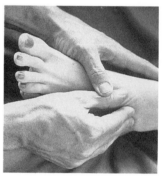

Reach down to your partner's ankle with all four fingers of both hands. By pressing in with the tips of your fingers while circling the ankle, you can combine three very important stress-reduction techniques. First, accumulated acids and other waste products are pressed out of the tissues. Secondly, the production of synovial fluid, an important joint lubricant, is stimulated. And finally, the stroke feels very good.

Circle the ankle four times in each direction. You can sometimes feel fluid draining from the joint as you massage. When that happens, follow the draining movement with a hard four-finger spot friction stroke to the whole calf.

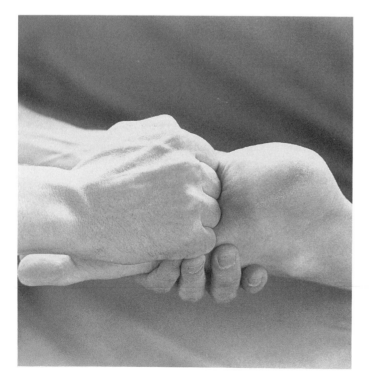

Rotating the Foot

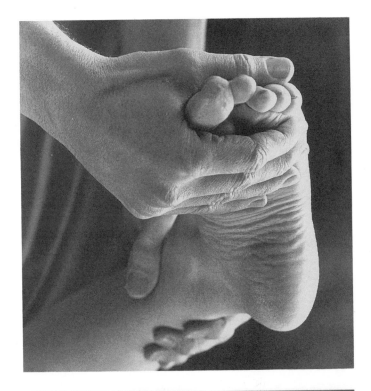

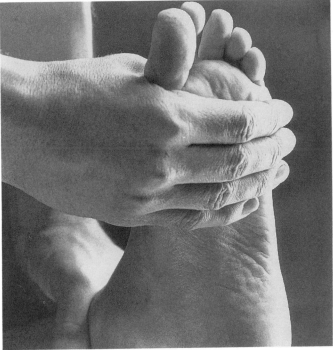

For every ankle that's sprained during a strenuous sporting event probably two are twisted stepping off a curb the wrong way. As stress levels mount throughout the body, tension is transmitted directly to tendons and ligaments inside the joints. The less mobility inside a joint, the more likely painful sprains become. We don't usually think of our ankles after a hard day at work . . . until it's too late.

Sprains can't be entirely prevented with massage, but we can make them less likely simply by keeping the ligaments inside the ankle supple. If a sprain does occur, frequent massage will shorten the recovery time by as much as 60 percent. More on that later. Stretching the ligaments inside the ankle must be done gently. The following foot rotation movement— practiced by sports masseurs

all over the world — is an ideal passive exercise for the whole ankle. You do all the work, your partner does nothing at all.

With your partner lying on her stomach, place a pillow under the knee. Lift and support the leg with one hand just above the ankle. Now grasp the top of the foot with your free hand and begin turning it. If you turn from just below the toes, the complex joint at the middle of the foot will be flexed as well. Like all joints, the foot turns in an irregular arc. Test the limits of the arc the first time around, then turn just inside the point of tension. Bend the top of the foot outward (as shown) and rotate it three times in each direction.

Multiple Joint Stretching

With a single movement, the foot can become a useful handle for stretching all the joints from the ankles to the hips. With your partner on his back, hold the top of his foot just below the toes while grasping the heel with your other hand. Lift the foot slightly and, smoothly, pull straight back with both hands at once. As the joints at the ankle, knee, and hip are flexed, the effects of this simple pulling motion can be felt halfway across the body. Pull until you feel real resistance, then hold for a silent count of ten. Release the foot gradually, but just before you break contact start pulling again. That way what your partner feels is an uninterrupted wave of pulling and release, pulling and release. Repeat the movement at least three times on each one of your partner's feet.

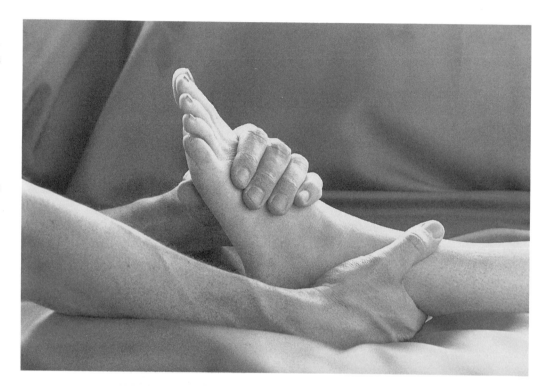

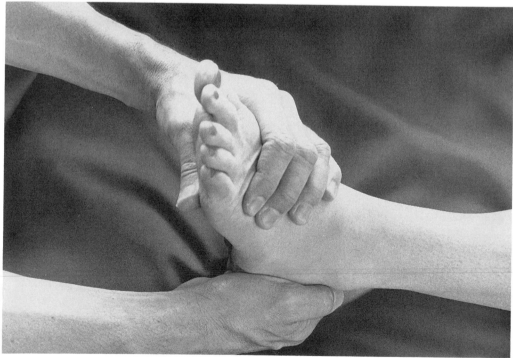

Quick Relief from Sprains

Much of the discomfort of simple sprains comes from the intense concentration of fluids in the injured area. The familiar sprained ankle that swells to several times its normal size cannot recover until the fluids are dispersed. If the pain is considerable, check first with a doctor to be sure a local fracture isn't the real problem. Once you get a medical clearance you can begin massage as soon as the usual cold compress has been removed. You would expect the amazing fluid release techniques that drain wastes from exhausted muscles to be particularly effective around a sprain, and you won't be disappointed. A hundred years ago, when physicians still routinely massaged their patients, Douglas Graham, an American physician, had remarkable success with friction, kneading, and circulation sequences in speeding a patient's recovery from sprains.

Graham records patients with severe sprain under his care recovering the full use of the sprained joint in five days when massage was begun at once. In seven hundred cases of sprains and joint contusions treated by French, German, and Scandinavian army surgeons, comparative statistics reveal that we can reasonably expect that sprains treated by massage will recover in one third the time

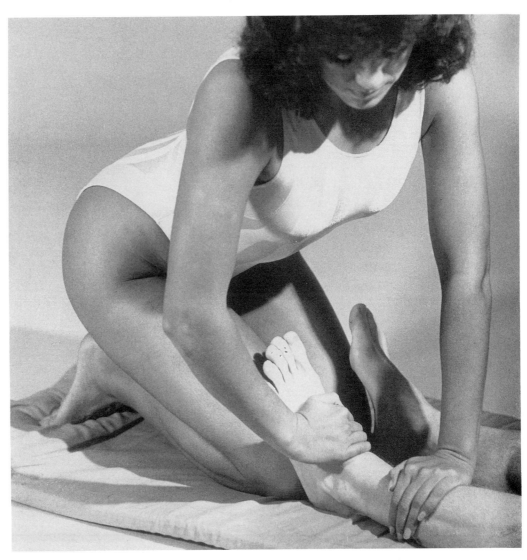

than those will where the part is kept immobile. — Kathryn L. Jensen, *Fundamentals of Massage*

You'll find nothing mysterious in the techniques that

worked so well for Dr. Graham; just a few minutes of hard work are required several times a day. To disperse the irritating fluids, Graham depended on concentrated fingertip kneading from midcalf to midfoot followed by light friction to the joint and a few full hand circulation strokes from the foot to the

knee. Use light pressures while the area remains tender and repeat the massage three times a day. As the swelling begins to recede, increase the pressure and frequency of massage. Each session need only last a few minutes. Massaging a sprain will save your partner days of recovery time.

3
LOOK BETTER,
FEEL BETTER,
SLEEP BETTER

7.
Four-Minute Insurance from Wrinkles and Worry Lines

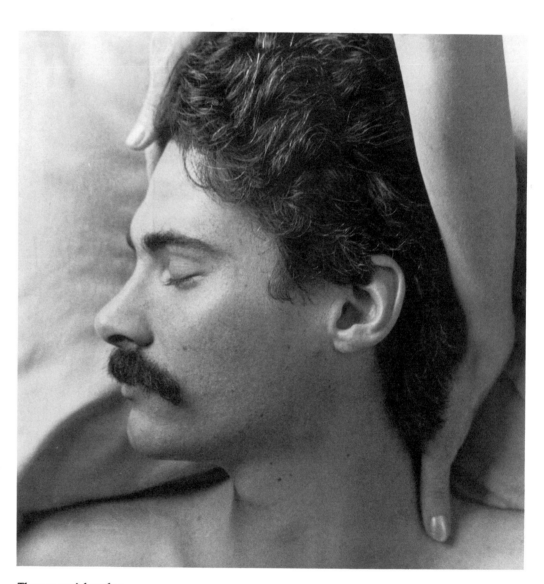

Three essential strokes
One minute each, fifty repetitions

☛ Pressing the forehead
☛ Rotating on the temples
☛ Fingertip kneading the face

Inside the Face

We have seen how stressed muscles are stretched tight, then pumped up with adrenaline and bathed in acids until relaxation becomes nearly impossible. With no relief from tension, the muscles will finally lose their natural resiliency and begin to sag. Small ones usually collapse first, which is why the ravages of stress are so apparent on the surface of the face. But if the source of stress is removed soon enough, fatigued muscles may be able to recover and you will witness a dramatic change; wrinkles that looked permanent begin to fade — transforming the whole face. Every massage facial must deal with a curious, often ignored phenomenon: wrinkles are rarely caused by imperfections in the skin, but rather by a weakening of the underlying muscles. Masseurs who do facials regularly begin to understand several cost-effective facts of life:

1. Mud, clay, and various specialized masks generate a unique feeling. They do not, however, provide a more effective way to clean the face than ordinary soap and water. Too much mud can destroy your hair.

2. Dabbing expensive cream, jelly, powder, oil, sauce, or extract on the face does nothing for existing wrinkles.

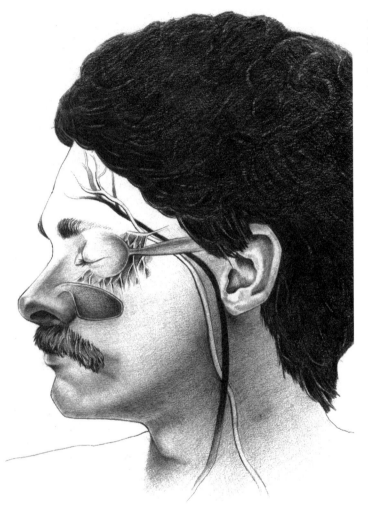

Major nerves and blood vessels converge at the temples.

Too much dabbing can deplete your checking account.

3. Steaming the skin makes it look red for a while. This is not a sign of health, just a sign that the skin has been overheated. Too much steam can burn your face.

4. Contorting the face with specialized exercises once a month or so has no useful effect.

5. Silicone travels.

As certain as death and taxes, when the tiny subcutaneous muscles of expression lose their tone, the surface of the face will wrinkle. Exactly the same thing happens, on a larger scale, around the waist-line or thighs when local muscles get flabby (try rubbing bee jelly on your thighs to tighten them up). Any treatment that is confined to the surface of the body will have little effect on wrinkles. You must reach inside the body to the source of the trouble. With certain modifications, massage techniques for firming up the fleshier parts of the body will work on the face. At its best, a facial massage can actually fulfill the promise of beauty creams and lotions by changing, in minutes, your partner's appearance. Wrinkles and crow's-feet may be permanent or they may be held in place by stress-tensed muscles. You'll find out which one after a first facial massage. Relax stressed muscles and the wrinkles may vanish.

The strokes that follow are focused on the part of the face that controls the precise way your partner looks — the tiny muscles of expression. All the movements are confined to a small area — in some cases just a single finger is used. Nevertheless, the effects can be just as dramatic as strokes that require half an arm. Your partner will feel the difference immediately after you finish a facial massage.

Then he'll see the difference.

A Simple Tension Test

Occasionally, a masseur can discover precisely how much tension a partner has by simply observing the body during massage. Long after local muscles yield to massage, certain parts of the body stubbornly refuse to relax, indicating that stress still rules. One of the most obvious, here on the head, is the jaw. If the mouth refuses to open when you press down gently on the chin, your partner is not relaxed. Resist the temptation to share this piece of intelligence; people do not become relaxed when told to do so. Instead, continue massaging the muscles of the face, adding extra repetitions everywhere you feel the slightest tension. Try pressing down on the chin again in a minute or two. When the mouth opens easily you've succeeded in relaxing the head and face.

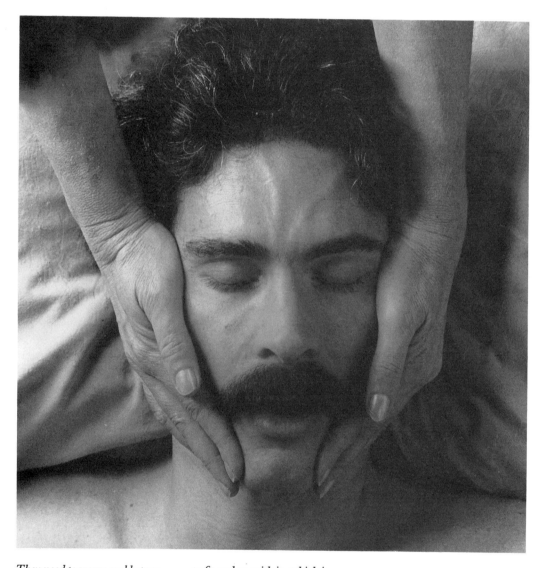

They need to worry and betray time with urgencies false and otherwise, purely anxious and whiny, their souls really won't be at peace unless they can latch on to an established and proven worry and having once found it they assume facial expressions to fit and go with it, which is, you see, unhappiness, and all the time it all flies by them and they know it and that too worries them no end.
— Neal Cassady, *Scenes Along the Road*

Muscle and Mood

Scalp Friction

When we read a face we're simply noting the current state of the subcutaneous muscles. The tiny muscles of the face, some of the most delicate structures anywhere in the body, are just inches from the brain itself. Normally the facial muscles reflect every emotional nuance, but under stress they will involuntarily freeze into a kind of rigid mask, an effect known as "body armor"; few Americans reach middle age without experiencing it. The supremely animated faces of children can trade tears for joy in seconds, but with the onset of body armor later in life all that changes. Suddenly the facial muscles must go through a ponderous shifting of gears with each new emotion—even smiling becomes complicated. As various moods flicker by during the day, muscles that once stretched effortlessly quiver with nervous indecision. Attempts to moderate the expression inevitably backfire. What good is a stiff upper lip if the lower one is quivering violently?

Tension is contagious. The fact is, if you're carrying too much body armor people start avoiding you. An expression or two can be faked, but,

as every actor knows, the transitions *between* expressions are much more difficult. Facial body armor doesn't respond to creams, ointments, lotions, or powders. The only escape is to relax the tiny subcutaneous muscles of the face; five minutes of work for your masseur.

Say you're so nervous before a very important meeting that you feel like climbing the walls. You find yourself pacing back and forth in your office like a caged animal. All that tension goes directly to the muscles of the face, where it becomes terribly public the moment the meeting begins. If you can't relax, others will find it difficult to do so as well. Suddenly, instead of sharing ideas you're sharing anxieties, and the whole tone of the meeting is changed. The next time you get wound up before a meeting, lean back and close your eyes for five minutes while somebody massages your face. Unwind with Super Massage. You'll go into the meeting rested and relaxed; your face will be more natural, more convincing.

Think of the scalp as the top of the face. If your partner is tense the scalp will feel tight, and that tension is transmitted directly to the delicate muscles of the face. You can't hope to relax the face if the scalp is tense.

Be sure your partner removes earrings and contact lenses before you begin massage of the scalp and face. When you're planning on massaging with oil, do this stroke at the beginning while your hands are still dry. Reach into your partner's hair and press down against the scalp with your fingertips—careful not to pull the hair. Other friction movements avoided bony parts of the body; this one seeks them out. You should be able to feel the surface of the skull throughout scalp friction. Don't rub the scalp, push through it against the bone. Test the movement a few times before you begin. Scalp friction works best if you press the thumb and four fingers toward each other repeatedly. Move slowly from

the front of the hairline all the way to the back of the skull. After a few passes you will feel a tangible difference in the range of available movement beneath your fingertips.

Once the scalp becomes more supple, press down against it with the flat part of your open hands and circle, first with one hand then the other. Half the scalp will move under each hand.

Scalp massage also benefits the hair. Just beneath the surface of the scalp a rich group of blood vessels supplies the roots of the hair. After a few minutes of vigorous scalp friction the scalp is so oxygenated that the hair takes on the glossy textured look one usually expects to see only after an exercise session.

Pressing the Forehead

Have frontal headaches been a problem for your partner? This sumptuous two-hand press puts direct pressure on the whole surface of the forehead from temple to temple. Directly under your hands a large set of nerves emerges from the brain. Steady pressure will effectively soothe them.

Support your partner's head from below with a soft pillow, then get comfortable yourself. Sit above the top of your partner's head, close enough so you can reach all the way down to the chin. Carefully establish contact with one hand from temple to temple, distributing pressure from the fingertips to the base of the palm. This is your contact hand, the other hand is called the pressure hand. Adjust your contact hand until the pressures from the fingertips

to the base of the palm are equalized. When your hand feels comfortable and well fitted to your partner's forehead, bring down the pressure hand on top of it. Press moderately hard from above with your pressure hand. Hold at the point of maximum pressure for a silent, slow count of ten or twenty, then release your hands very slowly. Repeat this sequence three times — that's often all it takes to get rid of some frontal headaches.

But whether or not the pain disappears right away, continue with facial massage for a while. Everyone wants a relaxed face.

Rotating on the Temples

If you do nothing else on your partner's face you should at least rotate your fingertips on his temples. Stressed people automatically reach for the temples to get relief, but it feels so much better if somebody else does it for you.

Begin by pressing down lightly on the middle of the forehead with your thumbs. Then bring your fingertips around to rest on the two temples. Locate the definable ring of bone surrounding the temples and massage just inside the ring. Depending on the size relationship between your fingers and your partner's head, two, maybe three, fingertips will fit comfortably inside the ring. Reach for the soft inner tissue. You can rotate both hands in the same direction or move in alternating directions—one hand circles up while the other moves down. Maintaining contact with your thumbs at the center of the forehead ties the stroke together and adds to your contact area. Facial strokes on the jaw, sinuses, eyes, and cheeks all begin with the thumbs centered on this spot. As various strokes move out from the center of the forehead, your facial massage acquires symmetry.

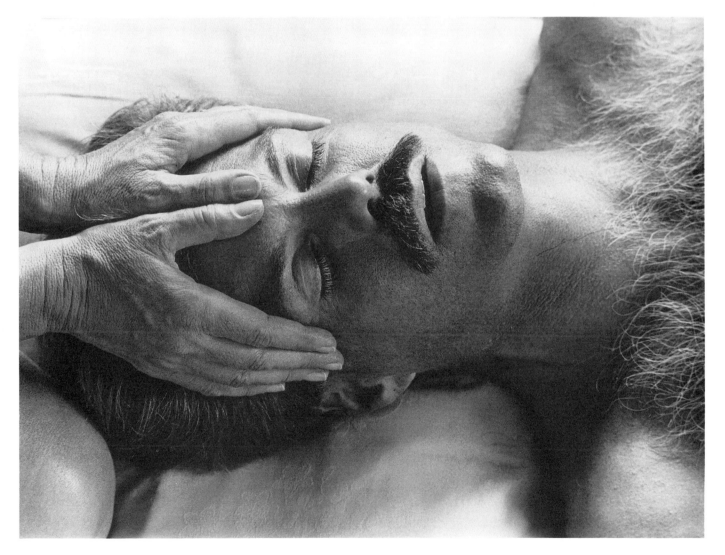

Fingertip Kneading the Face

Stroking the Sinuses

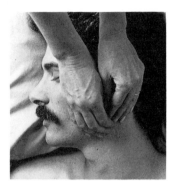

Kneading the muscles of expression is one of the most delicate operations in massage. Your partner will be very aware of *your* mood, so take an extra moment to compose yourself before starting—a gentle, confident manner is always helpful. Oil carefully; one or two drops on the fingertips will do. Have a soft towel ready to take off any excess.

Since the whole skull can move at almost any time during a facial massage, it's especially important to anchor each stroke. People are simply not accustomed to being touched anywhere on the head. However, the face, one of the most sensitive parts of the body, grows accustomed to massage rapidly. This stroke spreads sensation from the temples down to the jaw.

Knead the face from the corner of one eye to the chin. Pick up a tiny fold of flesh between your thumb and forefinger. Near the forehead you will be limited to two fingers, lower on the cheeks you can add one or two more. Avoid pinching or forcing the skin up. The rhythmic kneading motion here is exactly the same as it is on the fleshier parts of the body.

The thumbs and fingers of one hand pick up a fold of flesh while the fingers of the other hand remain open. Cover a whole side of the face from the forehead to the chin, kneading in small circles. This area is small enough to permit easy repetition of any stroke that your partner enjoys. At the back of the jaw, just below the ear, you will always feel a certain amount of extra tension. In fact, the muscles of the jaw are one of the points where stress registers first. Knead it a few extra times. You'll be returning to the jaw muscles soon with more specialized movements. As you knead your partner's face, subcutaneous circulation is stimulated and the muscles beneath the skin grow more supple. Kneading prepares the face for the strokes to follow.

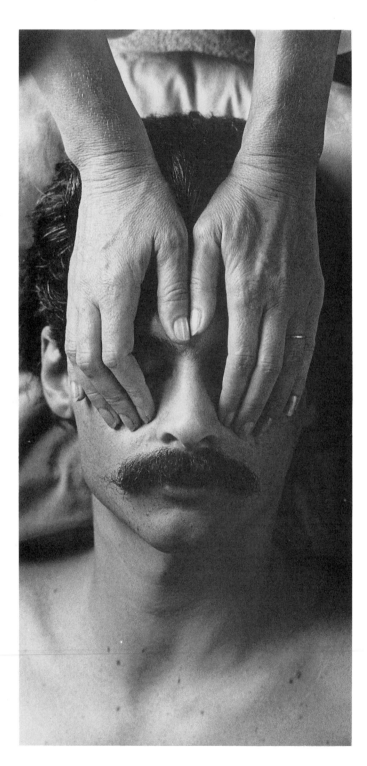

Friction to the Jaw

One of the more unfortunate side effects of stress is a nagging low-level congestion — cold symptoms without the cold. The general tightening that closes down the vascular system during vasoconstriction also affects the sinuses. Breathing becomes more difficult, the voice breaks, and the throat is cleared to no avail. The best solution is to relax the whole body, but one can sometimes achieve satisfying results by massaging the area around the sinuses. Relax the face, and your partner's congestion may vanish.

Begin, once again, by lining up your thumbs at the middle of the forehead. The eyes, like the temples, are set inside a ring of bone. Below the bottom of the ring, almost against the nose itself, you can feel the tissue soften. This is just below the spot where the lower sinuses begin. Reach down into that soft spot with your middle finger and trace an arc outward under the bony ring (as shown on p. 90). Then trace the same arc with all four fingers. Repeat the arc with all four fingers, staying just below the bone, at least three times. After the third repetition, reach into the sinus area with two fingers of each hand and apply spot friction. Finish with a long, leisurely forehead press.

The muscles of the jaw are one of the first areas of the face to register stress. Once the most powerful muscles of the face become tense, a kind of negative undertow is exerted on surrounding tissues. You see the effects immediately around the corners of the mouth and eyes, where smaller muscles are literally pulled out of shape by the inflexible jaw muscles. And they will stay that way, forming all kinds of alarming wrinkles, until the jaw is relaxed.

Center your thumbs on the middle of the forehead and reach down to the base of the jaw with all four fingers of each hand (as shown). The contact area for this spot friction movement is just below the ear and slightly forward. Have your partner grit his teeth for a moment and you will feel a marked muscle concentration at the base of the jaw; this is the precise spot to focus your friction stroke. Anchor the head on one side of the face while applying pressure with your friction hand on the other. Rotate all four fingertips against the thick jaw muscles and don't be afraid to use extra pressure. After massaging one side of the jaw, turn the head slightly, and massage the other side of the jaw. You may want to cover each side of the jaw several times before moving on to the next stroke.

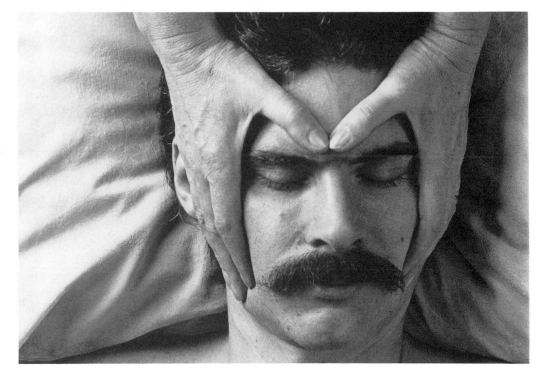

Relaxing the Muscles of Expression

Tension is stored in the shoulders, scalp, and jaws, but it registers first around the eyes and mouth. The muscles here are simply too delicate to resist the powerful forces exerted from above and below during stress. When they yield, people start looking stressed all the time: the expression freezes, smiling becomes awkward, and where clear-eyed serenity once prevailed, a half dozen cross-purpose facial twitches suddenly appear. Happily, if you start massaging soon enough, all of these nasty little afflictions are only temporary. Once you've relaxed the neck, scalp, and jaw muscles, you're ready for the tiny, exquisitely sensitive muscles of expression.

Again, most strokes will work best if you keep the thumbs centered on the middle of the forehead. Reach down with your fingers to do the massage.

The muscles of the face before and after massage.

The Eyes

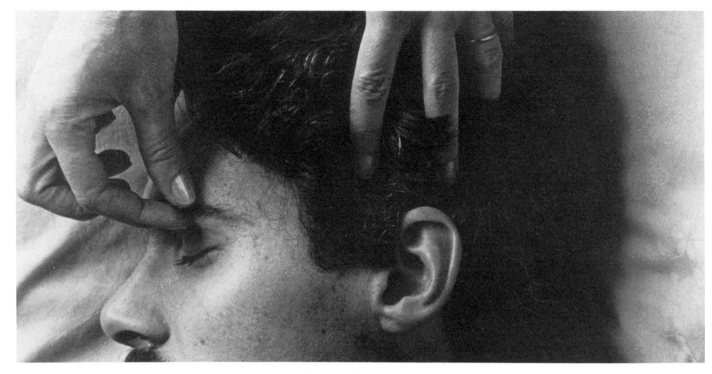

Eye massage works above and beside the eyes as well as directly over the eyelid itself (the thinnest-skinned part of the body). Begin directly above the eyebrow with a four-finger friction stroke. To isolate the effects, anchor close by over the other eye. Rotate your friction hand in tiny circles. The skin will form tiny folds in front of your hand. Move back and forth across half the forehead, then switch hands so you can apply friction above the other eye. Then reach down and do the sides of the eyes with what is, really, a variation of the temple stroke. To get closer to the eye your rotating hand works outside the bony circle.

This is the home of the infamous crow's-feet wrinkles. As you massage, depleted muscles are flooded with oxygen while acidic wastes are driven out of the tissues. Sometimes you can actually see your partner's coloration change from a pale, sickly hue to a vibrant glow as you massage.

Did you know that you can actually put down all four fingers on the top of your partner's eye? Direct eye massage is a delicious experience, all the more so since most people have never even con- sidered it. Center your thumbs on the forehead, then carefully lower both little fingers onto the inside corners of the eyes. Move out toward the corner of the eye, resting the balls of your fingers against the bony upper rim of the eye. Very light contact with the eye is sufficient. As the little finger begins to move, bring down the other fingers one at a time. Turning the hands as your fingers slide out toward the corners of the eyes permits all four fingers to descend and glide, one after the other, across the eye. As you repeat this stroke, return to the starting position and try it on the bottom rim of the eyes.

The Cheeks

This movement will distort your partner's lips into some strange and wonderful shapes. Relaxing the general area around the mouth makes strokes for specific muscle groups at the corners of the lips far more effective.

Begin by extending one hand against a cheek, holding it still, and rotating with the other hand on the opposite cheek (as shown). Once you get a sense of how far the cheeks will move, begin rotating both hands. With your thumbs centered on the forehead, reach down to the cheeks and rotate slowly, using the flat surface of all four fingers. The stroke works best when the hands turn in opposing circles: one hand up while the other is down.

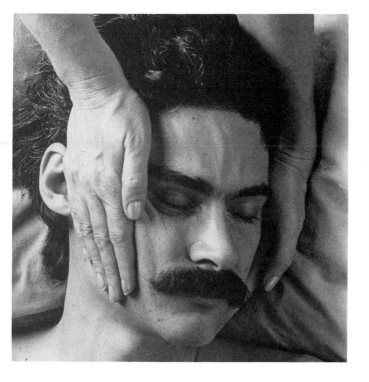

The Mouth

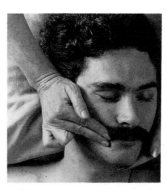

Normally one of the most animated and mobile parts of the body, the area around the mouth is always noticed socially. When the expression changes it usually happens here first. In stressful situations, however, local muscles are kept so unnaturally taut that their resiliency begins to disappear. When relaxation finally does come, the face simply collapses. Precisely because it is so visible, this is one of the most distressing stress patterns anywhere on the body. Stress begins to pull the expression out of shape at the corners of the mouth. Here's how to put it right.

Once again, don't massage the mouth until you've relaxed the larger muscles of the face and shoulders. Tension here is always amplified by outside forces.

Anchoring on the side of the face gives extra support to your partner's head throughout this delicate movement. Reach down to the corner of the mouth with the forefinger and middle fingers of one hand. Right next to the corner of the lips you can feel the spot where the muscles converge. Press there and begin rotating your fingertips, first in one direction then in the opposite direction. This will momentarily distort your partner's features, but, in fact, the rubbery effect is exactly what it takes to restore the natural mobility of the face. Turn your partner's head to one side and, beginning at the corner of the lips and working outward, knead each side of the mouth with your fingertips (as shown). Then turn the head to the center and grasp both cheeks with the whole surface of your hands. Rotate slowly. Finish with a hand-over-hand pulling stroke, starting at each corner of the mouth and ending all the way back at the base of the ear. Maintain tension on the corner of the mouth as you pull.

8.
Four-Minute Relief from Nervous Tension

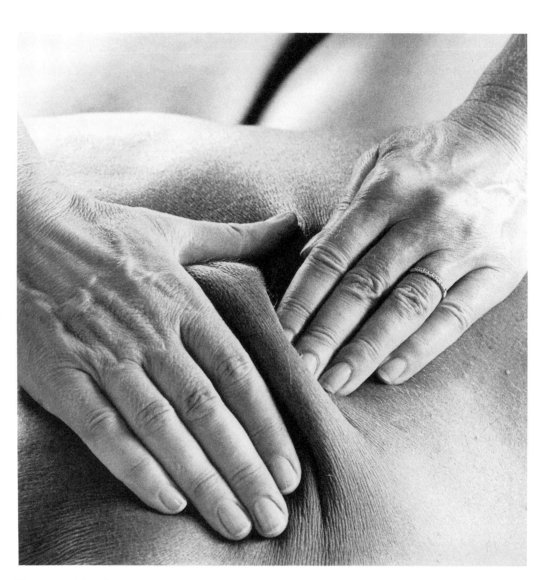

Three essential strokes
One minute each, fifty repetitions

- ☛ Local (or full body) circulation
- ☛ Spot friction
- ☛ Pounding

Massaging the Stress Addict

He seemed to look at us from a zone of weariness where not even despair is felt, because that is feeling, and such weariness is fathoms deeper than feeling.
—C.J. Koch, *The Year of Living Dangerously*

Probably the most difficult challenge you will face when massaging overstressed people will come from the individual who must constantly rush in order to achieve meaning in life. He needs a massage badly but never manages to find time for one. It's so much faster to gulp a few aspirin or tranquilizers, then rush off to the next appointment. The very fact that he's always rushed is supposed to show how committed, successful, and thoroughly modern he is. Snappish, combative, obsessed with clocks, he wears his perpetual tension like a badge of honor. He's the latest medical time bomb, the stress addict.

In the office, on the farm, or in the kitchen, the stress addict is eternally far behind schedule and rushing like mad to catch up. Whenever you meet him you feel pressured: you're wasting his time, you're doing unimportant things that could have been finished long ago, *you're never busy enough.* Alcoholics and drug addicts can sometimes manage to leave the

Do

Ask your partner to close his eyes.
Give your partner permission to relax and do nothing for five minutes.
Keep preliminary conversation to a minimum.

Don't

Give orders. Instead, make suggestions.
Argue about anything.
Talk about how good it will feel after the massage.
Discuss massage techniques.

rest of us alone for a while— not the stress addict. He enjoys bugging other people; he actually seems to thrive on conflict and arguments. Nevertheless, family and friends are often deceived or intimidated by a busier-than-thou air which accompanies almost all activities.

At first, the stress addict may simply appear to be a committed, rather ambitious individual to whom time is money. He's dynamic, perhaps a bit too intense, driven, and fiercely competitive. He finds tension motivating, adrenaline exciting, and delays of any kind infuriating.

Those who live with him, however, soon discover other, more disconcerting traits. He bolts meals, races through meetings, hurries conversation without listening, and charges into lovemaking as though it were an Olympic competition. Vacations and leisure-time activities become a marathon of high-pressure events with winners and losers at every turn. Music, art, and literature hold little interest—they're too time consuming. In fact, nothing matters as much as the process of rushing itself. If something can't be rushed it isn't worth doing.

The rush reflex:

- ☛ Heart rate increases.
- ☛ Blood pressure increases.
- ☛ Adrenaline increases.
- ☛ Arteries and veins contract.
- ☛ Bodily secretions decrease.
- ☛ Oxygen supply to the brain decreases.
- ☛ Judgment and thought become erratic.

- ☛ Muscle tone decreases.
- ☛ Subcutaneous facial muscles collapse, causing early wrinkles.
- ☛ Digestion becomes slow and incomplete.
- ☛ Body experiences constant fatigue and anxiety.

Inside the stress addict an invisible stopwatch ticks away, reducing each day to a series of deadlines which, like hurdles in a hundred-yard dash, must be executed at precisely the right moment. Family, friends, and co-workers with other ideas are accused of being dull, slow, or lazy, then pushed relentlessly. Spare time is for new activities so that additional deadlines and schedules can be crammed into every un-committed moment. All opportunities for leisure are instantly eliminated. Work hard, play hard.

The stress addict wears his tension like a medal from an honorable war. He's fought the good fight and earned the right to a perpetually stiff neck and six cross-purpose facial twitches. You'd be tense, too, if you weren't so lazy. Finally, when rushing becomes a kind of reflex almost as automatic as breathing, the inevitable physical penalty must be paid: whole sections of the body become permanently tense and everything starts to hurt. Unwinding is then so physically diffi-cult it is all but abandoned.

What remains is a furious scrambling from one deadline to the next, attempting to achieve the stress addict's ulti-

mate goal: *total busyness.* Exhaustion, which sets in late at night and sometimes yields to sleep, takes the place of relaxation. During the day stress generates more stress as all problems are solved by pressuring somebody. "The squeaky wheel gets the oil," insists the stress addict as he bellows out an order, checks his watch and, grabbing at the phone, swallows a hand-ful of Valiums.

The confirmed stress addict invariably blames others for his problems. He needs faster cars, faster food, faster serv-ice, and faster-acting pills. He also desperately needs relief from lower back pain,

nagging headaches, persistent neck and shoulder tension, and sore feet. He's having frequent digestion problems and his blood pressure is ris-ing. How do you get him to sit still for a massage?

Not by talking about it. Try-ing to talk the stress addict into slowing down is frustrat-ing because he will lie (like other addicts) when con-fronted with his excesses. Things are always "crazy" at the office but the job is "great." Marathon weekends in the country, which might

include eleven hours of driv-ing plus a daunting roster of sports, specially prepared meals, entertainment, and leftover office work are "fun, relaxing." Again, like other addicts, he tries hard to feel superior to everyone else. His life is so "full" compared to yours.

The first clear sign to all that a stress addict has been push-ing the limits can, of course, be a heart attack. Of all the debilitating effects during stress none is more dangerous than the abrupt venous and arterial contraction known as vasoconstriction. When adrenaline is squirted into the blood vessels, the entire venous system immediately contracts. The heart then speeds up in order to force blood through the body, and all secretions decrease. The pulse grows weaker and the skin turns deathly pale as blood moves away from the surface. This is the "fight" impulse that permits mam-mals to become ferocious at a moment's notice. It isn't meant to continue for days, weeks, or months at a time, and when it does the body must pay. Stress addicts learn to enjoy the adrenaline rush and try to ignore the pound-ing heart that goes with it. The aches and pains, the fre-quent infections, the insom-nia, and the shattered rela-tionships are harder to ignore.

Three Steps to Prepare the Stress Addict for Massage

Masseurs look for a solution to stress addiction inside the body. The immediate problem — muscle tension so pronounced it may be near spasm — is physical, not psychological. Eventually, as co-workers, family, and friends fall behind, the stress addict is driven entirely by his own adrenaline; the body becomes a stress factory. Masseurs seek to change all that by dealing with what the stress addict is actually feeling.

What does it feel like to walk around in his body all day long? The terrific tension in the neck, shoulders, or lower back broadcasts the answer. By focusing on the stressed area with Super Massage, you can reverse the vasoconstriction effect in just a few minutes. Relaxation then takes the place of tension — you substitute one set of feelings for another.

A stress addict can get so wound up that he forgets the difference between tension and relaxation; resting becomes rushing less. Discussing this, however, will only provoke an argument and postpone the massage. Again, *never comment on how tense your partner seems to be.* A better approach is to begin with a simple three-part sensory-awareness exercise that feels so good it becomes a part of the massage.

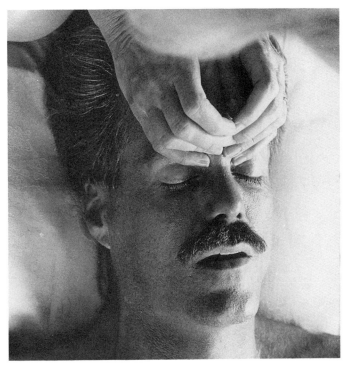

Silence

Since doing nothing may be the greatest sin for a stress addict, it sometimes helps to provide assurances that it's OK to relax. When you do, be prepared for a strange reaction. Ordinary relaxation can be so threatening that to find familiar territory your partner may try desperately to start a stress-generating argument — whatever it takes to get the adrenaline going again. Most masseurs have seen a stress addict, about to surrender and melt as a massage begins, suddenly become completely rigid, sit bolt upright, and demand the time of day. Moments later he's on his feet, searching frantically for his watch, appointment book, and a phone. Giving a stress addict permission to relax is a crucial point in your preparation. By proceeding diplomatically you can defuse an argument, calm irrational fears, and greatly enhance the massage. Here's how.

Most likely the last time your stress-addicted partner experienced real play, leisure, or idleness was as a child. If he's got problems as an adult, why not let him be a child again? Begin by giving your partner permission to relax while playing a simple children's game called "Stiff as a Board." He begins by walking like a wooden soldier, exaggerating each movement. Then, on command, he sits on a rug and immediately becomes a "limp noodle," so limp that he cannot support any part of his body and must collapse to the floor. Repeated several times, this little fantasy clearly demonstrates the difference between tensed and relaxed muscles. Next time you "give him permission" to relax, just before the Super Massage begins, he will know something about how it should feel. And he won't fight the feeling when it starts to happen. The final time your partner becomes limp, ask him to do so without speaking. Silence quiets the mind and allows the feeling of relaxation to take over.

Darkness

Accomplished as the stress addict may be in other areas, his sensual awareness is crude. He will focus on the loud, the aggressive, and the speedy. Simply closing the eyes, as though he were in the presence of an exotic scent or exquisite music, will tune your partner into a more subtle level of sensual awareness. It also releases him from a host of familiar demands. Turn off the lights. Darkness intensifies the sensual.

Breathing

Slow, rhythmic breathing is a luxury that stress addicts almost never allow themselves. It's far too relaxing. By simply asking your partner to breathe deeply during massage you allow her to "do something" while relaxing.

You make breathing into a little job. Still, it's important that your partner realize that breathing itself is not goal oriented. You won't be asking her to increase the speed or giving her other special instructions. It's not a test she can somehow fail. Later, when you do the massage, you can adjust the rhythm of your stroking to your partner's breathing. Right now it's enough just to breathe deeply and slowly.

Quietly, in the warm darkness, your partner will surrender slowly to the natural rhythm of her own breath.

Are high-strung individuals condemned to be forever jittery? It's tempting to dismiss constant nervousness as a stubborn personality trait that simply cannot be changed. It's not. We have seen how a few minutes of Super Massage can transform acid-ridden, fatigued muscles and dramatically improve your partner's mood. At no time are the positive mood swings more apparent than when massaging nervous people.

Masseurs view nervous tension as a physical, not a psychological problem, and work through the body to bring relief. The muscles,

nerves, and brain are so intimately connected that any irritation to one system instantly affects the other two. After many hours of tension, oxygen levels in the muscles are seriously depleted, which means that paralyzing cramps can strike at any time. One can cope with jittery nerves but not with the excruciating pain of cramped muscles. Think of nervous tension as a valuable warning sign: relax the body when muscles begin to tighten, and you should be able to spare your partner the painful cramping that will otherwise inevitably follow.

Strokes in this chapter should be chosen according to your partner's profession and sex. Active and sedentary people experience different kinds of nervous tension. More on that later. When massaging tense women, pay close attention to the pressures you use—a woman's nerves are usually more easily stimulated than a man's. The strokes that follow are designed to provide quick ways of altering tension-induced anxiety and depression. Think of nervous tension as the fuse, and cramps, stomach disorders, and circulatory problems as the bomb. Taking a few minutes to cut the fuse of nervous tension can alter your partner's whole day.

Spot Friction

While most massage movements can travel from one part of the body to another, spot friction is designed to focus on a single tense location. It's useful on the heavily muscled parts of the back as well as in areas where working with the whole hand is awkward. Hard-to-reach nerves just beneath the shoulder blades and at the base of the skull are common sources of headaches and other nervous complaints. Focus on them with spot friction whenever you're dealing with nervous tension.

To be truly effective, friction strokes require plenty of repetition. Get comfortable before starting so you won't have to interrupt the stroke. Generally, women experience tension in the neck and shoulders while male complaints center on the lower back. Check with your partner to find out if any painful areas require special attention.

Uncontrolled spot friction can shake your partner's

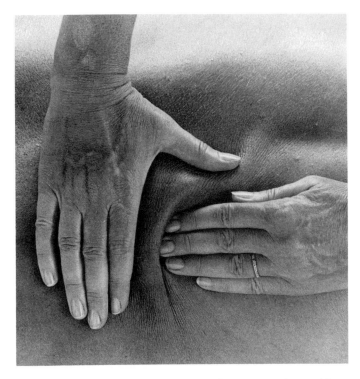

whole body. Confine movement to a single location by pressing a small fold of flesh toward the friction area with one hand (the anchor hand) while you apply friction with the other. Open your thumb whenever possible (as shown). Forget about oil. Remember that friction strokes turn against interior tissues instead of gliding across the surface of the body like other massage movements. Keeping your thumb tight against your

forefinger, press down with your fingertips until you feel muscles beneath the skin. Then, with your fingers pressed tightly together, rotate against the muscular surface. Circle, choosing a moderate speed that you feel comfortable maintaining for a minute or more.

Full Body Circulation

This is the most ambitious stroke in massage. It's also, often, the most appreciated. Get it right and you can treat your partner to one of those delicious experiences that is unique to massage: an uninterrupted wave of sensation traveling all the way from the bottom of the feet to the neck, turning across the shoulders, then returning along the sides of the back and legs to the feet. He *was* experiencing nervous tension. All at once he's experiencing pure pleasure.

Unless you're much bigger than your partner you will need to change position several times during a full body circulation movement. Spread out a few small pillows along your partner's side and move as quietly as possible. Remember: the best masseur, like the best waiter, is invisible. Bend your fingers, throughout this stroke, to follow the changing contours of your partner's body.

Begin on the bottom of the feet. Cup your hands around your partner's foot with your fingertips facing each other. Press up onto the calves and across the back of the knees to the upper thighs (as shown). Then, without interrupting the stroke, move forward, repositioning yourself near your partner's waist. As you move up the back, your fingertips should come close to touching the sides of the spine. At the base of the neck, let your fingertips turn until they are pointing toward

the ground. Move out to the edge of the shoulders, turn again, and begin your descent along the sides of the back. Careful not to cut corners at the feet—your partner will notice if you rush. Continue down all the way to the toes, then turn your hands and get back into the starting position with your fingers facing each other.

Take your time and let your partner savor the ascending and descending waves of sensation. Repeat the whole movement three times. After your final return to the feet, if your partner asks for more, it's easy enough to keep going.

Vibration — a Spot Friction Variation

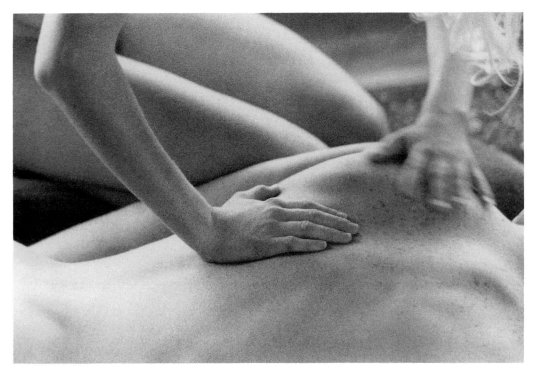

Nervous tension usually spreads from an irritable area to the whole body. Before you begin massage, see if your partner can pinpoint certain spots that feel more tense than others. Work on them first. If it's difficult to isolate tension in a single area, start by paying special attention to the neck and shoulders, the small of the back, and the muscular part of the calves.

You can choose one of two spot friction variations. For deeply knotted interior muscles you will need to press down fairly hard as you turn with a regular spot friction movement. But if the skin seems taut and the muscles beneath are slack, tension is probably limited to the surface of the body. Try a minute or two of vibration, an open-fingered friction variation that produces a pleasant glow across the surface of your partner's body.

Vibration breaks one of the hard-and-fast rules of massage: it's done with the fingers spread apart. However, you do make use of nearly the whole surface of each finger throughout the stroke. Anchor near the friction area with one hand. Since you won't be pressing down into the tissues, don't bother picking up a large fold of flesh with the anchor hand. Simply concentrate on confining the effects of the vibration to a single area. Holding steady with the anchor hand, turn your vibration hand rapidly from side to side at the wrist. Be sure to break the movement at the wrist. Vibration with the whole arm becomes awkward . Let your fingers brush across the surface of your partner's body as you turn the vibration hand. As you approach the side of a limb, bend around the curve with your fingers.

Move as fast as you can while maintaining a comfortable rhythm. As always, consistent rhythm is more important than raw speed. This stroke allows you to blanket a joint or muscle group with intense sensation for a minute or more. When you stop, your partner will realize that cold, clammy tightness has yielded to a warm, spreading glow.

Full Hand Cupping

Pounding

Eventually, nervous tension will dominate almost any personality. If your neck and shoulders are seldom relaxed, you're simply not going to feel very good about life. Massage brings relief via the fluid release effect and by substituting an intensely pleasurable experience for the enervating tension. Tense people are impatient, even snappish, so you need to reach inside the body and make things happen fast. One way to do this is with a series of high-intensity percussion strokes.

Full hand cupping works on most broad, fleshy areas, but it's especially effective on the heavily muscled parts of the back. Cup your hand (as shown) to form a small hollow area in the center. When contacting your partner's back, listen for a slight popping sound as a tiny vacuum is formed between your hands and the surface of the body.

As in all percussion movements you must cushion each "blow" by breaking the downward thrust at the wrist. Move up and down the sides of the back, methodically keeping your hands close enough for the thumbs to brush each other. Cover the whole back up to the muscular ridges that run parallel to the spine, but stay off the spine itself.

Pop, pop, pop. Full hand cupping brings blood to the surface where you can see it.

Pounding really comes into its own on the back. Massaging from the center of your partner's body (as shown), you can usually reach from the midthigh to the shoulders. Pressures should vary depending on what's under your contact hand. Reserve your lightest strokes for the soft area between the lower ribs and the hips.

Pounding is a versatile stroke: you can cover an entire leg or limit the effects to a single aching muscle group. Either way, the effects reach deep within the body to interior muscles, nerves, even organs,

The Pinky Snap

providing the dramatic changes you need to eliminate nervous tension.

Obviously one can get carried away with pounding. Cushion the stroke two ways: first, by striking the back of your contact hand instead of your partner's body, then, by breaking the downward thrust at the wrist. Pounding is most effective if you reach across the spine to massage the far side of your partner's body. Use your contact hand to feel for bony areas like the rib cage and shoulder tops before you begin. Never pound on the spine itself. To focus on the long muscles that run parallel to the spine, it's important to limit the pounding to your fingertips. Let the palm of your contact hand ride lightly over the spine while pressing down on the muscles with your fingertips. Then pound the back of the fingertips with your other hand.

Thanks to Hollywood, the pinky snap (a.k.a. hacking) is probably the most misunderstood massage movement. We see it in movies while people talk on the phone, drive, eat, and play cards—in short, always while doing something else. Suddenly the neck and shoulders are besieged with a flurry of quick karatelike chops to the soft tissue while the vital pinky snap, which is supposed to moderate the blow, is invariably left out. No wonder the obligatory sigh of pleasure afterward seems false—a little closer to the spine and the scene would become impossible to reshoot.

Real pinky snapping is always cushioned by the little finger, which hangs down as the hand descends. Actually, there are two cushioning points during this stroke: at the pinky and at the wrist. When bringing each hand down, make sure to break at the wrist. The effect you want is a light, snapping motion. One hand is always up while the other is down.

An agreeable rhythm is more important than raw speed, so find a comfortable rate of repetition and stay with it. As the pinky closes against the fingers, listen for a crisp snapping sound—when it's consistent so is your rhythm. The stroke should move slowly across the body, covering each area thoroughly. Dazzling jumps from, say, the upper back to a leg à la Hollywood may impress onlookers, but will confuse your partner. On the other hand, repeating the stroke over a small area three or four times provides a pleasant warming effect that will last for hours.

Pressing the Spine

Muscles along the nerve-rich spine are extremely sensitive to stress. In fact, when tension persists, the lower back is one of the first parts of the body to suffer. Women generally experience tension around the neck and shoulders; for men the most sensitive area is the lower back. Normally, the vertebrae are held in place by the long muscles that run parallel to the spine. When stressed, however, the muscles tighten, pulling, even jerking the spine to one side. A vicious circle of mounting tension then begins: direct pressure to the spine irritates the nerves, thereby causing more muscle contraction which, in turn, generates more stress. Eventually, an excruciating lower back muscle spasm can result. If the pain is intense always check with a doctor before beginning massage.

Once you're satisfied that there's no structural damage, use back pressing with fingertip kneading and friction movements to relax over-tensed muscles and bring peace to the lower back. Sometimes you can actually feel the muscles soften as you massage.

There are several ways to press along the spine. Both hands can rise together to the shoulders, spreading sensation evenly, or the hands can ascend one at a time, limiting the sensation to a single side of the back. Either way, confine your pressures to the raised muscular ridge that runs parallel to both sides of the spine. Stay off the spine itself. Push forward into the muscle with the heel of your hand. Lean into this stroke. Flatten out your hands at the shoulders and move out across the shoulder tops. Maintain light contact with your partner's sides on the return to the waist.

Vibrating the Whole Upper Body

It's always best to be sure the neck is relaxed before doing this stroke. If your partner struggles to "help" when you start lifting the head, her neck is still very tense. Remind her, gently, not to help when she feels her head being lifted. You do all the work—she does nothing at all. If tension remains, spend a minute or two fingertip kneading the thick muscles at the base of the neck (see p. 47). Lift again and repeat the neck kneading if necessary. When your partner's head falls back gracefully as your hands press up between the shoulders, she is ready to surrender to the luxurious feeling of being lifted into the air while her back vibrates slowly.

Kneel above your partner's head. Oil your hands, then slide them under her shoulders, spreading the oil as you move, down to the area between the shoulder blades. Begin by simply lifting up with the fingertips of both hands until the rib cage begins to rise. The vibration effect is produced by raising and lowering your fingers rapidly. Keep your fingers pressed tightly together and pull up toward the neck as you vibrate. Once you get comfortable with the pulling-up motion, try increasing the frequency so what your partner feels is a subdued percussion from beneath the ribs. Pull your hands up toward the neck as you vibrate. This stroke moves in only one direction: from the shoulders to the neck. Return to the starting position between the shoulder blades each time you reach the neck. Reach halfway down her back for the final lifting-pulling sequence. Feels as great as it looks.

9.
Four-Minute Relief from Insomnia

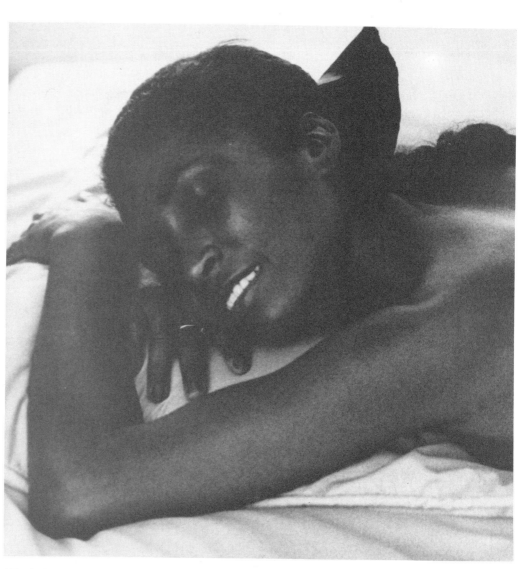

The feeling of loneliness and depression that is so apt to come in the nighttime when people are run down or in ill-health is usually dispelled very promptly by means of massage. In this and other respects its action is similar to the primary and agreeable effects of opium and alcohol in restoring tone to the respiratory centre and vascular system, without, however, the injurious aftereffects of these internal remedies. In place of headache, drowsiness, and disordered digestion, which are so apt to result from the use of hypnotics and stimulants, after sleep from massage the patient is refreshed and buoyant in mind and body. Massage does more than this: it will often counteract the disagreeable feelings that result from the necessity of taking sleep-producing medicines or too free indulgence in alcoholic stimuli. —Douglas Graham, M.D., *A Treatise on Massage*

Massage at Midnight

Perhaps no malady is more closely tied to stress than insomnia. How does one slow down after rushing all day? When the tensions of the day end up in bed, unwinding becomes yet another stressful chore. But, of course, sleep is the one goal that cannot be rushed or forced.

Bedtime is an ideal setting for massage; a comfortable mattress, a darkened room, silence. For centuries only the rich and powerful could summon a masseur at midnight. A hundred years ago the President of the United States, arguably one of the more stressed individuals around, found that sleep would come in minutes when he had himself massaged at bedtime. We now depend on habit-forming drugs with unpredictable side effects to do the same thing. Certain pills will knock you out, but what about the next morning? The massage solution has no unpleasant side effects.

Take a few special precautions when massaging an insomniac. Be careful not to be distracted by nervous conversation. Your focus should remain on the body, especially on the limbs, where poor circulation can leave the muscles very tight. Avoid the natural tendency to favor very delicate movements, which seem more soothing late at

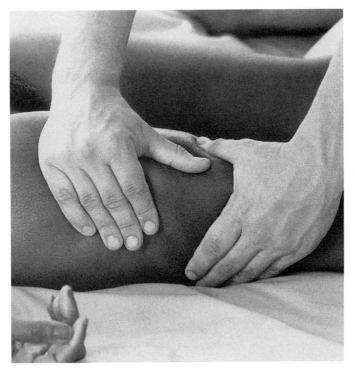

Do

Keep the lights low.
Take the extra time to heat the oil.
Be sure to keep your partner warm; use blankets on part of the body if necessary.
Give extra attention to the limbs.
Be silent.
Be generous with massage.

Don't

Discuss your partner's problems.
Complain about being up late.
Make the experience complicated. Skip the food, drinks, music, magazines, and aspirin. This is massage, not air travel. If all goes well, your partner will be asleep very soon.
Stop massaging the moment breathing becomes regular. Asleep, your partner's body continues to benefit from the massage.

night. Insomniacs are almost always *over*stimulated. The more flamboyant massage movements, even strokes that vibrate over large parts of the body, are more likely to break a mental logjam and relax the muscles. The larger, more dramatic massage movements will also distract your partner from nagging anxieties. Remember: the brain has been racing, generating stress at a furious rate. With massage you create physical events, tangible *feelings* that are far more immediate and significant than any kind of mental static.

If it's been a particularly stressful day for your partner, you may have to disperse large quantities of irritating acidic wastes. Concentrate on repeating the kneading and circulation sequences in this chapter wherever you find tensed muscles.

Professional masseurs take it as a compliment when a client falls asleep during a massage. What better sign could you get that tension has been relieved? (The only problem is finding a graceful way to make room on the massage table for the next client.) If your partner does drift off after a minute or two, continue massaging for a while. It's not the conscious mind you're working on, it's the body.

Energize the Limbs: Super Circulation

The adrenaline released by stress dilates blood vessels in our muscles so that blood drains from our body to our legs.
— Dr. Claire Weekes, *Peace From Nervous Suffering*

We have seen how stress constricts the circulatory system, trapping irritating acids deep within the muscles. Eventually, when the muscles are not permitted to relax, the acidic buildup itself becomes a source of stress. The body is under constant attack from within. At the end of the day, when stimulants and mood enhancers wear off, tension should finally yield to exhaustion. But what if some of the stress-hardened muscles refuse to relax and sleep doesn't follow?

During most insomnia episodes, stale, poorly oxygenated blood and various toxins clog the limbs, producing a leaden feeling that is especially troublesome in the legs. Before your partner will feel any real relief, you must clear irritating acids from the tissues and reinvigorate both legs. A high-intensity circulation movement will immediately oxygenate the legs, eliminating the "deadness" in less than two minutes.

Begin with a series of rapid circulation strokes. Start at the ankles and press all the way up to the buttocks. At

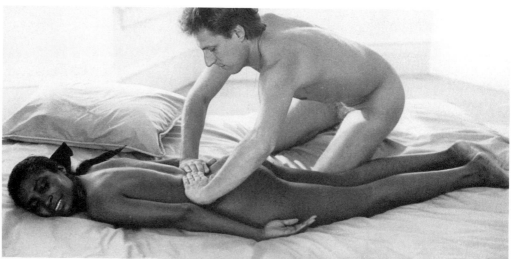

the hips, turn your fingers out and return to the ankles, maintaining light contact on the sides of the legs. Do each leg separately at least twenty times, then finish up with three or four luxurious full body strokes, covering both legs at once. At the top of the last circulation stroke, continue up over the buttocks

(as shown) and across the back all the way to the shoulders. With light, full-hand pressure, turn your fingers out again and return to the ankles down the sides of your partner's body. Maintain full contact with your hands when turning at the feet and shoulders. A full body stroke allows your part-

ner to feel truly pampered. As you move up and down the body, you may need to reposition your body. Do so without breaking the rhythm of this, the longest of all massage strokes. Feel for knotted muscles along the whole length of the body. That way you know exactly where to begin with the next stroke.

Relief for Tensed Muscles: Compression

Rock-hard muscles cry out for a minute or two of compression. Often, you can actually feel them soften under your hands.

This is a friction variation, so you will need to anchor from above or below. You can do compression on the back or the back of the legs without oil, but it usually works better with light lubrication (particularly if your partner has hairy legs). Make a fist and press down firmly with the flat part of your knuckle. For a softer effect, press down with one hand on top of the other (as shown). Turn slowly as you press. Confine yourself to the thigh on the front of the leg—from the knee down it's too bony. Compression really comes into its own on the muscular back of the leg. Here you can begin just above the ankle and work up all the way onto the upper back.

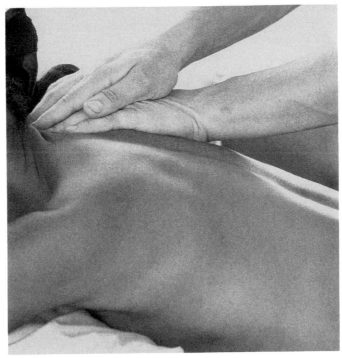

One area bears special watching during back-of-the-leg compression. The Achilles tendon, largest tendon in the body, wraps around the heel and extends halfway up the calf. If it's too tense the whole leg will be affected. Be sure to circle all the way down the heel itself when you're massaging the lower part of the leg. If the tendon feels tight and requires extra attention, put a small pillow under the ankle to raise the foot.

Deep Friction

Ask your partner how she feels. If she's uncertain, do a final full body circulation stroke, checking, once again, for knotted muscles. Again, insomniacs have trouble pinpointing exactly what is bothering them. Feel for the tension. Are the muscles of the neck rigid even when the head is supported? Do you feel more tension on one side of the spine than on the other? Does the calf remain tight when the rest of the leg is relaxed? You've found the spots where she needs deep friction.

Skip the oil. Keep in mind, during friction, that unlike most massage strokes, your hands should *not* glide across the surface of the skin. Friction movements rotate on the muscles beneath the skin. Feel for them; let the muscles, not the skin, ripple under your fingertips as your hand turns. On the thicker leg muscles, press down with the flat part of your knuckles; use just your fingertips over the long muscles that run parallel to the spine. Anchor the stroke with one hand as the other applies friction (as shown). Start slowly and find a comfortable pressure for

plenty of repetition. It's tempting to push down very hard on larger muscle groups, but the extra pressure can tire you out. When poor nighttime circulation depletes the oxygen supply inside major muscles, extended friction is a wonderful gift. Take a break with a light fingertip kneading stroke, maintaining contact and rhythm while

you get ready to do some more deep friction. If there are no specific complaints, concentrate on the lower legs, where circulation is likely to be the poorest. Three or four rotations on tensed muscles make a difference — one hundred and the tension vanishes.

Flexing the Legs

With your partner lying on her stomach, lift both her legs at the ankles, bending her knees until the feet are straight up. Fold the ankles over each other (as shown). Then grasp both ankles and press down slowly until you feel tightness. The point of tension, where you feel a tangible strain, will vary from one individual to another. The heels can touch the buttocks without a trace of resistance or they can grow tight just a few inches beyond the upright position. Once it's established, the point of tension indicates just how far to press the legs without causing discomfort. On the upward part of the stroke, take the legs all the way back to the original position with your partner's feet on the bed.

Then, lift with both hands and press again. After repeating this movement a half dozen times, press *slightly* beyond the point of tension just once. The legs can also be flexed from the other side of the body by simply pressing forward against your partner's knees (as shown).

Knead the Whole Side of the Body

Once you've relaxed the legs and applied deep friction to areas of obvious tension on other parts of the body, your partner will probably be more than halfway asleep. Try some more of the luxurious full body strokes. Be generous when massaging an insomniac. An extra few dozen repetitions will go a long way toward relaxing her.

Reach across your partner's body and knead the entire opposite side. Start at the ankles and move all the way up to the shoulders. Pay special attention to the fleshy areas around the hips. Whenever possible, use the whole surface of your hands from the fingertips to the base of the palm. Between the rib cage and the knees you'll find it's easy to pick up a fold of flesh between your thumb and forefinger with each stroke. On the bony sides of the knees and near the ankles don't bother forcing the flesh to come up if it doesn't do so easily. But whether or not the flesh is actually lifted, keeping the thumb movement consistent with each stroke maintains the hypnotic mood you're working to create. When kneading the side of the body, you can relax muscles that operate the arms, legs, and back (as shown).

Shaking the Body

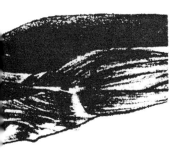

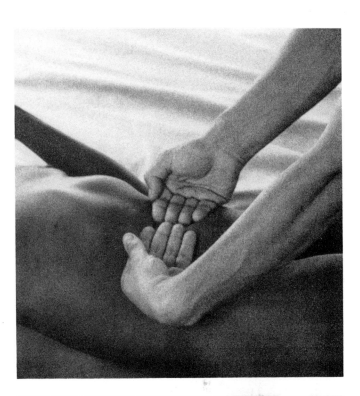

Does your partner complain of feeling stiff in bed? No reason to let that keep her awake. Here is a simple lift that flexes the major joints of the lower back and hips while your partner does nothing at all. As the whole center of the body rises slowly, feelings of tension give way to an expansive light sensation.

With your partner lying on her back, head raised on a pillow, get comfortable by her side. First, cup your hands (as shown) then slide them under the small of your partner's back until the fingertips nearly touch the spine. Lift with the entire flat surface of your fingers. Spread your knees slightly for balance during the lift, and be careful not to "dig in" to her back with your fingertips. Bring the center of the body up about one foot and hold for a moment. Then shake gently from side to side a half dozen times and lower her slowly. When shaking the body, be especially careful to avoid sudden, jerky movements — keep everything slow and measured. Take extra time between lifts if you need it.

Lift and shake three times. Then, maintaining contact with a knee or one hand, sit back, rest for a moment, and watch your partner smile. Levitation is the perfect escape for insomniacs.

Thumb Kneading

Squeezing and Rolling the Arm

Sometimes insomniacs are able to identify a single source of tension, such as a stiff neck, a sore arm, or aching muscles in the calf, which calls for a single, concentrated massage solution. Thumb kneading, one of the most adaptable strokes in massage, is ideal for all these problems. It's especially

Thumb kneading travels well. With your partner lying on her stomach, you can begin kneading the Achilles tendon at the ankle, move up the fleshy back of the calf, and end on the broad surface of the thigh. Or start at the wrist, move up the inside of the forearm, and knead all the way to the shoulder.

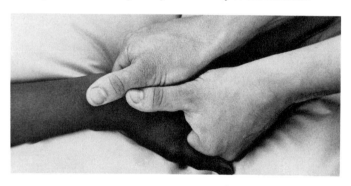

effective in tight areas that full hand kneading strokes can't reach.

Thumb kneading works best on the limbs, although it can be adapted for parts of the torso as well. Reach under the limb with all four fingers of each hand, resting your thumbs on the surface (as shown). Rotate the thumbs in opposing circles: one up while the other is down. While you knead, try to keep the thumbs as close to each other as possible without pinching the flesh.

Always knead the soft, fleshy areas — avoid the bony parts of the body.

A unique thumb kneading variation sometimes called "the violin" frees up both of your hands to massage the upper arm. It also elevates the upper arm while you massage it, which makes the stroke considerably easier to do. Lift the arm you want to knead and put all four fingers under the armpit, the thumb on top (as shown). Holding your arm tight against your body as you knead will keep your partner's hand in place.

If your partner enjoyed body shaking, these two arm movements are sure to please. They stimulate without becoming jarring and they do wonders for aching arm muscles. Here is something unusual for your partner to *feel* instead of something abstract to worry about. See these movements as a simple alternative to anxiety as well as one more step toward eliminating the irritability that comes between your partner and deep sleep.

Circle the wrist with your thumb and forefinger, then lift your partner's arm straight into the air. Reach over with your other hand and circle her arm near the shoulder. Squeeze between your thumb and four fingers. Concentrating on the soft tissue areas, move up the arm all the way to the wrist. Squeeze every second or so.

Rolling also begins near the top of the arm, but with an important difference. This time you use both hands to bring the sensation surging upward. First, fold your partner's arm across her chest (as shown). Then, with your fingers straight out, reach forward and grasp both sides of her upper arm as close to the shoulder as possible. Gently at first, then more vigorously, rock your hands back and forth as they move up the arm. Your partner's arm will straighten at the elbow as you move up toward the wrist. When you reach the wrist, lower her arm, supporting it above and below the elbow with both hands, and begin again from the starting position.

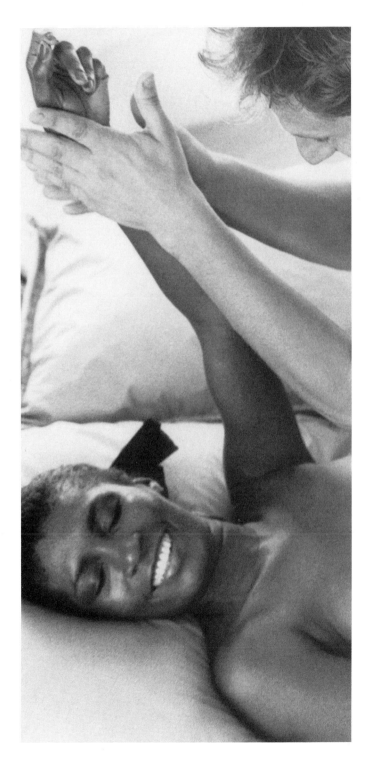
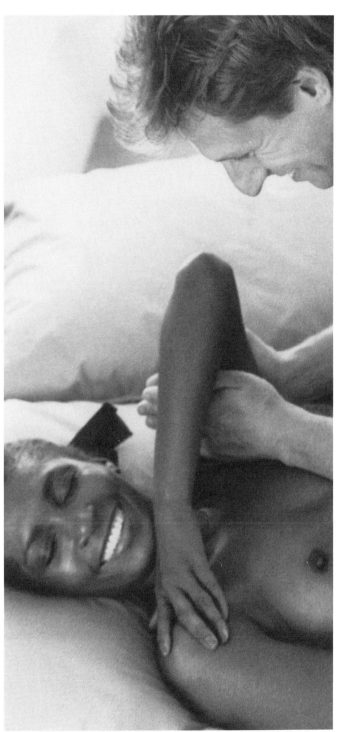

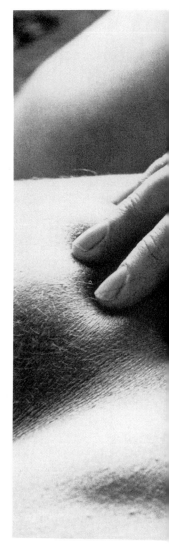

Covering an entire leg with a series of quick full hand strokes, this movement is the longest fast stroking variation anywhere on the body. It's an ideal way to complete a leg massage; your partner experiences waves of sensation moving from the top of the leg to the bottom.

Reach straight down and grasp the top of the thigh with both hands (as shown), bringing your thumb around as far as it will go comfortably. Pull down, hand over hand, as far as the knee, then over the knee onto the lower leg. Stop at the ankle. Build up speed gradually once you get comfortable. Pressures should be light to moderate, even at high speeds, during this stroke. The trick is to grasp the leg firmly without grabbing at it. As you move closer to the feet, reposition yourself quietly without interrupting the movement. What your partner should feel (again, the final test of any massage) is a cascading wave of sensation beginning near the hip and descending all the way to the feet.

Fast stroking — the decisive way to move off a leg.

To be lomi-lomied *you lie down upon a mat or undress for the night. [A native], beginning with your head and working down slowly over the whole body, seizes and squeezes with quite peculiar art every tired muscle, working and kneading with indefatigable patience. . . Whereas you were weary and worn out, you find yourself fresh, all soreness and weariness absolutely and entirely gone, and mind and body soothed to a healthful and refreshing sleep.* —Charles Nordhoff, *Northern California, Oregon, and the Sandwich Islands*

Generally, massage during insomnia ranges from deep, penetrating strokes to very light contact. The most delicate stroke of all is the delightful full body brushing movement. Save it for the end.

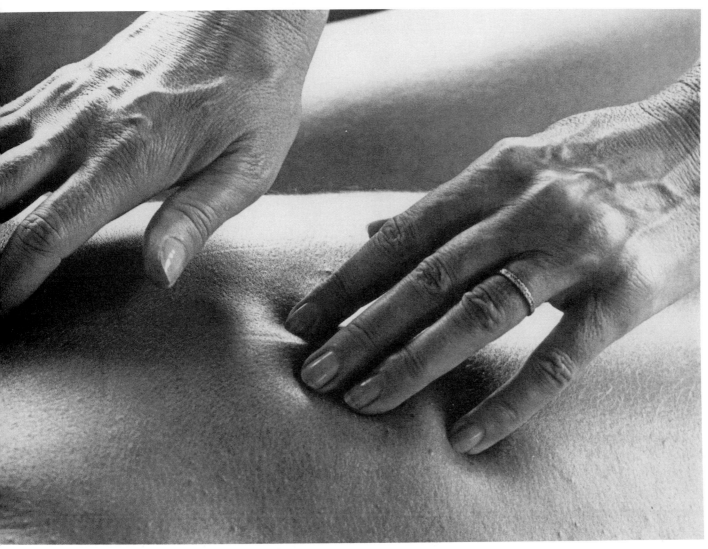

Begin by centering your hands at the top of the spine just below your partner's neck (as shown). Simply hold your hands in place for half a minute or so without moving. Open your fingers and begin moving down the spine with one hand, then the other over the same route. Two hands following each other enhance the sensation. Make contact only with the tips of your fingers. Brush slowly, pulling straight down the spine, covering each area several times as you descend. Continue over the buttocks and move down the backs of the legs. The feet are especially sensitive to a light, brushing movement, perhaps because most people cannot remember the last time they felt anything light or delicate on the feet. Complete the stroke with your fingertips in contact with your partner's toes. Pick one toe for your final contact, the same one on each foot. Now the stroke stops again, just as it did at the beginning of the movement. Maintain single-finger contact with a single toe on each foot for a silent count of ten. Then, very slowly, break contact.

Be silent.

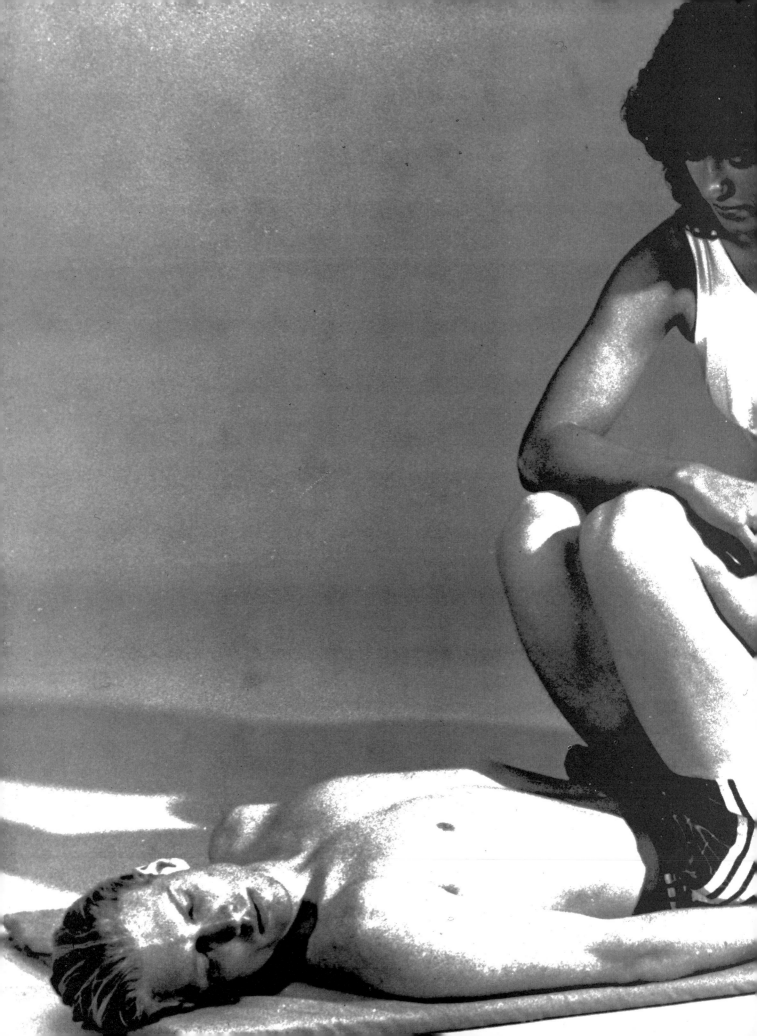

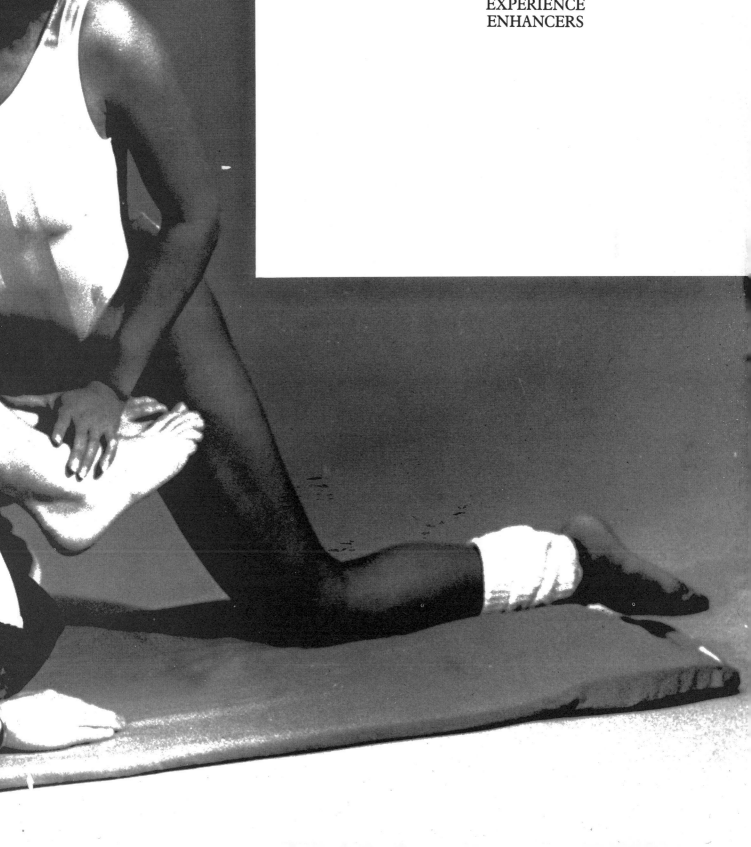

4
EXPERIENCE
ENHANCERS

10.
Five-Minute After-Exercise Conditioning

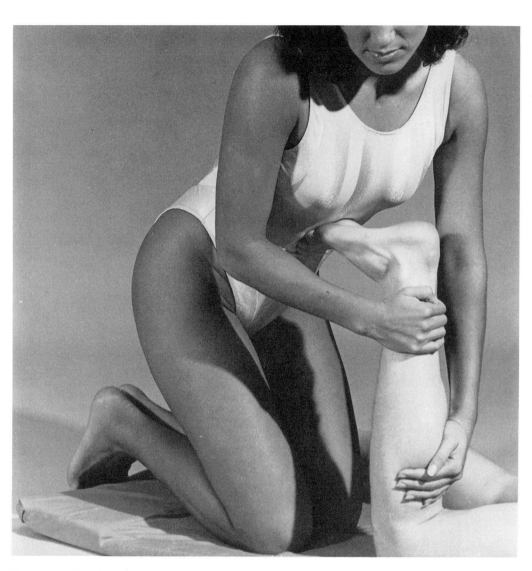

Three essential strokes
Three minutes each, fifty repetitions

☛ Flexing the top of the back
☛ Pumping the legs
☛ Forearm percussion

Exercise Without Pain

Fitness programs, especially those designed for the novice, come with a hidden cost: when the exhilaration that follows exercise begins to fade, nagging aches and pains can pop up all over the body. You get up an hour earlier to run, only to discover that your knees hurt all day. An invigorating bicycle ride leaves your legs so tense that sleep becomes difficult. And we're told that this is exactly as it should be — getting in shape means living with an aching body. In fitness, as in life, there is no gain, according to the joyless Puritan ethic, without pain. Eventually, pain becomes an end in itself, a sought-after goal — press on until your muscles burn, because only then are you finally getting somewhere. Staying fit is reduced to an excruciating ordeal, something one endures like unpleasant medicine "because it's good for you." Suffer or get fat.

We know that the dreaded lactic acid, a by-product of increased combustion rates during exercise, will irritate the muscles for hours, even days, after a workout. The question is: are aching, acid-drenched muscles the price we *must* pay for fitness?

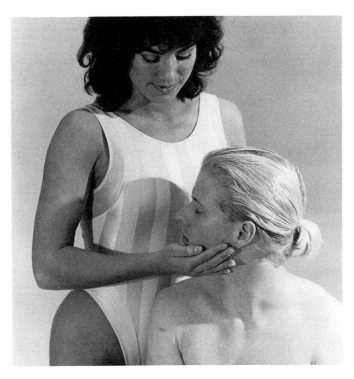

Ergographic tests, used to measure muscle recovery rates after exertion, point the way to the missing link in the modern exercise program; a specialized kind of Super Massage that works in stages. First, the enhanced blood supply created by massage acts as a natural analgesic; it relieves pain. Then, once tensed muscles begin to relax, circulation strokes become far more effective, boosting the oxygen content of tissues in the massaged area by more than 15 percent. Extra oxygen means irritating wastes can be burned off more quickly, but a more significant change

After-exercise massage:

Relaxes tensed muscles.
Oxygenates internal tissues.
Boosts the combustion rate of acidic wastes.
Increases the white and red blood cell count in the massaged area.
Boosts the muscle recovery rate from 75 percent to 125 percent.

comes about when you concentrate on eliminating the cause of after-exercise pain.

During Super Massage, when lactic acid is literally squeezed out of the muscles, the normal metabolic process is accelerated. In minutes, you can accomplish what it would take hours or days for the body to do by itself. After the massage, your partner goes through the day invigorated instead of in pain. But there's more . . . don't stop massaging when stress-hardened muscles begin to yield. By continuing for just a few more minutes you will discover why Olympic teams all over the world have become intensely interested in massage.

The effects of several minutes of Super Massage on fatigued muscles simply has to be experienced to be believed. Again, typical muscle recovery rates after exercise are no more than 20 percent. A person capable of doing fifty push-ups will, after five minutes of rest, be capable of doing only ten more. But if five minutes of fluid release

Flexing the Top of the Back

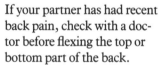

massage is substituted for the five minutes of rest, muscle recovery rates jump to between 75 percent and 100 percent!*

Originally documented by scientists more than eighty years ago, this significant data was largely ignored by generations of antitactile Americans. Until very recently serious athletes were expected to put up with aching muscles after every workout. In 1980, when I introduced a program of fluid release massage for runners in *The New Massage*, only a few teams throughout the world traveled with a masseur. Not surprisingly, the East Germans, Israelis, and (a few) American swim teams who massaged their athletes dominated the competition. The news spread with their track records, and today nearly every major competitor recognizes the value of massage as a natural training aid. All over the world, swimmers, runners, dancers, weight lifters, and boxers have discovered a drug-free way to radically alter the effects of fatigue on the muscles.

One way to overcome the puritanical fear of massage is to start with a dramatic effect that cannot be duplicated in any exercise program. At first, back flexing feels more like exercise than massage, but you will notice important differences; this is a passive exercise — you do all the work while your partner does nothing at all. Muscles and tendons that are often ignored in a workout are stretched, making the whole upper body more flexible. The smiles usually outlast the stroke, maybe even the whole massage. No pain and plenty of gain.

If your partner has had recent back pain, check with a doctor before flexing the top or bottom part of the back.

During this stroke you will be twisting the whole upper back; first to the right, then to the left. Begin by pushing forward on your partner's right shoulder with the heel of your right hand while you pull back on her left shoulder with your left forearm. Some backs twist much further than others — stop as soon as you run into real resistance.

Back off slowly from the point of tension, and try the movement again. With just three or four repetitions you should feel the point of tension begin to retreat as little-used muscles are gently stretched. Flex the right side of the back four times, then reverse the whole stroke; push forward on your partner's left shoulder with the heel of your left hand while pulling back on her right shoulder with your right forearm.

*Graham, *Massage: Manual Treatment, Remedial Movements*, p. 83.

The Full Back Flex

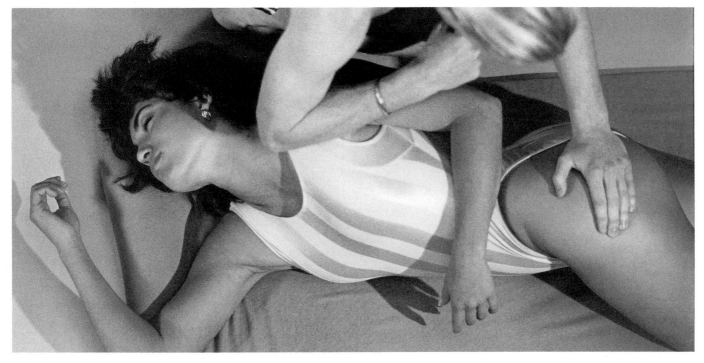

Since back flexing works best on supple muscles, the period just after exercise is ideal. Athletes are quick to recognize the value of a long stretch that occurs at both ends of the back simultaneously. No exercise can provide this extraordinary effect — it's unique to massage.

Once again, stretching is accomplished by pushing forward with your hand while pulling back with your elbow. When flexing the lower back, however, you're manipulating the whole area from the shoulders to the hips, a much larger part of the body. This doesn't require a great deal more effort than upper back

flexing; nevertheless, a moment or two of careful preparation will definitely make things easier. Before starting the movement, your partner should be reclining on her side, facing away from you and relaxed. If she seems nervous, say a few words about the stroke so she has a general idea of what to expect. First, the hips will move forward while the shoulders move back, then, as you reverse directions, the hips move back while the shoulders come forward. The actual twisting occurs at the top and bottom of the spine.

Start by pulling back on the shoulders while you push forward at the hips. Make a fist, then press your right elbow across the front of your partner's shoulder (as shown). Using the heel of your left hand, push forward gently on the bony crest of your partner's hip. Try to equalize pressures as you push and pull. Usually, the top of the body will move further than the bottom. To compensate for the difference, flex the top and bottom of the body at the same rate until you reach the point of tension at the hips. Then hold steady at the hips and continue twisting at the shoulder. Be especially

careful during this stroke to avoid short, jerky movements. When flexing any part of the body, always move deliberately and slowly.

To flex the back in the other direction there's no need for your partner to move. Simply reverse the hand positions you just used; press forward on the back of her shoulder with the heel of your right hand while pulling back on the hip with your left elbow.

Sometimes, as the joints of the lower back are moved, you will hear a little pop. It's usually followed by a long, satisfied sigh of pleasure.

Flexing the Leg

Flexing the leg effectively stretches out a wide range of lower body muscles where the leg and lower back meet. Near the point of tension every major joint of the lower back will move far enough to extend nearby ligaments — the fibrous bands that connect bones to each other.

With your partner on her side facing away from you, reach straight down and grasp the inside of her bottom leg just above the knee, then reach forward with your other hand into the small of the back. Start slowly so you can carefully equalize the pulling and pushing pressures. Leg flexing requires pressure in two almost opposite directions: pull straight back on the lower leg while pushing forward against the small of the back. If the stroke feels awkward, simply rearrange yourself and your partner. On the first try you will notice that the leg and lower back have different points of tension — adjust your pressures accordingly. Leg flexing stretches

the powerful four-part quadriceps muscles on the front of the thigh. In fact, most of the resistance you feel when pulling back on the leg comes from this large muscle group.

As the bottom leg is flexed, the top leg usually moves forward, bending the back into a graceful arch. Flex the leg three times to the point of tension, then have your partner turn over so you can do the other leg.

Pressing the Leg

With your partner comfortable on her side, it's easy to lift the top leg straight up in the air and press both sides with a squeezing motion. The precise amount that you will be able to lift the leg will of course vary. Never force the leg. As always, massage just inside the point of tension. Supporting the leg with one hand at the ankle leaves the other hand free to squeeze away. Follow the contours of the muscles as you squeeze, avoiding the bony surfaces of the leg and the knee. Move up and down the inside of the leg, squeezing every few inches, then reverse your hands and massage the outside of the leg.

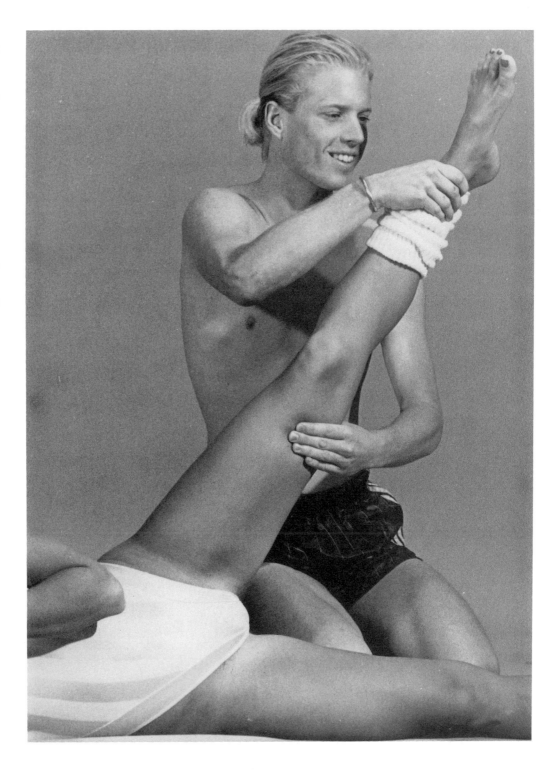

Pumping the Legs

We have all seen the athlete whose earnest exercises are performed within the sad limitations of a body completely dominated by tight muscles. His stride, although vigorous, is short and choppy. Throwing, swimming, or dancing are quirky and unbalanced. In fact, every movement seems to take place in a space that's rigidly defined by perpetually tense muscles. Instead of becoming more supple after exercise, the body merely becomes more obviously stressed. As we have seen, fluid release massage can provide an athlete with a way to transform the exercise experience. Muscle stretching movements,

although not as dramatic, do accomplish something similar: here is a kind of conditioning that your partner simply cannot do as well for himself.

Leg pumping after exercise is a much more energetic movement than the variation used to relieve insomnia. After exercise it's more important to stretch tight muscles, tendons, and ligaments than it is to improve circulation. Leg pumping stretches the large hamstrings on the backs of the thighs, along with a wide range of smaller muscles around the knee. Inside the knee, the body's most complex joint, tiny tendons and

ligaments are extended each time you pump the leg. Note the point of tension on the first pass and pump the leg within its limitations. After a few repetitions the point of tension will usually begin to recede without additional pressure. If it does, don't hesitate to press a bit further as you continue this movement.

With your partner lying on his back, pump one leg first, then the other, and finally, both at once. Lift, using both hands to support your partner's leg above and below the knee, until the knee is straight up. Steady the leg with one hand at the ankle while pressing forward on

the knee with the soft inner part of your forearm (as shown). Lean into this stroke. Hold the leg for a silent count of ten at the point of tension, then release it slowly. It's best to bring the leg all the way back to the full prone starting position. Be sure to provide support above and below the knee as you lower it.

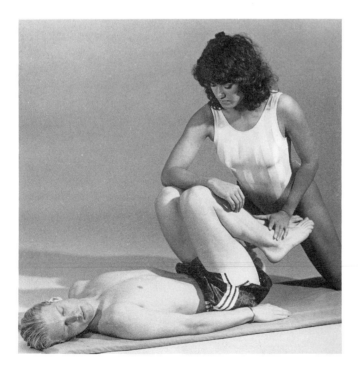
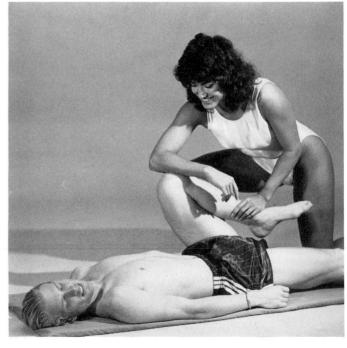

Controlling Cramps

Legs

Cramping becomes a serious threat the moment the oxygen supply to a muscle drops precipitously. Low temperatures, tight clothing, and excessive exercise can interfere with normal blood circulation. More commonly, however, cramping strikes because stress (and therefore vasoconstriction) has been allowed to continue unchecked. For athletes, the problem usually begins with an overly ambitious workout. If, say, the muscles are not properly warmed up, they can easily fail to meet the extra demands of a long run in cold weather.

Controlling Cramps (cont'd)

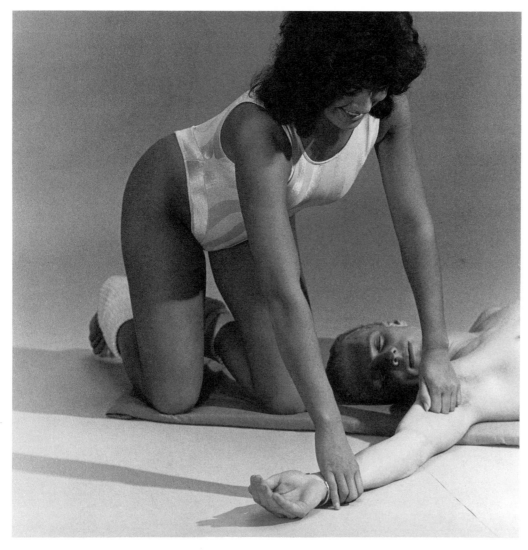

Excruciating muscle cramps deliver the message: the leg muscles are out of oxygen.

Most sports-related cramps occur in the arms or legs. Before you attempt any massage, use part of your own body to straighten out the afflicted limb. With your partner lying on his stomach, straighten a cramped calf by pressing your knee hard against the bottom of his foot. Hold it in that position while you massage. Anchor the leg just above the ankle (as shown on p. 129) and press down into the hardened muscle with the flat part of the knuckles. Rotate your hand slowly. Don't stop, even though you may feel the muscle soften as you massage. Move in with friction strokes (p. 32) to the center of the muscle. Fingertip knead the whole area (p. 56), then press down with your closed fist and circle with a deep compression movement (p. 67). Try a simple circulation movement (p. 74), pressing blood toward the heart along the whole length of the affected leg. Finish by pulling down from the back of the knee to the ankle with a fast hand-over-hand movement (as shown on p. 129). Squeeze the calf as you pull.

Arms

Stretch out a cramped arm and support it with one hand while you do compression with the other (as shown). Rotate the flat part of your closed fist on the raised muscles of the arm. Stay off exposed blood vessels and the bony shoulder top.

During hand-over-hand pulling, grasp and pull vigorously with each stroke if the muscle has been cramped.

Help your partner rise slowly after the massage — leaping to one's feet the moment the pain diminishes can bring the cramp right back.

Forearm Percussion

The whole range of percussion strokes becomes useful after exercise, especially if muscle cramping is a problem for your partner. If you can't isolate a specific problem area, a forearm percussion stroke is more generally effective than any of the hands-only variations. The wide muscular center of the back is the perfect place for this movement. Percussion here increases the blood supply to all the vital organs and relaxes the long muscles that run parallel to the spine. By using the whole forearm you substantially increase the contact area, covering half the back with each stroke.

If you're larger than your partner, sit comfortably near his waist but if you're smaller and lighter, try straddling him and sitting back on the hips (as shown). This gives you better balance throughout the stroke and makes reaching forward easier.

Make a fist and, with moderate pressure, snap your whole forearm against your partner's back. Begin on the long muscles that run parallel to the spine and work outward to the sides of the back. The trick is to bring the entire contact surface, from the flat part of the knuckle to the elbow, down at once. Naturally, this stroke will move more slowly than the hands-only percussion movements, but, as always, consistent rhythm is far more important than raw speed.

11.
Instant Energy
at Home
and at Work

Three essential strokes
One minute each, fifty repetitions

- ☛ Mixed percussion
- ☛ Fast friction
- ☛ Walking the back

The Coffee Break Vs. the Massage Break

If your partner has been depending on stimulants for a pickup during the day, massage will open up a new world of possibilities. The following strokes are ideal for hard-working people who want a quick energy boost—without a crash afterward.

In the kitchen, living room, or office, a variety of percussion and friction movements, none of which require oiling or special preparations, can be used to alter your partner's mood. In fact, major changes start happening inside the body even before you finish massaging. In minutes, as oxygen levels throughout the massaged area climb, fatigue is diminished and a wonderfully energetic feeling takes its place. Stiffness in the muscles and joints yields to the sort of fluid ease one usually experiences after a strenuous physical workout. Finally, as acids are flushed out of the tissues to be replaced by oxygen-enriched blood, irritability gives way to an optimistic can-do attitude.

The effects are particularly impressive in situations where people must sit and concentrate for long hours at a telephone, typewriter, or computer. As fatigue departs, endurance levels are dramatically improved. Apple Computer, Pacific Telesis, and Raychem, to name just a few,

Do

Schedule the massage when your partner is not likely to be interrupted. Be punctual.

Get feedback on stroke and pressure preferences.

Appear confident and organized. Bring with you everything you will need.

Take whatever simple steps are possible to quiet the environment.

Take all of your partner's requests seriously.

Leave quietly as soon as the massage is finished.

Don't

Massage while your partner does something else. Don't get flustered if interruptions do occur.

Encourage conversation.

Comment on how tense your partner seems to be.

Randomly explore your partner's body—people dislike being probed.

Impose a complex routine of strokes to impress your partner.

Introduce complicated rules or exotic theories.

Needlessly take up your partner's time.

have already begun regular massage programs for their employees. A masseur visits the office and either moves from desk to desk or massages in a company lounge. Employers and employees alike realize that massage keeps everyone in good spirits while improving productivity.

If you have a few extra minutes during the day, you don't need to hire a professional masseur to relax a tense worker. You can do all of these strokes yourself. At home or at work your reward is that next time you may be the one getting the massage.

If you're pressed for time, however, or have many employees, a good professional masseur is invaluable. But given the wide proliferation of quackery in the field, finding the right masseur or team of masseurs can be tricky. The guidelines that start on p. 142 are designed to help you make the right choice.

Team Massage

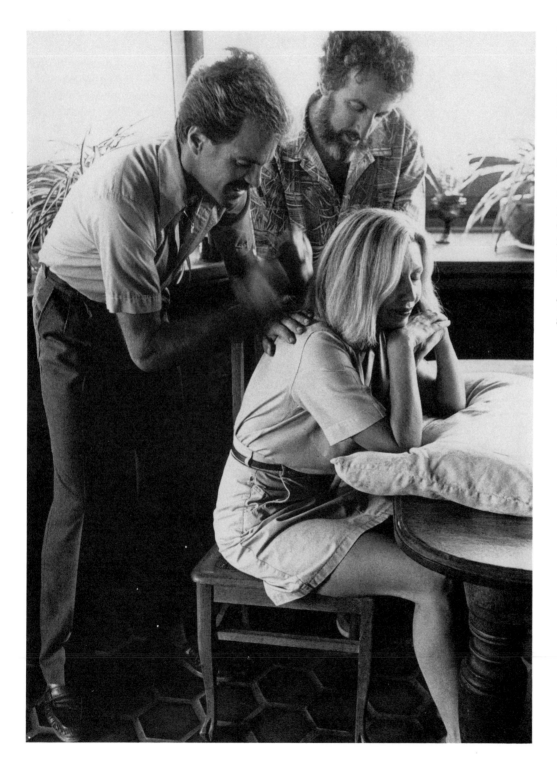

The most common problem one encounters when massaging busy executives is the overbooked itinerary. If your partner is too busy to sit still for a massage, try ganging up on her. Two pairs of hands can deliver twice as much sensation as one. The feeling of *four* hands thundering up and down the back during a pounding movement is so overwhelming that even the most self-absorbed type will stop talking and surrender to massage.

They always thank you afterward.

The Office Pillow

If you can't locate a lounge in which to sprawl out, the massage pillow becomes very important. With it, percussion and friction strokes for the upper back, the staple of on-the-job massage, become much more effective. Every worker needs a pillow large enough to support the full weight of the upper body when placed across the surface of a desk. Subdued colors are most inviting. The pillow should give good support during any of the common percussion movements, but remain firm enough to retain its shape. A removable cover makes occasional oiling possible, although a large towel can serve as well.

Some offices have nothing at all that can be used as a massage pillow, so it's wise to inquire ahead of time and provide one, if necessary, whenever you do massage at work.

Mixed Percussion

Percussion strokes are probably the easiest to prepare for in massage. Don't bother having your partner lie down or remove any clothing; just grab a pillow and you're ready to go. In fact, if no pillow is handy, the head can be supported on the hands without seriously compromising the stroke. For offices without lounges, or for a quick burst of energy around the house, nothing satisfies like a few minutes of intense percussion.

Move up and down the back on both sides of the spine, but stay off the spine itself. Save your greatest pressures for the thickest muscles at the top of the back and across the shoulders. Generally, these movements are more effective over the rib cage, where bones provide a kind of natural cushioning effect. If you move to the lower back, follow the elevated ridge of muscles that runs parallel to the spine. Be careful not to pound on your partner's kidneys. Choose a percussion speed that you can comfortably maintain for a while. Rhythmic consistency is more important than raw speed.

Start with pounding, the most intense percussion movement, and let it give way to a more gentle full hand cupping stroke (see p. 104). A light pinky snap (see p. 105) is nice across the top of the shoulders. Your partner may want to direct the percussion to a specific part of the back; listen for feedback. If nothing is actually said, remember

that pleasurable moaning means that what you're doing feels good—keep it up for a while.

Percussion strokes set up a vibration that carries right through the body. Work on the back for two or three minutes, and the feeling goes on after you stop.

Fast Friction

Raking the Back

Immediately after percussion, while your partner is still relaxing on a pillow, try some fast friction. It's the perfect stroke for that stiff neck or nagging pain at the top of the back. This energetic, immensely versatile friction variation can be used on almost every part of the body. It penetrates easily through clothing and works in nearly any setting, making it ideal for on-the-job massage. Fast friction is one of the rare massage strokes that takes some real effort to sustain. However, the extra exertion is always appreciated; no other stroke in massage produces a more intense feeling. It's shown here on the top of the

back, the area most frequently requested by office workers, but the stroke is equally effective on any fleshy part of the body.

The key to successful fast friction is good anchoring, without which the movement becomes sloppy and random. To cover the whole upper back, push down between the shoulder blades with the flat surface of one hand, then work up to the lower neck (as shown). Anchor near the shoulder, pushing flesh toward your friction hand. You'll need to reposition your anchor hand frequently during fast friction. Rotate the friction hand while pressing down moderately hard. Remember: friction strokes turn on the interior tissues, not the surface of the skin. You will feel the muscular interior of the upper back as you turn. Press in constantly with your anchor hand to confine the movement to the area under your friction hand — you don't want to shake the entire body. Your partner should feel an intense vibration that is confined to a single spot. Once you get the feel of the stroke, try increasing the speed. Fast friction can move almost as fast as you're able to go, but never push it to the limit — you'll have trouble sustaining the speed and controlling the stroke. Check with your partner to find out just how much speed he likes.

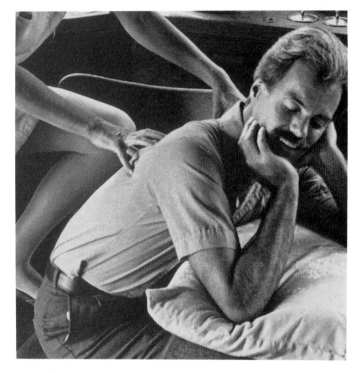

Generally, most massage strokes stay off the spine itself, focusing instead on nearby muscle groups. Whenever they get tight, the long muscles that run parallel to the spine pull directly on spinal nerves. Repeated frequently enough, this stroke will go a long way toward relieving direct muscle pressure to the spine that keeps the nerves irritated.

Have your partner lean forward and support the weight of his head either on his arms or a desktop pillow. Forming a rigid arch with both hands, begin stroking down both sides of the spine with your fingertips. Keep your fingers

flexed and rigid throughout this stroke. That way you can glide across the surface of clothing while penetrating deep within. Start at the neck and pull straight down in a series of alternating, foot-long strokes. The stroke moves slowly down the back, covering every portion five or six times. When you reach the bottom of the spine, start again from the top. Rake the whole back at least three times.

Walking the Back

Traditional back walking works only if you're considerably smaller and lighter than your partner. With a bit more effort much the same effect can be created using the fists. In fact, you can feel tensions with the hands that would go unnoticed beneath the feet. As your hands travel up and down the back, pressures can be directed with great precision—you can actually feel tensed muscles begin to relax.

This movement follows the same path you took during the raking stroke. You can stand directly behind your partner and do both sides of the spine at once (as shown). Make a fist and press the flat part of the knuckle into the long muscles that run parallel to the spine. As your fist sinks into the muscle, roll it forward slightly, pressing down hard as you roll. Start at the base of the neck with one fist, then repeat the movement immediately below with the other. Move all the way down the spine, pressing down first with one fist, then the other. Do each side of the spine twice; more if your partner asks for it.

They usually do.

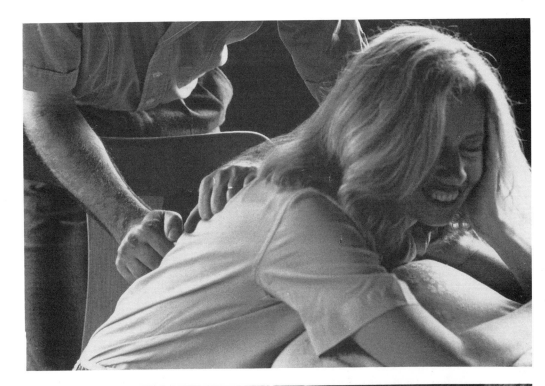

Quick Friction
for the Arms and Hands

Although the hands and arms are used constantly at work, we tend to ignore their aches and pains, focusing instead on the shoulders or lower back. Given just five minutes to work, most masseurs will settle for the lower back and shoulders. Before you do, look closely at your partner's job. Are typing, computer

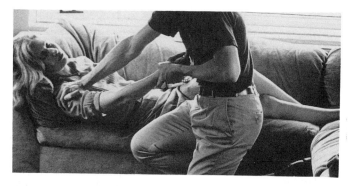

work, or extended telephone conversations required? After massage, the feeling of new-found energy will be just as invigorating in the hands and arms as in the high stress areas of the back.

This stroke also provides an excellent introduction to on-the-job massage. Even the most harried executive can be persuaded to rest an arm on the desk for a few minutes, or better yet, collapse on a couch in the company lounge.

Remember: you need only a few minutes to get the fluid release effect started. With your partner lying on her back, anchor her extended arm at the wrist (as shown) and press down on the fore-arm with the flat surface of your knuckle. Rotate slowly, moving up and down the arm from the wrist to the shoul-

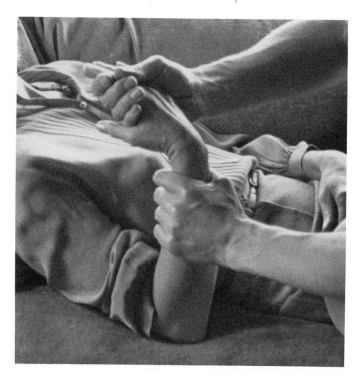

der. Ease up over the exposed blood vessels at the wrist and inside the elbow, reserving your real pressures for the muscular forearm.

To massage the shoulders, circle your partner's wrist and pull it straight out until the whole arm is extended (as shown). Then rotate the same flat part of your knuckle on the muscular shoulder top.

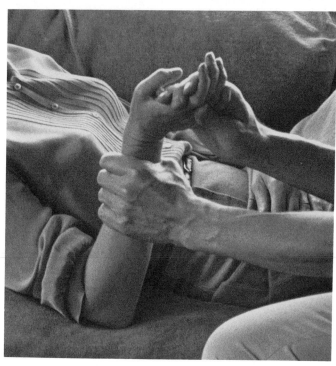

Rotating the Bones of the Arm and Hand

When was the last time your partner had her bones rotated?

The hand is operated by remote control via long tendons and bones that begin at the elbow. As the hand and arm turn, the two descending bones, the radius and ulna, demonstrate one of the more extraordinary aspects of human anatomy by actually crossing at the center of the forearm. During massage, however, the bones of the forearm can be made to cross while simply rotating the complex joint at the wrist.

Just as an effective foot massage starts up at the knee, massage for the hand must consider parts of the body between the wrist and elbow. Grasp your partner's hand around her loosely clenched fingers (as shown on p. 138) and rotate the wrist once just to test the limits of the turning arc. Pay close attention to the real limits of the arc, which will change several times in a single rotation. As you turn the wrist, the bones of the forearm will cross and uncross themselves.

Rotate the hand three times in each direction. Then grasp your partner's hand tightly between both of your hands, keeping your thumbs on top (as shown) and rotate your hands slowly. The bones inside her hand will move with your hands. Massaging on a couch, you can rotate the bones of her other hand by simply reaching across her body. There's no need for your partner to move at any time during this stroke. You do all the work for her.

Throwing the Arm

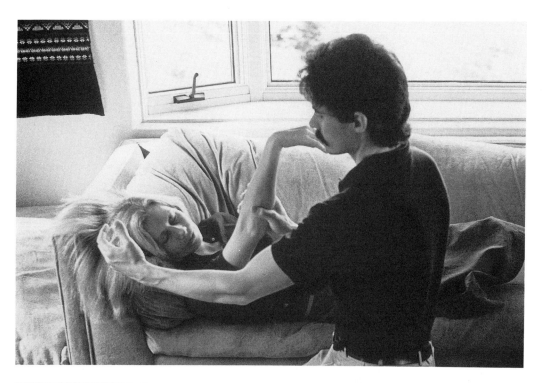

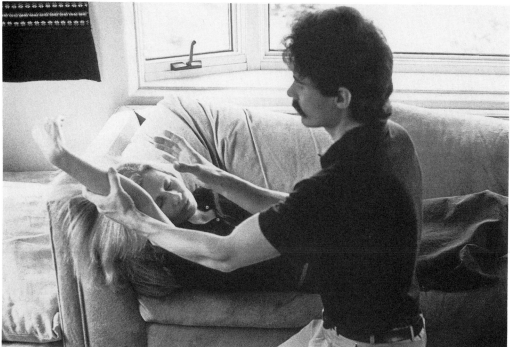

Here is the perfect movement to break the monotony of desk work. While an arm flies through the air, your partner does nothing at all. The large ball joint at the shoulder is vigorously exercised as circulation throughout the limb is stimulated.

Lift your partner's arm first above the elbow (as shown), then at the wrist, until it's straight up in the air. Continuing to hold steady at the wrist, bring the arm up over her head until you feel resistance. Then move the wrist and arm all the way down to a point near her waist. Move the arm back and forth several times until you are completely familiar with the limits of the arc. Only then are you ready to begin the throwing part of the movement, starting with a small arc and enlarging it gradually. With your partner's arm fully extended, toss the wrist from one hand to the other. As you increase your throwing arc to the previously established limits, increase the speed. Let your arm give way a bit each time you catch your partner's wrist. Reach across your partner's body to throw the other arm.

This is the fastest passive exercise. Arm throwing — a thriller.

Real and Imaginary Massage

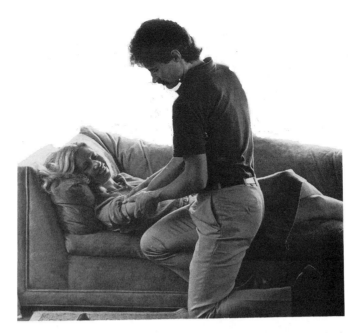

Our Puritan heritage has assigned all physical contact between adults to two rather narrow categories: sexual or commercial. You're either making a sexual advance or you're making money when you touch other adults. Those engaged in commercial touching are careful to remain as impersonal as possible lest they be accused of making a sexual advance. This unfortunate stereotyping has created serious confusion in the massage profession. We have massage as a familiar euphemism for prostitution vs. massage therapy in which the body is manipulated as impersonally as a collection of auto parts. Real massage, the kind that has been practiced everywhere on earth since biblical times, is a sensual art: it works because it feels good. Sensuality is part of the wide spectrum of human feeling between sex and therapy. We live in a society that tries to deny its existence.

In massage, this denial has created some bizarre imitations. A prostitute posing as masseuse fiddles around with a leg or an arm for a minute or two before getting down to business. The customer really didn't expect massage and none was offered. But the massage therapist posing as doctor has even less use for real massage. Any gadget that will confer authority on the

practitioner and distance him from the sensual is embraced wholeheartedly. High-speed electrical devices, magnets, bits of stone, and vials of uncertain chemicals are solemnly pressed against the body. Hands are waved back and forth in the air in order to "balance" mysterious forces.

When flesh finally does meet flesh, it's always to demonstrate an exotic theory, never simply to please. Bursts of nasty finger-poking alternate with violent manipulation of the joints because "blocked energy" must be liberated. Strokes wander aimlessly across the body, departing from the map of the circulatory system, from nerve paths, and, finally, from all known systems. As the confusion mounts, charts covered with exotic oriental characters are rolled out, indicating that dozens of independent lines converge on the bottom of the spine, the side of an ear, or the back of one toe. And of course the magnets and bits of stone converge on

those spots with full liturgical ceremony.

Through it all the practitioner advances relentlessly on his helpless "patient," self-righteously poking, jabbing, and pulling at the body in the name of "healing." In manner, if not in practice, the therapist seeks to emulate the high priests of the medical profession (usually his sworn enemies). Ask a question and the authoritative bullying begins: your therapist knows things you don't know about: "meridians," "auras," "energy imbalances," and "pressure points." It's all very mysterious and complex, and if it hurts, well . . . it's good for you.

Quackery, not prostitution, is the biggest problem facing massage today. We're in the process of rediscovering an ancient health principle that can enrich our lives, but for many people the quack and his spooky bag of tricks will be the first and last contact with massage. The human

body, perhaps the most complex arrangement of matter in nature, remains a mystery to the quack. He usually has little understanding of anatomy and no appreciation for the simple, sensual beauty of massage. Those who love massage understand that something primal pervades the experience — this is one of the most ancient human activities. Unfortunately, so is quackery.

Thousands of years ago, when people massaged by the light of open fires, bead strokers and body pokers concentrated on purging the body of evil spirits. Proving? That, in quackery, little has changed over the past few millenniums; self-promotion remains far more important than healing. The quack has always sought power by transforming the body into a supernatural freak show that only he can understand.

But there is a gray zone, too, between quackery and real massage. Many earnest practitioners, concerned that their efforts will be confused with prostitution, go to great lengths to "dignify" massage. The airs and exotic terminology are usually abandoned the moment a partner begins to sink into that profound state of relaxation that only real massage can bring.

How to Find a Good Professional Masseur

Thinking of hiring a professional masseur for yourself or your company? The rewards are great, but it pays to shop carefully.

The right masseur, or team of masseurs, can change the whole working environment for a small or large company. Employees are happier, more relaxed; the workplace becomes a pleasant environment where one feels good. Absenteeism declines, and productivity, that elusive goal, goes up. Do something this nice for your employees, and they're going to return the favor.

How much is stress costing you? Are your employees attempting to tack ambitious exercise programs onto the workload — failing — then turning to drugs to relax? Professional massage is less expensive and time-consuming than any of the standard medical services. You'll see dramatic results after just five minutes of massage two or three times a week; each session takes less time than the average coffee break. If stress is a serious problem at your company, massage can become a kind of preventive medicine, permitting the doctor to do other things. Which would you rather pay: the masseur or the workman's compensation claims?

The number of good professional masseurs is growing every year, but with no standardized licensing procedures, you have no way of knowing what to expect until the massage begins. Nevertheless, setting up a corporate massage program is one of the most pleasant tasks in business, simply because the interviewer will be massaged by so many of the job applicants. But there's more to the interviewing job than collapsing on a couch in your office while your neck and shoulders are kneaded. Use the following guidelines to pick the right professional for your company.

First, find out if any companies in your area have already set up massage programs — their recommendations are a good place to begin. Larger companies require a team of masseurs with a common philosophy — a program. Choose a program that's flexible enough to fit into your business day. If there's no separate lounge area in your company that can be used for massage, a team should be able to adapt to conditions in the office itself without causing any problems. If necessary, massage can be going on at one desk while work proceeds at the next. Again, the best way to audition a masseur, once

The Massage Bill of Rights

You have the right:

To remain silent and to expect the same from your masseur.

To refuse phone calls or other interruptions.

To uninterrupted pleasure throughout a massage.

To walk out if the massage is unpleasant.

To direct the massage, requesting specific strokes and timings if you so desire.

To be warm and comfortable.

To choose the music if you're in the mood for music.

To be alone afterward.

references have been checked and preliminary interviews completed, is on your own body. Each masseur should be able to continue any stroke for at least five minutes without breaking rhythm. Ideally, he (or she) should be as efficient and invisible as a good waiter. And as silent.

If you're planning an extended massage program for a larger company, hire masseurs who keep simple records concerning the condition and special needs of each employee. Finally, look closely at your masseur's general presentation. A calm, confident manner will help put your employees at ease,

while an officious, overly busy approach will ruin the experience. A masseur should be clean, with carefully trimmed fingernails, and a pleasant personality.

How do you separate the quacks from the serious masseurs? *Beware of any practitioner who attempts to justify painful treatments in the name of massage.* The quack shows up with an incomprehensible program that invariably includes plenty of nasty poking and twisting "because it's good for you." At best the quack is annoying and a waste of time, at worst actually dangerous. Turn one loose in your office, and your

employees become a testing ground for excruciating "body therapies," thereby creating more, not less, work for the company doctor. The responsible practitioner, on the other hand, will respect your rights throughout a massage (see "The Massage Bill of Rights"). It is, after all, your body, not a pet theory, that matters most. Above all a masseur must be flexible enough to meet your personal needs. This means that you should get exactly what *you* desire (even if it means skipping the masseur's forty-seven-point program). If you want your shoulders kneaded for five minutes straight, ask, and if you get an argument, move on to another masseur.

Much the same criteria can be used to hire a personal masseur. Naturally, it becomes even more important to be sure the masseur will be sensitive to your own specialized needs. People come in various body types, and a good masseur will recognize yours, immediately seeking out the trouble spots and lingering on the most pleasure-sensitive areas. Nevertheless, your requests, if you feel like making any, should come first. And afterward you should feel much more relaxed than before.

12.
A Ten-Minute Erotic Massage

Three essential strokes
One minute each, fifty repetitions

☛ Local circulation
☛ Pumping the legs
☛ A full body stroke

Banishing the After-Work Blues:
The Sex Enhancer

*. . .why do I yield to that
  suggestion
whose horrid image doth unfix
  my hair
And make my seated heart
  knock at
my ribs against the use of
  nature?
Present fears are less than
  horrible imaginings.*
— William Shakespeare,
Macbeth

If the mind is the greatest aphrodisiac, then fear and tension are the principal enemies of good sex. We yield to our fears when we're over-tired and overstressed. Without relaxation and the trust that follows, good sex is rare. The familiar "after-work blues," a combination of headaches, muscular aches and pains, and general irritability, can easily turn sex into a joyless chore. The trick is to find a way to leave your problems, anxieties, and fears at the office so they don't end up in bed. You must find a way to relax after work without working at it.

The after-work blues, like other stress-related complaints, originate in the body, not the mind. Deal with the physical manifestations of stress, and the emotional problems, which may seem terribly deep-seated, begin to disappear. Has your partner been sitting for long periods with little opportunity for

Focusing your erotic massage

Does the base of the neck or the lower back hurt?
Is your partner in pain from a recent accident?
Has your partner been wearing tight shoes?
Can you see visible marks from tight clothing?
Does your partner complain of being continually overstressed?
Is your partner taking stimulants or tranquilizers?
Is your partner wearing contact lenses?
Is there a hot bath or shower near your massage area?
Can you eliminate telephone calls and visitors?
Are children and pets cared for?

any kind of exercise? Has constant scheduling pressure reduced him to a nervous wreck? Have many arguments occurred?

If the answer to any one of these questions is yes, you can be certain that concentrated acidic wastes are trapped in the tissues. Inside the body the hidden source of most stress is usually marked by a peculiar concentration of nasty chemicals. With or without drugs, it is virtually impossible for anyone to relax while the muscles are bathed in lactic and carbonic acids. To vanquish the after-work blues, you must get rid of those acids. If you don't, there's no hope for real relaxation. And not much chance for good sex.

If the acids are hidden, their effects certainly are not. You can usually anticipate the quality of a sexual encounter by simply observing your partner's mood before sex. Look carefully at the response to tension after an exhausting day at work. Do you see a general collapse on a comfortable chair with a cocktail or three (just enough to take the edge off, you understand)? Sex after heavy drinking will be tense because alcohol doesn't bring true relaxation, it simply depresses the nervous system. And turning off the mind

Banishing After-Work Blues (cont'd)

with vast stretches of uninterrupted TV doesn't get rid of a stiff neck, lower back pain, or congested feelings in the legs. Selected tranquilizers may distance one from various pains (for a while) and from sexual desire as well, but in a few hours, when the tranquilizers wear off, all of the discomfort returns with an extra measure of anxiety. And good sex is more remote than ever.

Should sex itself be reduced to a vehicle for releasing tension, a kind of rudimentary physical therapy for burned-out bodies? That approach transforms the "therapist" into a martyr, an unwilling, even resentful, sexual partner. Happily, you can find a better way.

Your partner can experience an extraordinary release from tension after just a brief fluid release sequence. The massage will immediately become much more real than any fears or anxieties. As you massage, real relaxation courses through the body, the muscles become receptive instead of resistant, and, in minutes, the after-work blues suddenly vanish. This, of course, is precisely the kind of "instant" relief that's promised by painkillers and tranquiliz-

ers, but somehow never quite delivered. With Super Massage it's easy to scrupulously clear internal wastes from the tissues, then oxygenate the entire stressed area. Here is a quick way to vanquish the after-work blues and present your partner with an exceedingly considerate gift: drug-free relaxation; an easy transition from anxiety to blessed peace. At the end of a long day give your partner a massage instead of a drink or pill.

This is not an argument for tacking on a few minutes of massage as a kind of extra foreplay to help seduce the unwilling. Use massage as a two-stage sex enhancer. One, as a means for relaxing your partner and clearing acidic irritants from the body. Two, as a part of sex itself. Ideally, in part one, massage should be separated from foreplay and sex, lest it be viewed as manipulative by a stressed-out partner. Never make demands on your partner during massage. Massage is not sexual ammunition. Instead, see it as a means for transforming an exhausted, stressed-out body. With massage, you focus on the entire body, not just the so-called erogenous zones. Afterward, one feels pampered, perhaps even a bit spoiled. And once relaxation comes, all else becomes possible.

Your partner's not ready for sex if he or she is:

Argumentative.

Rushed.

Having trouble sitting still (compulsive foot tapping, teeth grinding).

Sitting with one leg wrapped around the other.

Complaining of vague aches and pains.

Accident prone.

Unable to concentrate.

Constantly talking about work.

Pale or out of breath. Exhausted.

Reducing Erotic Stress:
Local Circulation

Pressing blood back toward the heart on all the limbs accomplishes several things at once. First, your partner's blood pressure is lowered — you're doing some of the work usually done by the heart. Secondly, the massaged limb is oxygenated, which leaves it feeling light and energetic. Most important, however, your partner experiences a new kind of touch. Perhaps for the first time since childhood somebody else is paying attention to, say, the lower leg. Forget the so-called erogenous zones and concentrate instead on basic sensory awareness. The arms can be a source of great pleasure. So can the legs and the feet.

Begin at the wrists on the arms, or at the ankles on the legs. Wrap your hands around one limb, making contact from the base of the palms to the fingertips. Move up toward the top of the limb, using the hands-opposed position common to all circulation strokes. Turn at the top of the limb and descend along the sides (as shown), making contact all the way back to the starting point. The pressure part of this stroke is always on the way up, toward the heart.

Reducing Erotic Stress:
Fast Stroking the Knee

The knee is the most complex joint in the body. Its smooth operation depends on keeping supple both the tendons that connect muscles to the knee and the ligaments that connect bones within the knee. This becomes difficult if the large muscles above and below the knee are perpetually tense. But once you've massaged the whole leg and the large muscle groups begin to relax, the knee will benefit from a fast stroking movement that makes things happen inside the complex web of ligaments, blood vessels, and tendons.

Use two contact points for this movement: on the fleshy back of the knee and just below the kneecap itself. With fingers pressed together, lift up slightly on the bottom of the knee with both hands, then slide the sides of your thumbs into the groove just below the kneecap. Stroke back and forth with your fingers under the knee while your thumbs make light contact above. One hand moves forward while the other moves back. With a little practice, great bursts of speed behind the knee are fun. As you build up speed, you can sometimes actually feel the warmth generated by your hands. So can your partner.

Reducing Erotic Stress: Forearm Compression

Does your partner worry too much about sex? Curiously, erotic stress seems to generate tension in the muscles of the calf. If nothing is done to relieve the tension, excruciating calf cramps, which usually strike suddenly in the cold hours of the early morning, will follow. Here is a stroke that flexes the leg while you relax all of its major muscle groups. Forearm compression travels well, spreading very pleasant sensations up and down your partner's leg all the while.

Oil the inside of your forearm before starting. Use extra oil if you have hairy arms. Begin on the thigh, then move down to the inside of the calf. Lift your partner's leg with both hands (always use two hands when moving a limb), then hold it in place with one hand just above the ankle (as shown). Lean forward, make a fist, and press down against the front of her thigh with the fleshy part of your forearm. Circle as you press. Move slowly up and down the thigh until you have covered the whole area between the knee and hip at least three times. Then, without breaking the compression

rhythm, move down to the inside of the calf.

Turn your forearm so the same fleshy inner surface makes contact with your partner's calf. Once the knee is raised, the calf will become much more relaxed than the thigh was. Nevertheless, you can often feel tension draining out of the muscles as you

massage. Press down into the muscle tissue and begin rotating your forearm. On this part of the body you can travel all the way from the ankle to the back of the knee. Here again, make at least three passes over the entire lower leg. To complete the movement, use both hands to provide support above and below the knee, then slowly lower your partner's leg to the massage surface.

Reducing Erotic Stress: Pumping the Leg

Pumping the leg flexes joints at the knee and hip and helps to stretch out a quirky lower back. Don't be surprised if your partner sighs with pleasure when you're through.

With your partner lying on her back, position yourself so you can easily reach the center of her body. Then,

using both hands, lift one leg (as shown). While steadying the leg with one hand around the middle of the calf, press forward just below the knee with the fleshy inside of your other forearm. The point of tension, the spot where you encounter resistance, will vary. Feel for it the first time you press forward and don't

press far past that point on successive strokes. A slight stretch feels good, but be careful not to force your partner into an uncomfortable position.

Pump each leg at least four times.

Awakening the Body:
A Full Body Stroke

Pure deepening whirlpools of sensation swirling deeper and deeper through all her tissue and consciousness, til she was one perfect concentric fluid of feeling. —D.H. Lawrence, *Lady Chatterly's Lover*

In massage we think of the erotic strokes as a gentle way of opening certain doors — the experience may or may not culminate in actual sex. Therapists have begun experimenting with erotic massage in the hopes of offering highly stressed couples an attractive alternative to lovemaking that has degenerated into a furious race to orgasm. First, couples are encouraged to relax and simply make physical contact with each other. No drugs, no pressure to perform — just touching. But the touching is educated, not random; circulation is boosted, aches and pains vanish, a joint becomes more supple.

People who have lived together for years discover, perhaps for the first time, each other's knees, feet, and scalp. Gradually, of course, the nonthreatening physical contact becomes a delightful little time bomb. You can use the same techniques that work for couples on a single highly stressed partner, but be aware that this is a very powerful tool. At its best, a first erotic massage can come close to redefining the sexual act.

Try to avoid conversation during an erotic massage. Now, more than ever before, words will come between your partner and the feeling. Conversation will almost always bring on a certain anxiety, which cheats both partners and generates even more stress. The secret of erotic massage is the gratifying way it can expand the range of feeling before sex. In just a few minutes your partner will experience what he or she has been missing. And of course the strokes are just as effective on a relaxed partner who simply wants to feel more.

Erotic massage works best on a firm bed or warm, well-padded massage surface. Surely the bedroom is the one place where we should all be completely free. But we struggle, even there, with each other's desires; the anti-tactile legacy of Puritanism manages to intrude on our most private moments. Expecting erotic feelings to be confined to the immediate area around the genitals,

A Full Body Stroke (cont'd)

we abandon the other 95 percent of the body during foreplay and sex. But not during erotic massage . . .

To soothe the nerves, you massaged the whole back of the body. Now you can massage the entire front of the body with a single movement that passes over most of the well-known erogenous zones. Erotic massage is supremely democratic; a breast should receive no more attention than a shoulder. By not stopping, not emphasizing the obviously erotic, you can make some electrifying connections. As you press up the legs, your partner waits with terrific anticipation and then . . . your hands move on. The moment you pass over a traditional erotic zone, the familiar intense feelings spread to the next part of the body. A feeling of excitement builds as you massage; it travels with your hands. Erotic massage animates the whole body and turns it into an instrument of pleasure.

First, oil her entire body. With your partner lying on her back, start on the front of the ankles with your hands wrapped over your partner's legs, fingers facing each other. Throughout this stroke, try to make contact with the

whole surface of your hand, from the fingertips to the base of the palm. Push up the legs slowly, allowing your hands to flatten out above the knees to meet the broad expanse of the thigh (as shown on p. 151). Use moderate pressures. Be

prepared to reposition your body several times as you move up from the feet to the shoulders. (Try not to interrupt the movement.) At the waist your fingertips will nearly meet. Press up to the very top of the torso and turn

out over the shoulder tops, allowing your hands to follow the precise contours of the shoulders (as shown). Turn in at the armpit and, with your fingertips pointed straight down and your fingers pressed tightly together, pull down the side of the torso and legs to the feet. Turn again at the ankles, maintaining maximum contact right through the turn, until your hands are back in the starting position.

This is the longest continual stroke in massage. Be especially careful not to rush any part of it. What your partner feels is a delicious wave of sensation sweeping back and forth across the body. Be generous. Let the feeling go on.

Awakening the Body: The Full Body Lift

Is your partner skeptical about the power of massage? This is the stroke to begin with even if you're planning to do only two or three others.

The spectacular full body lift is usually employed to flex the spine and lower back, but it has a very useful side effect for headache sufferers; large quantities of oxygen-enriched blood are moved down into the head. Here is a fast way to get oxygen into the brain by simply dumping it there. The full body lift also permits your partner to experience being lifted entirely off the ground by another person, perhaps for the first time since childhood. In fact, if you can hold your partner up for a full minute, you will see an unmistakable difference afterward. The face appears ruddy, almost flushed, and some of the tension lines around the eyes and mouth have already vanished. This is one of the rare massage strokes where physical strength is important. Obviously, if your partner is a great deal larger than you, a full body lift will be awkward. Fast stroking the neck (see p. 46) will accomplish the same thing—you'll just need a bit more time.

If size is no problem, don't miss the full body lift. The effect is dramatic and nearly instantaneous. Lift from a tripod position, with one knee and foot down, and the other knee up (as shown). Clasp your fingers together basket style under the small of your partner's back. Then lift slowly, allowing her head to fall back gracefully. Pause at the top of the lift for about thirty seconds. You may want to reach forward with one hand and support her head as you lower her. Don't break contact if you're going to lift a second or third time. With her eyes closed, your partner will experience the lifts as a single uninterrupted movement during which she floats up and down into space.

Awakening the Body: Hair Brushing

A strand of your hair touches my cheek.
How much better for the world had nothing else ever happened in it.
— Kenneth Patchen, "The Great Birds"

The luxurious feeling of animal fur only approximates the real thing: human hair. People love being touched by each other's hair, but seldom have an opportunity to experience it. Did we turn to animals and their furry coats because we couldn't depend on each other? Give your partner the chance to change all that by using your hair as part of the massage.

You don't need very long hair to do this stroke; with care, just a few inches will work nicely. Hair brushing usually has to be done from a kneeling position, which may be difficult to hold for long periods. Nevertheless, even a half minute of this delicious sensation will enhance any erotic sequence. Kneel near the center of the area you want to cover and lower your head until the top is nearly parallel to your partner's body. It helps to rest on both hands whenever you need to lean forward (as shown). Then, let your hair fall, slowly, onto naked skin. Move up and down the body, keeping your head in the same position. Hair brushing is a long, leisurely stroke that can cover the entire body. Make it last.

An Extended Erotic Massage

An epicurean who wishes to follow the ancient Greek model doesn't simply wallow in sensuality but rather distances himself from the world in order to experience pleasure more fully. We all understand why music sounds better in a symphony hall than a cafeteria; to really know a beautiful thing you must first remove unnecessary distractions. The epicurean isolates a pleasure; then, at his leisure, enjoys its essence.

No society in recorded history has offered greater opportunities for the pleasure lover than ours. Nevertheless, stress levels continue to climb. We have seen how pure sensual pleasure can relax the body and provide quick relief from stress. But when was the last time your partner allowed himself just fifteen minutes of pure sensual pleasure? Perhaps our pleasures are elusive precisely because we fail to follow the epicurean example. We are surrounded by an array of glittering toys; the trick is to play with them properly.

Most professional masseurs will recognize the client who specializes in a wholly materialistic approach to pleasure. Every sensation becomes a kind of possession — tasted

for a moment, then discarded in the greedy rush for new experience. But purely sensual pleasure can't be rushed, compressed, or collected.

Make that point with your hands during erotic massage by creating feelings that will reach any human being on the most profoundly personal level. An extended erotic massage can redefine your partner's whole concept of pleasure.

To establish the right mood, begin with long unhurried stroking movements (see p. 37) repeated dozens of times. Watch the pleasure register from one end of the body to the other as tensed muscles relax beneath your hands. Closing his eyes, your partner abandons the familiar senses and settles into the most private place of all — the body itself. Soon the clock stops and pure sensation takes over. The best erotic massage takes place in a world of its own, the exquisitely private world of touch where everything that is known is simply felt.

The traditional erogenous zones, a mere 5 or 10 percent of the whole body, exclude nearly everything beyond the sex organs themselves. Massage offers you the chance to break out of these ungenerous restrictions by turning the entire body into an instrument of pleasure. Taking the time to extend the limits of erotic feeling introduces your partner to an essential sensual experience: pure pleasure from head to toe. Extend the massage and the feeling will continue.

5
MASSAGE AND
LIFE EXTENSION

13.
Stress, Aging, and Massage

And after she had bathed him and annointed him with olive oil, and cast about him a goodly mantle, he came forth from the bath in fashion like the deathless gods. — Homer, *The Odyssey*

A Regular Program of Massage

Thanks to research on the fluid release effect, we know precisely how powerful massage can be. In minutes, pain is transformed into pleasure, and fatigue gives way to feelings of great energy. Muscle recovery rates after exercise increase so dramatically that one almost has to experience the effect to believe it. And every part of the body that is massaged becomes totally animated, perhaps for the first time since childhood. Whether it lasts a few minutes or several hours, the massage experience is one of continuous pleasure. Expect no unpleasant aftereffects; no secret price must be paid.

Nevertheless, all of these wonderful effects are temporary. The chemical changes inside the body such as increased oxygen supply, more efficient combustion and elimination of wastes, more supple joints and muscles, have been observed as long as one full week after a thorough massage session. Then they vanish.

We have seen how stress can literally kill people. And perhaps by now a few readers have experienced, firsthand, the way massage can be used to control, even eliminate stress. The question is: what if one were massaged all the time? Hippocrates, who had himself massaged daily, lived

to the age of 104. Could it have been the massage that kept him going?

We have come a long way since the golden age of Greece — with the same bodies. As millions of people struggle to cope with stress that seems to come from all quarters, the speedy space age could degen-

erate into the pill age. The differences between us and the Hunzas, perhaps the most long-lived people on earth, are instructive. They live in a beautiful place with little noise, pollution, or crime. Rushing, for its own sake, is virtually unknown. The Hunzas also have an extremely stable family structure. In

short, as a society, they are far less stressed than we are.

Of course we cannot hope to duplicate the utopian environment of the Hunzas, but we can look closely at the lives of very old people in our own society. Not surprisingly, a similar low stress pattern emerges: they don't worry

A Regular Program (cont'd)

sage, by ridding the body of various wastes and toxins, super-oxygenating the tissues, and lowering stress levels does, in fact, slow the aging process?

Can we expect a massage renaissance to equal the fitness craze? Will the parks and beaches ten or twenty years from now be filled with massaging couples? Will massage be taught to children at home and in school? We have "fat farms," what about massage farms? Will we see daily team massage lasting perhaps several hours for stroke and nervous breakdown victims? Will massage-medicine clinics take their place beside sports-medicine and other specialized facilities? Will regular massage actually extend one's life?

Stay tuned.

too much, they know how to relax, and they aren't angry all the time. In fact, even in the most chaotic societies certain individuals somehow manage to stay relatively peaceful. And relatively stress free.

A program of *daily* massage is not part of any major health plan, but it is, perhaps, the missing link in the modern health equation. Diet, exercise, and massage. Over the past few years we have seen a tremendous surge of interest in fitness-oriented exercise, and today our parks are filled with determined runners.

Athletes, we are told, will probably live longer. A scientific evaluation of the relationship between massage and longevity would, of course, take years to reach a conclusion. *But what if it were clearly demonstrated that frequent mas-*